Strength

AND

Glory

T. Elizabeth Renich

Emerald
Books

P.O. Box 635
Lynnwood, Washington 98046

Scripture References are taken from the King James Version of the
    Bible
The Glory of Fathering a Daughter (poem)—original work by the
    author, dated 1997
Program from National Cemetery Dedication
Gettysburg Address "Spoken Text"
found in <u>Lincoln at Gettysburg</u> by Garry Wills

Strength and Glory

Copyright © 2000 T. Elizabeth Renich
Published by Emerald Books
P.O. Box 635
Lynnwood, Washington 98046

Publisher's Cataloging-in-Publication
(*Provided by Quality Books, Inc.*)

Renich, T. Elizabeth (Tammy Elizabeth), 1964-
        Strength and glory / T. Elizabeth Renich. --
    1st ed.
        p. cm. -- (Shadowcreek chronicless ; bk. 4)
        ISBN: 1-883002-40-0
        1. United States--History--Civil War, 1861 - 1865
    --Fiction. 2. Virginia--History--Civil War,
    1861 - 1865--Fiction. 3. Confederate States of
    America--History--Fiction. 4. Women--United
    States--History--19th century--Fiction.
    5. Historical Fiction. 6. War stories. I. Title.
    II. Series: Renich, T. Elizabeth (Tammy
    Elizabeth), 1964- Shadowcreek chronicles ; bk. 4.

    PS3568.E593S77 1999   813'.54
                        QBI99-300522

Dedication

*F*or my Momma
 —because she loves me...

*F*or Jessica
 —because I love her...

*F*or Alicia, Lindsay, and Ann
 —because they wrote to me...

*T*his story is dedicated in part to the memory of

> former Chargers linebacker
> David Griggs
> (killed in a car accident, June 19, 1995)
>
> former Chargers running back
> Rodney Culver and
> his wife, Karen
> (victims of the ValuJet crash of May 11, 1996)

*T*heir strength in this life was a reflection of God's glory.

☆☆☆☆☆☆☆

Other Books by T. Elizabeth Renich:

Word of Honor
Matter of Trust
Not Without Courage

Acknowledgments

*T*hey *that wait upon the Lord shall renew their strength...* That reassuring promise from the beginning of Isaiah 40:31 contributed to part of the title for this final volume of *The Shadowcreek Chronicles*. It never ceases to amaze me that the Lord does indeed bestow just the right amount of strength we need depending upon the particular events in our lives, but I can indeed testify to the fact that He is faithful and He will provide. This story took longer than I dreamed it would or could, but here it is at last, and for it I give God the glory.

Emerald Books tolerantly extended my deadlines in order to accommodate circumstances that concurrently transpired during the researching and writing of this book. Warren Walsh, Marit Holmgren, and Sara Mike never gave up on me—and neither did the many readers who repeatedly expressed their interest in the conclusion of Jeremy and Salina's tale. Thanks for waiting.

I've said this before, and I'll say it again: I am *not* Margaret Mitchell, and it has never been my intent to rewrite *Gone With the Wind*. The years of research, study, frustration, elation, blood, sweat, and tears invested into this volume have certainly been an adventure. In this work of historical fiction, as in the three that precede it, accuracy and details are very important to me. This project was successfully completed as a result of the willing aid from the vast array of people who took the time to assist me in what I was striving to get accomplished. I believe it is fitting to give credit where credit is due, and my heart felt thanks belongs to ALL those who have contributed in both large ways and small—a special thank-you goes out to each one for their efforts on my behalf. The following are those who deserve more than I can hope to ever repay but will have to make due with honorable mention:

Carol Alston; Vickie Beane; Ray & Vicki Bentley/Maranatha Chapel (San Diego, CA); Jimmy Blankenship/City Point Unit, Petersburg National Battlefield (Petersburg, VA); Members of the Brandy Station Foundation; Danny & Holly Brisco; Margaret-Ann Brown; Art Candenquist; Bruce Carney; Mike & Linda Sue Carroll; Joan & Sal Chandon; Myrtice Chavis; Conference on

Women and the Civil War; Roger Delauter/Stonewall Jackson Headquarters Museum (Winchester, VA); the late John Devine; Rebecca Ebert, Archivist/Handley Library (Winchester, VA); Rich & Beverly Ellsworth; Cal & Betty Fairbourn; Ruth Fairrington; Carol Drake Friedman; Glenn, Judy, Sarah, & Rachel Gillette; E. Jane Griffin; Clark "Bud" Hall; April Havens, Ranger/Point Lookout State Park (Scotland, MD); Patrick Heelan, former Curator-Administrator/Stonewall Jackson Museum at Hupp's Hill (Strasburg, VA); Dr. Susan V. Heumann/Stuart-Mosby Historical Society; Evelyn & Tommy Hicks; Donna Holmes; Bobby Horton/Homespun Songs (Birmingham, AL); Michelle Hughes; Sharon Ibex; Joe, Irene, Lauren, & Jenna Jacoby; Dave & Beth-Anne Jahnsen; Dawn Johnson; Wes Johnson; Todd Kern, Curator/Stonewall Jackson Headquarters Museum (Winchester, VA); Doug Knapp, Director of Development/Museum of the Confederacy (Richmond, VA); Robert E. L. Krick, Historian/Richmond National Battlefield (Richmond, VA); Robert K. Krick, Chief Historian/Fredericksburg & Spotsylvania National Military Park (Fredericksburg, VA); Stan Kwan/Detroit Lions; Carol Land; James Lester/City Point Unit, Petersburg National Battlefield (Petersburg, VA); Dale & Èva Lindsey, former San Diego Chargers/then Washington Redskins/current Chicago Bears; Dana MacBean, Exhibits/Museum of Charleston (Charleston, SC); Carl Mauck/Buffalo Bills; Scott Mauger; Susan McCabe, Archives Staff/Handley Library (Winchester, VA); Tom McColl/Stonewall Jackson's Headquarters Museum (Winchester, VA); Patty McDermitt-Endres/Gettysburg College Athletics (Gettysburg, PA); Chip & Stacey Morton; the late Jim Moyer; Chris & Phil Osburn; Kim Palmersten; Thomas D. Perry, Founder/J.E.B. Stuart Birthplace Preservation & Trust (Ararat, VA); Marilyn Piper-Brosch; Gary Plummer/former Chargers Linebacker; Nancy Proclivo; LuAnn Pushic/Barnes & Noble at the Arboretum (Charlotte, NC); Eric and Bonnie Ransom; Carol Elizabeth Renich; Jessica Elizabeth Renich; Ken Renich; Sheryl Renich; Waldo & Leta Renich; Steve Ritchie; Colleen Ritter/Old Town Welcome Center (Winchester, VA); Friends and Co-workers at Schlafhorst Inc. (Charlotte, NC); Henny & Vic Schuster; Linda Shimamoto; June Shreck/Stonewall Jackson's Headquarters (Winchester, VA); Suzanne Silek/Warren Rifles Museum (Front Royal, VA); Kelvin Smith, Pastor & the Believers at Steele Creek Church of Charlotte (NC); Pat Smith, Librarian/Stuart Hall (Staunton, VA); J.E.B.

Stuart, IV; Jan Tornell; Robert J. Trout; Lenora Varela; Virginia Historical Society Archives Staff (Richmond, VA); Sharon & Dale Wisner; Patricia Walenista, President/Turner Ashby Society (Richmond, VA); Friends of the Wilderness Battlefield/Ellwood Volunteers (Locust Grove, VA).

I am indebted to you all, for I couldn't have done it without you.

T. Elizabeth Renich
October 30, 1999

Prologue

Late July 1863
West of the Rappahannock River
Culpeper County, Virginia

*M*ajor General J.E.B. Stuart stood near a crackling campfire with his booted feet braced apart, arms crossed over his chest. His usually merry blue eyes were somber; the crinkles at the corners indicated the depth of his thoughts. As dusk settled over the green landscape, the general listened intently to a report given by Private Kidd Carney. Stuart's lips pursed together tightly, all but disappearing between his full cinnamon-colored mustache and long-whiskered beard.

Carney's tale bordered on the incredible. The Confederate private had been taken prisoner during the late Battle of Gettysburg and escaped. He was caught a second time and escaped a second time, only to be captured yet *again*. Carney's third escape had been successful—and aided by one intrepid young lady profoundly loyal to Virginia, Stuart, and his Southern Cavalry.

"What was our Miss Salina doing in Gettysburg in the first place?" Stuart wondered aloud, accepting a mug of coffee Kidd

Carney had poured. The last time the general had seen the young lady in question was in early June, not quite two months ago, at a review of his cavalry near Brandy Station.

"I believe, sir, you are aware that her mother married a Federal major—Duncan Grant by name—shortly after the death of her first husband?" Kidd Carney's explanation turned inquiry. "Well, it just so happens that the Yankee major's family is from Gettysburg, and he sent Miss Salina's mother there for safety's sake. Mrs. Grant was with child, and she expressed a wish for Miss Salina to be with her during the final days of her confinement. Miss Salina went north out of deference to her mother's request, but then she found herself entangled in the middle of the battle."

Stuart digested Carney's narration. "And you say she went out in that downpour on the Fourth of July and found Captain Barnes on that bloody cavalry battlefield all by herself?"

"Aye, sir. Miss Salina told me she had a *feeling* Captain Barnes was out there, needing her, and she did manage to find him—still alive," Carney reported, "but terribly hurt."

General Stuart rubbed his chin, toying with his long whiskers, deaf to the sounds of picketed horses and men preparing for a rare evening's rest. "So Captain Barnes arranged to finally marry Miss Salina after all?"

"Aye, sir." Kidd Carney's affirmation was accompanied by a wide grin. "In their case, the fighting at Brandy Station merely postponed what Gettysburg could not. Reverend Landstreet did the honors. I myself was witness to their ceremony."

Stuart flashed a broad smile and slapped his leather gauntlets against his thigh. "Well, well! She's quite the lady, isn't she?"

"Indeed, sir, I reckon she is. Never even batted an eye when we pulled off the charade she willingly performed to get me out of that confounded Yank hospital," Kidd Carney marveled. "On that day, sir, Miss Salina acted in a manner both brave and heroic."

"She's her father's daughter," Stuart interjected by way of explanation.

"So I've heard. Unfortunately, I did not have the privilege of knowing Captain Hastings before he was killed, but by all accounts, I understand Miss Salina is a good deal like him and shares his sense of adventure and streak of independence." Kidd Carney produced an envelope addressed to General Stuart in Salina's fine, flowing script. "In exchange for her assistance in making my escape possible, I promised to bring this letter to you.

She wants you to know that Captain Barnes is alive, though his wounds will no doubt keep him out of service for some time."

"Knowing Captain Barnes, he'll be back with us as soon as he's recuperated," Stuart predicted confidently, but his amused grin evaporated by the time he finished reading the firelit lines:

Maj.-Gen. J.E.B. Stuart, C.S.A.
Cavalry Headquarters

July 24, 1863

Dear General Stuart:

In light of the recent, horrible cavalry clash, I trust that you are well and have survived to fight another day. There has been no mention that you sustained any injury to yourself, so I will take that to mean that you are in good health and planning the next campaign against the enemy.

I am writing, sir, to let you know that my husband, Captain Jeremy Barnes, has not been so fortunate as to come through the fight unscathed. In truth, he is in a bad way, but I am determined that he will live through this—with all the caring I can give him, and with much prayer. To the best of my knowledge, he went down when his horse was shot out from under him during the cavalry fight on the third day of the Battle of Gettysburg. He has suffered a broken leg, broken ribs, a dislocated shoulder, a severe sabre cut along his brow and cheek, and a frightful concussion due to a blow to the back of his head. Symptoms accompanying the concussion are loss of memory and loss of sight—both of which the doctor says may be temporary—but he offers no substantial guarantees. If I may entreat you, sir, when duty allows, to please keep us in your thoughts and prayers, as I would be much obliged.

May the good Lord bless and keep you safe. Please mention me to your wife when next you chance to see her. Tell her I do hope that all is well in her present condition. I look forward to the day when we shall all meet again.

Thank you for your understanding, General. If you should have need to contact me or Captain Barnes for any reason at all, please do so by way of one of his men, *or send word to Shadowcreek, near Chantilly. They will know how to find us.*

> *I remain your devoted friend and compatriot,*
> *Salina Rose Hastings Barnes*
> *Grant Farmstead*
> *Gettysburg, Pennsylvania*

Grieved to learn the alarming extent of Captain Barnes's injuries, General Stuart silently vowed to keep the young couple in his prayers. "She seems optimistic that in time he will recover."

Kidd Carney's eyes reflected the flames of the campfire, yet his tone was somber. "You know her, sir. Miss Salina is resolutely determined. If anyone can help Jeremy, she is the one."

"Aye," the general agreed, his keen eyes focused on a point somewhere far beyond the surrounding cavalry encampment. "Indeed, she is the one."

☆☆☆☆☆☆☆

> *August 19, 1863*
> *Old Capitol Prison*
> *Washington, D.C.*

Lost in blessed reverie, Ethan Hastings sat on the dirty, straw-covered floor of the cell with his back against the corner walls, elbows balanced atop his knees. Both sets of joints were visible through holes in his shabby jacket and woolen britches—the gray fabric having seen better days.

Images of home at Shadowcreek and of his much-loved wife paraded behind his closed eyelids. God only knew when he'd be able to hold Taylor Sue in his arms again.

Incessant prattle and the noisy jangle of a key ring alerted Ethan to the overly gregarious guard making nightly rounds in the corridor. Footsteps, two pair, halted at the door. Murmured conversation between the guard and a blue-clad officer was masked by the jingling keys, several of which the guard fumbled with before selecting the appropriate one, pushing it into the lock, and twisting it with a grinding turn.

Ethan jerked his dark head up from its resting place on his crossed forearms. The swiftly opened door crashed handle-first into the wall. The musty cell vibrated with a resounding *SLAM!*

The senior officer, decidedly the taller of the two silhouetted forms, entered the prison cell.

Lantern light shone into Ethan's wary eyes, all but obliterating the shadowed features of the man who'd come for an unexpected nocturnal visit. Squinting, Ethan raised a grubby hand as a shield against the light, but he was still unable to distinguish the visitor's face.

"Good evenin'." Ethan's pronounced Southern drawl intoned sarcastic pleasantry. "Bit late for a *social call*."

"This is *not* a social call, I can assure you," the tall silhouette spoke. "Though I'm given to understand that you've had your share of company in the last few days."

Ethan knew the voice: It belonged to his Yankee stepfather, Major Duncan Grant.

Major Grant allowed himself to be locked in the cell with Ethan and the lantern, then summarily dismissed the guard. He cast a doleful glance around the dank space. His senses revolted at the malodorous atmosphere. The stench and filth took some getting used to, and he opted to breathe through his mouth rather than his nose.

Ethan waited until he was certain the guard was gone. "If you're referring to the two *gentlemen* who were here yesterday morn, I'd hardly define their visit as a *social call*. Those two vultures came to find out how I plan to repay the money I owe them. You see, creditors have little compassion for a man locked away with no means to pay his debts."

"Creditors?" Duncan Grant arched an eyebrow in question, not believing a word of Ethan's glib story.

"Creditors," Ethan repeated, feigning seriousness. He knew Duncan would howl if he discovered the true identities of the men who'd come in disguise to his cell.

Duncan stared at his stepson for a dreadfully intense moment, but whatever he was thinking remained tactfully unsaid. It pained him greatly to see Ethan in his present circumstance; it reminded him too much of the last time he'd ever seen Ethan's father.

The Confederate captain tardily stood, brushing off errant pieces of straw sticking to his ragged gray uniform, and met the Union major's glance without flinching. "Is that why you're here? To interrogate me about the visit of two money-minded creditors?"

"No," Duncan answered in a low voice, choosing to let the suspicious matter rest. He held an envelope in his hand. "I came about this."

Ethan's scrutinizing eyes never left Duncan's face as he plucked the envelope from his stepfather's gloved fingers. "I'm honored, Major, that you'd take the time to *personally* deliver this." The sarcasm was thinly veiled.

"You should be," Duncan returned pointedly. With a remorseful sigh he added, "You didn't have to bribe a guard to get a letter through the lines to your wife, Ethan. I'd have seen to it, if you'd trusted me a little."

Ethan grimaced wryly. "I had to try on my own, Duncan. I don't expect *you* to get me out of this scrape. I've got to fend for myself in here because you are *not* in a position to offer any intervention in this particular instance. It poses too great a risk—for both of us." By unspoken yet mutual agreement, their relationship was not known to anyone inside the prison, especially since it would benefit neither if the truth were disclosed. With that firmly in mind, they each went along pretending to be the enemies they supposedly were. "I understand your dilemma, Duncan; I don't hold it against you."

"Before your father died, I promised him that I'd look after you Hastings'—your mother, your sister, *and* you," Duncan needlessly reminded Ethan.

"I know," Ethan acknowledged, feeling the tide of belligerence toward Duncan slowly recede. "And you have done so—even while none of us has made it easy for you." He averted his eyes, making deliberate work of opening the envelope that contained a letter from his wife. Taking a step closer to Duncan's lantern, Ethan angled the pages to better catch light.

While Ethan pored over Taylor Sue's handwritten words, Duncan covertly surveyed the imprisoned man's unkempt beard and shaggy hair. Ethan undeniably favored his sire: He and Garrett shared the same towering height, rangy build, raven-black hair, intense eyes, squared jaw, quick mind, and Rebel sympathies. Each also held the identical rank of captain in the Confederate Army.

A sudden, perplexed expression appeared in Ethan's dark blue eyes, and his bearded jaw sagged in startled disbelief.

"I trust everything is well?" Uncertain, Duncan made it a question. "Is everything all right at Shadowcreek? You haven't had bad news, I hope."

"No! No. It's not bad news." Ethan shook his shaggy head in reply. "According to this, Taylor Sue is...fine. Shadowcreek is fine.

Everything is going to be just fine." A faint smile flickered at the corners of his mouth. "Duncan, may I ask you a question?"

"Of course," the Yankee major nodded, curious.

"How did you feel when Mamma announced to you that she was going to have your baby?"

"Shocked; a bit overwhelmed," Duncan clearly recalled. "Why?"

Ethan's partial grin spread. "I reckon you could say I'm feeling a little shocked and overwhelmed."

Understanding caused Duncan to chuckle heartily. "Had your father lived, I believe he'd have been quite amused at the prospect of becoming a *grandfather*."

"Yeah." Ethan agreed. "I'm sure he would have—but he's dead." He took a hard look at his dismal surroundings. "I wonder if I'll still be in this wretched hole when it comes time for her to be delivered..."

Duncan cleared his throat. "If you wish to write a reply back to Taylor Sue, I'll see that it gets through the lines."

"Duncan, I don't mean to sound ungrateful for your efforts on my behalf," Ethan protested, "but it's not worth jeopardizing your army career on my account."

Determination glinted in Duncan's eyes. "I would do whatever is in my power to help you. I gave my word of honor to your father."

"Then get me out of here!" Ethan retorted—yet admittedly the challenge was an empty one. He knew that Duncan was doing for him all that could be done without exposing either of them.

Ethan's audacious demand went unanswered. Instead, Duncan informed him: "I've written to the Confederate States War Department requesting verification of your identity, rank, and commission. To date I have received no response. When Major Barnes planned to have you locked up, he knew what he was doing by ordering Lieutenant Everett to strip your uniform of insignia and burn your belongings. No one here will believe that you are anything more than an enlisted private, let alone a doctor, without proper proof. Until I have something more substantial, my hands are tied."

Ethan clamped his jaw, stifling any reply. He put Taylor Sue's letter back in its envelope and tucked it into the jacket pocket closest to his heart.

"I know you're not overly fond of waiting, Ethan, but that's the best advice I can offer you. Wait and see what happens. Be patient."

"I have little choice," Ethan commented dryly. His troubled eyes settled on his naked ring finger, acutely missing the gold wedding band that had been stolen from him. "But nothing's going to happen, Duncan. You know it, and I know it."

"That's where you're wrong." Duncan took a step closer to Ethan and whispered conspiratorially. "I have it on good authority that you're to be transferred out of here. You're to be moved to the new prison camp at Point Lookout in Maryland."

As if that'll be any better?! Prison is prison! Ethan wisely kept his thoughts to himself. "When?"

Duncan shrugged. "That part I'm not certain of—yet. It could be as soon as tomorrow or not for several weeks. Do you know what day tomorrow is?" he asked out of curiosity.

"The twentieth of August," Ethan answered without the slightest hesitation. The look of surprise on his stepfather's face was apparent. "Duncan, I may have been locked up in here for over a month already, but I haven't yet forgotten how to count the days. Sure, the monotony is rather tedious—it provides one with the solitary opportunity to do an *awful* lot of thinking, whether one wants to or not." He added, "Salina will be seventeen years old tomorrow. I've no way of knowing when I'll see her again—or my new little brother, for that matter."

"While you're thinking so much, I hope you're not thinking of doing anything...rash," Duncan cautioned.

"I won't do anything rash," Ethan assured the Yankee major. "In truth, I'd venture to guess that it's my darling little sister who would consider doing something—*impulsive*—shall we say? Duncan, you've got to keep Salina out of this."

"I heartily agree, but keep in mind that where your sister is concerned, it may be easier said than done." Duncan knew the intelligent young lady who was his stepdaughter all too well. He knew the boundless measure of her determination once she set her mind to something. "I intend to send a wire to wish Salina a happy birthday. With your permission, I'll pass along your greetings to her as well as to your mamma."

"Please do."

"Any additional message?" Duncan inquired.

There were a hundred things Ethan wanted Duncan to tell them. That Taylor Sue was going to have a baby topped the list, but Ethan refrained. Prudently he replied, "Let them know I'm all right and doing as well as can be expected. Tell them I'm not starving at present and I have yet to become infested with lice." His effort to find some small humor in his predicament was a weak one.

"Duncan, make sure Salina knows she's to sit still on this one. If you don't make her see reason, she might attempt something we'll all regret."

Duncan's jaw was firmly set. "Rest assured, I'll make sure she understands."

"Good. Tell her to watch her step—especially if Lieutenant Everett is still on the loose and working for John Barnes. Make her see that she must always be on her guard. He can't get to Mamma anymore, and he's got me right where he wants me. I have no doubt Barnes will go after Salina again, or Jeremy. The man's crazy; he won't leave us be. If Salina plans on going back to Virginia anytime in the near future, she's going to have to be *extremely* cautious."

"I'll remind her," Duncan nodded. "If I hear anything else concerning your transfer, or if I get any confirmation from your government, I'll be sure to let you know. Rest assured."

"Godspeed, Duncan." Ethan wiped his palm on his trouser leg, then extended his hand to the Yankee major.

At first Duncan shook Ethan's proffered hand, but then he pulled the younger man into a quick embrace. "We'll be praying for you."

"I'm counting on that." Ethan, a bit uncomfortable with the unexpected display of affection, stepped back and squared his shoulders. "Thank you for stopping by."

Duncan nodded curtly. He turned away from Ethan, blinking back the unexpected sting of tears, and called for the prison guard.

Chapter One

Late August 1863
Shadowcreek near Chantilly
Northern Virginia

*C*aptain Jeremy Barnes restlessly kicked at the broken brick curb bordering the garden walkway. Dandelions pushed up through the cracks in the herringbone patterned masonry; weeds on either side of the paved path had grown waist-high. Once upon a time this patch of acreage had been a lush sea of colors and fragrances—roses, gladiolas, gardenias, azaleas, wisteria, dogwood, and pine. It was not so now. Leaning his shoulder against one of the remaining upright arbor posts, Jeremy impatiently studied the face of the open pocket watch cupped in his gloved hand. He'd allow her ten more minutes, but then they were moving on. Something didn't feel right.

Jeremy raised his sandy-blond head, his glance sweeping the slope of the hill until he located his wife. Salina stood, her dark head bowed, in the midst of the burnt rubble—all that was left of what had been her home. Jeremy presumed she was reliving a bittersweet string of old memories, calling to mind a time when this place was whole and beautiful, filled with love and laughter. Shadowcreek was a part of her as much as she was a part of it. Along with the strength of character she'd inherited from her father, Salina had inherited a natural love for this land.

Seven more minutes... Jeremy snapped his watch closed and stuffed it into his vest pocket. He harbored his own fond memories of Shadowcreek. It was more than just a place to him—it had been a tangible representation of warm acceptance mingled with heartfelt caring. The Hastings family had befriended him years ago, and because of their genuine welcome, he'd never been made to feel a stranger. Shadowcreek was his definition of what *home* should mean—and that definition ultimately included the family who had resided here. It saddened him to recall the night nearly a year past when the elegance of the Hastings manor house went up in flames, reduced to utter devastation on account of a malicious Yankee torch.

With four minutes still to go, Jeremy started his assent up the hill. Although he was keenly aware of the breeze whispering in the trees overhead and of the gurgling rush of the stream in the distance, it was not the peacefulness of the past, but disquiet that filled him.

When Jeremy reached the top of the rise, Salina was not there. Only the chimneys, the lasting sentinels, stood tall among the debris. "Sallie Rose?" he spoke aloud his habitual nickname for her.

Leaves stirred, cicadas droned. A chill of indescribable dread traveled the length of his spine. "Sallie!"

"I'm right here, Jeremy. No need to shout."

Jeremy turned in the direction of his wife's lilting voice. Salina had come from his right—his blind side—and he hadn't seen her approach.

Salina studied Jeremy with luminous emerald eyes. She sensed the momentary panic in him ebbing, supplanted by a hint of frustration. "What's the matter, darlin'?"

"Nothin'." He didn't want her to know how uneasy her sudden appearance at his side without his knowledge made him feel.

Salina tipped her head, peering at him through her thick lashes. "You're not happy to be home?"

"I'm glad we're back in Virginia," Jeremy replied.

"I am, too! It's been far too long since we've been where we belong." Salina was quiet for a moment, instinctively listening for something she didn't yet hear. She scanned what remained of the treeline that divided the estate from the turnpike a few hundred yards away. "Are we being watched?"

"You tell me," Jeremy quipped. "You're the one who usually knows things like that, Sallie Rose."

Salina hugged her elbows and took a deep breath. "I think we ought not stay out in the open any longer than necessary. Especially you."

Jeremy smiled to cover his renewed wonder at her flawless intuition. "See what I mean? Perceptive."

Her laugh was brittle. "It doesn't take a genius to figure out that since we're in precariously close range of a Federal outpost that you, being the Rebel cavalry officer you are, would make a prize catch for the Yankees." Salina placed her hand in Jeremy's. "I want to visit the cemetery before we go. Come with me?"

"Sure." Jeremy allowed Salina to drag him along to the fenced plot where the Hastings' had buried three generations of their dead. With his good eye, he kept a more observant watch.

Salina opened the gate in the wrought-iron fence and hastened onward, leaving Jeremy to follow. By the time he caught up, she had cleared away the weeds crowding the base of a stone monument. She reverently placed a bouquet of wildflowers tied with a narrow strip of ribbon at the marker, which had been erected as a memorial. The remains of the late Captain Garrett Hastings were in fact interred elsewhere.

Jeremy stood apart, respectfully giving Salina some time to herself. He wasn't able to clearly make out what she was whispering in the one-sided conversation, but he knew how badly she missed her daddy; Jeremy missed the man, too.

Wandering among the other graves, Jeremy tripped over a miniature marker that had been swallowed up by the tall grasses. Hunkering down to push the weeds aside, he uncovered two diminutive gravestones. He read the carved words aloud: "Son of Garrett Hastings and Annelise Spencer Hastings; Stillborn, 1843." The second bore a similar inscription: "Daughter of Garrett Hastings and Annelise Spencer Hastings; Stillborn, 1856."

"Mamma lost four other babies, too. All miscarriages," Salina murmured, this time approaching Jeremy from his left side, where he would see her right off. "My mamma was married to Daddy for just over twenty years, was with child by him eight times, and has only me and Ethan to show for it."

"Sallie, your folks could've had a whole passel of young'uns and your daddy would still have doted on you most of all." Jeremy wasn't sure what the deep brooding he detected in her eyes meant.

A sentimental smile replaced her pensive expression. "I miss him so much, Jeremy."

"We all do." He brushed her temple with a kiss and gave her shoulders a firm squeeze. "Are you ready?"

"Almost. There's something else here you need to see." Salina led him to a corner, to a space separate from the family markers. In this spot two newer graves had been dug and marked not with stone but with wooden crosses. One of the markers was for a former rider in Jeremy's little band who'd died of wounds suffered at the Battle of Kelly's Ford. The other cross stood at the head of a grave completely free from the tangle of weeds. It was new—in fact, according to the date, it was but two days old. The name lately carved into the wood was *Charlie Graham*.

"What do you make of that?" Salina queried, wondering what had caused the demise of this long-time family friend and one-time potential suitor.

"I don't know." Jeremy took Salina firmly by the hand. "Come on. We've dawdled here long enough. Surely someone at the cabin can tell us about this."

Roughly two hundred yards down the hill from where the main house used to stand was a clear, cold, winding stream that meandered through the Shadowcreek estate. Hand in hand, Jeremy and Salina crossed the footbridge that arched over the swift-moving water. On the opposite bank they were taken aback to find that the white-washed cabin, which Salina had painstakingly renovated and lived in prior to her sojourn north, was reduced to a blackened, still smoldering ruin. Nothing at all remained of the other structures that the old slave quarters had comprised.

"Stay put, Sallie," Jeremy ordered, placing a restraining hand on her arm. Through the soles of his boots he felt the heat of spent flame emanating from the wreckage.

"This was no accident," she stated adamantly.

"No, I reckon it probably wasn't." Jeremy poked at piles of ash with a booted toe.

Somberly Salina declared, "John Barnes strikes again."

"Aye, it does appear to be his handiwork—I recognize his calling card," Jeremy remarked caustically. "And in light of this," his glance swept over the charred destruction, "we can only assume that he must know where we are."

"By last report Lieutenant Everett was in Gettysburg. Do you suppose he followed us from Pennsylvania and told Barnes we were on the move?"

"But," Jeremy interjected, "Everett might not have known that we stopped in Maryland; therefore, Barnes mistimed his attack."

"Taylor Sue, Mary Edith, and the twins would have been here—what about them?"

"If they were here, they'd have gone down the passage under the fireplace and through the tunnels beneath the cabin to safety. They're probably at Ivywood with your Aunt Priscilla and Uncle Caleb even now," Jeremy guessed, hoping he was right. Charlie Graham, however, remained the mystery.

"I reckon Charlie probably resisted and got caught in the backlash," Salina said, practically reading Jeremy's mind. "You know Charlie: He always wanted to go in a fight. It appears he did."

Salina stooped to retrieve a broken bit of rose-patterned china. Too quickly she stood again, and a rush of dizziness threatened her balance.

Jeremy pulled her close to steady her. "Sssssshhh," he smoothed her hair as a torrent of tears spilled onto his shirtfront. "It'll be all right, Sallie."

"We shouldn't have come here directly." Salina suddenly felt as if the trees around them had all grown eyes and were observing their every move, mocking them. "It was too predictable an action on my part..."

"It's logical for you to want to come home after being away for so long," Jeremy answered, aware that *something* besides the fire and Charlie's death was bothering her. "Come on," he whispered. "Let's head on over to Ivywood. Surely that's where your cousin and Taylor Sue have gone. They'll tell us what happened."

☆☆☆☆☆☆☆

If one were required to judge by the apparent tranquility and marginal prosperity of the Armstrong estate, it would be difficult to ascertain that there was a war on. Contrary to the conditions at Shadowcreek, Ivywood looked much the same as it always had. The white columns of the mansion's porch gleamed in the afternoon light; the gardens were well tended; the fields would soon be ready for harvest. Smoke poured from the kitchen chimney; the laundress, seamstress, and weaver each worked steadily while a handful of black-skinned children played nearby.

"Caleb Armstrong must be doing something to give his people initiative to stay on and work for him." Jeremy nodded toward where two dozen fieldhands were toiling.

"I wouldn't be at all surprised if Uncle Caleb has taken to using his blockade-running profits to hire them," Salina speculated.

Jeremy halted the mule-drawn wagon. After securing the brake, he jumped down and assisted Salina in her descent from the buckboard seat.

The front door of Ivywood flew open. Taylor Sue Carey Hastings hurried across the veranda and down the stairs. "You're safe! Oh, thank God!" She took one of each of their hands in her own, so grateful to see them both alive and well. "If you've been to Shadowcreek already—which I'm sure you have, or you wouldn't have known to come here—you're already aware that John Barnes has been looking for you again."

"Aye," Jeremy squeezed his sister-in-law's hand. "We figured that had to be it."

"Come inside," Taylor Sue invited. "Maraiah is just fixing supper—she'll set extra plates for the two of you. Mary Edith is in the nursery with Annie Laurie and Bonnie Lee, and Aunt Priscilla and Uncle Caleb will be pleased to see you, too. Not half so pleased, though, as your men."

"My men are here?"

"Yes, and have been for two days now. It seems that practically everybody knew you two were due to return. The Remnant forwarded a message saying you'd left Gettysburg over a fortnight ago. I was actually starting to worry, especially when Jeremy's men arrived at Shadowcreek without him. I was told they, too, had received word that you and Salina were on your way back, but it seemed that you had up and disappeared. No one knew precisely where you were, or if you were safe. If it hadn't been for your men, I doubt very much if Mary Edith and I could have gotten out of the cabin with the twins on our own."

Taylor Sue acutely remembered the ferocity of the fire, then immediately dismissed the nightmarish scenes from her mind. "It was most fortuitous that they arrived when they did." She looked up at the sandy-haired man who was her best friend's husband. "It's an answer to prayer to see you looking so well, Jeremy. It was my understanding that you almost died in the cavalry battle at Gettysburg."

"Almost," Jeremy acknowledged, fidgeting under Taylor Sue's amber-eyed scrutiny.

"Kidd Carney reported you were blind and couldn't even recall your own name," Taylor Sue prodded in her delicate way.

"I was indeed blind when Carney left Gettysburg. Since then, however, the good Lord mercifully bestowed a healing. The loss of memory and loss of sight proved to be temporary."

"The Lord faithfully answered my prayers and restored him," Salina added.

"Glory be!" Taylor Sue exclaimed, then teased coquettishly, "But if you ask me, Jeremy, I'd say that eyepatch makes you look more like a pirate on the high seas than a horse soldier."

Salina giggled. "I've told him the very same thing."

"Pirating is not my forte, and I'm happy to leave that aspect to Randle Baxter," Jeremy said, referring to Mary Edith's husband who was captain of a Confederate privateer. Jeremy remained with his wife and sister-in-law for a few minutes more, but he was anxious to see his men. He wanted to find out what was going on, where General Stuart was. "You go with Taylor Sue," he encouraged Salina. "I'll take the wagon around to the stables."

"Your riders are in the barn loft," Taylor Sue informed him. "They've politely declined the offer to stay at the house, as there's rarely any warning as to when the bluebellies might stop and water their horses. They reckoned there was no need to provide the patrols with even the slightest reason to search the place."

"Those people come around that often?" Jeremy didn't like the sound of it.

"The Yankees have been a bit overzealous in trying to track down Mosby and his partisan rangers as of late," Taylor Sue explained. "The Federals are wont to search homes with the very slightest provocation. It's their way of keeping local Rebel sympathizers on their best behavior."

"Can you get word to Reverend Yates to have him meet us here?" Jeremy inquired.

Taylor Sue nodded toward the house. "He's already here. I'll let him know you've arrived and send him to join you." She slipped her arm through Salina's. "I'm so pleased that you have come home safely. It's an answer to many a prayer—but you've got a lot of explaining to do!"

☆☆☆☆☆☆☆

"He is a beauty." Jeremy ran a currycomb over a dappled gray gelding, inspecting the steed with a practiced eye. "Has he got a name?"

"Tristan calls him Tucker," Weston Bentley replied. "Swears it would take a hundred-mile race to tucker this horse out."

"Mmmm...good endurance. How about speed?" Jeremy queried. "Can he outrun the Yanks?"

"Not to fear. Tucker'd be the winner of that hundred-mile race and still have enough juice to run circles around those people," Bentley boasted. "It's mighty good to have you back, Captain."

"It's good to be back." Jeremy saw Bentley hesitate and said, "What is it, man? Speak your mind."

Bentley lowered his voice. "I don't want to sound like I'm a softhearted old fool..."

"But you are." Jeremy grinned at this man who had been a fellow beneficiary in a prisoner exchange orchestrated by General Stuart. Bentley was old enough to be father to any one of the other riders, and though Jeremy held a higher rank, he, too, acknowledged Bentley as the esteemed mentor of the ragtag little band.

"Well, sir, I guess all I'm trying to say is that I'm real pleased you didn't die."

Appreciative of the sentiment the elder rider sheepishly conveyed, Jeremy grinned. "My wife saw to keeping me alive, what with her nursing and her prayers. She insists that God hasn't finished with me yet, so He's allowed me to live."

"She's probably right," Bentley nodded. "If you'll permit me to say it, I believe she's good for you, sir. Miss Salina's got just the right touch of determination to match you and yours."

"Aye," Jeremy conceded with a nod. "Lucky me."

Together the two men unloaded the contents of the wagon, stacking and sorting the various-sized wooden crates. "Miss Salina know about these guns?" Bentley inquired.

"Do you know how difficult it is to keep a secret from my wife?" Jeremy arched the brow above his black leather eyepatch. "She hasn't come right out and said anything to me about them, but neither have I volunteered how I came to possess them. Salina's smart enough to figure out that they were—*taken*—as lawful prize, the spoils of war."

"How *did* you come by these crates?" Bentley wondered.

"Drake found an abandoned stash, which he handed over to me. You see, any weapons found on the battlefields surrounding Gettysburg were to have been gathered by the provost guard to be turned in to the Federal quartermaster. These particular guns—well, they just happened to get away."

"And she's said *nothing* about them?" Bentley scratched his head.

"My wife's never been fond of my dabbling in guns—bought, sold, or stolen. Her daddy and I used to run guns in California; it can be a messy business." Jeremy searched the shed for a tool to open the crates. "But Salina's no fool. She's sensible enough to understand what firepower like this can do for our side. It's that understanding that keeps her from voicing her objections."

The elder rider whistled low when he took stock of the contraband inventory in the remaining crates: coffee, tea, sugar—both brown and fancy white—flour, dried fruit, canned beef, and jerky; quinine, chloroform, bandages, and salves; candles, matches, kerosene, two spare lanterns; socks, heavy work gloves, worsted yarn, knitting needles, a sewing kit, a shaving kit, hairpins, two pair of boots, a pair of shoes; bolts of calico, gingham, flannel, corduroy, jean-cloth, and oilcloth; needles, thread, buttons—and a bag of lemon drops, presumably for Jeremy's sweet tooth. "Quite some accumulation you've got here."

"Entirely Salina's doing," Jeremy chuckled. "While Drake and I collected arms and ammunition, she was stockpiling items that are not easy to come by since the Northern blockade of our Southern ports has been in effect. She had planned to smuggle goods back through the lines even before the guns became an issue."

Jeremy pried the lid off one of the two crates containing Spencer repeating rifles. He brushed off the straw packing and caressed the glossy wooden stock. "Fine piece of workmanship, wouldn't you agree?"

Bentley muttered, "For an instrument of death."

"The way I see it, we've one of two options: We can either shoot with 'em or get shot by 'em. *Those people*," Jeremy made reference to the enemy Yankees, "brag they can load these on Sunday and fire all week: twenty-one rounds a minute. Guns such as these could make a small detachment of men like us seem double—or maybe even *triple*—their strength."

Bentley voiced his skepticism. "But the South don't manufacture ammunition for them—leastwise not yet she don't. What happens when ordnance runs low or completely out? The Spencers become disposable?"

Jeremy had pondered that point. "I suppose they might—but that will depend on whether or not we can acquire more ammunition for them. We'll just have to take care to use them when it's most prudent to do so."

"Oh, aye," Bentley nodded. "And from now on we'll only raid Yankee supply wagons that carry the kind of ammunition they use."

Jeremy returned the rifle to the crate, ignoring Bentley's sarcasm. "These are what the Union cavalry was shredding our columns with at Gettysburg. We couldn't stand up to fire like that."

"We got drummed out of our saddles up North at Gettysburg," Bentley said. "Charges and countercharges—it was *awfully* reminiscent of Brandy."

"We carried the day at Brandy—we held the field." Jeremy studied Bentley for a moment. "What's eating at you? I've not heard you talk like this before."

Bentley brushed Jeremy's concern aside. "Maybe I don't particularly care for seeing my comrades die or get hurt. Browne Williams, Pepper Markham, Harrison Claiborne, Archer Scarborough." He ticked each dead man's name off on the fingers of his left hand. "It seemed you was sure and certain to be on that list, too, but instead you got yourself tallied in the 'wounded' column with C.J. and Kidd Carney."

"This is war, Bentley," Jeremy whispered. "We made a commitment we are bound to uphold. There is duty and honor to be considered."

"Well, I'm getting heartily sick of it, just the same!" the elder man bellowed. "Commitment or no."

"We all are. It's been three summers now, and God knows how many more are yet to come. You always seemed so focused before." Jeremy didn't cotton to such defeatist talk.

"Ah!" Bentley growled. "I'm just running on at the mouth. You've come back, mostly in one piece, and we have that to be thankful for. Don't mind me."

"When I go back to serve as courier and scout for General Stuart, I need you by me, old man."

"Duty and honor drive us," Bentley remarked. "You can count on me, sir."

"Good." Jeremy breathed a little easier. They'd all had doubts and trials, yet they'd been there for each other to stand strong and make it through. They'd do so again. "Where are the others?"

"I set them to watch," Bentley answered. "Barnes got to Shadowcreek only a short time after we did. You just barely missed the homecoming party he threw in your honor."

"Yes, fortunately I did."

"That man is obsessed with his hatred of you." Bentley stated a simple fact.

"I know." A determined light flickered in Jeremy's unpatched eye. "But he hasn't finished me off yet—and I'm not about to go down quietly or without a fight."

☆☆☆☆☆☆☆

When Salina was agitated, she had a habit of twisting her wedding band around in circles, as she was doing at present. Sitting opposite Taylor Sue on the window seat, she relayed the events that had transpired in Gettysburg and their departure thereof. "Lieutenant Everett came after Jeremy with an arrest warrant from the provost marshal's office," she recounted. "A Federal warrant holds no jurisdiction over a Rebel captain, but we decided it more sensible not to take any unnecessary chances. Drake and Jeremy got out of Gettysburg, but then they came back to fetch me—they figured it wasn't safe to leave me behind, what with Everett at large."

"Wasn't it Everett's underlings who took Ethan?" Taylor Sue queried.

"It was," Salina nodded. "Taylor Sue, during those four days, Drake and Jeremy went to the Old Capitol Prison."

"They did *what*?!" Taylor Sue's hand flew to her throat, her reaction identical to what Salina's had been upon learning of the impractical stunt. Her amber eyes began to dance. "Did they…?" She was almost afraid to ask the question burning on the tip of her tongue. "Oh, Salina, they didn't somehow manage to get Ethan out of there, did they?"

"No," Salina shook her head slowly. "Unfortunately, they did not. Drake and Jeremy told me they hadn't actually planned to go as far as Washington when they left me at the Grants. They went purely on a whim, relatively certain that if Everett was searching high and low in and around Gettysburg, he'd never dream of hunting them in the Union capital itself. What they did do, however, was carry off a preposterous charade, pretending to be creditors needing to talk to Ethan about some unearthly amount of money he supposedly owed. The ruse enabled them to infiltrate the prison long enough to see for themselves that Ethan was at least tolerably well. A rescue would have required far more time than they had and more extensive, detailed plotting. They had a difficult time making me accept that it was not feasible for them to undertake a half-cocked attempt to spring my brother and bring him back. I understand now that they did what they thought was best, especially in light of the level of risk involved for each of them."

Taylor Sue shook her russet head. "It wasn't meant to be, then. Not yet, anyway. So," she took a deep breath and denied the tears that might have otherwise collected in her eyes, "I will continue to cling to the promise that all things work together for good. I will strive to be strong and courageous for Ethan's sake, and I beg you, Salina, to keep him lifted in prayer with me."

"You know I will. I do," Salina affirmed.

Taylor Sue squeezed her sister-in-law's hand with assurance. "There is a reason in all this. We just don't know it at the moment." With an effort at lightheartedness she didn't fully feel, she commented, "All things considered, Drake and Jeremy are absolutely...*amazing!*"

"Or utterly stupid."

Taylor Sue smiled knowingly. "Surely *you* can differentiate between plain stupidity and bold daring. You just told me you believe they did what they thought was best."

"Daring?" Salina's ire kindled anew as she remembered long hours-turned-days of fear for Jeremy and Drake's safety while they were off on what they perceived as a lark. "Oh, let me show you *daring.*" Salina fished in her carpet-sided satchel and produced a small, black lacquered case hardly measuring bigger than the palm of her hand. "They were so exceptionally sure of themselves that they *dared* take the time to stop and have their likenesses made."

Taylor Sue unfastened the brass clasp and spread the hinged case open flat. "My word, would you look at that!" The *carte-de-visite* depicted an impeccably dressed Jeremy posed in a Napoleonic stance with the fingers of his right hand tucked between the pearl buttons of his tapestry vest. His expression was a blend of audacity and arrogance. "Drake's clothes?" Taylor Sue inquired at last.

"Indeed, they were."

Taylor Sue looked askance at her friend. "But you don't fault them for making the most of the unexpected opportunity, do you?"

"The chance to see Ethan?" Salina twisted her wedding ring again. "No. In truth, I'm glad they went to see him—but the mess they could have landed in if the caper had been discovered..." She shut her eyes tightly. "The deed was already committed; no amount of obejection on my part would have done any good. Jeremy merely laughed, told me I had no cause to worry because it had all gone off without a hitch. The thing is, I know he'd do it again if he could."

"But?" Taylor Sue prompted.

A smile slipped past Salina's restraint. "My only regret is that there was no way to get Ethan out."

Taylor Sue nodded, equally sharing that regret. The two friends fell silent, each harboring her own thoughts until Taylor Sue observed, slightly puzzled, "This photograph was taken after Jeremy was wounded—yet there's no hint of his scar."

"Drake got his hands on some greasepaints, stage makeup that actors use. He applied them to his own scar and to Jeremy's. At least they had the foresight to reason that neither of them could waltz into Washington with those telltale markings of theirs and not later be identified by them. The paints concealed the scars from plain view, as well as from detection by the camera."

Taylor Sue handed the encased portrait back to Salina.

Salina perused the handsome picture for a moment before snapping the case shut. The words imprinted across the bottom margin of the *carte-de-visite* still sent a chill down her spine: *Brady's National Photographic Art Gallery, Washington, D.C.* "The anger I felt when Jeremy first told me where they'd been was overshadowed by the fact that his sight had returned. His memory had started to come back just before he'd left Gettysburg, and then the vision, too, was restored."

Taylor Sue's curiosity got the better of her. "Then why does Jeremy wear an eyepatch if he can see?"

"His right eye was the more damaged of the two. The area around it was terribly bruised and battered, and though the sabre cut didn't do any harm to the eye itself, it left the telltale mark for all the world to see. Dr. Warrick—the Yankee surgeon who tended Jeremy—gave Jeremy the patch primarily to cater to his sense of vanity, to conceal the scar as best he could. Jeremy's sensitive about it, and I can't say as I blame him. In time the mark should fade, but it will always be there. As Jeremy healed, his vision came back by degrees—he still has a blind spot on his right side. We both hope that over time that will dissipate, too."

"At least he is alive," Taylor Sue said.

"Amen!" Salina agreed. "I hadn't been a wife for a full twenty-four hours before he rode out to fight that day. I thank God I didn't end up a widow in the same amount of time!"

"You might yet if John Barnes keeps up this senseless vendetta," Taylor Sue hastened to point out. She continued to tell how the cabin came to be destroyed. "As I said, Jeremy's men came through the secret passageway. Mary Edith and I fixed supper and listened to them tell of where they'd been as of late—you know they've been riding with Mosby again. They participated in the Boot Raid and saw action near Billy Gooding's tavern on the night Mosby was shot."

A panic-stricken look filled Salina's face. "Is he...?"

"Mosby's not dead," Taylor Sue clarified. "He's gone home to recuperate. One of his subordinates is in charge of the 43rd Battalion for the interim. C.J. told of all the happenings in Richmond, and Curlie relayed to us how Rooney Lee had been taken prisoner by a detail of Yankees who'd slipped through the lines with the express intent of capturing him. They took him out of his sickbed at Hickory Hill, his in-laws' estate—right in front of his wife, mother, and sisters! Can you imagine?"

"Poor Rooney!" Salina breathed.

"Poor Charlotte Lee!" Taylor Sue aligned her sympathies with the wife who'd had to endure the ordeal. "Her husband has been imprisoned with no hope for exchange."

"Too familiar a tale," Salina remarked bitterly, thinking of her own incarcerated brother. "How do you suppose Barnes knew that we were on our way back to Virginia?"

Taylor Sue shrugged. "I'm convinced he believed you were already back, not just on your way. He came out of the darkness like a demon out of the pit, screaming the most horrendous things. That sorry excuse of a man is a raving lunatic." She rubbed her arms to ward away the gooseflesh that prickled along her skin. "We're still not sure exactly how many men he had with him, but I'm positive Everett was among them. One man got close enough to the porch to hurl a stone through the front window. It knocked over a kerosene lamp. The draperies caught fire, and once that happened, there wasn't much we could do to keep the flames from spreading out of control. It all happened so fast... Mary Edith and I gathered up Annie Laurie and Bonnie Lee while Jeremy's men returned fire in I don't know how many volleys. One by one they gave up the fight and followed us out through the tunnels—all except Charlie. Reverend Yates found his body the next morning, and we had a proper burial for him."

"Charlie stayed behind deliberately?"

"You know how he's been since he lost his leg at Stones River. Staying on the Shadowcreek property gave Charlie a sense of being needed. We did need him—Mary Edith and I couldn't keep the place going on our own. We relied on Charlie." Taylor Sue shook her head sadly.

"But he couldn't pass on the chance to prove he was still worth his salt in combat, even with only one good leg," Salina lamented. "What happened next?"

"Jeremy's men brought us here to Ivywood, safe and sound," Taylor Sue concluded. "They've ridden between here and cavalry headquarters half a dozen times at least since that night. Boone, Bentley, and Kidd Carney went out looking for you. They searched every possible route they thought you might've taken south."

"And didn't find us. We were holed up at a safehouse in Maryland, outside Frederick, not far from the Monocacy River. The family's name was Cobb. Jeremy..."

There was concern in Taylor Sue's eyes. "Jeremy...what?"

"Jeremy was rather sick." Salina picked at a button on the window seat cushion. "Very sick, actually."

"I don't understand what you're trying to tell me," Taylor Sue gently pressed.

Salina hesitated, trying to devise the best way to explain. "To go along with all his bruises, cuts, and broken bones, Jeremy had severe headaches induced by the concussion and the fever. Even after the healing process was under way, the headaches remained and plagued him cruelly. At first, Dr. Warrick prescribed morphine for Jeremy's aches and pains, but when the supply ran out, he administered laudanum instead. The laudanum eased the severity of the headaches, but in a short time Jeremy formed a dependency on it. I thought I had monitored him better—for I was fully aware that the treatment could result in addiction, and I wanted to prevent that. I found too late that he'd been taking the medicine without my knowledge far more than I realized. When I finally pieced together what was wrong, the cravings had a frightful hold on his system. By the time we reached the Cobbs, he was definitely struggling—I wouldn't let him have any more of the painkiller, and you know how stubborn I can be."

"I do," Taylor Sue worked to restrain her grin. For a moment, she almost felt sorry for her brother-in-law.

"Mrs. Cobb was very kind. She'd seen this sort of thing in recuperating soldiers before, after Sharpsburg, and had an idea what to do for him. Jeremy's system had to go through a process of detoxification to rid itself of the dependency. For nearly a week he was down with chills, fever, stomach cramps." Salina closed her eyes, but she couldn't block out the torment Jeremy had suffered. "It was hard on both of us."

"How is he now?"

"Now he's well," Salina answered with conviction. "Once he finally admitted to himself he didn't *need* the medicine, he became as determined as I to rid himself of the addiction. Now he's back to being his old self, for the most part. He still experiences drastic mood swings on occasion, and there has been a bit of uncertainty about him, but we're back home now, and I'm sure all that will pass. He feels guilty for succumbing to what he perceives as an abhorrent weakness in his character—but he also knows that healing and forgiveness are God-given. Acceptance is something he must come to terms with on his own and from there move forward. I'm just glad I was there to support him and help him fight through it."

"Jeremy thrives off your strength, Salina," Taylor Sue candidly observed. "How is he ever going to do without you once he goes back to Stuart's staff?"

"I'd rather not think of that," Salina hedged, fingering her gold, heart-shaped locket.

"You must think about it," Taylor Sue contended. "You know it's bound to happen, sooner or later."

"Well, I'd prefer it be later, thank you just the same!" Salina wrung her hands. It had been difficult for her to say good-bye to Jubilee, Mamma, and Yabel—her little brother who was half-Yank and half-Rebel—when she left Pennsylvania. She purposely didn't dwell on how much more painful it would be to say good-bye to Jeremy when the day came for him to go back to the front. Apologetically she whispered, "I'm a fine one to talk. It's trivial compared to what you're enduring with Ethan in prison."

"But at least I know where Ethan is—he's not out there getting shot at. Jeremy will be in far more danger in a cavalry charge or scouting behind enemy lines than Ethan will encounter in a Yankee cell."

"Don't discount starvation and brutal prison conditions. I'd say their chances for survival are about equal," Salina said ominously. "If only there were some way to get Ethan out of there."

Taylor Sue's expression softened as she stared out the windowpane. "Right now I'd be satisfied to know if he got my last letter. I'd have given a good deal to see the look on his face when he read that one."

Salina touched Taylor Sue's shoulder. "Meaning?"

"I'm going to have his baby, Salina," Taylor Sue confided, a bright glow in her amber eyes. "I pray constantly that Ethan might be exchanged before my time comes."

Salina enveloped Taylor Sue in a comforting, congratulatory hug. "Know that I am doing the same!"

Chapter Two

Jeremy lay flat on his stomach fast asleep, faintly snoring. Dreaming of Salina, he rolled onto his side, one arm unconsciously reaching out to embrace her.

A whisper-soft sigh escaped Salina's lips. Salina felt purely content as Jeremy's arm bound her securely to him, even as he slept. As the pale morning light filtered through the window, Salina couldn't help but grin, appreciating Jeremy's striking features. He appeared completely vulnerable and utterly at peace—a marked improvement over the anguish he'd suffered in the past few weeks.

Carefully, so as not to awaken her husband, Salina brushed a lock of his hair back from one of his black eyebrows and kissed the dark lashes resting against his sun-browned cheeks. Jeremy's was a handsome face, regardless of the new scar that started an inch above his right brow, missed the corner of the eye by a mere hairsbreadth, and trailed down his cheek for another two inches. Eventually, the pinkish mark would whiten, but it would be a lasting reminder of the violence of a Yankee-wielded sabre.

Unexpectedly, Salina's stomach knotted, churning fiercely, rendering her powerless to prevent herself from gagging. Salina began to climb out of the brass bed, but the instant she moved, Jeremy's arm tightened about her. Placing a tender kiss on his bare shoulder, she released herself from his hold. "I'll be right back," she whispered. Belting her dressing gown around her waist, she darted from the guest bedchamber and headed for the privy.

In his wife's absence, Jeremy blinked and stared up at the elaborate ceiling mouldings. He sat up, rearranged the pillows behind his back, and glanced at his surroundings. He put a hand over his left eye. The room immediately lost its distinctive definition—hard edges and lines blended together, hues blurred without specific form. When wearing the patch, Jeremy had to turn his head to the extreme right if he wanted to see anything beyond the bridge of his nose. What Dr. Warrick had called "peripheral vision" was greatly diminished as a result of the injury.

Yesterday at Shadowcreek when Salina had surprised him by coming upon him from the right, Jeremy had gotten a whiff of the perfumed rose water she frequently wore, though he hadn't realized it until now. Drake often seemed to have eyes in the back of his head, because he employed all his senses to their fullest, Jeremy mulled. Jeremy became determined to better use his other senses—particularly those of smell and hearing—to offset the deficiency of his sight.

A full twenty minutes passed before Salina returned to the guest bedchamber. She closed the door with care, letting the latch click lightly into place as the porcelain doorknob was released into its original position. Leaning her forehead against the door, Salina expelled a shuddering sigh. She felt better than she had a few minutes before—or so she endeavored to convince herself. She tiptoed across the wooden floor and seated herself at the vanity dressing table. Her thickly lashed eyes were wide and lucent, and if she wasn't on guard, their telling expression might reveal a secret she had not yet disclosed to her husband.

Salina's beringed hand trembled slightly as she reached for her silver-handled hairbrush. Staring into the mirror, she took several deep breaths in succession, willing herself to regain her composure. A movement stirred in the bed behind her. A pair of vivid, sapphire eyes caught and held hers in the reflective glass, but only the left eye viewed her with clarity.

"You're awake." Salina stated the obvious, a smile curving her lips.

"Yup," came Jeremy's gravelly reply. Crossing his arms over his chest, he remarked glibly, "I realize you were trying not to disturb me, but you failed, Sallie Rose. Miserably." He yawned. "I was awake the instant you wrestled yourself out of my arms and practically sprinted out of here."

"My apologies." Salina's smile was only mildly repentant. "I didn't intend to wake you, since you were sleeping so peacefully, but I am glad to see you awake nonetheless. There are a few things we need to talk about. Are you hungry?" Yet even as she uttered the inquiry, her stomach roiled at the mere thought of food.

"Yeah, I suppose I am," Jeremy said, rubbing his stomach. "But breakfast can wait."

In the mirror's reflection, Salina surveyed this man who was her lawful husband. Her profound love for him, regardless of their shared trials, was written all over her face.

Jeremy looked intently at Salina while she quietly sat in a gauzy cotton dressing gown. He detected an unusual degree of paleness in her otherwise rosy cheeks. Tentatively he asked, "You all right, Sallie? You seemed in an awful rush to get out of bed."

"I'm fine—really," she hastened to assure him. "Nothing to fret about."

Jeremy winked at her with his good eye. "Glad to hear it."

"You're certainly in an agreeable mood this morning." Intentionally, Salina broke eye contact with him and began pulling the brush through her curls. Jeremy knew her well and, like Ethan and Daddy before him, had the unsettling knack for reading whatever she was feeling or thinking just by looking into her eyes—the proverbial windows to her soul. *I will be no good at keeping my condition from Jeremy if he is determined to find out for himself what really ails me.* Her husband was obstinate and headstrong; he could be ruthlessly persistent, too, when the occasion called for it. Though she would not lie to him outright, she would do what she could to redirect his attention before he could initiate a serious interrogation. She wasn't ready for him to discover what she was just coming to terms with herself. Not yet.

Jeremy slipped from the bed, donned a pair of jean-cloth trousers, and pulled the braces up over his bare shoulders. "Aye, Sallie, we've got plans to discuss. Reverend Yates has confirmed that it was indeed John Barnes who had been around here again. He also brought up another point that we cannot afford to overlook: Taylor Sue is a Hastings since marrying your brother, and Barnes will probably regard her as fair game in his one-sided vendetta. In his twisted mind, he will see her as a threat."

"But Taylor Sue has no part in this feud—she only married into it," Salina argued.

"For better or for worse." Jeremy leaned over the washbasin to splash cold water on his face.

"Why would Barnes see her as any sort of threat?" Salina wanted to know.

"She has the potential to bear the next Hastings heir," Jeremy answered. "He's bent on annihilating your family because he wrongly believes your grandfather cheated him out of his birthright. It's common knowledge that your family came into possession of the Shadowcreek lands fairly and that the deed to the property is legal and binding. But we also know that John Barnes is not a reasonable man. He has his own brand of truth and justice; he takes the law into his own hands while using the war for cover."

"There must be a way to stop him."

"Sure: killing *him* before he can kill *me*!" Jeremy blurted out. "There are times, Sallie, when I'm downright sorry that I didn't kill him when I had the chance. It would've been ruled an act of self-defense..." He shook his head. "It would be far easier for me to leave you knowing that he wasn't out there lurking in anticipation of committing some unspeakable harm against us."

With Jeremy's shirtless back toward her, Salina was presented with an unhindered view of a long, white scar that ran low across Jeremy's narrow waist and right hip. She knew a matching mark ran along the back of his left leg. These scars were old, not fresh like the one on his face. The scars predated the war by a good five years—permanent examples of that "unspeakable harm" Jeremy spoke of: John Barnes frequently used to beat Jeremy, severely and without provocation. Barnes's murderous hatred for Jeremy was unrelated to land or title deeds, as in the case of the Hastings. John Barnes hated Jeremy because Jeremy bore the same surname without being a blood relation. Jeremy's mother had used her marriage to Campbell Barnes, John's brother, as a cover for her illicit affair with the man who was Jeremy's true father—a man enigmatically known only by the initials of *E.S.*

Towel-drying his unshaven face, Jeremy met his wife's troubled eyes. Tossing the towel aside, he took hold of the nearby chair and placed it behind the short stool Salina was sitting on. "Here."

He relieved her of the silver-handled brush and straddled the chair. "Allow me." He made several measured strokes through her long, raven curls with the hairbrush before he noticed she was staring at him intently.

"What else is going through that mind of yours?" she dared ask.

Jeremy saw no reason for hiding it from her. After all, she stoically shared all his other fears. "John Barnes would delight in destroying your family equally as much as seeing his name purged by ridding the world of me. It frightens me to think of what he would do if he ever found out that you and I were to have a child together." Threaded through his chilling words was an audible agony: "Our child would mingle your Hastings blood with mine. Barnes would stop at nothing..."

"Jeremy!" Salina gasped, absorbing the implication of his unspoken words.

"Ssshhhh," Jeremy grasped her trembling hands within his own. "I'm not going to let anything happen to you. The Lord is our defense, our strength, and our shield. He will see us through, of that I am sure." He kissed each of Salina's palms. "I was speaking of a hypothetical scenario, Sallie, about you and me having a child together. We got married in such haste that we never really gave that much thought, I reckon. But I do want a baby, someday, should the Lord see fit to bless us with a little one of our own."

Salina swallowed, and Jeremy went on. "When I was sick I had some bizarre dreams, but I had some comforting ones, too. One that occurred repeatedly was of a little girl—our own little girl." He dropped his gaze from her face to the wedding ring on her left hand. "I know you married me professing not to care what my name is or what it should be."

"I don't care," Salina reiterated.

Jeremy entwined his fingers with hers. "But a child would make things different."

"How?" she wondered. "Why?"

"I don't like bearing the name of Barnes in the least, but it's all I've got." He squinted, as if trying to discern something engulfed in a dense fog. "Sometimes I wish I knew what my name ought to be— for I don't cotton to the idea of branding our children with the name of a miscreant like John Barnes. I desire to give them a more honorable legacy than that! But I reckon there's little I can do about it."

"I've offered Hastings to you—or we could change our name to Barnett." Salina referred to an alias they had used on previous occasions. "Barnes, however, is the name you are known by. You've had the opportunity to bring honor to it, which you have admirably done. I'm proud to share it with you because it belongs to you."

"Forget about it," Jeremy muttered. "It's just as well to keep things the way they are."

"Would it really mean so much to you to learn what your father's name was?"

Jeremy's shoulders lifted and settled in a dejected shrug. "The man's dead, but the puzzle remains. Maybe it would ease my mind to know who he was—and then again maybe it wouldn't. Aunt Isabelle confirmed that Evan was his given name—which is where I get my second name from—but beyond that we only know he was a Union casualty at Shiloh. End of story. I shouldn't let it bother me."

Salina yearned to rid Jeremy of his confusion and doubt. Jeremy's mother had abandoned him in the wake of Campbell Barnes's death when he was a lad of fifteen years, leaving him nothing but debts and lies as an inheritance. Salina desired to shower Jeremy with her affection, to have him know that no matter who he was, no matter what his name was or should be, he would always be the one whom she loved best. It was on the tip of her tongue to share with him the revelation that his seed grew within her, but a stealthy knock disrupted their quietude.

"Who is it?" she called.

Jeremy stood, hastily wiped his eyes, and retreated behind the dressing screen to put on a clean shirt.

"It's me—Taylor Sue. May I come in?"

Salina opened the door, partially stepping out into the hall. "Good morning."

"Are you all right?" Taylor Sue asked in a low tone.

"I'm fine."

Taylor Sue pressed a half dozen crackers into Salina's palm. Her tawny eyes held a knowing look, and she whispered, "It's best to keep something down, even if you don't feel hungry."

Salina swallowed uncomfortably. She stuffed the crackers into the pocket of her wrapper. "Thank you."

Taylor Sue winked conspiratorially, then spoke loud enough for Jeremy to hear: "Reverend Yates has arrived. He was hoping that Jeremy was awake and would join him in the stable. You can tell him his men have already had their breakfast."

"If you'll be so kind as to tell the reverend I'll be down directly, I'll just grab something to eat off the buffet downstairs," Jeremy announced from behind the dressing screen.

"Aye." Taylor Sue retreated down the hall.

Jeremy pulled on his knee-high boots and buttoned up his vest. Snatching up a threadbare jacket, he mused, "I've got to get a proper uniform together."

"When the time comes for you to report to General Stuart, you'll go properly dressed," Salina declared.

Jeremy smiled, but he didn't say anything. He knew that look about her: She was up to something, and he deemed it best to wait until she was ready to tell him what it was. "I'll be back in a bit."

When her husband had left the room, Salina nibbled at the corner of one of the crackers.

Taylor Sue returned to the guest bedchamber. She studied her sister-in-law intently. "Doesn't he know?"

Salina shook her dark head, not bothering to pretend to misunderstand what Taylor Sue meant. "I was on the verge of telling him—just before you knocked."

Taylor Sue quickly apologized. "Bad timing on my part."

"Don't fret about it. I'm still not certain I'm ready to tell him—or if he's ready to hear it," Salina confided. "Please, Taylor Sue, don't say anything to him."

"You know I won't," Taylor Sue assured her. "But, Salina, you can't let him go back to the war without telling him he's going to be a father. That would be cruel."

"I'll tell him," Salina nodded. "I will."

"I know what you're feeling," Taylor Sue took hold of Salina's hand. "Like it can't be possible. It's so odd to imagine that there is life inside of you—a little one who'll depend upon you for love and nurturing..."

Salina pulled her hand away from Taylor Sue's comforting grasp. "No, you don't understand..."

"But I do. You're scared," Taylor Sue deducted. "I was when I first realized what was happening to me."

"Please, I don't want to think about this right now!" Salina insisted but then softened her tone. "Thank you for the crackers, and I do appreciate your concern—as well as your silence." Her fears were founded on something else.

"Salina, we have been through many an adventure together, and the Lord has seen us through them all," Taylor Sue softly remarked. "I'll grant you that motherhood will be a different experience altogether than being imprisoned at Fortress Alcatraz or working with your father's connections through the Remnant, but the verse applies nonetheless: We must be strong and courageous."

Salina mutely nodded, taking her sister-in-law's counsel to heart. Through the window, she saw her husband saunter across the yard below, then disappear into the stable.

Taylor Sue watched Salina's eyes as they followed Jeremy's ambling stride. "He'll be gone soon, Salina. At least we have each other to lean on."

"Aye." Jeremy had never kept from Salina his plans to return to service with Stuart's cavalry: He'd been honest concerning his intentions on that score.

Jeremy returned three-quarters of an hour later. Salina sat in the cane-backed rocker with her Bible spread across her lap.

"What are you reading?" he asked.

Salina recited the passage from Psalm 62 that had touched her heart:

> *My soul, wait thou only upon God;*
> *for my expectation is from him.*
> *He only is my rock and my salvation:*
> *he is my defence; I shall not be moved.*
> *In God is my salvation and my glory:*
> *the rock of my strength, and my refuge,*
> *is in God.*
> *Trust in him at all times; ye people,*
> *pour out your heart before him:*
> *God is a refuge for us.*

"Amen," Jeremy murmured.

"What word did Reverend Yates bring?"

"Tabitha Wheeler has learned that Barnes has left this area, though no one knows where he has gone. Now is as good a time as any to make our move," Jeremy stated.

Salina met his glance steadily. "I figured it had to be something like that, so I've already packed our bags. When are we leaving?"

A slow grin spread over Jeremy's face. He admired his wife's venturesome nature. "Within the hour."

"And where are we going?"

"Stuart's near Culpeper Court House."

"Aunt Tessa will give us shelter," Salina nodded with certainty. Tessa Carpenter was Daddy's sister. She lived in Culpeper with her two daughters, Delia and Clarice, and with Ruby Tanner, Salina's aunt by marriage.

"Us?" Jeremy asked, curious.

"Taylor Sue and I. I'm not leaving her behind, and you'll be going back to camp," she reminded him.

"If he'll take me back," Jeremy mused.

"Of course General Stuart will take you back," Salina insisted. "You're one of his most trusted scouts."

"Taylor Sue is willing to go along?"

It was Salina's turn to smile. "She has already assured me that she's ready for our next adventure."

☆☆☆☆☆☆☆

Reverend Yates was at Ivywood to say farewell and to pray over the Barnes couple and their comrades as they prepared to make their departure. "May God bless you and keep you. May He grant favor to your endeavors."

"Amen," came a resounding chorus of reply.

Jeremy's men mounted up while Jeremy tied the girls' horses, along with Tucker, behind the mule-drawn wagon. Taylor Sue hugged Mary Edith and kissed the twins good-bye. Salina did the same, thanking Uncle Caleb and Aunt Priscilla for their hospitality.

Caleb Armstrong gave his niece twenty dollars in Union greenbacks. "Federal money goes much further than Confederate bills."

Salina nodded, knowing the truth of his statement. "Thank you."

The minister pushed his spectacles up on the bridge of his nose as he smiled at the daughter of Garrett Hastings. "Rest assured that the goods you brought back from Pennsylvania will be distributed where they're most needed—Tabitha will see to that."

"I'm sorry I didn't have the chance to see her before we leave." Salina regretted missing the spritely old woman who was a friend and contact through the Remnant.

"She bid me to tell you once again that your efforts are to be commended," Reverend Yates said. "She would have liked to have been here to see you off, but Fairfax Court House is occupied, and she's got more than enough to do with handling the routine at the boarding house. Make sure you keep in touch, Miss Salina. Let us know how you're faring."

"I've not been an active participant in the Remnant for quite some time now, Reverend, but please remember that I haven't forgotten how to translate codes or create ciphers if necessary,"

Salina suggested in earnest.

"Your collecting that load of supplies was proof enough to remind us that you know what you're about, Miss. You'll do just fine. If we have need of your translation skills, we'll find you."

"Is there anything pertinent from the Remnant we should know before we leave?" Salina ventured.

"Concerning John Barnes, you mean?" the reverend inquired. "Nothing that you don't know already from your past dealings with that man. Watch your back, be on your guard, and know that we continue to lift you and the captain up in our prayers."

"Don't forget about my brother," Salina pleaded.

"He is high on the list, Miss Salina, never fear. Trust in the Lord; He will supply your strength."

Chapter Three

General Stuart's Headquarters
Cavalry Corps, Army of Northern Virginia

"General?"

"Yes, Major McClellan." Jeb Stuart did not pause, nor did he look up from the dispatch he was writing. "What is it?"

"It's Captain Barnes, sir," Henry B. McClellan began. "He's just arrived in camp and is requesting permission to report."

"Captain Barnes?" The pen halted in midstroke; Stuart shifted his attention from his portable camp desk to the face of his adjutant. "Have him wait. I'll see him directly."

"Very good, sir." Major McClellan exited the tent. The instant Stuart heard the order relayed to the young captain, his pen was in motion again, rapidly scratching words along the paper. When the dispatch was completed, Stuart refrained from folding the page until he was certain the ink was dry. In that time, he determined what had to be done where Barnes was concerned.

"Captain Barnes! I cannot tell you how pleased I am to see you well!" Stuart took note of the patch covering the horse soldier's right eye. Major McClellan stood near Jeremy Barnes under the tent fly. "Major, see that this dispatch goes to General Lee's headquarters as quickly as possible. Then come back. I have need of you here." Stuart whispered a set of instructions to his adjutant.

"Aye, sir," McClellan nodded, departing swiftly to carry out his orders.

Turning back to Jeremy, Stuart commented, "You look rested and healed. Private Carney brought me a letter from your wife not long ago that grieved me—yet your appearance here today is surely a testament of her determination to make you healthy again."

"To a degree, I suppose you're right, General," Jeremy grinned. "But I daresay my presence here is more accurately a testament of her answered prayers. I am blessed in having a wife who puts up with me and stands by me."

The general, too, smiled. "So am I."

While Jeremy recounted the details of his absence for his commander's benefit, Stuart's keen eyes took stock of the man before him. Jeremy Barnes stood proud, shoulders squared, and at attention. Despite the variance in their respective heights, Jeremy being slightly taller, the two men could very nearly look each other in the eye. Stuart detected a gleam of anticipation in Jeremy's unpatched eye—but the gleam did not burn as brightly as it once had.

"Sir, I've come to once again offer my services to your command," Jeremy asserted, "and I hope you will allow me to resume my duties of courier, scout, or aid, as you see fit."

Stuart appreciated Jeremy's willingness to volunteer, but he held strong reservations. At some point during the briefing, the returned Major McClellan had maneuvered behind Jeremy, around to his right, and—without any warning—now jerked the nine-round LeMat pistol clean from the holster. Jeremy realized too late that the sound of the hammer cocking behind his right ear was a telling sign to his commander.

Stuart folded his arms across his chest, shaking his head slowly from side to side. In a low, gentle tone he said, "I can't send you back out there, Barnes; not like this."

"You aren't going to let me scout?"

"Give it a little more time," the general suggested. "There are other duties that need attention here at headquarters. I will assign you enough responsibility to prevent you from being bored, rest assured."

Protestation from Jeremy was quickly squelched. "It's too dangerous, Captain," Stuart insisted. "If Major McClellan was able to sneak up on you from your blind side in broad daylight, what's to say some crafty Yankee couldn't do the same by less than the light of the moon? You could be captured or, God forbid, killed. And if you carried dispatches such as the one I just sent off to General Lee," Stuart pointed in the vicinity of Lee's encampment, "they'd fall into the hands of the enemy. I cannot afford that chance. Surely, you must realize that the risk is too great."

Jeremy's pride was stung. "Sir, I meant no disrespect. I would never want to do anything that would jeopardize battle plans, you know that, sir. But I really don't think—"

"Captain Barnes," General Stuart interrupted, "had I not already abolished the existence of Company Q, that's where you'd be temporarily reassigned along with the other recovering wounded. Since that no longer is an option, I will seek other duties for you."

"But, sir..."

"That is all, Captain. Debate is not an issue," Stuart stated.

"For how long?" Jeremy dared to wonder.

"For as long as it takes to prove yourself to me again. If I don't think you can handle reconnaissance or other courier assignments in a timely fashion, your new duties will be of a more permanent nature."

"With all due respect, sir, I am in your service on a voluntary basis," Jeremy said tightly. "If there is nothing I can do to prove my abilities meet your standards and you determine that I cannot be of use to you anymore, I would just as soon prefer to be released to Major Mosby's command."

"How would you serve Mosby any better than you can serve me?" General Stuart countered. "It's a tragedy, Captain, but if you are indeed blind in that right eye, it will take some adjustment on your part to deal with it. I'm not saying that you can never be a scout again. I'm merely pointing out that it might well be too soon after the injury."

Wisdom prompted Jeremy to hold his tongue.

Stuart continued, "I'll order Dr. Fontaine or Dr. Eliason to conduct a detailed examination—but if their findings leave any margin of doubt, I cannot send you out. Other lives depend on you; I have that to consider. I'll not knowingly put you in a position where your actions could endanger our strategy against those people."

Jeremy swallowed the lump of disappointment in his throat. "As I said, I meant no disrespect, sir."

General Stuart nodded, clapping the younger man on the shoulder. "Your resolve does you credit, Captain. Go see Fontaine or Eliason. When you've finished, have them report to me directly."

"Aye, sir." Jeremy saluted. He took his gun from Major McClellan's proffered hand and set out to find one of the cavalry surgeons.

Major McClellan sensed that the meeting had been a taxing one for General Stuart. Many of the staff officers—men who were friends of the general's—had been killed in action: Redmond Burke, John Pelham, Will Farley, Channing Price, to name a few. Heros von Borcke had been so severely wounded he had been unable to return to active service. Stuart's five-year-old daughter had died, but through it all, the general had taken care to keep his grief private, notwithstanding the black mourning band sewn to the sleeve of his jacket.

The adjutant knew that General Stuart took a special interest in Captain Barnes primarily because Jeremy had served under Garrett Hastings prior to volunteering with Stuart's cavalry. The letter Kidd Carney had brought to Stuart had disturbed the general, who, like every other commander, hated losing good men. He didn't want to see Jeremy Barnes's name added to the ever-growing list of deceased comrades-in-arms. Captain Barnes's reputation was that of a brave and strong warrior, a reliable and talented scout. Perhaps Stuart was right, and additional time to heal was all the man needed to return in top form.

"He's a good character," Stuart commented, nodding in the direction Jeremy Barnes had walked. "Fine soldier, that one. I honestly hope Fontaine or Eliason clears him."

A short while later, Dr. Talcott Eliason sat on a camp stool in General Stuart's headquarters tent submitting a verbal report. "Captain Barnes doesn't need the patch, really, for he does have some extent of vision in that eye, although it's not perfectly clear. He does admit to some degree of impairment, but he can determine shapes and colors and has a degree of depth perception, albeit slight. The patch he wears allows the eye to rest. His right eye isn't as strong as his left, but in time, I believe there's a chance that he may experience a total recovery."

"If you had it to do, would you send him out?" Stuart sought a professional opinion.

"Maybe not just yet—maybe only as a last resort," the surgeon admitted. "But I wouldn't eliminate all his duties, or he'll get discouraged and lose his will."

"And if he seeks a means of *proving* himself?"

"All the better," the surgeon nodded with enthusiasm. "That would be a clear indication that he still wants to fight. I would allow him to make the attempt, for I reckon it would not be an act meant merely to prove something to you, sir, but also to himself. Will that be all, sir?"

"Yes." Stuart contemplatively toyed with his long cinnamon whiskers. "That will be all. Thank you, Doctor. I'll keep your opinion in mind."

☆☆☆☆☆☆☆

Home of the Carpenters
Culpeper Court House, Virginia

"There's a man downstairs in the parlour come to see you," Clarice Carpenter, Salina's cousin, announced.

Salina looked up from the osnaburg shirt she was hemming.

"Claims his name's Drake Dallinger," Clarice continued. "But he didn't have a calling card with him. He insisted that you would know him. Do you?"

Salina set her sewing aside, a grin illuminating her face. "Indeed I do. He is our trusted friend, Clarice. One of the best." She gave her cousin no further explanation, making haste to reach the parlour.

"Little One." Drake greeted Salina in his customary way when she arrived to meet him. "You're looking as pretty as ever." He took her hand in his and gallantly kissed it.

"How you do go on, sir," Salina coyly replied. She took note of Drake's appearance. "And you're looking a little rough around the edges. An expensively tailored suit is one thing, but your hair is getting a little long for this part of the country, don't you think?"

"It's my understanding Taylor Sue is here with you—maybe she can be persuaded to give me a trim before I leave." Amusement shone in Drake's turquoise eyes.

"Leave?" Salina queried. "Where are you going?"

"To Kansas—back to the ranch," Drake replied with a decisive nod.

"I thought you were going to Boston with your sister and Elinor Farnham."

"That's where I've come from—and what an ordeal that was. There are all sorts of delays and connections that require traveling permits and passports if one hasn't got a military-approved pass. But," Drake grinned, "it was worth any effort to see you and Jeremy. I left Aurora and Elinor comfortably installed at Grandmamma's house on Beacon Street. They'll spend the winter there, no doubt immersed in their work for the U.S. Sanitary Commission. Grandmamma, however, is determined to launch the pair of them into high society. Rorie will not escape a coming-out ball, I'm sure." Drake visibly shuddered. "Just being in that city again reminded me how much I've missed my life out West."

"But you're the Dallinger heir since your father bestowed your inheritance. Aren't you required to keep up with the family business ventures?" Salina wondered.

"I pay my attorney an atrociously handsome retainer to manage all my affairs on behalf of the Dallingers. He'll keep things on track until I return."

Salina smiled at this man who had been Jeremy's friend long before he'd been hers, dating back to the two men's employment by Russell, Majors, and Waddell for the Pony Express. To see Drake now, dressed in all his finery like a proper gentleman, was a marked contrast to his old buckskins and boots. The absence of his gold hoop earring and the knife sheath he once wore strapped to his thigh proved Drake's outward appearance had become a bit more refined, but Salina knew that underneath the polished exterior Drake was very much the same rugged and incorrigible man she'd first met in St. Joseph, Missouri.

"So, you've come to say good-bye." Salina tipped her dark head to one side. "Neither your exorbitant fortune, a newfound sister, nor your kindled interest in Elinor Farnham can induce you to give up your affections for the untamed West, can they?"

"No, they cannot," Drake affirmed. "Besides, I'm needed at South Union. Lije is waiting on me. I'll miss you, Little One."

"Jeremy and I will miss you, too," Salina reciprocated. "I don't know what I would've done without you these past few months, Drake. You never let me give up, and you stood beside me all through Jeremy's recovery."

"It's never easy to see someone dear to you laid low like that," Drake nodded. "I'm just glad that you felt like you could count on me. Where is Jeremy?"

"He's at General Stuart's headquarters, offering to resume his duties. He's always got to be in the thick of it, you know."

A bright grin flashed in Drake's copper face. "That's where the action is."

Salina met Drake's turquoise eyes, but then she looked away.

Drake lifted her chin, making her meet his inquiring glance. "What, Little One? And don't answer 'nothing,' because there is something going on behind those deep green eyes of yours."

"I don't have any right to ask any more favors of you. You've done so much for us already."

"Let me be the judge of that."

Salina took a deep breath. "The next time you do go visit Boston, would you consider enlisting the aid of your attorney—Micah, isn't it?"

"Yeah, Micah Southerland," Drake clarified. "He's Lije's grandson."

"And Lije is the owner of the ranch in Kansas." Salina rubbed her arms to ward away the sudden, inexplicable chill that raced down the back of her neck.

"Uh-huh. So? What's Micah got to do with anything?"

"If he's an attorney, one might assume he would have access to certain...connections, shall we say?" Salina danced around the issue. "He might have the means to conduct an investigation of sorts."

"What kind of investigation?"

"Drake, I want to find Jeremy's name for him, to learn the identity of the man who was his real father."

Drake was silent for a minute. Salina witnessed his consternation, evident in the way the jagged white scar across his forehead puckered.

"You don't think that's a good idea." She jumped to the conclusion before giving him a chance to sort it through.

"Little One, I don't honestly know how you're going to find anything out about the man. You yourself did the translation of the pages in John Barnes's journal—they clearly said that Jeremy's father, known by the initials of E.S., was dead—a casualty at Shiloh."

"A murdered casualty," Salina qualified. "But Drake, I've been thinking: John Barnes is a crazed man. He's not known for telling the truth unless it suits his own purpose. What if he's lying? What if this E.S. isn't really dead?"

"E.S. is not much to go on," Drake repeated for the sake of argument. "There are hundreds of men who have those initials."

"According to Isabelle Barnes, John's wife, the E stands for Evan—which is Jeremy's second name. Isabelle has nothing to gain from lying to Jeremy. And we know that this Evan was fighting on the side of the Union. Beyond that—you're right. There is little else that provides a clue to his identity."

Again Drake was silent, contemplative.

"I know it would mean the world to Jeremy," Salina persisted.

"Little One, I've known Jeremy for a long time," Drake remarked. "He's never made a fuss over his name before."

"Of course he hasn't. Why would he? Up until a few months ago he didn't know that Barnes *wasn't* really his name. Oh, I don't know, Drake, it's just... Well... Perhaps your friend Micah knows a way to uncover something like this. Maybe he knows of an investigator who specializes in finding lost people—or one of those detectives like Alan Pinkerton had. Someone who could probe into the past?"

"You're talking about digging into a virtual Pandora's box," Drake cautioned. "You don't even know what ramifications an investigation like this could have."

Salina's stance betrayed her determination. "Jeremy and I have been through so much, Drake. Do you honestly believe that anything discovered could be worse than what we've survived together already?"

Salina had a point, Drake had to admit. Something had given her this notion, and he knew her instincts often proved right.

"Are you *sure* this is what you want?" Drake pressed. "You need to consider that it's not just your lives that could be impacted. What about the others involved? This family Jeremy is a part of, yet they know nothing of his existence? There are undoubtedly more than just yourselves who will reap the whirlwind," Drake predicted.

"Can't it be done discreetly? It might well give Jeremy a sense of peace in just knowing his own identity. Drake, he hates the fact that he bears the same surname as John Barnes—especially since they aren't even related. Barnes is merely the name his mother gave him when he was born."

Drake pounced on Salina's last statement. "What do you know about his mother? In the years I've known him, I've never heard him mention her."

"It's no surprise to me that Jeremy doesn't speak of her. She was never around much, but I remember her being beautiful and spoiled. She liked men and was liked by them. She married Campbell Barnes to cloak her affair with whoever Jeremy's father was and pawned Jeremy off as his son, even after making the discovery that Campbell was incapable of producing offspring of his own. When Campbell died, she turned Jeremy over to John Barnes, who beat Jeremy, sometimes almost to death. She never looked back—I don't believe she loved Jeremy a jot. How *could* she and walk out on him the way she did? She never wanted him. Campbell Barnes was *not* Jeremy's father—E.S. was."

"A name can have significance, Little One, or it can have none," Drake said sagely. "I knew my name was Dallinger all my life but never bothered to use it until now. I didn't have any need for it among my mother's people. By declaring it as my own, however, I've hurt some people and shocked others: Grandmamma is a point in case. She blames me for the grief and disappointment my father caused her by taking an Indian maiden to wife. 'Oh, the scandal!'" he decried, employing the falsetto voice of his dead father's mother. "'What *will* other people think?!'"

Salina smiled at Drake's mimicry, but her tone remained serious. "That all stems back to your name."

"That's right—that's what I'm trying to tell you. I'm asking you to consider the potential consequences of this request, to think it through carefully."

"But I have, Drake, or I wouldn't have brought it up in the first place," Salina reasoned.

Salina's earnest sincerity touched Drake's heart. If she truly believed giving Jeremy his name could do some good, Drake was willing to do what he could to help her. "All right, I'll look into the possibilities, Little One, for your sake. I'm not making any promises, mind you, but I'll see if there's anything Micah can do."

"No," Salina shook her head. "I don't want this done for my sake. I want it done for Jeremy's sake. It's *his* name."

"But you'll share that name."

"I've already told him I will share whatever name he decides to claim as his own." Salina put her hand on Drake's arm. "You're his friend. If you're going to do this thing, then do it for him."

Drake stared into her beseeching eyes for a long moment, then nodded.

In spite of the sunny summer day, there were storm clouds above Jeremy's head as he returned to the Carpenter house on the outskirts of Culpeper following his interview with General Stuart. Jeremy thundered up the veranda steps, and with barely leashed force, he swung the front door open wide. His expression grew even darker when he saw his wife and his best friend whispering conspiratorially together. Drake and Salina both jumped—almost guiltily—when he stormed through the parlour.

"We-ell," he drawled sourly, "what's all this?"

"I don't think I like your tone, friend," Drake said coolly, "any better than I like the conclusions you're jumping to."

Salina glanced from the stony expression on the face of her husband to the defiant challenge snapping in Drake's eyes. Jeremy wrenched his accusing gaze from Drake, harshly leveling it at Salina.

The room suddenly felt to Salina like it was more than a hundred degrees and tilting left of center. Salina was not aware that her knees had buckled under her or that she would have fallen into an inglorious heap at Drake's feet had he not acted quickly, gathering her into his arms. She never heard the rifle shot that broke a glass windowpane, tore through the draperies, nicked the chandelier, whizzed through the parlour, and slammed into the mantel shelf. She was entirely ignorant of the other residents in the house and of their uproarious clamor, shouting, and screaming. For a heart-stopping instant, her name was on everyone's lips.

A second shot rang out immediately after the faded echo of the first, then a third and fourth in rapid succession. Delia, Clarice, and both the aunts hit the floor, covering their heads, expecting a barrage of lead that didn't come. The ensuing silence was deafening, but as it stretched into greater length, they began to wonder whether the episode was over.

Drake wasn't taking unnecessary chances. Pulling his pistol from his holster, he shouted at Jeremy: "Get her out of here!"

"Bring Salina and come with me." Ruby tugged impatiently on Jeremy's arm. "There's a hiding place in the cellar."

Jeremy obediently scooped up his wife's unconscious form; Salina's head lolled against his chest.

Four of Jeremy's men reined up in front of the house, Spencer repeaters in hand, with the clear intent of riding out after the sniper. Drake joined the search party.

"I should be going with you," Jeremy insisted.

"Don't be absurd," Drake countered. "We don't know who's out there. If it's Barnes, he'll kill you just as soon as look at you. No, you stay here and make sure Little One is all right."

Drake had called Salina by that nickname since their first meeting. It had never bothered Jeremy before, but for some reason, today it made the hair on the back of his neck stand up. This inane jealousy had no founding, and he upbraided himself for casting both his wife and his friend in an unfavorable light. Surely his imagination was conjuring what didn't—couldn't possibly—exist.

Aunt Ruby and Jeremy settled Salina onto a pallet on the root cellar floor. In the cool dimness, Jeremy pressed a damp cloth to his wife's forehead, offering a glass of water when she came to. It was his concerned face that filled Salina's vision when she revived, and she saw the relief that flooded over him. She was horrified when he told her what had happened.

Jeremy murmured something unintelligible to Ruby, whose eyes flashed with instant disapproval. Then Jeremy kissed Salina's temple, instructing her to be still and rest.

"Where are you going?" Salina wanted to know, struggling to sit up.

Jeremy paused at the cellar door. "Don't fuss, darlin'. I'll be back shortly."

"Easy, child," Aunt Ruby placed a firm hand on her niece's shoulder. "You lie still."

"But he's going out to join the chase..."

"It's within his right to protect what is his," Ruby reminded her.

"But..."

Ruby shushed her.

Salina persisted. "Why would someone shoot at this house?"

"He thinks somebody was trying to kill you," Aunt Ruby answered plainly. "There's a bullet hole in the parlour mantel which might have hit you if you hadn't fainted when you did."

All the color drained from Salina's already pale face. "But *why?*"

Ruby outlined the obvious reasons; "One: You're the daughter of Garrett Hastings. Two: You're the wife of Captain Jeremy Barnes. Three: You're a former operative in a rather successful spy ring and had a prominent role in the Western Campaign, which, had it not failed, might've allowed the Confederacy to annex the northern states of Mexico and capture California along with the other Western territories. Take your pick, child; there are enough strikes against you."

"I'm proud of all those things, Aunt Ruby. I've nothing to be ashamed of. I've only acted and done what I thought was right, and I'll stick to my guns."

At that Aunt Ruby smiled. "Oh, I know you will. You've your father's strength and stubbornness."

"Someone must've followed us from Shadowcreek and pinned down our location to this place," Salina deduced. "We've put you all in danger."

"How could you have known?" Aunt Ruby countered. "You couldn't have. Don't fret. Your young captain and his friends will make it all come out right in the end."

Jeremy rode out in the same direction he'd seen Drake, Curlie, Jake, Boone, and Tristan go. A menacing thought belatedly came to mind: If whoever it was had wanted to take him, they could have done so easily on the road back from Stuart's encampment. He acknowledged with a sickening knot tightening in his gut that this was a deliberate attack on Salina herself.

☆☆☆☆☆☆☆

A few hundred yards from the Carpenter house stood a copse of trees large enough to conceal a sniper. The spot afforded an unhampered view directly into the parlour, Jeremy noted, looking from his position back toward town. He glanced first at the corpse lying facedown in the dirt, then at the jittery, wild-eyed horse that had apparently been spooked by the shooting.

"Lieutenant Malcolm Everett," Jeremy identified the deceased before Drake or any of the others could ask if he knew who the man was. "He works— worked—for Barnes."

Tristan pointed to the oozing hole in the man's chest. "Somebody killed him before he could get off a second shot at the house."

Drake looked askance at Jeremy. "You got some kind of guardian angel you're not telling the rest of us about?"

Jeremy shrugged, more than a bit unnerved. "At least there's one less madman I'll have to watch my back for."

☆☆☆☆☆☆☆

"Did you have your interview with General Stuart?"

Jeremy turned toward Salina's soft voice. Her form was swallowed by the cellar shadows until the lantern he'd brought down with him illuminated her face. "Aye. I saw him." He sat down on an upended barrel and ran an agitated hand through his mussed sandy-blond locks.

Salina knew her husband well enough to discern the difference between anger and hurt in his tone. She touched his shoulder with a reassuring hand. "I can't help you if you don't tell me what the trouble is."

Balancing his elbows on his knees, Jeremy leaned over, practically bent in half—almost as if he were going to be sick. As Salina kneaded the taut muscles at the base of his neck and across the wide expanse of his shoulders, he reluctantly narrated the outcome of his audience with the Confederate cavalry leader. It had not gone as well as he'd hoped it would have.

Salina could feel the heat of frustration and aggravation seeping from him. She moved to face him, kneeling at his feet, resting her hands on his knees. "Jeremy."

He looked at her squarely, saying nothing.

Her fingers, of their own volition, untied the string holding the eyepatch in place. She gingerly traced the red scar along his brow and cheekbone.

Jeremy grabbed her hand in a vicelike grip. "Don't do that!"

"Why?" Her question was an indirect challenge. "Does it still hurt, even now?"

He held her fingers tightly.

"It does, doesn't it? But not with physical pain. It hurts you here," she caressed his forehead, indicating his mind, and then pointed to his chest, to his heart. "And here." She silently dared him to refute her statement.

Her perception unsettled him. "What are you thinking, Sallie?" he ground out. "Contemplating just how ugly I've become?"

"You're not ugly, Jeremy!" her sharp rebuttal was instantaneous. "Far from it!"

"I might've been handsome to you once—but no more. Not with *this*." He deliberately retraced the angry red scar himself. "Doesn't it bother you to be married to a maimed man?"

"Jeremy, don't be absurd!" Salina framed his whiskered face between her hands. Her soft whisper belied the level of conviction that raised her chin. *"Maimed* is a strong word—and I hardly consider you that! *Maimed* might be losing a leg or having an arm amputated—though if either of those misfortunes had befallen you, I would still love you with all my heart!"

"Strong words," Jeremy purposely echoed her phrasing.

"Very strong," she murmured against his lips.

Jeremy's eyelids fell half-closed. The butterfly kisses he traded with her were administered with an effort that lacked much in the way of enthusiasm.

Salina sat back on her heels, confused by his cool reserve. "I can't read your mind, Jeremy."

"I've got to find something to prove to him. Something impressive." Jeremy's fisted hands illustrated his vehemence. "I reckon I'll have to accomplish something *impossible*, and that'll show him! Nothing ordinary for General Stuart—oh no! Definitely something that will catch his attention."

"Something impossible? Such as?" Salina was trying to ascertain where Jeremy's thoughts had rambled on to. "Such as sneaking behind enemy lines, capturing John Barnes, and delivering him to Libby Prison?" she facetiously queried. Sarcasm got the better of her. "No, I know! We'll send word through the Remnant to leak news to John Barnes telling him I'm here in Culpeper alone. That should be enough to draw him out. He tried to use me as bait to trap you once— I'm sure you could do the reverse: I'll pose as the bait to trap *him* instead."

"I'll not put you in the path of danger, Sallie," Jeremy said. "But as for going behind enemy lines...with the right plan, with enough men...this could work. I'm sick and tired of being hunted," he flatly told her. "Maybe it's time to become the hunter instead."

"Jeremy, I wasn't serious... I..." Salina stopped. Though she'd meant it as a jest, she knew nothing she could say would change his mind. "Oh, what have I done?"

Jeremy was already scheming. "And if Stuart still doesn't think me worthy to ride for him after pulling off a stunt like that, then I will just go over to the 43rd Battalion under Mosby's command. Mosby doesn't question his partisan rangers. He merely expects discipline and obedience from them. Plus, Mosby knows me—I've ridden with him before. Even you know all about how invalid soldiers in Fauquier County appear to be recuperating by day, their whereabouts fully known to the Yankees, and then secretly they go riding with the rangers by night. Well, I'm *not* an invalid anymore, Sallie. I won't sit here idle and let the action pass me by. That brilliant suggestion of yours is going to get me back into the general's good favor!"

"There is no cause to go borrowing trouble!" Salina protested. "Jeremy, if something ever happened to you..."

"What? What if something happened to me, Sallie?" Jeremy recalled the way she and Drake had been so *amiable* in front of the fireplace earlier. "If I had died in that cavalry battle at Gettysburg, would you have married Drake after I was dead and buried?"

"What?!" Salina's astonishment was plain. "What on earth are you talking about?"

"I've seen the two of you together," Jeremy said bitterly. "Not only today, before you fainted—but at your birthday party before we left the Grants. You two were as thick as thieves then, too." He closed his eyes, remembering the picture Drake and Salina had made, foreheads almost touching, as they'd pored over the scenic cards in the stereoscope he'd given her as a gift. "You two exchange confidences with regularity, I'm sure. You're always buzzing about something, laughing and whispering together."

"Drake is our good friend," Salina objected.

"You two were completely engrossed in discussing something when I came in this afternoon. Obviously something of great import—and yet you didn't feel you could confide in me about it."

"Aunt Ruby says that if Drake hadn't caught me when I fainted, I very likely would have smacked my head on the hearth!" Salina's indignation flared as she defended herself. "He's been very good to us, Jeremy. If he shows any partiality toward me, it's merely because he has your best interests at heart!"

"*My* best interests?" Jeremy asked snidely. "Drake's got a habit of looking after his own interests quite effectively."

Salina was dumbfounded. "Are you making some sort of accusation here?"

"No." Jeremy shook his head. "No, I'm just pointing out a scenario which is not as far-fetched as you seem to believe. Your mother married Duncan Grant in the wake of your father's death."

"What has that got to do with anything?" Salina demanded. "Duncan married my mamma so he could change her name and hide her somewhere where John Barnes wouldn't find her."

Jeremy knew that what Salina said was true, but he was stubborn. "I guess I just got to thinking that you and Drake must have been *very* close while I was recovering from my wounds. For weeks I couldn't see and I couldn't remember—you yourself had to break it to me that we were married, for Pete's sake, because I didn't know it myself! If I'd died, you'd have been free to love Drake instead of me."

It took every ounce of strength Salina possessed to prevent herself from unleashing an utterly scathing reply. "Yes," she confessed lowly. "We *were* exchanging confidences when you walked in, Jeremy. But they were about *you*." Her heart felt heavy, bruised, for there had been a time when distrust had been an issue between them, yet she was sure that rift had been sensibly mended. Could it be that the lingering effects of his past laudunum addiction still clouded his judgment? Salina simply wasn't sure if that was entirely the cause of his irrational assumptions. "It doesn't matter what I say right now," Salina asserted, "you aren't in the frame of mind to listen to reason. If you were, you'd realize how insane this entire conversation is! I love you! I always have—I always will. Come what may!" She stormed past him, scrambling up the cellar ladder before a torrent of angry tears overtook her.

Jeremy leaned his head back against the earthen wall. "But I love you, too, Sallie. So much it hurts." He checked the impulse to go running after her, reckoning it better to make appropriate amends when both of their tempers had cooled. He was at fault, and he would apologize—profusely. Reason reminded him that Salina was *not* his mother, and he knew that Salina wanted him, or she never would have agreed to wed him in the first place.

Jeremy sauntered into the stable to check the horses—anything to clear his head. Crossing the threshold, he failed to see the man on his right who brought the blunt end of a pistol down hard on the back of his head. Jeremy pitched forward onto the straw-covered ground, oblivious.

Chapter Four

*D*rake had overheard Jeremy's resounding disagreement with Salina, their voices having floated up through the cracks in and around the wooden cellar door. Salina's assent up the ladder had cautioned him to get out of her way, and she'd stalked past without even seeing him. She had a right to be angry, Drake allowed. He couldn't believe Jeremy had so little faith in her or in her love for him. With grim determination, he followed Jeremy to the stable with the intent of setting his friend straight on a few issues.

Drake was within a yard or two of the stable door when he heard the groan that preceded Jeremy's fall. Quick as lightning, he slammed the attacker's back against the stable wall, jamming a forearm under his jaw.

The man coughed and stammered in protest of the pressure Drake applied to his throat. The brim of his hat, dislodged by the blow, hindered his view of his assailant.

"Let the colonel go, sir," a voice behind Drake firmly advised. "Now."

Drake heard the click of a hammer pulled into position and felt the barrel of a revolver tickling the side of his ribcage. He closed his eyes, clamped his jaw, and silently berated himself for not considering the possibility of more than one person hiding in the stable. Deciding it would be in his best interest to do as he was told, Drake willingly released the colonel, held his hands away from his body, and slowly turned around to face the second man. "Consider it done."

"Much obliged, Brisco." Readjusting his hat, the first man nodded gratefully to his partner, who still held the gun aimed at Drake.

The blue-uniformed colonel breathed easier without Drake's forearm pressing against his windpipe. He stuck a finger between his collar and his neck, stretching the fabric to allow more adequate room to swallow. Clearing his throat, he looked Drake in the eye. "I'm afraid I haven't had the pleasure of officially making your acquaintance," he said with feigned politeness. "And just *who* might you be?"

"Drake Dallinger."

"Well, now, Mr. Dallinger. It just so happens I've heard of you," the colonel nodded. "Your philanthropic gestures in Gettysburg were quite beneficial to the widows and orphans in the wake of the battle. Reliable sources say that you're a very powerful man in Boston—owning controlling interest in nearly half of the city's industry—and that doesn't count the millions you have in other odd investments and hobby-type business ventures. Without a doubt, you are possessed of the wherewithal to put forth a great deal of time and expense in relief efforts—*most* commendable." The colonel thoroughly inspected the rangy, black-haired, turquoise-eyed man. "I've even heard that you dabble in cattle drives when it suits your fancy."

The mention of cattle arrested Drake's attention. This colonel had obviously done some extensive research. Drake's Boston involvement was common knowledge, as were his efforts in Gettysburg, but how this man knew of cattle drives was a puzzle. How would a *Yankee* colonel know of work he'd done for Lije Southerland way out west in Kansas?

Drake let the comment about the cattle drives go without inquiry. Instead, he tested another avenue to gain his own information. "What do you intend to do with me, Colonel, if I may ask? If you're thinking of holding me for ransom, let me tell you now that my attorney won't pay a dime. Between him and my sister, they know I'm not worth it."

"Oh no, Mr. Dallinger," the colonel chuckled, amused. "You quite mistake my purpose. I've no intention of holding you for ransom. I wouldn't *dream* of depriving any of your fortunate beneficiaries of your generosity. No, sir." The colonel clasped his hands behind his back and paced in front of where Brisco held Drake. "They say that you never sent supplies to one side or the other exclusively, but seemed to have a hand in lending aid to both sides in an attempt to be fair, equal."

"You are well informed, Colonel," Drake remarked. The colonel made him uncomfortable.

"It's my job to be informed." A contemplative expression crept into the colonel's dark blue eyes. "I know a man who tried like tactics in his business dealings—favoring neither the North nor the South, but both. He had a moderate measure of success."

"If we are thinking of the same man, then yes, you could say he's made a success of it," Drake ventured.

The colonel's eyes widened. "There are lots of men in this world, Dallinger. You and I travel in entirely different circles. I'd be very surprised to find that we are acquainted with the same people."

"But we must know *some* of the same people," Drake persisted.

The colonel was growing weary of the polite conversation. The very fact that Dallinger was here led the colonel to believe that he might have information that he sought. He braced his feet at shoulder width and balanced his fists on his gun belt. "We both know of Salina Hastings, don't we?"

Drake bolted toward the colonel. "If you so much as lay a hand on her, I'll..."

Brisco brought the butt of his pistol down on the back of Drake's head. Unconscious, Drake sprawled face first onto the floor, as Jeremy had. "They'll both have knots," Brisco commented, returning his gun to his holster.

"Aye," the colonel agreed. "Dallinger probably won't stay out for long. Lock him up in the shed."

"And this one?" Brisco turned Jeremy over. The outside light slanted through the stable door, falling across his face.

For a moment, Colonel E.S. Ridgeford thought he knew the unconscious man—but he couldn't possibly. "I..." he stammered. "I suppose we could tie him up, leave him in one of the empty stalls."

Brisco hoisted Drake's body over his shoulder and deposited him in the storage shed. He snapped the padlock shut.

"Did you see Dallinger's face? He looked like he wanted to kill me when I brought up Salina's name," Ridge pondered. "Almost like a jealous lover."

"Or a true friend. He doesn't have a wedding band on—this one does." Brisco pointed to Jeremy's left hand. "Husband?"

"Yes, as a matter of fact, he is my husband," a female voice piped up.

Both Ridge and Brisco looked over their shoulders, entirely unsure as to how long the young lady had been standing there, or to what degree she might have overheard their conversation.

"Put your weapons on the floor, both of you," she commanded. "Then raise your arms and turn around so I can see you. If you so much as flinch, I'll fire—and I don't think you'd *really* want me to do that."

The lady was absolutely right. Neither Ridge nor Brisco had any desire to be used as target practice. The two men did as she bid, then held their arms clear away from their bodies.

Salina put herself between the prone form of her husband and the two men she faced. "What have you done to him?"

"Oh, he'll be all right," Brisco said, "but I'm certain he'll have a bump on his head."

Ridge stood face-to-face with the daughter of Garrett Hastings. He'd been searching for over a month now and had found her at last. This might be his only opportunity. "I've been looking for you..." He took a step toward her. "We don't have much time, and there is a whole passel of things you and I need to discuss..."

Salina's shot slammed into the stable floor a mere inch from the toe of Ridge's boot.

Brisco whistled.

"Yikes!" Ridge yelped, glaring at Garrett's daughter. "Wait a minute—you don't understand. I just need to talk to you!"

Salina was sure the sound of the gun report would stir a commotion within the house. Aunt Ruby and Aunt Tessa would come to investigate, no doubt toting loaded rifles of their own.

"Where'd a little lady like you get ahold of a nine-rounder like that?" Brisco wondered.

"That's not important," Salina replied calmly, her emerald eyes somber, watchful. "What is important is that I can use it just as effectively as the little number in this hand." She brought his attention to the pearl-handled revolver she habitually carried.

"I believe you." Brisco didn't speculate as to whether she was a hair-trigger shot or just a nervous one.

"Who are you?" The countenance of the colonel disturbed Salina. His eyes were every bit as blue as Jeremy's, and he possessed some of the same facial features. The man's hair, however, was sable brown, not light like Jeremy's, but their black brows and bearded chins were uncannily similar.

Ridge declined to answer.

Salina looked to Brisco, but he, too, remained mute. She saw their tethered horses. "If you get out right now, I might prove generous and let you go free."

"But..." Ridge's chance to conduct his interview was slipping away. "I came to enlist your help. I just killed a man out there who was trying to kill you." He pointed toward the distant copse of trees. "Surely you could answer a few questions in exchange for saving your life."

"Mount up," Salina ordered. "Now!"

"Salina..."

"Look, I don't know how you know who I am, but I don't care! I said you're going!"

"Now's not the time, Ridge," Brisco intervened. "There's been enough noise that someone at the house is bound to come check. We can't afford to have anyone reporting us to the authorities. Miss Hastings here doesn't trust us above half, not that she should, considering the circumstances, but we haven't got the time to explain that we're on her side. It's time to take our leave!"

Swearing under his breath, Ridge mounted his horse and followed Brisco to the stable door.

Salina stepped into the colonel's path, knowing he'd rein to a halt before running her over. "Common sense does you credit," she remarked saucily.

Ridge locked his teeth together to keep himself from tossing back a rudely caustic reply. His ma had taught him etiquette, manners, and how to treat a lady; he was trying desperately to remember those lessons at present.

Standing her ground, Salina coolly stated, "I want your name."

That made Ridge laugh derisively. He shook his sable head, sapphire eyes glinting. "Your *father* was one of the few people who knew my name, Salina. Your *stepfather* has spent the better part of a year trying to discover it. Forgive me if I don't just up and blurt it out to you on demand." He snapped a mocking salute, then rode out of the stable without a backward glance.

Brisco touched the brim of his hat. "Until we meet again, Miss Salina," he dipped his head in deference.

Salina shuddered. She was as certain as that man Brisco that there would be another encounter. It was only a matter of when and where.

When she was assured the two Yankees had gone, Salina gathered Jeremy into her arms. She traced his brows, the scar, the curve of lips between his whiskers. Her feathery touch brought him back to wakefulness.

"I owe you an apology," Jeremy admitted.

"I know," Salina nodded, patiently waiting.

A hard lunge at the shed door made the jamb shudder. Surprised, both of them started at the loud *CRACK!* of splintering wood and scrambled to their feet as Drake kicked the door down. He emerged from the shed gingerly rubbing his head.

"They got you, too?" Jeremy put his fingers to a like lump behind his ear.

"The two of you are quite a pair," Salina muttered affectionately. "Come on, both of you. I'll fetch some ice for those thick skulls of yours."

Drake and Jeremy stood watching Salina sashay back to the house, her skirts and petticoats swinging like a bell.

"Have any idea as to who those men were?" Jeremy asked.

"One called Brisco, the other called Ridge," Drake answered. "Dressed as Yankees, but I'm not so sure." Again, he pressed his fingers lightly against the swelling lump on the back of his head. "They knew me—and they knew her."

"But how?" Jeremy wondered.

"I don't know." Drake shrugged. "But you can rest assured that I intend to find out."

☆☆☆☆☆☆☆

Supper was over, the dishes done, and the Carpenter household settled in for the night. In the stable, however, Jeremy and Drake examined maps, read current newspaper articles, and discussed strategy at length with the assembled riders. They would wait only until word came through the Remnant verifying the whereabouts of John Barnes—and then they would go get him.

When Jeremy came upstairs to the room he shared with Salina, he found she was not asleep; in fact, she was not even in bed. Salina stood at the window, silhouetted in the moonlight, staring out at the landscape below.

"I still owe you an apology, darlin'," Jeremy drawled. He made a detailed study of the Oriental carpet covering the wooden floor. "I said some things earlier today that were uncalled for, and I hurt you."

"You did," Salina readily agreed. She looked up into her husband's troubled face. "But I forgive you."

Jeremy hung his head, properly chagrined. "May I ask you something, Sallie?"

"Anything." Though Jeremy stood but a few inches from her, Salina couldn't quite bring herself to reach out to him. He was going to have to make an effort to bridge the distance between them.

"Why do you love me?" Jeremy wanted to know.

"It's a bad habit I have," Salina quipped.

Jeremy looked quizzical, trying to gauge whether she was serious or merely being sarcastic.

A slow, clement smile curved Salina's mouth while the tiny bit of merriment grew from a spark to a blaze in her emerald eyes. "I have always loved you, Jeremy Barnes, since I was about twelve, I think. In fact, I can't rightly remember a time when I didn't love you."

Jeremy tentatively caressed her cheek, then slid his fingers to cup the nape of her neck.

Salina kissed the arm he rested on her shoulder and voluntarily elaborated on her reply to his question, intuitively sensing that hearing the words spoken might help him believe: "I may not have loved you then as much as I love you now, but I'm sure that's when my affection for you first took root. You were tall, sure of yourself, more than a little attractive—certainly not difficult to catch an admiring girl's fancy with those qualities in your favor. You're an intelligent man, Jeremy, a good-hearted, God-fearing one at that. You were Ethan's friend before you were mine, but you didn't laugh at me, no matter how silly or schoolgirlish I might have seemed to you, and we built the foundation of our friendship. Your past has never interfered with the way I feel about you. I love your pride, your independence, and your daring. Your courage intrigues me, along with your strength and confidence."

Jeremy withdrew his hand from her neck and stuffed it in his pocket. He turned away from her, unable to face her when he admitted, "I don't feel very confident now, and I can't hide that from you."

"Why?" Salina gently pressed. "Because of the residual effects of getting free of the laudanum? Or because we had a disagreement and heated words got the better of us? The latter is bound to happen from time to time, Jeremy—we're too strong-willed for it not to. We both knew that before we said our vows."

"I'm not even the same man you married," Jeremy asserted, eyes downcast. "The war has changed me. I've seen things that I can never forget, done things either because of orders or self-preservation..."

"Ssshhhh..." Salina put a finger to his lips to shush him. "Yes, I'll agree that you've changed—but so has war changed us all. Look at me—I've done things I'd *never* have dreamed myself capable of doing in peacetime: I've served in field hospitals, worked on relief efforts with the Women's Assistance Guild, and I've operated as a translator for Daddy's old Network and the Remnant. They say desperate times require desperate measures. The Confederacy, I'm afraid, may end up being quite desperate before all is said and done." Salina took one of Jeremy's large hands between her own. "I know the deep-down you, Jeremy. I know you'll laugh again, and your smile will appear to warm and thrill me. Your confidence will return. We'll rely on each other, love each other. You'll continue being the brave cavalier, the tender poet, the man of my dreams."

Jeremy smiled, appreciating her bravado on his behalf. If she was trying to bolster his confidence, it was working. His voice shook slightly on account of the raw emotion welling within. He blinked away tears. "You make me feel ten feet tall, you know? Like I could whip fifty Yankees single-handedly. What have I ever done to deserve a lady like you?"

Salina's lilting laughter was music to his ears. "Oh, I have my moments, too; don't forget that."

Jeremy drew his precious wife into his arms, mingling kisses with their shared tears, increasing their strength of will. Salina sensed, rather than heard, him explain that he'd been wrong in his hasty conclusions. He silently begged for her forgiveness, promising to love her the best way he knew how.

With dawn's early light came a certain chill. Salina missed the warmth of the body that had lain next to hers. Opening sleepy eyes, she found a pink rose on the pillow where Jeremy's head had rested only an hour before.

Panic threatened. "You can't have gone yet, Jeremy!" she whispered into the empty room. "I've still got something I *must* tell you." With those sentiments hanging in the air, Salina made a hasty dash for the privy.

☆☆☆☆☆☆☆

Jeremy had not left the vicinity, but he had opted to return to the cavalry encampment, visiting Salina at her aunt's house whenever duty allowed. Over the course of the next fortnight, Jeremy divided his time between performing his limited responsibilities at Stuart's headquarters during the days and training with Drake in the evenings. He readily grasped the lessons Drake taught him to hone his other senses to make up for the insufficiency of the vision of his right eye.

Target practice was another pastime, and along with his men, Jeremy drilled to achieve deadly accuracy in the use of the Spencer rifles. Salina was present at these shooting lessons, for Jeremy had made up his mind to leave one of the guns and accompanying ammunition with her. She needed to be prepared to use it if necessary.

One morning Aunt Ruby caught Salina in the pantry collecting crackers from the cracker barrel. In the other hand Salina held a fat, dill pickle. "You're not having an easy go of it, are you, child?"

"Am I so transparent?" Salina was alarmed.

"To one who's had four children of her own, yes, I can easily identify your symptoms. That husband of yours, however, doesn't have a clue," Aunt Ruby observed, "does he?"

Salina shook her head. "He's got other things on his mind right now. I haven't... We haven't had much time to talk lately."

"You must make the time, child," Ruby said firmly. "If you don't, he'll see it before he hears about it."

Salina had gained a little weight, but not so much that it was noticeable—yet. The drawstring skirts that Jubilee had fashioned would allow her to gradually let out the waistband as it became uncomfortably tight around her middle. She'd been sleeping a good deal, was tired the rest of the time, and usually went to bed early. The mornings continued to feature a trip to the privy, where she would empty the meager contents of her stomach, then stop off for a handful of crackers from the pantry—all before she believed anyone had seen her. She stood corrected. Her routine had given her away. "I'll tell him."

"Today," Aunt Ruby insisted.

"Today," Salina repeated.

"This arrived after you'd gone to bed last night," Aunt Ruby produced an envelope. "It's addressed to Captain Jeremy Barnes, but the rest is in code. I thought it might save some time if you translated it for him now. Then you could ride out to headquarters and deliver it to him yourself."

Salina had had a feeling that she already knew what the message, forwarded by way of the Remnant, would contain. Diligently she decoded the lines, and her suspicions were realized: John Barnes had been located, traced to where he was currently operating out of a tavern on the outskirts of Alexandria. Along with Barnes's whereabouts, confirmation was enclosed stating that Lieutenant Malcolm Everett had met his end, the deed attributed to and reported by a Colonel E.S. Ridgeford.

The initials of E.S. fairly leapt from the page, dancing before Salina's eyes. Perhaps she was overly sensitive to those particular members of the alphabet as a result of the translation she'd done of John Barnes's journal, where those letters had first come to have significance.

The image of the Yankee colonel in the stable swam behind Salina's closed eyelids. "Ridge," she whispered with a shiver. Short for Ridgeford? *E.S. Ridgeford.*

Salina spent the better part of the morning rummaging through a packet of papers Daddy had left to her. Letters, memos, reports— but none of the documents contained that name.

In the afternoon, Taylor Sue, Clarice, and Delia accompanied Salina to cavalry headquarters, where Jeremy and his band were encamped.

As Jeremy read the Remnant's message, a sense of purpose settled over him. "I'll be home tonight in time for supper." He tucked the missive into his pocket. "We'll discuss this then."

☆☆☆☆☆☆☆

Salina occupied her time by laying out the new uniform she had painstakingly assembled with the assistance of Mama and Jubilee prior to leaving Gettysburg. Now that it was certain that Jeremy was soon to depart on his mission, she intended to see him properly attired and equipped. Across the quilted comforter she arranged the collection of accouterments. There was a pair of new gray britches and a shell jacket that sported two rows of mismatched brass buttons—some bearing the letter "C" for Cavalry and others patterned with Union eagles on them. A Jefferson-style blouse, an osnaburg shirt, and another of sturdy flannel lay neatly stacked next to knitted socks and a used pair of gloves. When she heard her name being called for supper, Salina set the remainder of the equipment aside and hastened down to join the company.

Drake, Jeremy's men, Taylor Sue, the cousins, and the aunts spent the next several hours together reveling over familiar stories of the Pony Express, hair-raising accounts of Rebel victories, and tales of Mosby's incredible exploits. Salina and her cousins marveled over C.J.'s tale of an instance in which the wily partisan leader had advantageously hidden under a leather apron and a face full of foam while reclining in a chair at the Warrenton barber shop. A Yankee officer came into the shop to interrogate the barber as to rumors of Mosby's whereabouts—utterly unaware that the Rebel guerrilla he sought was literally under his nose. Boone told of another episode in which Mosby had climbed out a bedroom window to hide high in a tree while a Federal detail conducted a search of the Hathaway home, where Mosby's wife and children were staying at the time. The Yankees discovered Mosby's boots and uniform in Mrs. Mosby's room that night—but they still hadn't managed to catch *him*.

"Hurrah for Mosby!" the young ladies chorused, enjoying the narrative. It was that brand of daring and bravado that kept Southern hopes for ultimate victory over the Federal forces alive.

A while later Tristan took out his fiddle and Kidd Carney provided accompaniment with his harmonica while the others danced. Aunt Ruby joined in with the pianoforte. *Nick Malone*, *La Belle Catherine*, and *Bobby Casey's Hornpipe* were among the lively tunes performed, and of course there was the *Cavalier's Waltz*.

When the dancers paused for refreshments, Bentley started singing *Lorena* and—just as he had done on the night of Jeremy and Salina's wedding—he intentionally substituted Salina's name in place of Lorena in the lyrics. *Jine the Cavalry* and *Riding a Raid* were added to the repertoire. The longer the merriment continued, the more Salina was convinced that the singing and dancing served only to postpone the inevitable good-byes. She instinctively guessed that the men were leaving, probably before daybreak.

The men sang their final number a cappella:

> *Way down in the valley where the lily first blows,*
> *Where the wind from the mountain ne'er ruffles the rose,*
> *Lives sweet Evelina, the dear little dove,*
> *The child of the valley, the girl that I love.*
> *Dear Evelina, Sweet Evelina,*
> *My love for thee shall never, never die.*
> *Dear Evelina, Sweet Evelina,*
> *My love for thee shall never, never die.*

She's fair like the rose, like the lamb she is meek.
She never was known to put paint on her cheek.
In softest of curls hangs her raven black hair,
And there never was need for perfumery there.

Dear Evelina, Sweet Evelina,
My love for thee shall never, never die.
Dear Evelina, Sweet Evelina,
My love for thee shall never, never die.

Three years have now passed and I've not got a dollar,
Evelina still dwells in that green, grassy hollow.
Although I am fated to marry her never,
I've sworn that I'll love her forever and ever.

Salina and the other ladies applauded the pleasantly harmonious efforts. "You've been practicing!"

"Aye, Miss, and so we have," Bentley nodded, winking at his captain's lady.

"But I'm disappointed that you haven't taken to deliberately mispronouncing my name as *Sa-lie-na* for that one," she goaded.

"We tried that, Miss," Bentley confessed. "But you're short a syllable: Sa-lie-na, Ev-a-lie-na. With all due respect, your name fits better in *Lorena*." He picked a pertinent verse with which to demonstrate:

Yes, these were words of thine, Salina,
They burn within my memory yet;
They touched some tender chords, Salina,
Which thrill and tremble with regret.
'Twas not thy woman's heart that spoke;
Thy heart was always true to me:
A duty, stern and pressing, broke
The tie which linked my soul with thee.

Salina agreed with a somber nod. "I see your point."

Within the quarter hour, Jeremy went out onto the veranda to give last-minute instructions to his riders. Salina and Taylor Sue covertly watched through the open window.

"They're up to no good," Taylor Sue predicted.

"They're going to go after John Barnes," Salina confided.

"Oh, dear..." Taylor Sue breathed. "Salina, you've *got* to tell Jeremy about the baby tonight."

Salina was quick to agree. "Yes, I know. I don't want him to leave me without knowing that he's *got* to come back. I have no wish to raise our child without its father."

"The war will keep separating you, Salina. You might as well get used to that right now," Taylor Sue advised. "It's inevitable."

"Inevitable, yes. But that doesn't mean I have to like it."

"None of us do," Taylor Sue replied. "Well, good night, Salina. I do hope Jeremy finds your news most welcome."

"Aye, me too," Salina whispered. She bravely stepped outside into the cool night. Her presence caused a quick scattering of the riders, all offering fond farewells.

"I'll be right back, Sallie." Jeremy followed his men to the stable. Drake was the last to leave.

"You will watch out for him for me," Salina requested of their friend.

"I'm not going with him, Little One," Drake broke the news to her as gently as possible. "I offered, and he politely but firmly declined. This is something he wants to do on his own, without any help from me."

"Is he ready?" Salina inquired, expecting an honest assessment.

"Aye," Drake nodded. "Your husband's determination has driven him to learn his lessons quick and well. If you want to test him, you go ahead and try to sneak up on that right side of his—but don't say I didn't warn you."

"Drake, that man in the stable—the one called Ridge..."

"Looked familiar to you, did he?" Drake guessed. "I'm going to set that investigation we discussed in motion. I'll wire Micah from St. Louis on my way to the ranch. I'll let you know if anything turns up."

"Please do." Salina's eyes were solemn. "And please take care of yourself."

A grin spread across Drake's copper-colored face. "I always do. I'll be in touch, Little One."

"I'm counting on that."

With Drake gone, Salina wandered into the garden, taking a seat on a bench under the wisteria arbor while she awaited her husband.

"'In softest of curls hangs her raven black hair, and there never was need for perfumery there...'" Jeremy echoed the lines of *Evelina*.

"Please sit down, Jeremy. I need to tell you something before you leave."

"You're not going to argue me out of doing this," Jeremy insisted.

"I couldn't even if I wanted to," Salina acknowledged. She patted the space next to her on the bench. "Please."

"This sounds serious," Jeremy noted, sitting next to her.

"It is." Salina didn't know how to tell him except in a straightforward manner. "Jeremy, I'm..." She paused to swallow her apprehension. "We're going to have a child."

"What?!"

"A baby," she whispered. "Between us, we've managed to create a baby." Salina watched his face, waiting on pins and needles for him to say something. The shadows hindered in gauging his reaction to the news.

"A baby?"

"A baby."

"Glory, glory!" A joyous smile illuminated Jeremy's whole face. "Sallie Rose, this is wonderful! Unexpected, but wonderful nonetheless." Jeremy stopped suddenly. "You must think me a fool for not putting the pieces together: the dizzy spells, the fainting, the morning sickness...is that why you've taken such a liking to crackers as of late?" He laughed, chiding himself for not seeing it sooner. "Ethan would've pegged what's been ailing you right off."

"My brother's a doctor," Salina allowed. "He should have been able to make a proper diagnosis. As for you, well...I was trying very hard not to let you guess what was wrong with me."

"But why?" Jeremy rubbed the pad of his thumb across her knuckles. Her hands were ice-cold.

"I guess I wanted to be absolutely positive," Salina confessed. "I..."

"How long have you known about this, Sallie?"

"For a few weeks," she answered. "I began to realize something was amiss while you and Drake were in Washington."

Jeremy hauled Salina onto his lap, cradling her in his arms. "Oh, Sallie—a baby!" After a few seconds, he looked down at her, puzzled. "Darlin', tell me honestly: Aren't you happy about this?" He lifted her chin and gently forced her to look at him. "Why were you keeping this from me? Because of what I said about Barnes wanting to destroy a child of our making?"

"That is a consideration," she conceded, "but it's not the sole reason."

Jeremy waited, sensing there was more to it. "I'm listening."

"I am delighted and amazed that in me grows a part of you," she confided. "It's just that... Well, you saw the graves of the still-born babies at Shadowcreek yourself, Jeremy. You know my mamma never had an easy pregnancy until she had Yabel—she had a miscarriage last September..."

"That was an accident, Sallie. Your mamma was thrown from a carriage in the middle of a thunderstorm after the horses bolted and a battle raged on Ox Hill less than a mile away."

"It happened to her before, though, too," Salina maintained. "I'm scared, Jeremy. What if my body has the same propensity to reject a child growing inside of me? What if I can't carry this baby to term?" Her shoulders shook as she began to cry. "Daddy was utterly devastated each time a little life was lost—a part of him died, too. His bouts of depression never lasted long, but they hurt him deeply." Salina rested her brow against Jeremy's. "I had to wait to tell you about the baby until I was sure. I didn't want to say something and then have something bad happen."

"I think you're putting the cart before the horse, darlin', don't you? It's going to be all right, Sallie," Jeremy crooned, rocking Salina gently. "I can understand your misgivings, but you don't have to be afraid. You're not your mamma. It'll all work out, you'll see." He slipped a possessive hand to the slight swell of her belly. "This child will be our source of hope."

"I do love you." Salina wrapped her arms around his neck.

They shared a prolonged kiss, one that spoke volumes beyond their whispered words. A new bond was forged between them. Their love would be made manifest in the months to come—a new life of their own making. A wondrous notion. They conspired together concerning the future they longed for, of one day rebuilding the main house at Shadowcreek, and which of the rooms they would select for the nursery. They laughed over potential names for their child, bickering over whether the baby would be a boy or a girl. They even spoke of peace after the war.

It was that mention of war that forced reality into their idyllic imaginings. "Come to the house." Salina got to her feet and pulled on Jeremy's hand. "I've got some things for you upstairs."

Jeremy appreciated the clothing, but he doubly appreciated the equipment Salina presented to him: a leather belt with a frame buckle, a cartridge box, cap pouch, canteen, oilcloth haversack, and a new hat—complete with band and ostrich plume. In addition to these treasures were a new cavalry sword and scabbard.

"Sallie, when did you... How did you...?" Jeremy stammered. "You did all this for me?"

A smile twitched at the corners of Salina's mouth. "I can't take credit for it all—I had help in compiling this outfit even before we left Gettysburg. Consider it a tribute to your determination. You never gave up, and I'm very proud of you for that, my darling."

"You wouldn't let me." Jeremy unsheathed the sword and held the blade up for inspection in the light from the hurricane lamp. On the hilt her initials entwined with his, carved over a small emblem of a rose encircled by curling wisps of ivy.

While he read the words on the blade to himself, Salina recited them from memory: "What God has brought together, let no man tear asunder—come back to me, my own Horse Soldier." She took the sword from Jeremy's hands, sending it to rest in its scabbard. She held the end of the scabbard in one hand and the basket handle of the sword in the other. Lifting the weapon to her lips, she christened it with a kiss.

Jeremy relieved her of the sword, leaning it against the rocker. He gathered the four corners of the spread like an oversized knapsack and set it with its contents on the floor at the end of the footboard. "God willing, Sallie Rose, I'll come back to you every opportunity I can." He plucked the hairpins free from her chignon to loose the cascade of her raven-black curls.

They lay in each other's arms. Jeremy was quiet, distant, and lost in his own turbulent thoughts, calculating and rehearsing plans in his head. Salina did not intrude into the silence, nor did she press him into idle conversation. She was simply content to savor their brief closeness. Beneath her cheek, Salina could feel not only the steady beating of his heart but also the tension coiled within him.

It was no great surprise, once she did drift off to sleep, that Salina had a nightmare. She'd had them before, horrendous and violent visions that caused her to bolt upright from a dead sleep, usually chilled in a cold sweat. This time Jeremy was at hand to chase away the dark illusions and soothe her fears, but Salina knew, without him saying so, that this would be their last night together for a good long while.

Sooner than Salina would have liked, Jeremy put on that new gray uniform, singing lowly as he packed his bedroll, valise, and saddlebags:

Our flag is unfurled and our arms flash bright,
As the sun wades up the sky;
But ere I join the doubtful fight,
Lovely maid, I would say "Good-bye."
I'm a young volunteer, and my heart is true
To our flag that woos the wind;
Then three cheers for our flag and our Southland too,
And the girls we leave behind.
Then adieu, then adieu, 'tis the last bugle's strain
That is falling on the ear;
Should it so be decreed that we ne'er meet again,
Oh, remember the Young Volunteer.

Jeremy believed his wife asleep when he laid a pink rose on the pillow beside her and placed a loving kiss on her shoulder, but Salina's mournful eyes opened and held his sapphire glance for a long moment. "I love you, Sallie Rose."

Salina's tears didn't fall until she heard the cadence of Tucker's pounding hooves carrying her beloved Horse Soldier on his way.

Chapter Five

Sixth Street Wharves
Washington, D.C.

"*Y*ou've been acting stranger than normal since we left Culpeper, Ridge. What's gives?" Brisco Cobb wanted to know. "You looked like you'd seen a ghost that day, and you've been spooked ever since."

"Maybe I did see a ghost," Ridge retorted offhandedly, staring out the grimy window toward the docks.

Brisco Cobb had known and worked with E.S. Ridgeford for more than a year now. He'd grown accustomed to Ridge's dark, brooding moods when they descended. "It was Salina's husband, wasn't it? He reminds you of someone."

This was one time Ridge was not appreciative of Brisco's exceptionally accurate observation.

"He had eyes as blue as yours, Ridge," Brisco stated outright.

"So? Lots of men have blue eyes, Brisco. You do."

"Yeah, but not *that* color. You told me once that all your brothers and your father share that same eye color—that it was a particular family trait," Brisco pressed.

76

"And so it is."

"So what would that make Salina's husband to you? A long lost brother or something? I saw him for myself, Ridge. If you had blond hair instead brown, the two of you could almost pass for twins, though you are more than ten years his senior."

"Shut up!" Ridge roared. "You're talking nonsense!"

"Am I?" Brisco goaded. "I must be hitting pretty close to the mark, if you ask me, or you wouldn't be so testy about the mere mention of him."

With deadly calm Ridge said, "Don't push it, Brisco. Leave it be."

Brisco glanced away from the blue fire in his partner's eyes. He took in the maps, the handwritten notes, and the translated pages strewn across the tabletop. "You've been going through Salina's transcriptions again. Let me guess: the passage of the journal that is John Barnes's confession for murdering your brother?"

"I'll see that he pays, Brisco. With his own life. If Everett hadn't been aiming directly at Salina and I hadn't had to kill him to keep him from killing her, we might've been able to make him talk, to tell us where that scum commander of his is hiding out."

"The Remnant can offer you no help with that?" Brisco queried. "Or haven't you thought to ask?"

"Up until now, I've been more preoccupied with the plans for California, if you must know," Ridge shot back. "Two of the operatives who were involved in Garrett's Western Campaign have been located and summoned to Washington—undercover, of course."

"Of course," Brisco nodded. "But you *have* been reading through the journal again."

Ridge confessed that he had. At first, all that had registered with him was the part dealing with his brother's death. It wasn't until just a few days ago that he'd reread the entry in its entirety:

My orders sent E.S. to the front at the head of the charge. He never had a chance. Got himself blown away in the first volley fired by them Rebs. He's dead 'n gone 'n he'll never find out thet he got himself a growed up son. J.'s secret'll go to the grave with her. She won't never let on thet her youngest weren't of C.'s seed. She mightn't care what folks'd say 'bout the whelp, but she cares mightily what folks'd say 'bout her. C. was a fool over her. J. preyed on his ignorance time 'n again. I swear I won't let J. or her Wrongful Act stain the proud name of Barnes she done covered herself with 'n passed on to her misbegotten brat. I shoulda kep her from marryin' C. all them years ago. Besotted with her, thet he was—just like his likker 'n his cards. She was poison to him, that match was doomed from the start, 'cept he wouldn't see it. At least I made a good match with S. til G.H. killed him outright. Things mighta been powerful difrent if H. hadn't killed B.J. in thet duel on account of A.S. Shoulda been the other way round. I swear I'll see G.H. an' his kin pay fer his deeds against us Barnes, one way or another...

Admittedly Ridge didn't know enough about John Barnes or his family to know who the initials *C., I.,* and *S.* belonged to, nor did he know the identity of *B.J.* But Ridge was a savvy enough detective to know that if he dug deep enough, he would no doubt uncover the answers he sought. Simple logic, however, led him to believe that *G.H.* stood for Garrett Hastings, and therefore, *A.S.* was likely his wife, Annelise Spencer. The tenuous connection between Ridge's brother and Barnes was obviously in who *J.* was.

Ridge stared out the office window, mutely observing the activity at the docks below.

"That's the English packet just arrived with mail, freight, and passengers from London," Brisco commented. "If gossip is to be believed, some titled earl is onboard; brought his whole entourage with him. Reports say that he's here to meet with President Lincoln, though I didn't hear precisely why..."

A particular woman in the parade descending the gangway caught Ridge's attention. The beautiful, high-toned redhead was dressed in splendid, regal glory. Ridge could almost smell the cloud of perfume and powder, even from this distance, and it made him queasy. A memory more than twenty years old—the face of a handsome, red-haired woman to whom his eldest brother had been engaged—flashed before him. Then it dawned on him. This woman on the dock was the woman in his memory, and he *had* seen her before—years before. He hadn't liked the picture she made then any more than he did now.

Ridge turned his back to the window, ignoring the view of the other disembarking passengers fresh from England's shores: diplomats, aristocracy, young men eager to join in the fight for the sheer thrill of it. He'd heard accounts of foreigners accompanying high-ranking officers in both the Northern and Southern armies, conducting their personal observations of the American conflict, offering their advice based on their own recent experiences from battles in the Crimea. Ridge took another glance, just to see if he'd seen what he thought he'd seen or if he'd conjured the whole thing. But she was gone, disappeared, and he couldn't differentiate between reality and imagination.

"I'm going to Boston for a few days," Ridge said offhandedly. "I have some business there. It will take a week at least. Why don't you go home and pay a visit to your family."

"All right." Brisco didn't argue. It had been a good long while since he'd seen his kinfolk in Maryland. "With your permission, Colonel, I'll leave straightaway—before you can change your mind about letting me go."

"Don't forget to take a gray uniform with you," Ridge admonished. "I heard the tongue-lashing your ma gave you for showing up last time dressed like a Yank."

"You don't have to remind me of that! Mum made her point quite clear." Brisco saluted. "What's in Boston, Ridge?"

"Maybe nothing," Ridge evaded. "Maybe I'm just chasing the wind. On the other hand, maybe I can validate some information, and then I'll have legitimate reason to hunt Barnes down like the mongrel he is."

"I wish you wouldn't brood on the entry in the journal," Brisco remarked. "It's not healthy. I'm sorry that your brother is dead, Ridge. My own pa's gone. This is war; men die. It doesn't lessen the hurt or loss, I know; but life goes on." Bluntly, Brisco continued while he had his partner's undivided attention. "For what it's worth, Ridge, I don't much care for this revenge aspect. It's a side of you I've never seen before."

Ridge's sapphire eyes blazed. "I've asked you before what *you'd* do if you'd found out that Barnes had murdered one of your brothers—you had no answer. Until you can think of something befitting, don't you condemn me for wanting to make the man pay for his crime."

"It's not up to you to play God," Brisco parried. "You already have Malcolm Everett's death to your credit. John Barnes will get his in the end—with or without the assistance of your trigger."

"You knew what you were getting into when you started working with me, Brisco. You didn't have any qualms then; don't go soft on me now."

Brisco's chuckles filled the office. "You're so ornery you couldn't get anybody else to ride or work with you like I do." He cleared his throat. "Do me a favor: Once you finish your business in Boston, get your mind back on the plans for California. Forget about John Barnes."

Ridge seethed inside, rebelling at his partner's well-meaning interference, but he allowed himself to go along with Brisco's suggestion. "Fine," he acquiesced. "I'll meet you back here in a week. Then we can move forward with California."

Brisco nodded. "In the meantime, you know where to find me if you need me. Take care, Colonel."

Ridge cleaned up the papers and put away the maps after Brisco had gone. He answered a knock at the office door.

"This came for you, sir. Thought you'd want to see it right away."

"Much obliged," Ridge accepted the envelope from the hand of another of the men he worked with. Closing the office door again, he read the cryptic lines that turned his blood cold:

Colonel:

> *Go to Union Hospital at Georgetown. There is a man there who has been identified as your oldest brother. You alone will be able to substantiate or denounce a living form attached to a name belonging to one believed long dead.*

> *Friends through the Remnant*

There was no other signature, no return address. There never was where such missives were concerned, but never once had information conveyed in such a manner been in error.

Ridge didn't think twice. He departed immediately for Georgetown. Boston would wait.

☆☆☆☆☆☆☆

Ridge furiously wiped the side of his stubble-roughened face, obliterating the hot trickle of a rare tear. He hadn't cried in twenty-five years at least. Not since the day his ma had given him a gloomy letter to read, written by Maida's husband, bluntly announcing that she'd died in childbirth. Guilt tugged at the recesses of Ridge's mind. He'd never once made an effort to see his sister's son, whatever his name was. Heaven help him, he couldn't even remember the name of his own nephew!

He paid the carriage driver for the ride. Just inside the entrance of the hospital Ridge faltered. His mission was to substantiate or denounce. What if his oldest brother was truly here? How could it be that Evan was alive after he was reported dead more than a year ago? His ma often used to say that the Lord worked in mysterious ways... In this instance, he certainly couldn't argue with that.

Resolutely wiping his face with both hands, Ridge rid himself of the last of the tears he hadn't known he could shed. He took a deep breath and determinedly entered the ward. Sparing a cursory glance at the cots lining the walls, the smell of death and decay assaulted him. Feverish eyes latched onto him, pained moans filled his ears.

"May I help you, Colonel?" A plain-looking woman garbed in black approached.

Dorthea Dix, Superintendent of Female Nurses in Union Hospitals, required nursing volunteers to be at least thirty years of age, the less attractive the better. They could not wear bright colors, ribbons, bows, or jewelry; were banned from wearing hoops to support their nondescript dresses; and need not have any notions of romance on their minds. The nurse at Ridge's side satisfactorily met the harsh standards—maybe even surpassed them.

"Colonel?" she inquired a second time. "May I be of assistance to you?"

Ridge only pretended to hold the rank of colonel, supposedly from an Illinois regiment. On previous infiltrations of Washington he'd been a corporal from Ohio, a sergeant from New York, and a major from Indiana. He'd learned that rank did indeed have its privileges.

"As a matter of fact, ma'am, I am looking for someone," he answered. "I was told I could find a man here by the name of Evan Southerland. Do you know where that man might be found?"

"Certainly, right this way. You're not the first who's come to visit since he's arrived."

"Not the first?" Ridge had expected to be the *only* visitor. Who else knew his brother was still alive? Had his killer come back to finish what he'd failed to accomplish the first time around? "Another one of the boys from the 9th Illinois come by to check on him?"

"Oh no. It wasn't a soldier, sir, it was a lady." The nurse volunteered the information as readily as she had her assistance.

Ridge kept a tight leash on the incredulity that suddenly threatened to choke him. "A lady?" he asked, thankful that his voice sounded calm.

"Yes, sir. Just an hour ago, at most. Beautiful to behold, dressed real fine, and all that gorgeous reddish hair—I've never seen a more striking woman," the nurse admitted with an understandable twinge of envy. "She claimed to be his wife."

"Wife?" Ridge cautiously inquired.

The nurse's fingers curled around the gold coins in the bottom of her apron pocket, belatedly remembering that she'd accepted a bribe from the woman to say nothing of her appearance at the hospital. The nurse lowered her eyes from the colonel's probing sapphire stare. "Perhaps I heard her incorrectly," she replied in a small voice. "I did not get her name."

Ridge instantly conjured the image of the woman he'd seen descending the gangway of the packet ship at the dock. Whoever the woman was, if indeed the selfsame one, he was fairly certain she'd be well away by now—especially since she'd deliberately deceived the nurse. Evan's wife was *not* red-haired, nor had she ever been much to look at.

"May I see him now?" Ridge persisted, ignoring the fact that he was shaking.

"But of course, right this way."

☆☆☆☆☆☆☆

September 13, 1863
Culpeper Court House, Virginia

The ominous scream of a lone cannon shot set the inhabitants of the Carpenter house on edge early on Sunday morning. The aunts were already awake, as was Salina, but Taylor Sue and the cousins came scurrying into the hallway from their respective rooms rubbing the sleep from their eyes.

"That was from Brandy Station," Delia yawned.

"It sure did sound like it," Aunt Tessa agreed.

"If there's to be another engagement here," Clarice commented, "we are fortunate to have the supplies Salina brought. We'll be prepared this time."

"Aye." Salina was grateful that she'd listened to Reverend Yates's advice and kept some of the bandages, canned goods, and medicine with her instead of giving it all to Tabitha Wheeler. "Pity, though, that we might have to use them so soon."

Taylor Sue eyed Salina inquisitively. "Is this how it started at Gettysburg?"

"Not exactly," Salina shook her head. "But my experience there taught me to hate that sound nonetheless." Without realizing it, she'd gripped the banister until her knuckles had turned white.

The ladies all waited expectantly, certain that some sort of reply in the form of an answering shot would follow, but none came. When it became clear that no retalitory action would transpire, breakfast was consumed as usual, and afterwards they all went on to attend the service at St. Stephen's Church on East Street. The initial shock and scare of the lone cannon blast had dissipated.

During the sermon, Salina had difficulty keeping her mind anchored on the words of Reverend Cole's teaching as she sat in the pew staring up at the colorful stained-glass windows. She was to have been married in this church, but Jeremy had not shown up at the appointed time. Their wedding had been postponed until weeks later, during a lull in the fighting at Gettysburg.

Shivering, Salina wondered at the portent of the shot heard from Brandy. Vaguely she remembered overhearing some of Jeremy's men, before they had departed, saying that if Pleasanton, commander of the Union cavalry, crossed the river with his columns, the blue horsemen were closer than anyone realized. If Jeremy had been out scouting instead of chasing the elusive John Barnes, he would know and probably would have already reported his findings to Stuart concerning such a matter—but Jeremy was not out there conducting reconnaissance for the Chief of the Cavalry. Jeremy should have reached Alexandria by now, or better yet, maybe he had succeeded in bagging his quarry and was well on his way to Richmond.

The floorboards beneath Salina's feet trembled a split second before the high-pitched wail of a shell rent the air. The ear-piercing whistle that preceded the explosion underscored the fact that a strike had made impact not far from the church building. Confusion erupted in the pews at St. Stephen's. Reverend Cole wasted no time in dismissing the service. Filing out of the vestibule, Taylor Sue and Salina clung to each other to keep from being swept away by the tide of panic pressing on all sides.

"Come, quickly!" Aunt Tessa called after her daughters and nieces, motioning them to hurry. She shouted to be heard above the cacophony, "The Episcopal rectory has a very large cellar. I want you all to go there; it will be safer for you. Ruby and I will be along directly. If this turns into another affair such as Brandy, we'll be ready to take in the wounded that are bound to come needing our aid. Clarice, Delia, go with your cousin and Taylor Sue. We'll meet you there."

People in the streets of Culpeper converged on the rectory cellar from every corner of town, not so much for spiritual refuge as for bodily shelter. Huddled below ground, the gathered citizens apprehensively waited out the bombardment that threatened their homes and property, not to mention their very lives.

"On August first, some Billy Yanks came 'cross the river on a pontoon at Kelly's Ford; they burned the Rappahannock railroad bridge. For the past six weeks now they've been movin', scoutin', carryin' on all manner of reconnoiterin'," one of the old gentlemen remarked to his neighbors. "I reckon this time it's come to a head."

Salina pressed her fingertips to her temples to rub away the headache that descended on her as the thunderous cannonade continued. She vividly remembered the long hours spent in the Grants' cellar beneath the farmstead on Oak Ridge a mile outside of Gettysburg proper. She prayed earnestly that this present ordeal would be over shortly and not last for three days.

Lips moved in silent prayer. Hushed voices whispered together. Hands clasped together in comforting reassurance. Ladies fanned themselves. Babies were rocked but unfortunately not induced to be silent. And outside the din roared.

Reverend Cole was worried. His daughter was not among those gathered for protection in the rectory cellar.

"Excuse me, Miss Carpenter, but you haven't by chance seen my girl Fannie, have you?" the reverend anxiously inquired.

"No, Reverend, I'm afraid I haven't," Delia replied. "But then, I wasn't looking for her either." She sat up a little straighter, scanning the faces nearest her.

"Is Fannie not here?" Clarice, too, searched for Fannie Cole. "Surely she would know to come here and not let herself get lost in the shuffle."

Reverend Cole forced a smile. "Well, never mind. I'm sure she'll turn up." But the minister failed to mask his obvious concern over the absence of his daughter.

Not long afterwards, Fannie Cole did indeed arrive at the rectory cellar.

"Where have you been, daughter?!" Reverend Cole's demand was tinged with relief. "I've been worried sick about you!"

Fannie put her hand to her heaving bosom as she tried to catch her breath. "Why, Papa, *someone* had to look after the church bell. I certainly didn't want the Yankees to get it!"

Curious, Reverend Cole eyed his exultant daughter. "What've you done, girl?"

Fannie euphorically pronounced her patriotic deed: She had climbed the bell tower armed only with a few yards of black cloth. She had draped the cloth over the top of the bell, completely covering it, and upon her descent from the belfry cut the bell rope. Triumph snapped in Fannie's eyes and shaped her grin. "From ground level looking up into the steeple, one can't even ascertain that the bell is still hidden there—and what those dirty Yankees don't know about, they can't steal!"

"Oh, Fannie!" Reverend Cole hugged his brave daughter's shoulders, leading her to a place to sit and wait out the bombardment.

Taylor Sue, Clarice, and Delia each glanced at Salina. "What?" she wanted to know.

The three were wholly unable to conceal their amusement in spite of the dire situation they found themselves in. Delia put words to their stifled laughter. "There was a time when I wouldn't have put it past *you* to do something equally as hazardous as climbing a bell tower yourself, Salina."

"If that's what was required of me to act on my convictions, I just might have," Salina resolved. She looked at her sister-in-law. "But things in my life are different than they once were."

☆☆☆☆☆☆☆

The shelling of Culpeper Court House lasted the full day. Several of the buildings in the northern and eastern sections of town sustained direct hits from the Federal artillery fire, but no structural damage was done to the home of the Carpenters.

Salina paced in front of the wide staircase in the entryway, hands stuffed in her apron pockets to keep from wringing them in utter agitation. She felt ill, and not just because of morning sickness. She dreaded being behind enemy lines again.

The enduring sounds of moaning and groaning, shrieks, cries, and muttered curses narrowly preceded the clatter of feet ascending the veranda stairs. Aunt Tessa was at the front door to direct the orderlies as to where the wounded men should be placed. A contract surgeon and several members of the Confederate medical corps muttered curt introductions as they filed past, hastening to set up their stations.

A steady stream of stretcher-bearers brought in close to three dozen men from the ambulance wagons parked outside. The hurt men needed immediate care, and Salina moved toward her first patient. She'd taken only two or three steps into the parlour before abruptly fainting at the sight of the bloody bodies.

"Stretcher-bearer!" an orderly shouted.

The man who answered the orderly's call graciously picked up Salina's unconscious form and hurriedly followed Aunt Ruby up the stairs.

"You may put her in there," Aunt Ruby pointed to Salina's bedchamber. "My apologies for the trouble, sir."

The stretcher-bearer tipped his cap. "No trouble, ma'am. Just hope the little lady is all right. We didn't scare her, did we, with all the blood and gore?" He spared a concerned expression for the young lady lying so still on the bed.

"She's been feeling a bit under the weather these past few days," Ruby explained, "but I reckon she'll be right as rain again real soon."

The orderly returned below stairs, but Aunt Ruby stayed at Salina's bedside, administering the customary cool cloths to her niece's forehead. She was much relieved when Salina stirred to a state of wakefulness.

"This is absurd." Salina weakly pushed away the damp cloth. "I've worked in field hospitals before. I know what needs to be done. I know what is required."

Ruby's firm hand on Salina's shoulder blocked her attempt to get up. "Now, that's enough, child, hear? You lie still until I say you can be up and about."

"But, Aunt Ruby..."

The look Ruby slanted at Salina stifled all further objection. "You just don't seem to understand, so let me make it as plain as I possibly can: You are going to have a child, and *that* is what's affecting you. I know of your skill in nursing, but the timing is not in your favor in this instance. You'll be no good down there to anyone if you don't rest." She pushed a sticky curl back from Salina's face. "Your body is going through a vast deal of change, child, and some things you used to do simply cannot be done for now. It's one of those cases where your spirit is most willing, but the flesh is weak. For the moment, we have enough hands; we're not overwhelmed. We'll be all right without risking you."

"But I feel so helpless, and I don't like it," Salina pouted. "Aunt Ruby, isn't there *anything* I can do?"

Ruby paused for a moment. "There is. I'll bring up some linens for you to tear into strips and roll into bandages. That will be a tremendous help to us, since no one else has the time to do it."

Left alone, Salina's wandering mind again contemplated the fact that carrying a baby was much different than she'd imagined it would be. The little life inside her was altering her normal routine of living, and that was something she would have to get accustomed to.

Taylor Sue brought up the bandage linens. "Aunt Ruby sent me to help. My stomach isn't as strong as it used to be either," she admitted. "I was fixing soup for the men, but it suddenly got to be too much for me."

"I'm glad for the company." Salina bit a tear in the muslin yardage and ripped off a long strip. "Have you heard any word of the fight itself?"

There was a troubled expression in Taylor Sue's amber eyes. "It's my understanding that the railroad cars at the depot were the cause of the battle."

Puzzlement creased Salina's brow. "Those General Lee sent up from Orange Court House to evacuate the supplies from here so they wouldn't fall into enemy hands?"

Taylor Sue nodded. "Apparently the Union scouts that approached Culpeper this morning met with little resistance. As they came in sight of the train station, they spied the cars parked on the tracks, and they assumed—without conducting a thorough reconnaissance—that the cars contained Rebel reinforcements instead of supplies. Shortly after reporting that erroneous calculation, their artillery opened fire."

"Those people launched an all-out attack on this town because they *thought* there were more gray troops stationed here when there aren't?" Salina shook her head, appalled.

"Our Rebel force was outnumbered," Taylor Sue glumly added. "As they moved out, the Yankees marched right in behind them."

By the time darkness fell over the beleaguered town, Taylor Sue's report was confirmed: The Army of the Potomac under

General George Gordon Meade—the victorious Union commander of Gettysburg—occupied Culpeper.

☆☆☆☆☆☆☆

Richmond, Virginia

As Jeremy stood with his back to the James River, the rushing of the water was nothing compared to the roaring in his ears. Jeremy looked up at the warehouse-turned-prison in front of him, at the paneless, barred windows where hundreds of unseen eyes peered down. He could feel the belligerent hatred, like dozens of fiery darts, pricking his skin, piercing his heart. Not a face showed, not a shadow shifted. The inmates knew that the sentries posted below were apt to shoot at even the slightest motion—a routine called "Sporting for Yankees."

Libby Prison, a converted warehouse at the corner of Cary and 20th Streets, was a notoriously hellish place. Formerly a ship chandlery and grocery owned by Libby and Sons, the building currently housed captured Federal officers. The capacity, in the best of terms, could be described as monstrously overcrowded. Beyond that, the conditions inside were reported to be indescribably bad.

Though it had taken a day more than a week to accomplish, the successful mission had been worth the effort when measured by triumph's standard. Jeremy and his men had employed the intelligence gleaned from the Remnant. Behind enemy lines, they had apprehended John Barnes and his two remaining lackeys at the tavern on the outskirts of Federal-occupied Alexandria. Surprise—along with the Spencer repeating rifles—was a powerfully persuasive weapon that Jeremy used to best advantage. Barnes never imagined Jeremy would have the gall to come after him.

The journey had been slow going, especially since Jeremy ordered that the prisoners *walk* the entire distance of roughly a hundred miles—all bound and, except for Barnes, gagged—behind the horses of Curlie, Boone, and Jake. The remainder of Jeremy's men rode in a confining perimeter around the three captives, eliminating any chance of escape.

For most of the miles, Jeremy was silent and stern-jawed. He did not allow himself to get ruffled over the incessant and vicious taunts of the hate-crazed major.

"I'll gladly shut him up for you, Captain," Curlie had volunteered, holding his rifle at a meaningful angle.

But Jeremy had been adamant: No one was to shoot unless one of the prisoners tried to make a break for freedom. For all he cared, Barnes could talk until his throat was raw or his tongue swelled in his head—Jeremy wanted only that Barnes be alive by the time they reached Richmond.

"But he makes no sense, Captain," Tristan complained, failing to understand the basis for Barnes's guttural oaths and maniacal threats. "Or am I right in that Barnes's favorite topic is your questionable parental origins?"

An apology had been issued to his trusted men. "I don't mean to bore you with his inane chatter about my colorful past. Maybe I'm being a little perverse, but I want to hear what it is he has to say." And it had been an education, Jeremy reflected, digesting what Barnes's twisted mind perceived. "Crazy" didn't do the man justice.

Erasmus Ross, the prison clerk, logged the names of John Barnes and his two lackeys into the record books in the commandant's office. At Jeremy's request, he handed over a signed and dated endorsement, vouching that these three prisoners of war had indeed been delivered for confinement. The two lackeys would be transferred to Belle Isle, where enlisted men were held, but Barnes, being an officer, would be an indefinite "guest" at Libby. As an armed guard came forward to take John Barnes away, Barnes spat at Jeremy and railed, "You no-account son of a dead Yankee..."

The guard halted Barnes with the tip of his bayonet. "That's no way to talk to a captain of the Confederate Cavalry, you blue-bellied scum. If you don't keep a civil tongue in your head, you'll be punished for a lack of proper respect."

Barnes glared at Jeremy. Through tobacco-stained teeth he snarled, "Ya shoulda killed me when ya had the chance! When I get out of here, I'll come after ya *again*, and I will kill ya, for sure and certain, if it's the last thing I ever do!" The guard sent the butt of his rifle into the ribs of the Yankee major, but Barnes persisted. "I won't just stop when yer dead—I'll git all of ya: Ethan, Taylor Sue, and yer *precious* Salina—but not before ya git what's comin' to ya, ya misbegotten little whelp! I coulda killed ya the day ya was born—an' I shoulda! I tole Cam right off ya weren't even his seed. Yer nothin' but a disgrace, boy! An unfathered scoundrel with no name to call yer own!"

The guard again drove the butt of his rifle against the prisoner. "I told you that you need to show proper respect, and you will learn your lesson. If you say one more derogatory remark..."

"You go ahead and try to get out of here, Major Barnes," Erasmus Ross challenged, boasting a pair of revolvers and a Bowie knife. "Others have tried. They never get very far."

"Good-bye, *Uncle*," Jeremy emphasized the nonexistent relationship between them. "I'd wish you all the best, but that would be a mite insincere. Ross," Jeremy nodded to the prison clerk, "it's been an experience doing business with you."

"Put your mind at ease, Captain," Ross shook Jeremy's hand. "Dick Turner, the jailer, he'll handle this one from here on out. If he doesn't learn his manners, I'm sure Turner can find a nice dark cell for him to fester in."

Jeremy tucked the endorsement into a leather wallet that he kept in his breast pocket. The deed was done. Turning his back on Barnes's mottled face and a deaf ear to the litany of hurled insults, Jeremy felt a sense of relief in knowing the man was indeed locked up. Strolling past the tents where the guards had their quarters, he was satisfied that he'd be able to fight his battles in peace without having to constantly look over his shoulder for the next unexpected strike from Barnes—and without having to worry whether Salina was safe and out of reach. A last look at the warehouse caused him to shudder. Barnes would suffer the identical fate he had contrived for Ethan. The score was even.

Bentley stood waiting with both his own horse and Tucker. "It's done," Jeremy reported.

"Aye," Bentley nodded, handing over Tucker's reins. "And I know you. You're not one to gloat over what you just did. You're not regretting this, are you?"

"No," Jeremy shook his head. "He had it coming; he left me with no other choice."

"He had quite a bit to say about you, didn't he?" Bentley treaded lightly. "Did you know what he was talking about beforehand, or is this news to you?"

"What—that my parents weren't married?" Jeremy asked.

"That's one way of putting it: He used different terminology," Bentley gibed.

"No, it wasn't news," Jeremy replied. "Do you see me differently since my father was a Union officer?"

"I see you differently because I've witnessed firsthand the measure of compassion you possess and the strength it took for you to put up with him and his accusations," Bentley answered. "A lesser man would've shot him for being the low-down mongrel that he is."

Jeremy stuck his foot in a stirrup and swung himself into his saddle. "It's all in the past now, Bentley. Let's leave it there, shall we?"

Bentley saluted. "Aye, Captain." He, too, mounted.

"Where are the rest?" Jeremy queried.

"The boys went on into town, sir. I told them to meet us back at the Spottswood in two hours. Some of them went for the barber and a bathhouse, some of them went shopping. I also told them not to eat yet, seeing as how you were going to treat us all to supper."

"Oh, is that what I'm doing?"

"Aye, it is. I hear tell they fix a mighty tasty steak there at the Spottswood," Bentley nodded, "when it can be had."

Jeremy counted the number of Union gold pieces in a small drawstring pouch. "You're fortunate I've enough to cover the cost with this. I haven't got enough Confederate scrip to buy a loaf of bread, let alone supper!"

Bentley laughed; it was good to hear the Captain doing likewise, but the mirth was short-lived.

"You go ahead, Bentley. I'll meet you at the hotel."

"Where are you going, sir?" Bentley was curious.

"I can't be this close and not stop in to see Ethan's in-laws. They live on Franklin, near First Street."

"Very good, sir," Bentley approved. "See you at the hotel."

Jeremy adeptly maneuvered Tucker amid the other horses and teams pulling all manner of conveyances along the clogged and dusty streets of the Rebel capital city. Richmond crawled with military personnel and swelled with refugees from all over the Confederacy. Lodging was next to impossible to acquire, food prices were outrageous, anything pertaining to the war industry boomed. Even the devastating losses of Gettysburg and Vicksburg had not yet been able to quench the seemingly indomitable Southern spirit. After several blocks, Jeremy passed the columned capitol building and the impressive statue of George Washington in Capital Square.

Struggle for independence, Jeremy mused, raising a gloved hand to shade his eyes from the afternoon glare as he craned his neck to gaze at the sculpted figure of the first man to be President of the then United States of America. George Washington had been considered a rebel in his own day, fighting in the name of freedom from English tyranny. He was a symbol of revolution that the Southern people took to heart, but how vast the difference from declaring independence in 1776 as opposed to 1861. Jeremy clucked to his horse, prodding Tucker into motion and moving on until they made the turn onto Franklin Street.

Between Second and First, Jeremy halted in front of a certain brick townhouse, where he tethered Tucker at the spiked iron gate. Passing through, he went down three small steps, crossed the cobbled walk, and climbed the steps to the stoop, where he rang the doorbell.

Jeremy spent the next hour and a quarter in the company of Taylor Sue's mother and sister. He left the brick townhouse sooner than they wished him to, but with letters from each of them that he promised he'd see delivered to Taylor Sue when he returned to Culpeper.

"Oh, then you haven't heard," Jennilee, Taylor Sue's thirteen-year-old sister, said.

"Heard what?" Jeremy inquired.

"My dear Captain," Rachel Carey drawled. "Culpeper was fought over at length but a few days ago. The Yankees occupy the town."

"That means the girls are behind enemy lines..." Jeremy shook his head, his mind wildly adrift.

"If they are still there," Jennilee pointed out. "Perhaps my sister and Salina left before the battle?"

"Doubtful," Jeremy muttered. "Neither of them is in any condition to..." He stopped short. "Well, this is a bit distressing. I will no longer impose upon your time, and I must meet up with my men. Good day, Mrs. Carey, Jennilee." He kissed each of their hands. Surely some vendor on the street was bound to have a newspaper for sale.

☆☆☆☆☆☆☆

The lobby of the Spottswood Hotel was no less crowded than the streets outside. Jeremy navigated a path through the crushing throng, making his way to the table where Bentley, Carney, Curlie, Cutter, Boone, Jake, C.J., and Tristan waited. A server had already brought a round of drinks, and a tall glass of sarsaparilla greeted Jeremy.

The news they shared only corroborated what Jennilee and Mrs. Carey had told Jeremy of Culpeper Court House. The rest of what the men had to tell him wasn't any more encouraging. Events outside of Virginia had a dismal quality about them: Lawrence, Kansas, had been sacked by Quantrill's raiders, who caused over a million dollars' worth of property damage and massacred one hundred fifty men, allowing only women and small children to be spared. The Federals were bent on capturing Morris

Island and Battery Wagner in Charleston, South Carolina, having already initiated another bombardment of Fort Sumter. The Union Army of the Cumberland under General Rosecrans was out from Tullahoma and had flanked the Confederate-held city of Chattanooga, Tennessee.

Jake Landon reported the most disturbing scuttle of all: that General Lee had drafted a letter of resignation but a few weeks after the Rebel defeat at Gettysburg. President Davis, however, had flatly refused to consider anyone other than Lee to lead the Army of Northern Virginia. The resignation, if it truly existed, was denied.

"There can't be much credence to that," Tristan confidently argued. "We'd have heard something, or read something in the papers, wouldn't we?"

"Unless it was intentionally kept out of the press," Curlie speculated.

"Lee's still in command," Boone confirmed. "He's not the type to give up. So we didn't whip our weight in wildcats up Gettysburg way—there will be other battles we'll win instead."

Cutter shook his head. "We can keep winning battles, but do we have what it takes to win this war?"

Not a one had an answer.

Chapter Six

*T*he Bible story of Joseph and his coat of many colors was not unfamiliar to Ethan Hastings. Reverend Yates had taught sermons from the text in Genesis on past occasions, yet this was the first time Ethan remembered the words stirring his heart so thoroughly. Perhaps those words had a more poignant meaning, considering his present circumstance. Ethan paid closer attention to the chaplain's reading:

> *"And Joseph's master took him, and put him into the prison, a place where the king's prisoners were bound: and he was there in the prison. But the LORD was with Joseph, and shewed him mercy, and gave him favour in the sight of the keeper of the prison. And the keeper of the prison committed to Joseph's hand all the prisoners that were in the prison; and whatsoever they did there, he was the doer of it. The keeper of the prison looked not to any*

thing that was under his hand; because the LORD *was with him, and that which he did, the* LORD *made it to prosper."*

Applying the scripture to his own life, Ethan realized that as of late he *had* been favored by the prison's superintendent. He'd been allowed to work with the doctor in the infirmary twice a week, treating Confederate inmates, and he had the shallow satisfaction that he was gaining the confidence of the surgeon in charge. "They might not be able to prove you're a certified doctor on paper," the blue-clad physician had acknowledged, "but it's evident that you've got a talent for healing and medicine. I don't have much to work with, let alone the fact that the prisoners don't trust me. They might relate to you a bit differently, though, since you're one of them."

...because the LORD *was with him, and that which he did, the* LORD *made it to prosper...*

Ethan contemplated the idea for a long time, even after the sermon was concluded and the last hymns were sung. He spent the remainder of Sunday afternoon quietly in his corner of the cell in concentrated prayer and meditation, relentlessly petitioning the Lord for guidance and strength. *God, please reveal what my purpose is here. Don't let me rot in this stinking place without a means to serve if this is what You have chosen for me.*

The nights were getting longer and colder. Once the sun had set, the memories of home and thoughts of loved ones pressed heavily on the incarcerated men. Melancholic tunes oft took prevalence, and mournful voices routinely joined in. This evening, Ethan couldn't bear to hear the heartrending words. He stretched out on the straw with his back to the song leader and laid his unkempt head on his arm in lieu of a proper pillow. His positioning, however, did nothing to block out the sad lyrics or the accompanying lament of a harmonica.

Do they miss me at home, do they miss me?
'Twould be an assurance most dear,
To know that this moment some loved one
Were saying, "I wish he were here";
To feel that the group at the fireside
Were thinking of me as I roam,
Oh, yes, 'twould be joy beyond measure,
To know that they missed me at home.
To know that they missed me at home.

The guards passed through the corridors to announce lights out. The enshrouding darkness concealed not only that Ethan's eyes were wet with tears but also that dozens of other confined Rebels had succumbed to silent weeping. Tasting the salt on his lips, Ethan whispered, "Good night, my darling Taylor Sue..." And his dreams were of her.

☆☆☆☆☆☆☆

Carpenter House
Culpeper Court House, Virginia

The low rumble of thunder hinted that rain might soon fall, but the quick-moving clouds failed to empty themselves over the enemy-occupied town. Salina leaned one elbow on the arm of the divan, propping her chin up, as she read the most recent letter from Jeremy.

Cavalry Headquarters
Army of Northern Virginia
September 26, 1863

My Darling Salina—

I was able to make arrangements for these pages to come to you by courier through the Remnant. It is my hope that they find you well, with a smile to accompany your thoughts of me.

It pains me to know that you are there behind enemy lines and I can't get to you—but these words will, and that must suffice at present. Enclosed you will also find two letters for Taylor Sue. I visited her mother and sister when I was lately in Richmond and I promised to forward them on. Will you be so kind as to see that she gets them, and give her my best regards.

It is done, Sallie: John Barnes is incarcerated at Libby. I'm glad to say that he is now a closed book and we have nothing more to fear from him. Since reading the report of our activities on that score, General Stuart relented and has given me back my scouting responsibilities, though he insists that he will keep strict watch on me. I'm not to ride out on reconnaissance with fewer than three of my men with me at all times. Courier may take a little more proof, but in time, he'll come around, I'm sure of it. He knows the value of my talents.

I don't know how much accurate news of us you will be getting—or whether it is only Yankee propaganda that they are telling you. Whatever the case, do not believe the tales you might've heard concerning the scrap we got into near Jack's Shop on the twelfth of September. An erroneous report was circulated by Lt. Col. Grenfell—a British officer who ran the blockade to fight for the Confederacy—telling that General Stuart had been captured and all his command taken by the Yankees. It simply wasn't true.

Granted, it was a wretched fight. We battled against Buford's troopers, who'd come over from Madison Court House. Our mounted charges couldn't bend Buford's columns, they hit us hard, wave after wave. The dismounted skirmishers fared no better. Kilpatrick flanked our left, manueuvering between our position and the ford, cutting us off from the road that would have given us a route of escape. It came to the point where our artillery was firing into enemy cavalry approaching from both sides of the hill, with us in between the press of Yankees. Our squadrons went charging in opposite directions, and in the end we mercifully managed to slip by Kilpatrick and clear a way to a more secure position. Had that not been the case, we'd have lost those guns for sure. We recrossed the Rapidan River at Liberty Mills and found safety in the support of our infantry. None of my men were hurt. I've not seen Grenfell since the fight—apparently he doesn't show his face around camp with any ease. He'd been assigned to Stuart's staff for but a few weeks, serving as inspector, but due to his false report regarding the General's capture and whatever else he's done to make the troops dislike him, the alienation is almost palpable. Admittedly, it was a close call at Jack's Shop, but we successfully escaped with our hides intact.

I pray you are well and feeling better in the mornings than you were when we were together last. I imagine you and Taylor Sue have been comparing notes as the weeks wear on. Know that I think of you and our dear little one often. Take care of yourself, Sallie Rose. I'll write again soon.

Your own devoted Horse Soldier,
Capt. Jeremy Barnes
Stuart's Cavalry, C.S.A.

Uncle Saul, the Carpenters' butler, appeared at the door of the sitting room. "Missie Salina, dere's a Maj-ah Dun-kin Grant ta see ya. Ah done axed him if'n he needed ta speak wid da cunnel dat's quartered heah, but he says, no, dat he come ta speak wid ya."

Salina refolded Jeremy's letter. "Would you mind showing Major Grant up here."

"Will do, Missie," Uncle Saul complied. He was back a few minutes later, Duncan trailing in his wake.

"Hello, Duncan," Salina greeted her stepfather.

"Salina. My, but aren't you a sight for sore eyes," Duncan grinned. "You're looking well."

"Thank you. It is good to see a friendly face for a change. May I offer you some refreshment?"

"No, I'm fine," Duncan declined. "I happened to be in the area with dispatches and decided to stop by to pay my respects. I didn't have the chance to say good-bye to you in Gettysburg before you and Jeremy left. Your mamma says we missed each other by an hour."

"We had reason to leave rather suddenly," Salina allowed. Studying her stepfather's face, she softly asked, "Why have you come?"

"I'm headed back to Washington City tomorrow. I thought that, seeing as how Culpeper is in our hands now, it might be possible to take you and Taylor Sue to the capital with me. You could visit Ethan in prison, and then I'd bring you back."

Salina eyes widened. "You would do that? You can get us in to see my brother?"

"With proper approval," Duncan said pointedly. "Unlike Drake and Jeremy's last visit."

Though she tried to school her features to give nothing away, Salina's expression affirmed that she knew all about that episode.

"If I take you to see your brother, Salina, there can be no high jinks, no mischief," Duncan insisted, warnings flashing from his storm-gray eyes. "I want your word of honor that you will behave and you won't try to spring him. You'd only put us all at risk if you did that."

Salina thought for a moment. "Duncan, put your mind at ease. Taylor Sue and I are not presently in a position to instigate a prison break." Secretly, Salina felt a certain sense of gratification in knowing that she worried Duncan, for always in the back of his mind he would remember that she was a Hastings. He had erred in underestimating her once—a mistake he would not repeat. "You have my word," she reiterated. "No mischief."

Duncan heaved an audible sigh of relief. "And you'll brief Taylor Sue?"

"She'll behave as well," Salina assured him. "We'll be as good as gold, Duncan. I promise you."

"All right." Duncan had to take her at her word. As Garrett's daughter, she lived by the same code of honor and duty Garrett had lived by. Their word was their bond. This sentimental whim, Duncan supposed, was an effort to make up to Ethan that he hadn't been able to do anything to bring about his release. Maybe he *was* trying to appease his conscience by bringing Ethan's wife and sister to see him before the transfer to Point Lookout came through. "I'll call for the two of you first thing in the morning. There's an early train departing from the depot that will take us as far as Alexandria. We'll hire a hack from there. Pack a satchel," he enjoined. "You'll be away for one night at the least."

But in the morning, a note from Duncan arrived. Urgent business had compelled him to return to the Union capital late the night before. The opportunity for Salina and Taylor Sue to visit Ethan was indefinitely postponed. Their only consolation was that along with the note bearing Duncan's regrets were two undated, authorized traveling passes bearing Salina's and Taylor Sue's names. Salina read Duncan's missive with a knot tightening in the pit of her stomach.

> *I leave it to your good judgment as to when you deem it safe to come to Washington for yourselves. I wish I could guarantee safe conduct, but alas, the situation is too volatile at the moment. Forgive me for raising and dashing your hopes—that certainly was not my intention when I first mentioned the scheme. Ethan knows nothing of this, so at least he is spared the remorse I know you must be feeling. Convey my sincerest apologies to Taylor Sue. The*

traveling passes will enable you to pass through the lines, should that become a necessity. You, I'm sure, are aware of what may happen should the lines shift again anytime soon. Do come when you are able.

Regards,
Major Duncan Grant, U.S.A.

☆☆☆☆☆☆☆

"Not again!" Duncan muttered under his breath. He could hardly get his office door opened for the strewn mess of documents littering the floor. No one except his superior officer was to have known that he was going to be out of town delivering dispatches to General Meade's headquarters. But obviously someone had known—presumably the mole that Duncan had been chasing to no avail.

Although Duncan never had been the best of organizers, he did have a system all his own. He knew where everything in his office *should* have been. Within a few minutes of sifting through the avalanched paperwork, he determined what was missing: an entire file containing all his findings accumulated during his investigation of a man named Evan Southerland. His search for this man had terminated in what he believed to be a dead end; but judging by the condition of his office, evidently he stood corrected. What puzzled him was why the mole would be after scattered bits of information that pertained to a certain dead man. Unless he wasn't dead.

A brisk knock interrupted Duncan's train of thought. "Major?"

"Lance!" Duncan exclaimed. "Am I ever glad to see you!"

Lieutenant Lance Colby pressed his way into the cramped little office. "I haven't been in the field with Buford for that long, Duncan, but if this is your way of showing me how much I was missed, then maybe I ought to pretend I didn't receive the orders for my transfer back to Washington."

"I've been floundering without a good right-hand man," Duncan readily admitted. "I'm truly glad to have you back working with me. I hope your time riding with Buford's cavalry has cured your desire for field duty."

"I missed secret service work more than I thought I would," Colby confessed. "Besides, Lottie will be pleased to take up residence here for the winter."

"How is your wife?" Duncan belatedly asked.

"Ready to be over and done with being in the family way. In all honesty, the poor thing looked like she was going to pop when I saw her last," Colby irreverently commented. "But don't tell her I said so! She hasn't got much longer to go until her confinement."

Duncan was amused. "If I were you, I'd not want to be within a hundred-mile radius when she goes into labor."

"From here to Gettysburg isn't a hundred miles," Colby murmured. "But then, maybe you'll have orders for me, and Lottie already knows that duty comes first." It had been his *duty* to marry Salina's cousin to make an honest woman of her. He didn't regret the forced marriage anymore, because he'd actually grown to love his wife, and he fully believed that she loved him in return; she just didn't know it yet. He knew she dreaded the confinement that was to come, and his sympathy was with her, but they had made their bed and must now lie in it. For every action there is a consequence, and he and his Southern bride both paid the full price for their indiscretion. All he could do now was pray that she was delivered of a healthy child and that no life-threatening effects would arise from the birthing. His own mother had died when he came into the world, so he didn't remember her—but he had heard his father's dire stories.

Shaking himself free of his reverie, Colby declared, "We might as well start cleaning up this mess. It's going to take us a while."

☆☆☆☆☆☆☆

October 12, 1863

Mr. Drake Dallinger
c/o Lije Southerland
South Union Spread, Kansas

Dearest Drake:

Grandmamma has appointed Ellie as my assistant to serve on the committee for the Christmas bazaar at church. We're going to have a fund raiser to generate money for Soldiers' Relief through the U.S. Sanitary Commission. Ellie and I have made a dozen quilts since we've been home, and the Reverend Pastor will be forwarding ours, along with other donated blankets, to our troops at the front lines.

Is it too much to hope that you will be back in Boston to celebrate Christmas with us? The ranch must be keeping you busy, since no letters from you have arrived in over a month. I know we haven't known each

*other for very long but I find myself jealous of the time
you spend in Kansas. I wish you were here, brother.
Please consider a visit—even sooner than Christmas
would be welcome, but I will agreeably settle for later if
it cannot be sooner. Micah Southerland has been twice
to supper in recent weeks, and he was our escort to the
theatre again last Thursday evening. He's a very charming man, with such arresting eyes—almost like yours—
but bluer. I'm inclined to believe that he has taken a
fancy to Ellie. Please, Drake, do consider a visit.*

*The seamstress has arrived and yours truly is the dis-
inclined subject of the fitting. Grandmamma is insistent
that I put off my mourning for Mason once and for all.
She's trying to have me come out this season, but high
society no longer fascinates me as it once did. You have
influenced me, instilling a fondness for less pretentious
things. I will, however, play the role of socialite if it
makes Grandmamma happy—and you had better appreciate what a dutiful sister I am. At least she cannot find fault
with my work at the U.S.S.C., even though she objects
that I spend far too many of my waking hours either at
their headquarters or working at the hospital. We still
have patients who were with Colonel Robert Gould Shaw
and the 54th Massachusetts at Battery Wagner. That regiment suffered more than fifty percent casualties, Drake.
How committed the Negro soldiers are! I only wish my
commitment was equally as unwavering.*

*Do take care of yourself, brother, and hurry home to
us. Ellie sends her regards.*

Your loving sister,
Aurora

Dallinger House
Beacon Street
Boston, Massachusetts

☆☆☆☆☆☆☆

Culpeper Court House, Virginia

Delia Carpenter entered the dim sitting room and touched a burning candle to each of the lampwicks until the golden glow of light
dispelled the hovering darkness. "Shall I put another log on the fire?"

Salina pulled her shawl closer around her. "I'm off to bed soon. I've just got a few more of the articles to paste into my journal, and I need to catch up on two days' worth of writing, but that won't take long. What about you, Taylor Sue?"

Patting the quilt covering her lap, Taylor Sue replied, "I'm quite warm enough with this, thanks. Are you turning in, Delia?"

Salina's cousin flushed. "I... I was going down to the parlour for a game of chess."

Taylor Sue nodded. "It's that winsome private with the broken leg, isn't it?"

"Y-yes," Delia stammered self-consciously. She forced an airy lightheartedness: "He's the only one who'll let me beat him at it!"

"Do you ever talk with him, Delia?" Salina didn't look up from the page where she smoothed the edges of a pasted account of the Confederate victory at the Battle of Chickamauga.

"Talk with him?" Delia repeated dumbly.

"Yes, you know, carry on conversation?" Salina persisted.

"Well, yes, of course we talk," Delia confirmed. "Why?"

"Without him knowing, do you think you could get him to tell you where the blue cavalry has gone? Or perhaps where they intend to strike next?" Salina had noticed that the recuperating Yankees downstairs were briefed daily by their visiting comrades.

"Are you asking me to spy?" Delia's eyes flashed with surprise.

"And if I were?" Salina finally met Delia's astonished glance, seeing the dilemma mirrored there. "Forget I mentioned it, Delia. Don't say anything to him. Go play chess."

"You don't like him because he's a Yankee," Delia charged.

"I'm sure the man's a perfectly amiable character, Delia," Taylor Sue put in, "but he *is* our enemy. He's almost well enough to be sent home. How will you feel when that happens?"

Delia kept her chin from quivering. "All right, I might be fond of him—but you've each got your own husbands to love. Clarice is practically spoken for by Boone Hunter. But no one cares for me!"

Salina took Delia's free hand between her own hands. Her cousin was shivering not from the cold but from jealousy and hurt feelings. "Delia, I'm not dictating that you shouldn't like him, and if he has any feelings for you, it's only because he's already discovered for himself what a kind and gentle creature you are. Just take care that he's not asking questions of you in reverse, without your knowledge of it, in hopes of getting answers out of you. He *is* a Yankee, and they say all's fair in love and war. I just don't want to see you hurt by him."

"I believe I can determine when I'm being taken advantage of!" Delia lifted her chin. "He's never asked, not even once, anything of me that pertains to a military nature. He's not like that, Salina!"

"I hope you're right, Delia," Salina spoke sincerely but mentally added, *For your sake, Cousin, I do hope you're right!* "Please forgive my improper suggestions. I misunderstood the depth of your affection for him."

With an indignant huff, Delia turned to leave the room. She plowed squarely into her younger sister. "Oh! Out of my way, Clarice!"

Clarice was startled by Delia's abrupt tone as she stormed past. "My apologies." She looked askance at Salina and Taylor Sue. "What did I do?"

"It's something I said, and I shouldn't have," Salina confessed, then explained.

"Delia acting as a spy? I really don't think so, Salina. She might rave about your past exploits and adventures, but she's not got your strength. You're not wrong, however, in being suspicious of that Yankee private," Clarice whispered. "Mama and Aunt Ruby don't trust him a lick. Mama has already told Delia she would do well to stay clear of him. Our brothers would be *livid* in their disappointment in her for fraternizing with that Yankee so freely. She ought to know better."

After the household had bedded down, Taylor Sue slipped into Salina's room. "You awake?"

"Yes," Salina yawned. "I keep thinking about Delia."

"Me too." Taylor Sue climbed under the quilt on the opposite side of the bed. "I suppose the best thing to do would be to let her simmer down before you try to speak to her again. She's bound to know you were looking after her best interests."

"Or is it because of my having worked so closely with spies, Daddy's Network, and the Remnant that I assume every opportunity a chance for covert reconnaissance?" Salina groaned. "This Federal occupation is wearing on my nerves, that's all."

"I know what you mean." Taylor Sue optimistically added. "Don't fret so, Salina. It'll all work out, you'll see."

Taylor Sue's words were prophetic. By the end of that week, the Rebels retook Culpeper Court House and General Robert E. Lee reestablished his headquarters in the vicinity. Delia's Yankee—along with a handful of others—was evacuated moments before the returning gray soldiers surged through the streets. The Federal convalescents unfortunate to remain at the Carpenters' were collectively taken as prisoners of war and relocated to a brick commercial building downtown where the Confederate provost guard set up their jailhouse.

☆☆☆☆☆☆☆

Union Military Hospital
Georgetown

"I was finally able to get my hands on the passenger list of that English packet: There was only one Justine on board—the wife of a Lord Colin Wentworth, Earl of Chetenham. If this countess is indeed your Justine, brother, it just goes to prove that her ambition knows no bounds. To think that she turned down your marriage proposal and life at the ranch for the eventual earldom," Ridge commented sarcastically. He softened his tone. "Well, she's of little consequence now. She and her earl set sail yesterday afternoon. There is no indication that Lord Wentworth, or his *charming* wife, will ever return to this country."

Evan Southerland lay on his side, facing the wall. He offered Ridge no indication that his words registered. Inside, however, his heart constricted painfully. It shouldn't matter to know that *she* had once again left him without so much as a good-bye; it shouldn't matter a whit. *Countess Wentworth...* He never should have loved her and would regret it until his last breath.

Ridge sat on the stool beside Evan's cot and continued his monologue. "According to the nurse, Justine came here twice to see you, but each time you were sleeping, and she supposedly didn't want to disturb you."

Still no answer from Evan.

Ridge let a hint of his exasperation show. "I don't know what you ever saw in her in the first place."

Evan suddenly rolled over and grabbed the chalk and slate from the bedside stand. With uppercase letters, he rapidly wrote: *AS YOU SAID, SHE IS OF NO CONSEQUENCE. SHE WALKED OUT OF MY LIFE MORE THAN TWENTY YEARS AGO. I CAN'T IMAGINE WHAT POSSESSED HER TO COME HERE NOW.*

"Neither can I." Ridge's sapphire eyes locked steadily with those of his eldest brother. "It's all rather curious." He ventured that he was treading on thin ice, but he plowed on regardless: "I know you had an affair with her, Evan. I know you loved her once, very much."

THAT WAS A LONG TIME PAST. FORGET ABOUT IT.

"How do you expect me to do so when neither you nor apparently she has been able to?"

A grossly strangled sound—one of pure frustration—emitted from Evan's damaged larynx. Evan rolled over to face the wall again without bothering to answer Ridge's last question.

While he hadn't died at Shiloh, as John Barnes had intended, Evan had not come through the battle near Pittsburg Landing, Tennessee, without severe injury. A bullet had torn through his throat, causing irreparable damage to his vocal chords. The doctors, while amazed that he lived, predicted that Evan would never speak coherently again. Chalk and slate were his means of communication.

"You don't have to look at me, Evan. I know you can hear me," Ridge declared. "Let me ask you: Have you ever given any thought to the notion that there might have been certain—*results*—from such an affair?"

Ridge's inquiry earned Evan's undivided attention, and Evan sat up to face his brother. His strokes on the slate spelled out his hasty reply. *I CAN'T IMAGINE WHAT SHE TOLD YOU, BUT I WOULDN'T BELIEVE HER, IF I WERE YOU. SHE'S A CONSUMMATE LIAR!*

"She didn't tell me anything, Evan. Her ship sailed before I could get to her."

THEN WHAT MAKES YOU THINK THAT THERE MIGHT HAVE BEEN ANY SO-CALLED RESULTS?

"You're admitting you had the affair?"

Evan lowered eyes filled with compunction. *IT WAS A MISTAKE. I'VE NEVER CLAIMED TO BE PERFECT.*

"Neither have I," Ridge countered. "We're all human. We all make mistakes. None of us are perfect."

QUIT STALLING. TELL ME WHAT YOU'RE TRYING TO SAY.

"I have come across someone...some information," Ridge amended, "that, if proven reliable, would lead me to believe that you have a son Justine never told you about."

Evan blanched. His eyes flashed with lethal blue fire.

"I don't have all the evidence yet, but I plan to acquire it," Ridge disclosed. "She's just low enough to have done something like that to you, isn't she?"

NO—IF THAT WAS THE CASE, SHE WOULD'VE TOLD ME, Evan scribbled emphatically, shaking his sandy-blond head. *I'D NEVER HAVE LET HER GO IF I KNEW THERE WAS A CHILD ON THE WAY. I'M NOT ONE TO SHIRK MY RESPONSIBILITIES.*

"But if she'd confessed to you then, would you have believed her?" Ridge challenged. "You just confirmed that she was a consummate liar."

I DON'T KNOW THAT I BELIEVE YOU EITHER!

"I'm not asking you to believe me—not until I can get some tangible proof." Ridge rubbed his whiskered jaw. He had an idea of where to start looking. "If I find anything, do you really want to know about it?"

Evan hesitated, then wrote. *YOU STARTED THIS, YOU FINISH IT. HEARSAY IS NOT SUFFICIENT—I'LL WANT TO SEE THE PROOF FOR MYSELF.*

"If it can be arranged, you may count on me. Like you, I'd certainly want to see proof before I'd believe it." Unexpectedly, a picture of Salina's husband sprawled on the floor of the Carpenters' stable came to Ridge's mind. *What if he'd already seen the proof?* Ridge quickly changed the topic: Jeremy Barnes was another subject for another time. "The doctor has granted clearance for your release. Tomorrow you're leaving; I don't know that it's safe for you to be here. There is a madman out there who's already tried to have you killed once. I'm not about to let him have the opportunity to come back and make a second attempt. I'm sending you north to Maryland to stay with a family who are friends of mine. You'll stay there until you're fit enough to travel on your own. Eventually, we'll ship you home to South Union. In the meantime, I'll get word to Pa and let him know that you're not dead, like we were first led to believe." Ridge produced some papers, which he unfolded and showed to his brother. "Here. You've been honorably discharged from service in the United States Army. This is a commendation for your bravery and a letter of apology from the Secretary of War sorely regretting the misidentification of a corpse that was not yours and begging pardon for any undue heartache such a clerical error has caused your relations."

Evan eyed the documents without really reading them. It would be good to go home, to see Ma and Pa, his younger brothers, the ranch he loved. It would not be easy to come face-to-face with Ruth-Ellen, though—doubly so if this implausible idea of Ridge's held any water. *A son by Justine?* He had two boys of his own at home: Evan, Jr. and Jonathan. *They* were his sons, his legal offspring. Ridge could do all the investigating he wanted to; Evan was reasonably sure that his insinuations had no foundation.

Evan perused the documents more thoroughly. The implication was that his reported death had been an error, a case of mistaken identity. But maybe it would have been better if he had died, Evan thought darkly. At least then he'd have been spared the miserable life he had left to live. He'd argued bitterly with Pa before he'd left to join up to fight, and their parting hadn't been under the best of circumstances. Evan's only consolation was that Lije Southerland was well-known for giving a man a second chance—how much more willing would he be to forgive his own son?

"Don't worry about making things right with Pa," Ridge said, almost as if reading Evan's troubled mind. "When he learns that you're alive, he'll slaughter the fatted calf. It'll be nothing less spectacular than the return of the prodigal."

I'M TIRED, Evan wrote, refusing to acknowledge Ridge's view on how Pa would react to his homecoming. *I APPRECIATE YOUR STOPPING BY.*

"All right, I'll go." Ridge took the hint that Evan wanted to be left alone. "I suppose I've given you quite enough to think about for one afternoon. I'll see you tomorrow."

Evan retreated to the relative safety of the pillows that ensconced his sandy-blond head. He closed his sapphire eyes to eliminate Ridge's face from his line of sight.

☆☆☆☆☆☆☆

Near Cavalry Headquarters
Army of Northern Virginia

Relaxing in front of the campfire, Boone Hunter rested his weight on his palms, elbows locked behind him for support, his long feet extended toward the flames. He eyed his captain with a contemplative glance while lazily biting on the end of a piece of straw grass. Slowly he shook his head. "Nobody *gives* horses away."

"That's right," Jake Landon and C.J. voiced their mutual agreement.

"I don't doubt that this man is your friend, Captain. I'm saying that there must be a catch," Tristan presumed, nursing a tin mug of freshly ground coffee.

"Where'd Dallinger get a herd of two hundred horses that he's got no use for?" As he waited for an answer, Kidd Carney wiped the last bit of foam from his face with a towel, having finished shaping his goatee by the last threads of daylight.

"The telegram didn't get that specific," Jeremy hedged, kicking the end of the log Bentley was perched on.

The elder rider looked down at the annoyance, then pointedly up at Jeremy. The younger man placed both boots on the ground. Bentley inquired, "What, *specifically*, did Drake say?"

"Read it for yourself." Jeremy handed over the message that had been wired from St. Louis.

> *If you need to acquire horses—as rumored—come and get them. Meet me at Cobbs in Maryland in a fort-night. If you don't make it, I'll understand that you had other pressing duties, but it's good horseflesh, so if you're willing to take the risk, I recommend you come if you can.*
>
> *—Drake Dallinger*

"It says *acquire* horses." Bentley rubbed his chin in ponderance. "Knowing the man like you do, do you figure that to mean the animals are available for purchase? Or that Dallinger won't put up any resistance if we were to come and take them?" He passed the telegram to the man on his left, and it continued to circle around the campfire until each rider had viewed the lines for himself.

"I'm not sure what he means exactly." Jeremy stuffed his hands deep into his pockets, shrugging his broad shoulders. "But I am certain he can be trusted to deliver. How much gold do we have left?"

"What need have we for gold?" Cutter objected. "We're not buying agents. If we make a raid behind enemy lines for horses, the animals are spoils of war."

The others nodded in acquiescence.

Curlie grinned. "Our best supplier is the Union quartermaster."

They waited as Jeremy seemed to wrestle the issue, trying to decide what to do.

"Captain." Boone held the telegram toward the firelight, pointing. "It says right here 'if you want them, come and get them.' I believe, sir, that a statement like that is the equivalent of throwing down the gauntlet."

"We're going, aren't we?" Curlie could stand the suspense no longer.

"It's got to be unanimous." Jeremy's unpatched eye moved from face to face of the band circling the fire. "Are you all willing to take this challenge?"

"Of course we are," Kidd Carney answered for himself and his fellow horsemen. "Aren't you, Captain?"

"If your *wife* was here, Captain," Curlie drawled, "don't you reckon she'd be the first to ask, 'Where's your sense of adventure?'"

Curlie's perfect mimicry of Salina's voice caused Jeremy as well as the others to grin broadly. "Aye, she probably would," Jeremy admitted.

"What are we waiting for, sir?" Tristan inquired. He was on his feet in an instant and dumped the last of the coffee dregs into the fire.

Bentley turned Jeremy's shoulders toward the commanding general's tent and gave Jeremy a gentle shove in that direction. "If you can get an audience with Stuart, speak to him about it. If he approves, what have we got to lose besides a couple hundred horses?"

Jeremy didn't voice a reply to the rhetorical question. He went to see Stuart.

☆☆☆☆☆☆☆

Maryland

Ridge and Evan were safely across the Potomac River, traveling over the serene countryside. Once they'd cleared the Monocacy River south of Frederick, Evan watched in silent fury as Ridge peeled off his blue uniform and donned a gray one in its place. *SO, YOU HAVEN'T CHANGED SIDES AFTER ALL, LIKE YOU WANTED ME TO BELIEVE—YOU'RE JUST PRETENDING TO BE ON THE SIDE OF THE UNION. TO WHAT END?*

"I'm not asking you to understand, Evan. There's too much at stake for me, and you don't need to know the reasons why," Ridge obstinantly declared. He loved his brother dearly, but he wasn't about to confide in him. "Hate me if it makes you feel better, but that won't change my regard for you."

Evan glared at Ridge. *None* of what was happening made any sense at all to him.

The Southerland brothers continued their journey for a few miles more until Ridge turned the wagon from the turnpike onto a long gravel lane. Evan saw a rooftop and smoke curling from a stone chimney. A gust of breeze set a wind chime to tinkling, and then, like a thunderclap, a dissonant roar erupted. Ridge rode on, unruffled by the ruckus. As the team and rig neared the farmhouse, clamorous shouts and laughter were discernible above the yipping pack of hounds surging toward the gate. In the barnyard, geese and chickens squawked and crowed, hustling out of harm's way. Meowing cats, more preoccupied with pestering a cornered field mouse than partaking in the reception, contributed their share to the racket that announced the arrival of visitors.

"Look! It's Mr. Ridge!" cried a towheaded lad.

"Mr. Ridge!" pointed a second.

"Mr. Ridge!" four more hollered, racing across the pasture.

Mrs. Seraphina Cobb stood on the top step of the pillared porch, watching as a half dozen of her sons collected around the newcomers.

"Who's that with Mr. Ridge, Mum?" Dannie-Anne, Mrs. Cobb's twelve-year-old, asked.

"I don't rightly know." Mrs. Cobb put up a hand up to block the sunlight shining in her eyes.

Damaris, the elder of the two Cobb daughters, marched past her oldest brother, chin held high. "I'll be in the kitchen if you need me, Mum. I'm sure I don't know why you tolerate having that traitor here," she spat.

Brisco Cobb took hold of his sister's upper arm. "Mind your manners, Damaris. Colonel Ridgeford is a comrade of mine. He's entitled to share in our good hospitality."

"Colonel? Hah! He was a sergeant last time he was here—one can only imagine what he's done to *earn* his promotion!" Damaris yanked her arm free. "He's *your* friend, Brisco, not mine. I don't appreciate the manner in which he changes the color of his uniform more often than some people change their socks!"

"Damaris," Mrs. Cobb warned. But the nineteen-year-old had already retreated into the house. Mrs. Cobb turned to her eldest son. "Your sister neither knows about the work you do, nor does she comprehend why that work requires you to consort with some unsavory characters."

"You think Ridge unsavory?" That made Brisco laugh.

"I still don't know enough about the man to trust him any farther than I could throw him," Mrs. Cobb admitted. "Go welcome him. See who it is he's brought along. I'll ready the attic room for them."

"You know he wouldn't come here without good reason," Brisco said quietly.

"Aye," Mrs. Cobb nodded. "That much I do know. You don't have to tell me any more, son. That way you don't have to tell so many lies."

"Mum, you're the one person on the face of this earth I'd never lie to," Brisco declared. "But since you're wise enough not to ask, you've prevented me from having to tell you the whole truth."

"We all have our secrets, Brisco. Blame that on the war," bemoaned Mrs. Cobb. "And don't be so hard on Damaris, hear? I reckon she's still half in love with him, even though he doesn't reciprocate her regard. I'll not have him hurting her again, and you may remind him of that."

Brisco grinned. "Oh, but Mum, that's where you're wrong. I fear that Ridge is still quite smitten with our Damaris. They're just too ornery to see eye to eye on a few pertinent issues."

"Well, if you want to kindly spare him from a first-class tongue-lashing, you'll tell Ridge to keep a respectful distance of her."

Evan was ushered to the attic room and settled comfortably there. He ate his meal from the tray Damaris brought. As he savored each bite, swallowing carefully, he listened to the comforting commotion drifting upward as the Cobb boys got their fill of war stories told by Brisco and Ridge. It was a welcome racket, the boisterous voices, the tribal camaraderie. Here indeed was a crew who rivaled the volume once so prevalent at the ranch.

Later, outside on the porch, Ridge and Brisco sat in the rockers, enjoying their pipes in the cool of the night after the youngsters had been tucked into their respective bunks, beds, and trundles.

"I brought Evan here because I didn't want to chance Barnes finding out he's still alive," Ridge explained. "He tried to kill my brother once. I wouldn't put it past him to try again."

"What happened to your brother?" Brisco issued the tentative query. "Does he remember?"

"He's been through a living hell," Ridge replied. "I don't know how much he truly remembers or what he willfully blocks from memory. I've pieced together as best I can from the clues I uncovered, but there are dozens of questions surrounding the events that I reckon will never be answered."

He'd never spoken of Evan much, and when Ridge started, Brisco didn't stop him.

"My brother was shot during one of the charges made by the Rebels against a place they call the Hornet's Nest on the battlefield at Shiloh. Only it wasn't a Confederate bullet that got him—it was one fired by John Barnes."

"That was spelled out in the journal entry," Brisco nodded.

"Evan was left for dead until another wounded man found him and took him to Bloody Pond in search of water." Ridge closed his eyes. According to the grisly reports he'd read, the clear, once-tranquil pond had turned rusty red, tainted by spilled blood of dying men and dead horses.

"The wounded man died at Bloody Pond. Evan was too hurt to make sense of either where he was or whether he was surrounded by friend or foe. It was a mixed collection of bodies. Men from both sides had struggled to reach the only source of water around, and many of them ended up dying there. Evan was found—alive—and taken to a brigade hospital, then moved to the tent hospital, where he was misidentified. A letter was sent to a family in Chicago saying that their missing son had been located, but when the old couple arrived, they were disappointed to learn that the comatose man was not the son they searched for. Unable to speak for himself, even if he had been aware enough to do so, Evan was loaded onto a ship that sailed upriver to Cincinnati, and at a general hospital, he was tended to by the Sisters of Charity. He was there for months until finally one of the ladies from the Cincinnati Sanitary Commission thought she recognized him as the husband of a friend. But when the wife came to identify him, she knew immediately Evan was not her husband.

"Sometime after Evan regained consciousness, he was transported by rail from Cincinnati to Washington. Once there, his military records were procured, and he was positively identified by a surgeon from Evan's unit who'd been transferred to the hospital at Georgetown. The surgeon was able to aid Evan a good deal—he saw my brother through pneumonia as well as the surgeries that pieced Evan's throat back together.

"Another issue that is unclear to me is how the Remnant knew who Evan was. But I won't question. I'm just thankful that I was contacted when I was and that I was able to take him with me once he was properly discharged. The trip here set Evan back a bit; he's not real strong. Is it too much to trespass on your mum's hospitality and ask her to look after him until I can arrange to get him home to Kansas? Evan's been through a horrendous ordeal, but I believe he'll make it—providing Barnes doesn't launch another strike."

"You haven't heard: Jeremy Barnes and his band pulled off quite a coup," Brisco informed Ridge. "They went through the lines, captured John Barnes outside of Alexandria, and delivered him to the confines of Libby Prison. You have no need to fear that Barnes will find out that Evan isn't dead."

"Jeremy did that?" Ridge was surprised.

"The dispatches were properly confirmed through the Remnant. Suppose he got tired of being hunted and finally did something about it?"

"It's possible," Ridge theorized. "I'd wager he did it first and foremost to protect his wife."

Brisco folded his arms over his chest. "I might've done the same—had I a wife who needed protecting, that is."

"And what word is there of Salina Hastings Barnes these days?"

"Safe by the last report, still in Culpeper with her aunts. The Rebels have retaken the town."

"I've spent these last few days working to obtain my brother's discharge and release from the hospital. I haven't been keeping up with much else since you left Washington. Even California has been set aside," Ridge lamented. "Our associates from the West, however, are due before the week is out. It's high time to put the plans in motion again."

"Indeed it is," Brisco declared. "Put your mind at rest concerning your brother. He will be well tended here. Mum never turns anyone in need away. She will see that he is well, and safe."

Ridge nodded. "Tell her for me, if you will, that I consider it a privilege to be in her debt."

Chapter Seven

*W*ithin a week of the Rebels' return to Culpeper, a courier brought to the Carpenter home longed-for letters and an invitation requesting the honor of their presence at a review of Stuart's cavalry, scheduled for the fifth day of November.

Taylor Sue envied Salina when she saw the twinkle of anticipation light Salina's eyes. Jeremy would surely be among the gallant cavaliers on parade. Knowing this caused Taylor Sue to miss Ethan more profoundly than ever.

The review was attended by a vast number of spectators from Culpeper and the outlying areas. Though not equal to the showing put on five months ago on the selfsame plains near Brandy Station, it was still an impressive sight to behold, staged with military pomp and patriotic circumstance. Last June there had been ten thousand cavalrymen brandishing silvered sabres; on this instance only half that many passed the high command, General Lee among them.

Salina noted that the horses appeared thin for want of forage and that many of the riders looked as gaunt as their mounts. In spite of these conditions, the pageantry did not disappoint. Upon conclusion of the review, the entertainment commenced.

"Ah, here you are." General Stuart doffed his plumed hat and bowed at the waist as he welcomed Salina, kissing her gloved hand. In the same cavalier fashion, he greeted Taylor Sue, Delia, Clarice, and the aunts. "I'm so pleased that you were able to join us today, ladies."

"It is an honor to be here, sir." Taylor Sue and Clarice smiled brightly.

"I trust you'll stay to partake of refreshments. The band will strike up shortly, I reckon," Stuart commented as he replaced his hat. "Miss Salina, might I have a word with you?"

"Of course, General." Salina walked alongside the general a short distance away from her relatives until he stopped at a spot that offered some shade beneath a pitched awning. Salina fired off a hundred questions concerning the recent campaign and the obstinate fight against the blue cavalry at what was known as the Buckland Races. She listened intently to Stuart's animated telling of the rout of Davies's brigade and was delighted in hearing that on that occasion the Rebels had bagged two hundred fifty prisoners along with eight wagons and ambulances—one of those captured conveyances being the headquarters wagon of General George Armstrong Custer, filled with his personal baggage and official papers.

The battle anecdotes were not what Salina really wanted to hear, however, and Stuart knew that. "I assume you've already noticed that your husband is absent from the exercises this afternoon."

"Aye," Salina nodded. "And so are all the men who customarily ride with him." She could contain her curiosity no longer. "Are you at liberty to tell me where they've gone?"

Stuart casually rested a booted foot atop a camp stool, leaning an elbow across his bent knee. "To be honest with you, Miss Salina, I was dumbfounded when Captain Barnes returned to my headquarters bearing documented proof of successfully infiltrating enemy lines and delivering that reprobate uncle of his to Richmond. Oh, I know, John Barnes isn't really his uncle, but that's beside the point. The point is your husband set out to put the man in Libby, and he got the mission accomplished, ably proving that he is fit for service and illustrating that the patch he wears has done little to diminish his performance in the line of duty."

Salina nodded but impatiently implored the cavalry chief to go on.

"You've witnessed with your own eyes the sad condition of our horses." Stuart indicated a group of mounts tethered at intervals along a picket rope.

"It's enough to break the heart," Salina murmured. "Mounts are not easy to come by, and yet the army doesn't move far without them—let alone the cavalry."

"Which is precisely why I allowed Captain Barnes, along with his men, to take on another special mission. The scheme he outlined was of such a nature that had anyone else approached me with it, I would have flatly denied permission."

"Sir?" Salina's mind raced. *What could Jeremy possibly be up to this time?*

"He's gone after more horses, Miss Salina."

"North, behind enemy lines?" It was the only place Jeremy *could* have gone, she reasoned, knowing the Confederacy's supply of horseflesh was much depleted and, therefore, Jeremy was in a perilous situation yet again.

"I'm reluctant to disclose further details, but I've no doubt he'll confide the particulars upon his return," Stuart acknowledged. "I am well aware, as is he, that you can be trusted to keep the issue to yourself. Suffice it to say that if the plans actually work, it will indeed be a noteworthy caper. If he fails to pull it off, well..." The general met Salina's eyes squarely. "If it doesn't work, it will be construed as a severe error in both our judgment. I have confidence in the captain; he'll very likely accomplish his purpose, so there is nothing to worry about."

"Does anyone else know of this 'caper'?" Salina wondered.

"Aside from you, myself, and two of my staff officers? No." The look in the general's snapping blue eyes was a direct order for Salina to be strong, to be supportive, and to raise no verbal objections. Her disappointment over not seeing Jeremy gave way to resignation that he was out doing whatever it was he was doing because he believed it would benefit Stuart and his cavalry in some way.

"Thank you for confiding in me, General. I know you wouldn't have done so if you didn't seek to put my mind at ease." Salina abandoned the subject of her husband. "And how is Mrs. Stuart?"

"Flora is doing well, thank you for asking."

"If I remember correctly, she should have had her baby by now."

General Stuart beamed. He regaled Salina with the announcement of the recent birth of his second daughter, who bore the patriotic name of Virginia Pelham Stuart. His meeting Virginia had been unavoidably postponed, but he was anxiously looking forward to the day when he would see her for himself. "Flora says Jimmie adores his new little sister. I'm told she's quite a bit like our Little Flora—the daughter we lost." The general's eyes momentarily clouded with mournful reminiscence.

Salina saw one of the staff prudently approach. "Sir, it has been a pleasure to see you again, but I know duty demands your attention. I do want to thank you for sharing the news of my husband with me."

General Stuart, too, was aware of the waiting adjutant. "All my best for your continued good health," he winked; the proportions of her belly had not escaped his notice.

Salina nodded in acknowledgment to Major Henry B. McClellan. "Good day to you, Major."

"Mrs. Barnes." Major McClellan tipped his hat in deference.

Salina hastily left the officers to rejoin her family.

☆☆☆☆☆☆☆

The setting sun painted the sky above the Blue Ridge Mountains with streaks of apricot, mauve, and indigo. Spectators from the review remained to hear the jovial concert put on by Stuart's own band of musicians. The bonfire cast a warm orange glow over the scene while overhead the stars winked like diamonds in the darkness.

One particular song, *The Cavalier's Glee*, composed by Captain Blackford, stayed with Salina even after they'd embarked on the return to Culpeper, the words playing in her mind:

> *Spur on! Spur on! We love the bounding*
> *Of barbs that bear us to the fray,*
> *"The Charge" our bugles now are sounding,*
> *And our bold Stuart leads the way!*
> *The path of honor lies before us,*
> *Our hated foemen gather fast.*
> *At home bright eyes are sparkling for us,*
> *We will defend them to the last.*

On the stairs of the veranda, a boy sat waiting for the residents to return to the Carpenter house. "I've a pair of telegrams for Mrs. Ethan Hastings," the lad said.

Uncle Saul handed each of the ladies down from the carriage.

"I am Mrs. Ethan Hastings," Taylor Sue stepped forward.

"Then these would be for you, ma'am." He turned over the wire-transmitted messages.

Taylor Sue fished in her reticule for a coin tip, which she handed to the young messenger. With a hearty "Thanks, ma'am!" the boy disappeared into the shadows.

Salina touched her sister-in-law's arm. "Come inside. There's not enough light to read by out here."

The first of the two telegrams was from Mrs. Carey. Taylor Sue's father had suffered a stroke, and her mama was begging her to come to Richmond to help care for him. The second was from Jennilee, her sister.

> *Mama has been quite hysterical and still is, though the doctor says that the initial danger has passed. Papa has some degree of disability, his speech is slow, he cannot use his left arm, but he should otherwise recover. It would mean a great deal to him to have you near, but you must do what you think best. The reports in the papers say that part of Northern Virginia keeps changing hands, so you will have to deem whether it is safe to travel or not. Mama portrays a dismal picture, and I won't lie by saying that all is peart, but the urgency is not what she would have you believe. Come, if you will, but don't do anything that would be dangerous in your condition. I leave it to your judgment. I can handle Mama, rest assured.*

Tears streamed down Taylor Sue's cheeks.

"The damage the Federals did to the railroad bridge before they cleared out has been repaired," Salina whispered. "You and I can take the train out first thing in the morning."

"You don't have to go with me, Salina. If I were you, I'd want to stay in hopes of seeing Jeremy when he returns. I don't want to interfere by dragging you all the way to Richmond."

"What nonsense is this?" Salina chided. "Time and again you have stood by me when I was in need. If anyone was ever 'dragged' into something against her will it's you, Taylor Sue. You had no choice in some of the messes I've landed you in. It's my turn to stand by you. Besides, Jennilee is right. This part of Northern

Virginia is too inconstant for my liking—there's no telling when those people will come storming back for another go-around. And there's no way to know for certain when Jeremy will be back either. Richmond's as good a place as any for him to come looking for me, and a good deal safer than him having to risk fetching me from behind enemy lines." She reread the telegram over Taylor Sue's shoulder. "Jennilee says that the initial danger is past."

"Yes," Taylor Sue nodded. She knew Salina well enough to tell that her sister-in-law's mind was formulating a plan of some sort. "So?"

"So let's go to Richmond—but let's take a little detour on our way. What do you say to seeing if Duncan will honor his word to let us visit Ethan?" Salina suggested.

Taylor Sue's tawny eyes flashed with expectation. "You'd do that for me? Talk about being behind enemy lines—that's a waltz right into the enemy capital!"

"But we'll be safe with Duncan. He won't let any harm befall us. I believe he is as good as his word."

"You do have your traveling passes," Aunt Ruby reminded Taylor Sue. "And if you two don't go now, when will you have another such opportunity?"

"Ethan may be moved to another location, Taylor Sue," Salina goaded. "Now is our chance, and we must make the most of it."

"I'll send a wire to Jennilee. I'll tell her we'll arrive no later than the end of the month." Taylor Sue looked askance at Aunt Ruby. "Is this what you would do?"

"Indeed I would," Ruby said with assurance. "Salina is right: It's a chance you must make the most of. Give your husband my compliments when you see him."

Another rush of tears threatened to fall from Taylor Sue's eyes. Both Ruby and Salina hugged her. "It will all work out, you'll see."

Salina didn't sleep a wink that night. A gnawing pain tugged at her heart, a sense of unease plagued her. Instinctively she felt it had nothing to do with the impending journey to Washington; rather it was something to do with Jeremy. "Father God, please don't let him be hurt," she prayed earnestly. "In the Psalms it says, 'I will call upon the Lord, who is worthy to be praised: so shall I be saved from mine enemies.' Keep Jeremy in Your hand. Cause him to remember how much I love him—wherever he might be."

☆☆☆☆☆☆☆

Old Capitol Prison
Washington, D.C.

Morning dawned with the clamorous commotion that only the event of new arrivals entering the prison could generate; Ethan was familiar enough by now with the sound.

Old-timers referred to fresh inmates as "fish," and following a thorough search and interrogation by the Union guards, these newly imprisoned Rebels were pounced upon by cellmates and bombarded with endless questions. Those inside were eager to learn the latest news from home and the front lines, craving whatever intelligence could be had about what was happening outside the oppressive prison walls.

Normally, Ethan would have been part of the pressing crowd, tossing out his own inquiries to glean new information, but today he didn't much care. While the ruckus went on around him, he mutely finished off the last of the pound cake that had been in a care package Mamma had sent. She'd managed to enclose a medical textbook, which Ethan read voraciously—for the third time. The book had not been confiscated.

"You there!" The gruff voice of a guard called out.

Ethan looked up.

"Yeah, you. On your feet!"

Ethan closed the medical text, using a *carte-de-visite* print of Mamma and Yabel for a bookmark, and obediently stood. The chain between his ankle shackles struck the floor with a dull thud.

"You're wanted in the superintendent's office," the guard informed Ethan. "Move."

Ethan fell into step with one rifled guard in front of him and another at his back. Not a word was uttered until the threesome halted outside the office door. "Wait here," the guard instructed.

Duncan's was the face Ethan encountered as he entered through the office door. With a rapid quickening of his heart, Ethan dared to hope that at last some verification of his identity had been found. Such, however, was not the case.

"Hastings, you've got visitors," the superintendent beckoned him forward. "Come in, come in."

Ethan's pounding heart stopped altogether when he saw his wife anxiously awaiting him. "Oh, my darling!" He immediately scooped her into his arms, nearly crushing her, while joyous tears flowed unashamedly. It took him a minute to see that his sister was also present. "Little Sister!"

"Hello, Ethan!" Salina's voice was as choked as her brother's.

"What are you two doing here?" Ethan babbled in disbelief, hugging his wife with one arm and drawing his sister near to him with the other.

"We came to see you." Taylor Sue smiled at him.

Ethan exchanged a speaking glance with his Yankee stepfather. "I am indebted to you for this, Major Grant," he said hoarsely.

Duncan nodded curtly, then engaged in a lengthy discussion with the prison superintendent at the far end of the room.

"Let me look at you." Ethan held Taylor Sue at arm's length, his eyes roaming over her from head to toe and back again. He reached out to touch the obvious protrusion of her belly. "Lord, have mercy! What you girls must've gone through just to get here!" He buried his face in the curve of Taylor Sue's neck and wept, silently thanking God for answering his prayers. He'd dreamed of seeing her, once at least, carrying his child.

"I love you." Taylor Sue framed her husband's bearded face with her hands. "Oh, Ethan. Every day I pray God would somehow open the doors to get you out of this dreadful place!"

Ethan shook his head. He had no desire to spend their brief time together lamenting his woes, his struggles, or the testing of his faith. He'd be content just to look at her, hold her.

Taylor Sue couldn't get her fill of looking at Ethan, scraggly as his appearance might be. Aside from his thickened beard and the length of his hair, Ethan looked the same, though perhaps a bit thinner. Taylor Sue dismissed the image of his shackles from her mind.

The reverse was equally evident: Ethan couldn't wrench his adoring eyes from the form of his wife.

"Now I realize the two of you might wish me invisible right about now, but I'm not," Salina interjected. She literally had to step between them to get her brother to pay her any mind at all. "Are you being treated well?"

"Well enough," came Ethan's terse reply. "We're fed regularly, we have adequate ventilation, and there's no shortage to the supply of comrades with whom to share my miserable fate. I hate to say this, but I'm probably better off being a Southern prisoner in a Yankee prison than a Yankee prisoner in a Southern prison."

"John Barnes is in Libby," Salina informed her brother. "An eye for an eye, so to speak."

"Jeremy did that because of me," Ethan supposed. He had cautioned Jeremy against letting revenge drive him, for that would be stooping to the same low level John Barnes operated from. Ethan shifted uncomfortably.

"He did it for all of us," Taylor Sue insisted. "What Jeremy accomplished insured that we don't have to wonder which of us Barnes will attack next."

Ethan was silent. If the tables were turned, wouldn't he have tried to do the same—regardless of being taught to turn the other cheek? "Word from outside is that the spirit of the Southerners is strong, despite the losses at Gettysburg and the fall of Vicksburg. The new arrivals claim that their faith in General Lee and the Army of Northern Virginia is undaunted. I've heard it said that the army and civilians alike are in a perpetual state of need."

"It is not the best of times," Salina confirmed, "but we'll find a way to make it. We've got to; we have more to think about than just ourselves."

Ethan belatedly saw what the "more" Salina stated truly meant: His sister was presently in the same condition as his wife. "Well, well!" His teasing grin appeared. "I'd no idea you two planned to have a family off the reel, Salina."

His sister flushed. "We didn't exactly plan to have a family immediately, but sometimes things happen."

Ethan hugged Salina's shoulders. "My congratulations to both you and Jeremy. We must pray that this next generation of our family is born healthy and hale, and that these little ones of ours will one day benefit from our present struggles, which will enable them to grow up in a free and independent land."

The hour-long visit Duncan had arranged passed too quickly. Salina wished there had been a way to give Taylor Sue and Ethan even ten minutes of privacy, but the superintendent would not allow the prisoner out of sight even for ten seconds. Ethan made himself content with the brief time together. He would live off the memory of it for weeks to come.

When the guards came to see him back to his cell, Ethan cast a look of gratitude toward Duncan. Then he tossed a warning glance to Salina, wordlessly ordering that she was to abandon any and all schemes that she might want to implement for his possible escape. Even while Salina silently conveyed her reluctant resignation to Ethan's wishes, the rattling sound of his chained ankles etched itself deep in her mind. With a heavy heart, burdened for her brother's plight, Salina put an arm around Taylor Sue, who wept freely, and followed Duncan out the office door and onto the street.

While Duncan endeavored to hire a hackney, Salina noted that Washington was much the same as it had been on her last visit. The place was still full of people crowding the streets; refugees and contraband Negroes sought work and shelter; convalescent soldiers marched to rejoin their regiments in the killing fields. The undercurrent of the hub of the Northern war machine could be felt pulsing from the very cobblestones beneath her feet. The only change Salina detected in the city's skyline was that the construction of the dome of the Capitol building was nearly completed. Daddy had told her once that Washington was a Southern town shrouded in forced Union sympathies. With a wistful expression, Salina glanced back at the prison gate. Surely there *must* be connections through the Remnant even yet, here in this town, that would lend aid to an escaped Southern soldier...

A hackney driver halted at the curb. Duncan handed Salina into the four-wheeled rig first, followed by Taylor Sue. He instructed the driver as to their intended destination, but just before he climbed into the cab, he heard a shrill, bloodcurdling scream. With a stab of horror, Duncan saw the far door of the hackney swinging limply on its hinges. He stood rooted to the street while a closed coach rolled forward and away, putting rapid distance between them.

"*Sa-lee-na!*" Taylor Sue wailed, facing the open door. "Duncan! Duncan, they took her!"

☆☆☆☆☆☆☆

"Hey!" Salina pounded her fist against the locked portal.

Salina received no answer to her plea, and she was knocked back into the upholstered seat as the team lurched forward, racing at breakneck speed. A gloved pair of strong-fingered hands had grabbed Salina before she could get herself situated in the back of the hackney Duncan had hired. Those clutching hands had roughly pulled her through the open door on the opposite side and deposited her into a closed coach parked parallel. Her feet hadn't even touched the ground in between the two vehicles.

The coach door had been slammed and locked from the outside before Salina could react. Salina struggled with the handle, rattling it, and when she pushed the window curtain aside, it was only to find that the pane had been covered over. The only source of light came from a small lantern above the door. Extending both arms to brace herself, Salina maintained her balance as the conveyance continued to gain momentum on the straightways. One more screeching turn like the last, and the puny light from the flickering lantern might be snuffed out all together. From the noise and clamor, Salina imagined the chaos going on outside—pedestrians and other vehicles making a mad dash to get clear of the careening coach.

Salina had no clue as to where she was being taken or who was taking her there. Her thoughts were jumbled: Who in Washington knew her identity or that she was even here save for Duncan and Taylor Sue? Her heart slammed in her bosom; fear gnawed at the edge of her mind.

Without warning, the coach came to a clattering halt. Salina was at a loss as to how much time or what distance had been covered. When the door was yanked open, she encountered the face of a man she'd never laid eyes on before.

"Where are we?" Salina disembarked from the coach with the man's assistance. The fishy smell of water wafted on the late afternoon breeze.

"Sixth Street Wharves, Washington Canal," came the laconic reply. The man's fingers lightly bit into her arm, as if encouraging her not to make any foolish choices. "Come on. Someone wants a word with you."

Uneasily, Salina walked alongside the man toward the warehouse, supposing that if she didn't move under her own power, he could easily pick her up, throw her over his shoulder, and haul her into the building like a sack of potatoes. She was ushered past huge shipping crates, tangled cargo nets, craggy dock workers, and surly sailors who shot unsavory comments and glances at her until her escort scowled back at them, putting them in their place. In a dimly illuminated second-story office, she was offered a chair and told to wait. Through the frosted glass window she could see the broad outline of the man as he stood guard just outside the door.

Seating herself in the lone chair at a table, Salina nervously wrung her hands beneath her cloak. Trying to think rationally, she reviewed her circumstances: She'd not been blindfolded or gagged—as she had been on the occasion when Major Barnes had kidnapped her from Shadowcreek—and that in itself led her to believe that she was being dealt with by a completely different set of people. *But who?*

Salina took several calming breaths; her stomach felt odd. Deep inside she felt an unfamiliar fluttering. *Calm down!* she firmly told herself, recalling Aunt Ruby's last caution about undue stress and strain not being good for the baby.

The baby!

A spark of maternal intuition influenced Salina's verdict that the child within her was the cause of the fluttering, not her nerves. She squeezed her eyes shut to forestall a capitulation to tears of awe and relief. Her baby had *moved*! *Lord, grant me strength— shield me and my child from any harm these people might desire against me...* The heavy tread of footsteps on the stair interrupted her petition.

"She's here," the guard reported, opening the door. "A regular little trooper."

"Good evening, Miss Salina."

Salina was astonished to find the face of someone known to her. "Ben Nichols?!"

"At your service." The doctor from San Francisco removed his hat. "And I'm sure you remember Hank."

"Hank Warner." Salina stared in disbelief. "How did you two come to be in Washington of all places? The last I saw you was in Nevada Territory, at the stage stop in Carson City." She turned to Ben. "And I was told that you had signed an Oath of Allegiance and went to work as a regimental surgeon for the Union forces in Tennessee."

"I had done exactly so," Ben Nichols confirmed, "but then I changed by mind. I found Tennessee a tolerable enough place to visit, but I missed California too much, and deep down, my conscience wouldn't allow me to go against the Confederacy—oath or no. I'm serving in a strictly unofficial capacity these days, Miss Salina. There are plans in the making that will take me back to the West. Ah, but I'm getting ahead of myself. You chat with Hank for a minute. I'll go let our other associates know you've arrived."

"I hope our man didn't frighten you," Hank apologized after the fact. "But we could hardly issue an invitation for you to come along peacefully—not with Major Duncan Grant right there, you know?"

Salina assured Hank that she understood.

"The Remnant of your father's Network still flourishes," Hank affirmed.

"Yes. I can only presume that that's how you found me," Salina nodded. "I am honored to still be trusted—that in spite of my presidential pardon, I have not been shut out of the Remnant or cut off from pertinent information which may still be accessed through the chain of contacts."

"There is no one among those still active in the Remnant who doubts your devotion to Virginia, Miss Salina. We're all well aware that you are your father's daughter. We know your character, we know what you're capable of. That's why we've taken measures to seek you out."

Ben Nichols returned with the other associates, and Salina's eyes grew round as saucers. Her hand flew to her throat as her exclamation came out in a choked whisper: "You?!"

"Yes, Salina," the blue-uniformed man answered coolly. "It's me."

"And Brisco?" she queried incredulously.

"Ma'am," Brisco Cobb stepped forward and politely doffed his forage cap. "I tried to tell you we were on your side."

"I remember." Salina's glance riveted on Ridge. "Who *are* you?" she once more demanded of the man with sapphire eyes so like her husband's.

"Colonel Ridgeford."

"That's just an alias," Salina objected, shaking her head. "That's not who you *really* are!"

"Just suffice it to say that Colonel E.S. Ridgeford is who I'm playing for now," Ridge curtly declared. "I trust we didn't scare you too much on the ride over. I know it takes quite a bit to shake you."

"You flatter me, Colonel," Salina said saucily. "My sister-in-law, on the other hand, is probably beside herself, and my stepfather will no doubt comb this city until he finds me."

"Never fear. We'll have you back before Major Grant can release the hounds," Ridge assured her. "Have you told her anything?" He looked askance at Ben and Hank.

"No, we were waiting on you," the two men answered.

"You were brought here because we need your help, Mrs. Barnes," Brisco began in a kind, soothing way.

Ridge disliked the sound of her married name. It reminded him too much of the man who'd tried to kill his brother. He wasted no more time in getting to the point: "You translated all the documents for the Western Campaign your father was working on."

Salina nodded her confirmation.

Ridge produced a fat, wrapped package and untied the strings that bound it together. "We've restored Captain Hastings' original plans, embellished them, and are in the process of putting pieces in place that will allow us to make another strike." He then unrolled a series of maps and a set of copied blueprints of the California Powder Works. "Read," he commanded.

Salina obeyed, murmuring aloud as she skimmed the pages: "California Powder Works...incorporated December 28, 1861...John H. Baird, president...banker and stockholder John Sime engaged to oversee construction on a location situated half mile above the paper mill owned by M.A. Cohen on the San Lorenzo River." She glanced at the corresponding map. The San Lorenzo River was not quite a hundred miles from San Francisco. A black "X" marked the Mission Santa Cruz, another denoted the already established paper mill. Salina's head snapped up. "A powder mill in California? That might prove to be a potential target for the Rebel operatives."

"But the mill is not operational yet," Ridge worked to contain his grin. She was quick, intelligent. He'd heard it said that she had a mind like a steel trap. Perhaps the glowing praise had merit after all.

"Up and running or not, it is significant," Salina reiterated.

"Indeed," Ridge nodded. "What would you make of it?" He was testing her.

"Well, it's not difficult to piece together what's happening." Salina scoured her brain for fragments of things Daddy used to confide in her. "California's been purchasing blasting powder for her mines from Europe and the East, but with the war on, shortages are becoming more commonplace because the armies need the powder here in order to fight. The mines in California and Nevada, however, are producing the gold and silver being used to finance the Union war effort." She summarized in a roundabout way: "No powder, no mining; no mining, no gold and silver; no gold and silver, no purchase of powder. Without powder, no ammunition to fight against the Rebels."

"Precisely." Ridge pointed to a set of copied invoices. "According to these, the price of blasting powder has escalated to thirteen dollars a keg."

Thirteen dollars was the supposed monthly wage of a fighting private, Salina mused. "So?"

"So, that's expensive," Brisco reentered the conversation. "Besides, the U.S. government has forbidden powder shipments by sea for fear they might fall into the hands of the Confederate Navy. California needs a powder works of her own. It's a necessity and, according to these documents, an eventuality."

"Has it been determined when the works will be operational?" Salina was trying to follow the path of their thinking.

"They hope to have things running by early next year," Hank responded.

"The place lacks no investors," Ben added. "It's merely a matter of time to complete the construction and hire the requisite crew."

"So California could produce her own powder more cost-effectively," Salina concluded. Yet cost-efficiency wasn't the issue here, that she knew. "Essentially, *if* another campaign was launched with the intent to capture California as its primary goal, the powder works—*if* up and running—would be both a tactical and a strategic resource in the hands of the Rebels. Black powder would be as necessary to the campaign as firearms. The powder works would ensure that the supply was on hand, thereby eliminating the worry of having to transport it west."

All four men nodded. Salina had hit the mark—squarely.

Ridge crossed his arms over his chest. He wagered that if Garrett Hastings were alive today, he couldn't be more proud of his daughter than Ridge was at this moment. Salina clearly understood what was involved, what was at stake, and she could again be a serviceable link in their efforts to plot the campaign. "That certainly sums it up."

Salina bit her lip. With dread she anticipated what was sure to be coming next.

"You were in possession of the original lists of names of Southern sympathizers in Northern and Southern California, Nevada, and New Mexico Territory," Ben Nichols noted. "Do you happen to remember any of them?"

"No, I don't. When I was in San Francisco, I was working as fast as I could to make the translations by the light of a candle in the wee hours of the morning. I had to enlist the aid of my sister-in-law—I could never have completed the entire translation on my own—so I didn't even see all of the pages myself. At that particular time, mental retention was not my key concern, clarity and correctness were. I'm sorry I can't help you." She looked up, boldly meeting Ridge's intense sapphire eyes. "Before you share any more of the plans with me, I must tell you that I cannot serve the Remnant as I once did."

Four pairs of incredulous eyes demanded explanation.

"If you call upon me to translate or encode information, or even to create a cipher for you, that is possible, but beyond that, I must gracefully and respectfully bow out," Salina insisted firmly.

Ridge's eyes glittered coldly, his voice ominous. "You've been trained by Garrett Hastings, you know the operation, and if you have to be forced into cooperating with us, then unfortunately that is the way your participation will be achieved."

Hank Warner attempted another angle. "Now, Miss Salina, we all know there's a certain level of danger involved in an endeavor such as this—you've experienced it yourself firsthand—but sometimes we have to look beyond that to what must be done for the common good of all. We need you; it's your duty to your country."

Ben echoed the sentiment. "Southern independence is at the heart of the matter, Miss Salina, which would lead to freedom for Virginia."

Salina squeezed her eyes shut, obliterating the faces of the four men who counted on her. *Duty to your country...* The phrase taunted her. *...freedom for Virginia.* "Gentlemen, rest assured that if the circumstances in my life were different than they are at present, I would not argue with you. In fact, I wouldn't hesitate in the least to do what I could to lend my willing assistance. But things have changed for me—most dramatically. I can't do this type of secret service work anymore."

"Can't, or won't?" Ben pressed.

Slowly, deliberately, Salina stood. She unbuttoned her cloak, shrugging it off her shoulders, and with a protective hand, smoothed her skirt to reveal the gentle swell of her abdomen. "I would not think twice about risking myself; I've done so before. But I will *not* risk the life of my unborn child."

The four men gaped and groaned in unison, calamity and dismay clearly conveyed by the shaking of their disbelieving heads. None had even *remotely* considered a complication such as this.

"That does put a hitch in the plans," Ben ruefully acknowledged. He looked to Ridge. "We can't mandate she go to California, not like this."

Brisco stepped between Ridge and Salina and said sharply, "This settles it. She's off the hook."

"Point taken," Ridge conceded in sheer frustration. "And here I thought I had *everything* worked out to the last detail..."

"I am sorry to disappoint you," Salina lamely apologized. "But there's no going back for any of us. Therefore, in light of my condition and my inability to offer any additional aid for this new campaign, it might be best if you don't reveal anything more to me. You can be assured of my secrecy. I'll not tell anyone of this meeting or the issues thereof. You have my word of honor, as the daughter of Garrett Hastings."

"That's good enough for me." Brisco clamped a hand on Ridge's shoulder. "We've got her word, Colonel. Let her go."

Having no other choice, Ridge nodded, albeit reluctantly. "Brisco, see her back to her stepfather." He motioned to Warner and Nichols. "Come on. We've got work to do. It'll take some time to locate an alternative operative to substitute for Salina—if one can be found."

"Thank you for understanding, Colonel Ridgeford."

"Where there's a will there's a way," Ridge stated. "I don't give up easily, Salina. This is a setback, without a doubt, but it doesn't mean the plans have completely unraveled. We will persevere in our endeavor and not quit until we've achieved our goal—that's something I learned from my own father, as well as from yours."

"How did you know him?" Salina wondered.

"Our first meeting, strangely enough, was when I literally ran into him in the office of Duncan Grant at the War Department. On that particular occasion, Garrett and I were hunting the same bit of intelligence which was, at that time, in Duncan's possession. Your father and I became allies of sorts; we shared information whenever it was in our best interest to do so. Now, I'm just trying to pick up where he left off."

"Why didn't you say so in Culpeper?" Salina persisted. "Why didn't you tell me any of this then?"

"I didn't have all the information about you then that I do now," Ridge guardedly admitted, rolling up the maps and collecting his notes. "Our lives, you see, are more intertwined than you know, Salina. Soon enough, you'll see how the puzzle fits together." He flashed a lopsided grin hauntingly reminiscent of Jeremy's. "You won't believe it."

With that cryptic remark, Colonel Ridgeford spun on his heel. Hank Warner and Ben Nichols bade Salina a hasty farewell and followed the colonel from the office, leaving her alone in Brisco's company.

"I'll see you back, ma'am." Brisco thoughtfully held her cloak for her.

"Brisco..."

He shook his wheat-colored head and smiled sheepishly. "I'll tell you the same thing I tell my mum: Ask me no questions; I'll not tell you any lies."

☆☆☆☆☆☆☆

Duncan was downright furious, and Salina knew it. Her flat refusal to answer his repeated questions concerning where she'd been for the past two hours maddened him to no end. Salina felt guilty for deceiving him, but there was little else she could do. She was honor-bound to keep silent.

"Please, Duncan," Salina finally implored. "Let it go. Let's just all be thankful that my abductors meant me no harm and have delivered me back into your care, safe and sound."

"This has something to do with your father, doesn't it?" Duncan relentlessly pressed, his square jaw set with unwavering resolve. "Garrett's contacts in this town are still operating, aren't they? And you know who they are!"

Stubbornly, Salina held her tongue, unable to meet her stepfather's stormy eyes.

Duncan gave in to exasperation. "Even if you know the identity of the mole who keeps breaking into my office, you still wouldn't tell me."

"Duncan, I truly am sorry; but this is one of those times when the divided allegiances between us become insurmountable. Your country is at war against mine! You know where my loyalties are, what order my priorities are in. I've never made that a secret from you. I don't mean to be so hardheaded about it, but please understand that this time I cannot give you the answers you seek. I am sorry."

"Not half as sorry as I am!" Duncan raged. Threatening to have her arrested would do no good; he wouldn't follow through with it. "Go to bed, Salina," he ordered, as if she were a naughty child. "You, too, Taylor Sue. The sooner we get through this night, the better off we'll be."

☆☆☆☆☆☆☆

Lieutenant Lance Colby greeted the Southern ladies at the breakfast table the next morning. Duncan was conspicuously absent.

"I've orders to accompany the two of you as far as Fairfax Court House," Colby informed them. "From there, you're on your own."

Salina forcefully tore her gaze away from Duncan's right-hand man. In this light, had Colby been wearing a gray uniform instead of a blue one, she could almost have believed that Jeremy was standing before her. It was often like that upon first glance, but then gradually, the longer Salina looked at Colby, the less he appeared like Jeremy. It was unnerving how much the two of them looked alike; it always had been.

"Thank you, Colby. You're very kind," Taylor Sue nodded gratefully, speaking for herself and Salina. "We appreciate your protection through the lines."

Salina's stepfather appeared but a scant moment before Colby gave the order for the carriage to drive on. Stilted good-byes were exchanged through the carriage window.

"Duncan, I can't thank you enough for allowing us to see Ethan," Taylor Sue offered her heartfelt gratitude. "We are obliged to you for what you have done for us."

Duncan nodded curtly. "May God keep His hand on you both until we meet again."

"Godspeed, Duncan," Taylor Sue whispered.

Salina longed to erase the scowl her stepfather wore, but she full well knew that she was the cause for his annoyed expression. That he was still angry with her was painfully evident; that she was not going to back down on her stated convictions was equally apparent. She was her father's daughter, and Duncan knew it.

The carriage driver clucked to the team of horses. It was a long and quiet trip to Fairfax Court House.

Chapter Eight

Cobb Farm
Near Frederick, Maryland

*T*ucker munched on tall grass while Jeremy kept a loose hold on his reins. Though Jeremy sometimes still missed Orion, the mount that had been shot out from under him at Gettysburg, this steady-tempered gelding had proved himself well-behaved, was easy to drill, and minded commands with uncommon alacrity.

Standing at the edge of a moonlit millpond, Jeremy relived an incident that had transpired during his first stay here at the Cobbs. He looked beyond the silvered surface of the water back to a day when his fiesty wife had actually pulled a gun on him.

On the journey from the Grant farmstead in Gettysburg to the Cobbs, Salina had determined that Jeremy had no further need of laudanum to ease his headaches. Jeremy, however, had differed with her opinion of the situation and, while she wasn't looking, searched the back of the wagon for the supply he knew she had packed.

"Jeremy, no!" He remembered Salina's soft drawl, the scene in his mind as clear as if it had happened yesterday rather than three months ago. Salina had found him rustling through her boxes of medicine and had tried to take the laudanum from him like a mother attempting to take something harmful out of the hands of a beloved child. "Dr. Warrick said you have no need for that stuff anymore."

Jeremy had brushed her aside with about as much effort as it takes to shoo away a pesky gnat. He had told her to let him be; he didn't care what Warrick said, because the doctor wasn't the one plagued by the headaches. Stalking away from her, Jeremy had uncorked the bottle and paused for but a split second, waiting to see what she would do before he indulged his craving. He'd forgotten to reckon with the fact that he and Ethan had been the ones to teach her how to shoot—and she had learned her lessons well. Holding her revolver firmly in both hands, Salina had expertly shot the bottle of laudanum Jeremy held into shards. The medicine spilled. Some was absorbed into his shirt, but most of it was swallowed into the dry ground.

"Are you crazy?!" Jeremy could almost hear his past rage echoing from the depths of the pond. He'd foolishly taken a step toward her and had wanted to shake Salina for what she'd done. "Maybe I am!" she'd boldly answered back. "I'm tired," she'd cautioned him. "It's not been the easiest of journeys so far. I told you before, but I'll say it again: You *aren't* going to have any more laudanum. Please don't make me shoot at you again. I'm upset— and I wouldn't want my aim to miss."

At that Jeremy had stood stock-still, giving Salina's statement proper credence. He had pleaded with her to simmer down, but she was already beyond determined. She had stormed to the back of the wagon with Jeremy on her heels, though keeping a respectful distance. He'd watched her warily, knowing that it pained her greatly to waste the medicine, since it was not easy to come by. To his shock and amazement, she'd willfully dropped that second bottle, defiantly raising her chin as the brown glass broke into bits at her feet. She dropped a third bottle, then a fourth and fifth in rapid succession.

"Stop it!" he had yelled, almost lunging for her, but the revolver she held kept him at bay.

A sixth bottle fell from her fingers, crashed against the others, its contents, too, combining to make potent mud. The seventh—and last—bottle she had hurled down in sheer frustration. Only then did Salina's grip on the gun loosen. Jeremy did shake Salina then. He railed at her, "Look what you've done!" The expression in his eyes must have been purely wild, but Salina never flinched. It took all his strength to merely set her aside and march past without lashing out further. He'd been so angry he hadn't realized that in setting her aside, he'd actually shoved her away. Salina had stumbled backward over the satchel she'd set next to the wagon wheel. She had sat down hard, and the gun had hit the ground. Her revolver had gone off with a resounding bang.

Jeremy shuddered. That bullet had whizzed past his elbow and smacked into a tree just a few paces from where he'd stood, stiff as a ramrod. He closed his eyes, hearing her voice again, reminded of the great big tears that had streamed down her face. "I didn't do it on purpose." Regret washed over Jeremy. He'd convinced himself that Salina just couldn't understand how unmercifully his head pounded, how angry he was over her willful destruction, or how badly he hurt and would continue to, since there was nothing left to alleviate his pain. Why he had ignored the fact that she would never have done anything to hurt him was beyond him. He knew that she always only wanted the very best for him. Yet in that instant, instead of running to her, he had turned away from her without even bothering to offer her a hand up. He had gone only two yards before he passed out cold.

To this day, Jeremy couldn't rightly account for what happened after that. Neither he nor Salina had made an effort to go back and rehash the details. It was not a moment of which he was most proud. He recalled waking up several days later. Salina and Mrs. Cobb had somehow got him situated upstairs in the attic bedroom, where he suffered mightily with the shakes, stomach cramps, fever, and chills. Mrs. Cobb had cooked up a home-brewed remedy that she and Salina took turns feeding to him. Jeremy shuddered, recalling the vile taste of the concoction, yet without it he might not have got through the detoxification process. It had taken a good while to rid his system of the poisons and cravings once and for all, but he'd been free of them ever since—and the episode was in the past.

"You're sure we're safe here, Captain?" It was Bentley who voiced the inquiry.

"Safe enough."

"This must be a place you've been before," the elder rider surmised. "Otherwise you'd not be so trusting."

"On our way back from Gettysburg, Salina and I were guests of the family who reside here," Jeremy vaguely explained. "The

Cobbs took us in and gave us shelter. They're good folks, Bentley, rest assured. Mrs. Cobb'll put us up with no questions asked. She's..." he paused.

"She's what?" Bentley queried.

"She's...trustworthy," Jeremy said, amending the statement he'd almost blurted out. Inhaling deeply, he caught the aroma of brewing coffee. "Smell that? She already knows we're here. Let's see to the horses, then go on up to house, and I'll introduce you. Mrs. Cobb makes wonderful coffee—*real* coffee."

"Anything's bound to be better than the substitute blend we've had in camp lately," Bentley nodded. The older cavalryman didn't expect to be told everything in the captain's mind, but he had the strong feeling that Jeremy was withholding information.

Jeremy privately believed that Seraphina Cobb was a link in the Remnant, even though she hadn't come right out and said so. That wasn't standard operating procedure for the lines of communication that Garrett had established. Each link played a vital role in collecting and forwarding bits and pieces of valuable intelligence, but not every contact involved was aware of the identity of others who might be. Secrecy and trust were what had revived and kept the Remnant thriving on a smaller scale long after it had unraveled on a larger one. Pertinent information was generally relayed only to whom it was necessary, when it was necessary.

Jake, Curlie, Tristan, Cutter, Boone, C.J., and Carney were at the pump washing up before making their way to the farmhouse. Bentley remained with Jeremy, suspecting that while the young captain knew he was safe, he was not entirely at ease.

"Something happen here that you want to tell me about?" Bentley ventured.

Jeremy's unpatched eye traveled to the window of the attic room where he had suffered indescribable agony. "Not especially, but thanks for asking." He happened to glance up at the attic window a second time—and started when he saw the curtain quickly fall back into place.

☆☆☆☆☆☆☆

Mrs. Cobb kindly welcomed Jeremy and his men and—with Damaris's assistance—served up plates of mouthwatering creamed chicken over hot biscuits. Intermittently throughout the meal, Jeremy thought he felt an unseen presence. Behavior that was much more characteristic of Salina than himself prompted him to twice look over his shoulder toward the shadowed stairwell that led to the upper stories of the house. But there was nothing— no one—there.

"How long are you going to be able to stay with us this time?" Mrs. Cobb asked cordially.

"Not long, ma'am," Jeremy answered for all of them. "We'll be here only until we get word as to where we're to conduct a certain business transaction, and then we'll be on our way."

"Then allow me to bid a hasty good night to you all. I'm sure you all have spent the entire day in the saddle, and sunrise has a way of putting in too early of an appearance in the morning." Mrs. Cobb smiled. "Perhaps the message you anticipate will come soon. Good night, gentlemen."

Soon Jeremy's men lay sprawled out on their bedrolls on the parlour floor, comfortable recipients of the warmth emanating from the stone hearth. Though Jeremy had ridden just as far and as fast as the others to get here, restful sleep eluded him altogether.

The fire in the parlour dwindled to little more than a pile of glowing embers. Damaris had told Jeremy that more firewood could be gotten from the lean-to outside the back door, and Jeremy took it upon himself to bring in a fresh supply. He donned his jacket and gathered his boots before treading lightly across the kitchen's wooden floor. Out on the porch he pulled his footgear on.

The night was cold, the wind brisk. Jeremy passed by the lean-to without picking up a single cord of wood, opting instead to check on the horses. He was halfway across the yard when the front door of the house opened and closed behind him. The hairs on the back of his neck prickled, yet there was no one else seen.

"Drake?" Jeremy impetuously called. No reply was voiced. Jeremy continued to the barn, trying in vain to shake the feeling that he was under a most scrutinizing surveillance.

Jeremy propped his elbows on the edge of Tucker's stall. He rubbed the thoroughbred's nose, ran a gentle hand over the arched neck and mane, and murmured unintelligibly to the horse. Trust and loyalty between man and beast were bonds that once forged were not easily broken.

Suddenly Jeremy's instincts prodded him to seek a hiding place in the tack room. He waited, revolver in hand, watching for he didn't know what.

After a few interminable minutes, the barn door opened. A man slipped stealthily inside. An icy wash of chills ran down Jeremy's spine. Jeremy blinked repeatedly to dispel the image before him—but it would not vanish. The man's face was no illusion: It was *real*—and it was a mirror image of *his own*!

Jeremy's blood ran cold. The sound of his sharply drawn-in breath caught the man's attention. The man raised the lantern he carried higher, searching the stalls.

Leaning heavily against the tack room wall, Jeremy was wholly dumbfounded. Forcing himself to take a second glance, he saw in the unknown man a picture of what he himself might look like a score of years from now: They shared the same hair color, though the man's was a more faded shade; the same black whiskers, though the man's beard was salted with occasional streaks of gray; the same stature, though the man's shoulders were less squared and more rounded. The shape of their mouths, the size of their noses, the arch of their brows, and the blue of their eyes were identical.

"Who are you?!" Jeremy mustered enough courage to exit the tack room. Prudence dictated the aim of his LeMat revolver toward the intruder.

The man's sapphire eyes widened in astonishment, but otherwise he failed to answer Jeremy's question.

"I said, *who are you?!*" With an impatient stride, Jeremy closed the gap between them—and *still* there was no reply. Annoyed, Jeremy backed the man into the wall next to the nearest stall, forearm braced across his chest, pinning the man's shoulders. In the shuffle, the lantern globe scraped against the paneling. The unbuttoned collar of the man's shirt parted, displaying double rows of zigzagging scars etched across the man's throat.

Jeremy stepped back, his mind reeling. Markings such as that must have resulted from a severe wounding, and most likely one that should have been life ending. The question spilled from his lips of its own volition: "What did they do to you?"

Abashed and desirous to hide the repulsive scars, the mute man hastened to do up the buttons one-handed, fingers atremble. His eyes snared Jeremy's and held fast. With a deliberate yet sympathetic motion, the man put a finger to his own cheek, tracing a line equal in length to the scar Jeremy usually hid beneath his eye patch.

"Yeah, I've got my own scars—plenty of them. Seems we both bear permanent souvenirs from this blasted conflict," Jeremy muttered darkly. He paused, unsure as to what made him assume those hideous marks on the man's throat had been inflicted by battle wounds. His eyes snapped with fiery confusion; his forearm pressed a little heavier against the man's chest. "Who *are* you?!" he repeated with escalating impatience. "Why are you following me?"

The older set of sapphire eyes clouded with distress and misery.

"Answer me!" Jeremy insisted.

"I... I...needed... to...see...you... for...myself... Now... I...have."

The strangled rasp of the man's voice sounded like something straight out of the abyss—and it made Jeremy's skin crawl. Jeremy immediately turned the man loose, stepping back and away.

Without his slate or chalk to write down what he wanted to say, Evan Southerland made a tremendous attempt to explain himself to the horrified young man. He swallowed, in great pain, holding his throat while straining to work his damaged larynx into forming a coherent string of words. "I'd have...done...different...had I...known... I...swear it!" Lantern in hand, the man retreated toward the house, leaving Jeremy in the darkness, staring tongue-tied after him, rooted and unable to move.

"Maybe I'm dreaming," Jeremy told Tucker, overcome by an involuntary shudder. "That's it: I've dreamed up a man with my own face." Another cold chill ripped through Jeremy. "What would the face of my father look like if not my own?"

Completely unsettled, Jeremy left the barn. He shot a glance at the top story of the house, but the attic window was dark.

A bitter knot formed in the pit of his stomach that didn't go away even after he'd piled the wood cords, banked the fire, and lay down on his bedroll. He couldn't get the blue-eyed man out of his mind. E.S., the man who was supposedly his father, was killed at Shiloh—Jeremy knew that to be fact. "The man is dead and buried!" he muttered into the oppressive shadows.

"So you are awake." In the stillness, Mrs. Cobb's voice was hardly a whisper, but Jeremy heard it plainly. He raised his head to look at his hostess. "You and I," Mrs. Cobb continued, "we have some business to discuss."

"What sort of business?" Jeremy followed her into the kitchen.

"I view you as an intelligent man, Captain Barnes. You might not have been at your best the last time you passed this way, but you're healed and whole and once more have your wits about you."

"There's something to be said for keeping one's head clear," Jeremy acquiesced. "Much easier to keep alert that way."

"Aye," Mrs. Cobb smiled. Without further ado, she told him, "I have a message for you."

"You're part of the Remnant, then, aren't you?" he challenged, following her silent command to be seated across from her at the table.

Mrs. Cobb nodded once, placing a steaming mug of spiced cider in front of him. She went to the pie safe and withdrew a folded map from a tin canister stored there. "Take a look at that, and listen closely."

Jeremy struggled to focus on the map, putting aside the incident in the barn. "Your friend Drake did not leave St. Louis when he expected to," Mrs. Cobb informed him. "Apparently there was a delay in getting all the horses cleared to ride the stock cars on the Baltimore & Ohio—but that's all taken care of now."

"You knew why we were here all along," Jeremy deduced.

"Aye," Mrs. Cobb confirmed. "I was informed that you were on your way shortly after you'd left Stuart's encampment."

Jeremy shook his head, marveling.

Mrs. Cobb smiled and went on, "They left St. Louis yesterday. If all goes well, he should be arriving at Harpers Ferry with two hundred horses roughly two days from now. Drake and his drovers will move the herd to a farm owned by sympathizers to our cause, just a spitting distance from Harpers Ferry." She pointed to a mark on the map located close to where the Shenandoah and Potomac Rivers converged. "They'll keep the animals there while Drake comes here to fetch you. Drake's men will work with you and yours to drive the herd toward Front Royal. You'll note that it's not a direct route and certainly a detour, but the Yankees patrol a good portion of the territory north of the Rappahannock, and they have strong positions near Culpeper."

"Yes, we knew that much." Jeremy rubbed the whiskers on his chin, thinking.

"Front Royal should be safe; it is not presently occupied. Of course, you'll have to keep to the back roads. It wouldn't be prudent to parade the herd out in the open along the nearest turnpike. But if you move by dark..." Mrs. Cobb stopped short. "Well, it's not my place to tell you what to do, Captain. You've got the map and will have the intelligence. It will be up to you as to how you get those horses to your quartermaster."

"It might not be your place, Mrs. Cobb, but I would appreciate any insight you have to offer. If it were yours to do, how would you do it?"

Mrs. Cobb again glanced at the map, thinking. "I might attempt to drive the herd from Front Royal, up the Shenandoah Valley a piece, and then pass through the Blue Ridge by way of Chester Gap. From there the horses could be moved along less-traveled roads southward until you reach Stuart's headquarters."

Jeremy thought about it. What the matron said made sense.

"Don't tell me outright what plans you settle on," Mrs. Cobb instructed. "If by some remote chance I were to be questioned at a later time, I could honestly say I didn't know what you had in mind."

Jeremy's eyes narrowed with deep contemplation. "Harpers Ferry is nearly thirty miles from here—and garrisoned by Federal troops."

"I said 'spitting distance from Harpers Ferry'—I didn't say you all were going directly into Lower Town or sashaying down High Street yourselves," Mrs. Cobb retorted.

"Pity Drake couldn't have transported the horses by way of the Winchester & Potomac." Jeremy's finger traced the railroad route toward Winchester.

"Winchester is by no means stable; the Yankees and Rebels occupy and retreat at will on a daily basis. I pity the population there, waking up each morning never knowing which side is in control. It's a no-man's-land." Mrs. Cobb shuddered. "More cider?"

"No, thanks," Jeremy declined.

Mrs. Cobb watched Jeremy for a moment. "Are you quite all right, Captain Barnes?"

"I was just...thinking..." He wanted to ask her about the occupant of the attic room but thought better of it. Maybe he was so tired his mind was merely playing tricks with his vision.

"In the morning, I expect to receive an updated report on the Yankee outposts in the Valley and along the Blue Ridge which should be of some use, providing the information is current. I will leave it for you in Tucker's saddlebags. Good night, Captain," she bade him before she began her ascent up the stairs.

"Mrs. Cobb?" Jeremy could no longer curb his curiosity. "Is there someone staying in your attic?"

She replied, "Trust in the Lord with all your heart and lean not unto your own understanding. In all your ways acknowledge Him, and He will direct your path."

Jeremy took her quotation of that particular scripture as her way of indicating the discussion was closed. It was hers to supply the information he needed pertaining to the horses. Beyond that, she would offer no more.

"He'll provide the strength to sustain you: Your own experiences have taught you that," Mrs. Cobb reminded him.

"Indeed they have," Jeremy allowed.

"It would be best if you could get some rest while you can. Good night," she repeated.

Jeremy returned to his bedroll and rethought the events that had led him here. When he had first approached General Stuart with Drake's telegram, he expected refusal, an inarguable declaration that the scheme was too risky. Jeremy had been genuinely surprised to win his commander's approval. Stuart had had some initial reservations but nonetheless sanctioned the unorthodox excursion, granting Jeremy and his men the necessary furlough. Two hundred horses were a tempting inducement, deemed worth the gamble in light of the fact that good stock, unless furnished by raids on the Federals, was getting harder to come by. Horses were sorely needed not only by the cavalry but also to haul cannon and caissons, ambulances, and supply wagons. Without horses to move them, the army was paralyzed. Jeremy had confidence in his men; he was certain that if they enacted the proposed plans to the best of their ability, they would succeed.

Jeremy tossed and turned so much that Boone and Tristan threw pillows at him. "Some of us are trying to sleep," they complained groggily.

Jeremy lay awake a long time before repose claimed his senses...and then he dreamed. It was of little wonder that his fatigued mind conjured the vague form of a man with no face, only a pair of deep blue eyes staring from a scarred countenance with the initial E.S. branded onto his contorted features. "I am your father," the harsh, wheezing voice professed. *"I am your father!"*

☆☆☆☆☆☆

Breakfast was delicious, but Jeremy hardly tasted the sausage or the apple butter slathered over flaky buttermilk biscuits. Mrs. Cobb seemed aware that something was amiss, but Jeremy made no comment to either her or any of his men. His dream had shaken him, disturbed him almost as much as the confrontation in the barn had, what with the blue eyes, the scars, and the clarity of the initials. He thanked his hostess at the conclusion of the meal and went alone to the stables. When he got there, he tore down the note stuck on a nail in Tucker's stall. His heart lurched as he read the capitalized letters: *MY NAME IS EVAN SOUTHERLAND AND I AM NOT DEAD.*

☆☆☆☆☆☆☆

November 18, 1863
Gettysburg, Pennsylvania

The town of Gettysburg was crowded to capacity, but on this occasion the overflow was not caused by the frenetic chaos of the now famous battle or its aftermath. This instance was a solemn one, yet the atmosphere was far more festive than it had been last July. Every spare room, hotel suite, and loft was occupied by visitors from far and near. Local residents took strangers into their homes, and even the churches opened their doors so that visitors could sleep in the pews that night.

The draw was that the President was coming to town. Abraham Lincoln had been invited—almost as an afterthought—by Judge David Wills to give a few "appropriate remarks," following the featured presentation to be given by the renowned orator, the Honorable Edward Everett. Judge Wills, head of the planning committee, was responsible for overseeing the idea of a national cemetery transferred from paper diagrams into reality. Thousands were on hand for the next day's dedication of the ground selected as the final resting place for so many fallen soldiers who'd given their lives in the struggle.

All the schools had been let out early, and young and old in the community had pitched in to make Gettysburg township presentable. The streets were clean; the windows around the Diamond, as well as along the route leading to the cemetery, were draped with red, white, and blue bunting; patriotically displayed flags fluttered on angled poles.

President Lincoln arrived at the depot on Carlisle Street shortly after sundown. He was greeted with cheers from the assembled welcome committee. He and Judge Wills, closely followed by the presidential entourage, walked a narrow gauntlet between rows of protective soldiers to the Diamond, where Judge Wills's residence was located.

A serenade of martial music played well into the evening. Sometime past the hour of nine, the President leaned from an upper-story window and gave a polite, if meaningless, little speech.

"He has a rather sad face," Lottie Colby commented to her husband.

"He's under a tremendous amount of strain," Lance Colby needlessly explained. "How would you like to have the weight of running this war on your shoulders?"

"I wouldn't," Lottie replied as Lance led her toward Baltimore Street, then on to their High Street home.

"There's talk that Mr. Lincoln's son Tad came down with a fever just before he left Washington. Last year, his son Willie died. I suppose that could be weighing on him as well," Lance speculated.

Lottie felt a spasm low across her back, much like the one she'd experienced after dinner earlier this afternoon. It was painful—and it scared her. When her twin sister, Mary Edith, had given birth to twins, Lottie had spent a miserable day in bed with sympathy pains. Over the months, Lottie had gradually reconciled herself to having Lance's child, yet her fear of the actual delivery had not abated in the least.

With acute concern written all over his face, Lance looked down at his wife. "You all right?"

Lottie didn't realize she'd stopped walking. "Yes," she hedged. "Please, let's get home. I'm tired, and I want to lie down for a spell."

☆☆☆☆☆☆☆

The next day dawned bright and crisp, characteristically November in southeastern Pennsylvania. Annelise Grant bustled around the kitchen of the Grant farmstead, dictating a hasty list of last-minute instructions to Jubilee.

"Not ta worry, Miz Annelise," Jubilee kept assuring her mistress. "Jube'll keep dat liddle Mistah Yabel comp'ny, an' ever'thin'll be right as rain. Ya jist gowan inta town an' enjoy da parade."

Without warning, a lone cannon shot rent the otherwise placid morning, and Annelise gripped the edge of the kitchen table, her eyes squeezed tightly shut. "I *hate* that sound, Jubilee!" she declared when the ground stopped vibrating beneath her feet. "I truly do!"

"Yas, Miz Annelise, ah knows whatchya mean," Jubilee nodded. The two women had weathered the battle in this house on this ridge, and since that time, virtually any loud noise brought on a rush of memories from those three hellish days and the bloody weeks that had followed.

"It's ten o'clock." Duncan appeared in the doorway of the kitchen, tugging on his coat sleeves to straighten them. "Are you ready, Annelise?"

"Yes, dear." Annelise slipped her arm through the handle of the basket that contained their lunch. "Have you found out whether you have to sit up on the platform?" she inquired.

"Yes—and no, I don't have to be on the stage. My orders allow me to remain part of the crowd and keep watch," Duncan absently replied. He was already thinking about the upcoming ceremonies and responsibilities in seeing to the protection of the Union leader. "I told Lance we'd meet him and Lottie at the cemetery."

The processional started at the Diamond before oozing down Emmitsburg Road toward the graveyard. Dignitaries were seated on a raised platform surrounded on all sides by the spectators who turned out for the dedication. Edward Everett, the featured speaker, was late.

Annelise skimmed the event program while Duncan's eyes furtively shifted over the crowd. Edward Everett was considered a mesmerizing speaker; he inflected all the right tones and punctuated his oratory with all the accompanying gestures. But while the oration was in progress, Annelise's attention was diverted by concern for her sister's daughter.

Lottie, standing to Annelise's right, surreptitiously shifted her weight from one foot to the other, trying in vain to attain a comfortable stance. *Had no one thought of chairs for this event?* she thought irritably, rubbing the small of her back.

Annelise asked, "Is everything all right, Lottie?"

"I'm...I don't know. I feel..." She shook her golden blond head. "I'm fine, really. I don't want to miss hearing what Mr. Lincoln has to say. Do you think it will be much longer before he speaks?"

"I'm not sure," Annelise whispered back. "Is it the baby?"

"Perhaps..." Lottie sighed. "But the pain isn't so bad now as it was a minute ago."

"Lance." Annelise reached behind Lottie's back to tap the young lieutenant's shoulder.

"Yes, Mrs. Grant?"

"Mark the time," Annelise instructed, and Lance obediently consulted his pocket watch.

The honorable Mr. Everett's address measured one hour and fifty-seven minutes in duration. Lottie had three more contractions in that same span.

When it came time for the President to make his remarks, he donned his spectacles, left his stovepipe hat on his chair, stood on the rostrum, and unfolded his script. His tenor words, powerful and stirring, rung out over the crowd. Lincoln's speech took less than three minutes:

"Fourscore and seven years ago our fathers brought forth upon this continent a new nation, conceived in Liberty, and dedicated to the proposition that all men are created equal.

"Now we are engaged in a great civil war, testing whether that nation, or any nation so conceived and so dedicated, can long endure. We are met on a great battle-field of that war. We are met to dedicate a portion of it as the final-resting place of those who here gave their lives that that nation might live. It is altogether fitting and proper that we should do this."

Lincoln continued, "But in a larger sense we cannot dedicate, we cannot consecrate, we cannot hallow this ground. The brave men, living and dead, who struggled here, have consecrated it far above our power to add or detract."

Annelise thought of Ethan and Jeremy and the struggle that they withstood in this place.

"The world will little note nor long remember what we say here, but it can never forget what they did here," Lincoln stated. "It is for us, the living, rather to be dedicated here to the unfinished work that they have thus far so nobly carried on." The President was momentarily halted by the spectators' audible offering of accordance. "It is rather for us to be here dedicated to the great task remaining before us,—that from these honored dead we take increased devotion to the cause for which they here gave the last full measure of devotion,— that we here highly resolve that the dead shall not have died in vain," Lincoln paused to acknowledge another smattering of applause, "that the nation shall, under God, have a new birth of freedom, and that the government of the people, by the people, and for the people, shall not perish from the earth."

The trickle of applause that followed the conclusion of Lincoln's short speech grew in length and volume. Some, like an unprepared photographer, weren't paying attention and had missed the poignant message altogether. The President returned to his seat with a weary expression. It made Duncan wonder whether Mr. Lincoln was trying to gauge whether or not his meaning was fully understood by those who had heard.

"Aunt Annelise?"

"Yes, Lottie?" Annelise felt the pressure of Lottie's grip on her arm. "Lottie?"

Lance, too, called his wife's name, for she was clutching his arm as tightly as she was her aunt's.

"I think I need to get home," she stammered. "Right away!" She flushed hot with embarrassment, tears flooding her cornflower-blue eyes. "I'm standing...in a puddle!"

"Your water has broken," Annelise said gently, comfortingly. "Can you walk?"

Lottie nodded. "Yes, I think so."

Annelise saw the terror in Lottie's eyes. "This is your first child. You may have hours yet before the baby actually makes his or her appearance. But I daresay getting you home and comfortable is a priority."

Lottie was grateful to be settled in her bedchamber. Hannah Colby and Lottie's sister-in-law, Dulcie, made the necessary preparations for the birthing.

Duncan explained to Annelise that he could not stay. "There's a luncheon back at Judge Wills' house which will be followed by a service tonight at the Presbyterian church. Do you think she'll be delivered by then?"

"Hard to say for certain," Annelise shrugged. "Babies have a habit of coming in their own sweet time."

"Lance has orders," Duncan added, fidgeting.

"All the better. Take him away with you," Annelise encouraged. "I know my niece's temperament. If the pain becomes too unbearable, she's prone to say some harsh things and might possibly question why he got her into this predicament in the first place. It might be easier on Lance if he's not obligated to come up with plausible answers for such inquiries."

Duncan kissed his wife, grinning appreciatively at her tongue-in-cheek wisdom. "Lieutenant Colby, I'm afraid duty calls."

Lance glanced from the twisted face of his wife to that of his superior officer. He squeezed Lottie's hand. "Mother, Dulcie, and your Aunt Annelise will be here, dear. Unfortunately, I cannot disobey orders."

"Get out of here, then," Lottie whined. "Go and leave. I don't care!"

Hannah put a comforting touch on her stepson's arm. She sensed that Lance must be recalling the fact that his own natural mother was no longer gracing this earth because she had given her life that he would live. "Go on, son. Lottie will be all right. By the time you get back, I reckon you'll have a fine child of your own; you'll see."

Apprehension clouded Lance's pale blue eyes. "Are you *absolutely* positive she's going to live through this?" he demanded an honest answer of Hannah.

"Lance, there's always a risk involved." She would not lie to the younger of two men she looked upon as her own sons. "She is healthy, and I'm reasonably sure that there will be no basis for alarm here."

Lance leaned down to kiss Lottie's perspiring brow. "I love you," he murmured, and genuinely meant it.

☆☆☆☆☆☆☆

Surprised to see his wife in a matter of hours, Duncan slid over in the pew to make room for Annelise to sit beside him in the back row of the church. "What's that?" he asked in a dry whisper, pointing toward the small daguerreotype case in Annelise's hand.

"Pressed dried flowers from the battlefield." Annelise unfolded the hinged case to show him. "I bought it from one of the vendors on the street. I'm sure the newspapers will print Mr. Lincoln's address in their next edition. I intend to clip it and send it along with this to Salina. I think she's open-minded enough to grasp the meaning of what the President said."

"Open-minded?" Duncan recalled his latest disagreement with Garrett's daughter. "If you say so."

"Where's the President?" Annelise craned her neck to catch a glimpse of Abraham Lincoln amid the church crowd.

Duncan whispered directions for where she'd find him, seated next to Mr. John Burns, the seventy-three-year-old Gettysburg citizen who'd taken up arms to fight the Rebels on the first day of the battle. Both men were listening to what the governor from Ohio was saying at the podium. "How's Lottie?" Duncan remembered to ask.

"Lance has a son," Annelise reported. "A boy—not as hale as our Yabel, but a strapper nonetheless. She's named him for their fathers: Caleb Alonzo Colby."

"Caleb Alonzo," Duncan repeated. "Well, all's well that ends well?"

"For today at any rate," Annelise grinned impishly. "Duncan?"

"Yes?"

"Did you know Alonzo Colby's second wife's name was Maida Southerland?"

"Maida." Duncan recalled a name from a long time ago. "She was Lance's mother. Why?"

"I watched over Hannah's shoulder as she entered the baby's name into the Colby family Bible. I thought the name *Southerland* sounded familiar, but perhaps I was mistaken?"

Southerland!

Open-eyed, they saw each other's look of astonishment. A few months back, Duncan had tried to discover the identity of a man with the initials of E.S., only to run into a dead end with no further leads. He'd narrowed his search down to a man known as Evan Southerland and contacted the man's kin, only to receive an indignant reply denouncing even the remotest connection between Jeremy Barnes and this man named Evan. Duncan squelched an impossible notion: If there was no connection between Jeremy and Evan Southerland, certainly there would be no connection between Lance and Jeremy— unless someone was lying about the connection. Alonzo would know whether Maida had had a brother named Evan. And if Jeremy and Lance were sons of a brother and sister, the reason they favored each other could be their relationship as *cousins*.

"Duncan, do you suppose..."

"Ssshhhh." Duncan put his finger to his lips to quell Annelise's inquiry. "Say nothing of this for now. In fact, don't even think twice about it." He wasn't going to hold his breath, but he might have stumbled onto the lead he needed to reopen the file on the identity of Jeremy's true father.

President Lincoln was obliged to depart the rally before its conclusion to make his train. Duncan was detailed to escort him, and the President was accommodating enough to pause a moment to pay his respects to Annelise.

"Good man, your husband," Lincoln said as he tipped his hat in deference to her. "Can't imagine a finer, more trusted character than he. His services are highly valued, Mrs. Grant."

"You're kind to say so, Mr. President. I deem it an honor and a privilege to make your acquaintance. Thank you, too," she added, "for your inspiring words this afternoon."

"Oh, that," the President brushed Annelise's comments aside. "We'll see how well received all that was in time, won't we?"

By six-thirty that evening, the President was on his train, which chugged out of Gettysburg toward the Union capital. Whatever lingering thoughts or doubts he might have had over his brief address at the cemetery were instantly superseded by the glad tidings given to him upon his return to the White House: His own little Tad was much recovered from his bout with the mysterious fever. Over that, Mr. Lincoln rejoiced.

Chapter Nine

Harpers Ferry, West Virginia

*D*rake was seething. How any-
one in his right mind had "forgotten" to feed or water two hundred
horses was an outrage. As he walked through the livestock pens, he
intentionally prevented several of the mounts from drinking too
much, knowing they'd gorge themselves if they were left alone.
They'd been given the proper amount of provender at Wheeling,
but apparently the horses had not been suitably tended at any of the
station stops since that point.

The famished and thirsty animals had traveled the bulk of the
distance from the ranch in Kansas. Their destination, a farm outside
of Harpers Ferry and not far from Charles Town, was less than five
miles away. It would be nothing short of disastrous if starvation or
thirstiness became a factor at this stage.

Lije Southerland cautiously approached his foreman. He could
appreciate Drake's indignation over the negligent treatment of the
herd, but they'd made it this far, and once fed and watered, he was

sure they would make it the rest of the way. The Western horses were tough animals. "My wife and I are ready to leave when you are, Drake. The last of the drovers have returned from their evening meal. I'll give them their instructions and we can set out. Why don't you go and eat something yourself. I'll oversee the horses while you're gone, if that makes you feel better."

"All right." Drake was slow to nod. "I won't be long."

"Drake, mark my word: It will all work out," the judicious rancher assured him.

Drake nodded a second time. He wanted very much to believe Lije's assessment of the situation.

"Hey, boss." One of the drovers caught up with Drake between the stables and the hotel. "Federal officer was looking for you at the depot. Said his name's Colonel E.S. Ridgeford. He said for you to meet him in the lobby at the hotel."

Drake squared his shoulders. Ridgeford—here. That didn't surprise him. "Much obliged." He could see that Lije, along with a handful of drovers, was occupied with monitoring the horses while they continued to feed. "If Mr. Southerland asks where I've gone, just tell him I'll be back shortly."

"Right," the drover nodded.

Drake entered the hotel lobby, boots muffled by the carpeting. He spotted Ridgeford instantly, and for a full minute the two men shared a stark, cold glare.

"Mr. Dallinger."

"Ah, Colonel Ridgeford." Drake performed a stilted bow. "What a coincidence that we should meet again. Or is it?"

"No," Ridge shook his sable head. "It's no coincidence."

Drake sized up the man anew. "I received a most enlightening letter from my attorney before departing South Union. He took pains to explain who you are, what your name really is, and that on your last visit to Boston you took possession of a report summarizing an investigation pertaining to Jeremy Barnes. Don't worry, I won't divulge your identity if you're that intent on keeping it a secret. My primary concern lies within the contents of that report. Where's Micah's dossier?"

"I've a room on the second floor. Perhaps that which you and I have to talk about could be better discussed there." Ridge let his cool blue gaze bore into Drake's guarded turquoise eyes. Micah had repeatedly assured him that Dallinger had a good many secrets of his own. Ridge, like Drake, did not have the habit of placing his trust easily. "How is my father?"

"He is well, anxious to see you. Your mother, too, is here. Did you know that?"

"Ma?" Ridge's brow furrowed. "That stands to reason. She would insist on coming, for I'm sure she holds the opinion that she alone can properly care for my brother. Ma can be stubborn when she's of a mind to be."

"Seems to run in your family," Drake chortled. "May I suggest, then, that we get this report business taken care of first. Once we're through, you can have your family reunion."

Ridge and Drake managed to suspend the animosity instilled at their first meeting in order to delve into the dossier. Contained within the pages was the irrefutable *implication* that Jeremy was the son of Ridge's oldest brother Evan—but the report had a conspicuous lack of tangible proof to that end.

The bitter disappointment Drake tasted was a fraction of what he was sure Jeremy would feel. In the course of his investigation, Micah had succeeded in discovering what he *believed* to be Jeremy's rightful name, yet there was no legal way for Jeremy to lay claim to it until formal acknowledgment was bestowed by Evan Southerland. Evan alone had it within his power to grant Jeremy ownership of the name his mother had denied him at birth.

"I must warn you: My brother is not yet in the proper frame of mind to publicly admit his past indiscretions," Ridge announced with a degree of regret. "He has directed me to find *documented* corroboration for him, something to prove beyond the shadow of a doubt that Jeremy is indeed his firstborn. I can't say as I blame him: From a practical standpoint, there is a question of inheritance at stake. I have an idea as to where to begin searching for the proof Evan requires, although it will take me time to obtain it. I intend to see if there is any recorded evidence of Jeremy's birth filed at the Fairfax County Court House."

"Is that the best you can do?" Drake goaded. "A ledger entry, possibly a certificate, that will validate his existence? What if the records were moved to keep them from falling into Yankee hands? Ever thought of that?"

Ridge had. "I've also been keeping tabs on his mother's whereabouts. She's visiting from England with her current husband and has not yet left this continent. I believe, if approached in the right manner, she might be...*persuaded*...to see it as her best interest to tell the truth concerning my brother and their alleged son."

Drake continued to pore over the meticulously chronicled findings Micah had compiled. "Yet in itself, this report still tells quite a story, doesn't it?"

"It's a lot to stomach," Ridge acquiesced. "If I'd known who Salina's husband was back in Culpeper, I'd have found a way to better acquaint myself with him."

"If you'd told me your name and who you were then," Drake countered, "it might've gone easier for you. We might've been able to combine our resources and learned to work together months ago."

"I didn't know we were basically on the same side then," Ridge hedged. "Now I do. I'm willing to concede that a working relationship between the two of us might prove beneficial—for our own particular reasons."

"Agreed." Drake closed the folder. "What do you plan to do with this?"

"I'd like to show the file to Jeremy, but I can't give it to him. This copy will be delivered to my brother's hand. I've taken the liberty of sending an identical copy of the dossier south by courier to Salina. I've requested that she safeguard it for Jeremy until he is willing and able to accept the truths in it."

"And Lije? Do you think your father is aware he has another grandson?" Drake challenged. "And you might want to think about this, Ridge: Jeremy's to meet me at the Cobbs—and Evan is there already? What if *they* happen to meet in the interim? What then?"

Ridge shrugged uncomfortably. The mental image of match flame to tinder created a rather explosive picture. "I can't speak for my brother any more than I can speak for Jeremy. I honestly don't know what could happen, but something's bound to, and now's as good a time as any for a reckoning. I suppose we'll just have to hope that they don't find each other before one of us can intervene or, at the very least, explain."

"You know Ruth-Ellen will be shocked by all this," Drake predicted. Having met Evan's wife, he speculated that she would not take kindly to the disclosure of an illegitimate son of Evan's seed born on the wrong side of the blankets—even though it had occurred years before he'd married her.

Ridge thumbed through the pages of the dossier. "My father will draw his own inferences when he sees Jeremy: He can hardly fail to notice the resemblance, let me tell you!" A curious smile played on his lips, and he shook his head in wonder. "I had no idea Jeremy and Salina were connected to so many people, either by blood or by marriage. The only one involved without any direct relative tie to them might be you, Dallinger."

"But I'm their friend, and I'm the closest thing Jeremy has to a brother. My allegiance is with *him* first, your father and the Southerlands second. Do you comprehend that?" Drake pressed. "I want to make sure there is no question as to where I stand—before or after the dust settles."

"I quite understand," Ridge said with a brisk nod. "And you'd do well to remember that this is a *family* matter—one to be handled by my family, without friendly interference. There will be pain inflicted, no less hurtful in spite of its being unintentional. You let us Southerlands deal with this in our own way."

"Keep it in the family then," Drake scrupulously agreed. "That's fine by me. The catch is that Jeremy's Southerland blood makes him a part of it."

"Whether he wants to be or not," Ridge quipped.

☆☆☆☆☆☆☆

Grave silence accompanied the turning of the last page of the Southerland dossier. Drake held his breath, waiting for Jeremy to say something, anything. But Jeremy didn't. He merely closed the folder and handed it back to Ridge Southerland. The only sign of reaction was in his tightly clenched jaw. Jeremy refused to meet the sapphire eyes that were so like his own, staring at him from the face of a man who was supposedly kin. He also refused to meet Drake's gaze.

"Are you going to sit there and tell me that all this means nothing to you?" Ridge fairly taunted. "Have you nothing to say?"

"What's there to say?!" Jeremy instantaneously shot back. "This report *almost* identifies Evan Southerland as my sire. *If* the man upstairs is actually my father, that would then make you an uncle, and Lije..."

"I am your grandfather," the patriarch of the Southerland clan asserted from the head of the table. Lije was no fool. He'd already identified what his eldest son was unready to confess. Visible proof was before him; he had no need of a document to verify Jeremy's obvious heritage. "Evan tells me that the two of you have met."

"He *told* you that?" Jeremy queried, his black brows bunching together.

"He wrote it," Lije clarified. "You gave him quite a shock."

"Yeah, well, the shock was mutual," Jeremy ground out. His head was swimming. The report spelled out his rightful name, exposed his mother's lover, and revealed a closet full of skeletons that might have been better left undisturbed. Suddenly the knowing, while at first a relief, flooded through him with sour remorse. He knew that while he was a curiosity to these Southerland men, he wasn't accepted as one of them. "Has *he* seen this?"

"He's seen it," Ridge answered.

"But he hasn't acknowledged it." Drake's copper fist pounded the table. "What you're saying is that even after seeing the report Evan's still not willing to name Jeremy as his son?"

"Drake, this is a rather startling, even precarious situation." Lije tried to diffuse the temper of his foreman before it ignited into full fury. "Ridge has already stated that Micah was unable to produce any actual documentation that would prove without a doubt the connection between Jeremy and Evan."

Drake eyed his employer. "You've always been a fair man, and I owe you my life, sir, but this situation, as you call it, reeks of renunciation. You're going to allow Jeremy to know what his name ought to be but deny him the privilege of claiming it? It belongs to him, he has a right..."

"Sons have rights that are inherited from their fathers." A placid expression of resignation settled in Lije's troubled blue eyes. "Evan's been unwell for months. He's requested more time during which either Micah or Ridge might obtain irrefutable validation. Surely caution and levelheadedness would be well warranted, especially since there is much at stake for both Evan and Jeremy."

Jeremy removed himself from the table.

"Where are you going?" Ridge queried.

"I'm tired of being discussed like I don't exist," Jeremy retorted. "But then, maybe that would be best for all parties concerned: Forget I even do!"

Lije Southerland followed his grandson at a respectful interval. He sat down on the millpond bank next to Jeremy and balanced his elbows atop his bent knees. Jeremy threw a pebble into the pond. The splash sent countless ripples undulating over the mirrorlike surface.

"We must seem rather cold and unfeeling to you," Lije began.

Jeremy took a sideways glance at the rancher. Eyes the same color as his own answered back, pleading for a chance. Irritated, he flung another pebble into the millpond.

"Well, I'm sorry for that. It's a lot of information to digest all at once, I suppose. It's just..."

"Look," Jeremy said curtly, hurling another pebble. "Don't put yourself out. I'm quite used to not being wanted. My mother didn't want me, John Barnes didn't want me, my own father doesn't want me. It shouldn't have come as such a surprise."

"But it *was* a surprise, Jeremy," Lije abruptly affirmed. "When Ridge initially showed me Micah's report, well, you could have knocked me over with a feather. It might've been different had Evan known of your existence and Justine had taken you away from him; if you'd been lost to us for years and found again, it would be..."

"Acceptable?"

Lije sighed. "None of this makes much sense, does it?"

"No, it doesn't."

"No more so than your mother's reasons for keeping her condition from Evan. We never knew about you until now. Coming so close on the news that Evan was not dead as we had been informed...it's a lot to swallow," Lije tried again to explain.

Jeremy didn't look at Lije. "You don't have to make amends for him. I don't care if he claims me or not."

"Ah, but you do," Lije argued. "You're one of us, and you're used to fighting for whatever it is that you want most. I can see that about you—I know the trait well because it runs through all the men in this family. You move like he does, share his mannerisms..."

"Well, isn't that nice," Jeremy remarked tightly.

Again Lije sighed. They were getting nowhere. "In all honesty, I wouldn't wonder if the color of your uniform might have something to do with his inability to claim you as his own flesh and blood. Evan believes in the Union wholeheartedly. I imagine it rankles him greatly to know that you serve the other side. It makes the two of you enemies."

"And what about you?" Jeremy prodded. "Which side do you serve? Here you've managed to transport two hundred horses east, purportedly headed to the Federal cavalry depot at Giesboro—yet you're willing to turn them over to me to ultimately be used by the Southern cavalry. Doesn't that upset your son? To know that you're supplying his *enemy* with remounts?"

"I've been doing business with both sides, Jeremy. Cattle and horses. I'm not taking sides in this fight. I'm merely trying to aid both."

"And how does your conscience justify that?" Jeremy pounced. "Do you sleep well at night knowing your kin is divided equally between the Union and the Confederacy? Doesn't it bother you that Ridge wears a blue uniform but is gray at heart?"

Lije contemplated the surface of the millpond for a moment, trying to formulate the right words to describe how he felt to this furious young man. When he looked up, Jeremy had disappeared, not having bothered to wait for his answer. "Dear Lord, that was handled poorly on my part. Bless him with forgiveness, Father God. Please don't let him grow to hate us. Soften his heart for acceptance," Lije petitioned, "—as well as Evan's!"

☆☆☆☆☆☆☆

"Hey!" Drake easily caught up with Jeremy's long stride. "You all right?"

"I'm fine."

"Yeah, well, you don't look it. Tell me what happened with Lije."

Jeremy stopped walking. "I don't know how you stand to benefit from this performance here, but I came here to do a job, and I intend to see it through."

"Benefit? What are you talking about?" The scar on Drake's forehead puckered as his brow furrowed in confusion.

"Don't look at me like that!" Jeremy snapped. "You were in on this from the onset, weren't you? Did you make up this elaborate scheme all by yourself, Drake? Were the horses just a ruse to get me up here so you could show me off to your friends? You certainly picked the right form of temptation for me to risk my life— as well as those of my men—behind enemy lines, let me tell you! *Horses*. Yeah, I bit—hook, line, and sinker!"

"There *are* horses," Drake answered pointedly. "And I'm sorry you think so little of me or believe I'd outright lie to you about something like that."

"All right. Suppose I believe you, and you haven't lied about the horses," Jeremy countered. "It doesn't alter the fact that they are a sham for the real reason you wanted me here."

"The horses were my idea initially. Admittedly," Drake confessed, "I didn't tell Lije who the so-called buyer was going to be on this end, but he approved the plan of shipping them east. Once he learned of your existence, he wanted to meet you for himself. You mean something to him, Jeremy!"

"Aaaahhhh!" Jeremy turned to walk away, not knowing what he believed anymore.

Drake followed, undaunted. "It's a quality herd. We had a little trouble keeping them fed and watered properly on the way to Harpers Ferry, but that should be taken care of by now. Ninety percent of them are like the mounts we used to get out of the Express stables: pintos, mustangs, Morgans, Thoroughbreds—some prize horses in the bunch."

"And the other ten percent?" Jeremy eyed Drake critically. "Now what aren't you telling me?"

"The rest aren't exactly pacers or walkers, but they'll do in a pinch—and I hear the Southern Cavalry is in just that," Drake quipped. "How does your side keep surviving when the North has so much more in the way of matériel and manpower?"

"We manage because we have to!" Jeremy's jaw had a stubborn set. "Because we have honor and pride and devotion to a common endeavor—*esprit de corps.* We're not whipped yet!" Jeremy stuffed his hands deep into his pockets, an action that stretched the braces taut over his shoulders. "My men and I will be ready to ride in ten minutes. Time's wasting; let's get on with the rest of the grandiose plan of yours. If the horses you claim you brought with you are really where you say they are, it'll take us most of the night to get there from here. Are you riding with us? Or are you staying here with them?"

"I'll ride," Drake said. He shook his head sadly. "Ten minutes." This wasn't turning out like he'd planned. The whirlwind he'd cautioned Little One about was blowing out of control.

☆☆☆☆☆☆☆

Marietta Southerland stood with Seraphina Cobb amid Jeremy's riders, hospitably distributing food and kindly extending her best regards.

"Peace offering?" Jeremy inquired suspiciously, securing a full nose bag of feed in front of his saddle.

"I suppose in a way it is. I so wanted to bid you farewell myself." Marietta self-consciously tucked an errant silver curl back into her chignon as the steady, skeptical gaze of Jeremy's unpatched eye rested squarely upon her. "I know I wasn't overly gregarious upon our introduction, and for that I would like to apologize."

"No need." Jeremy dismissed her words. "Thanks for this," he politely amended, indicating the small burlap sack she'd given him.

He turned his back to her, stuffing the home-cooked sustenance into a saddlebag.

"Please forgive them, Jeremy. Southerlands are proud men, staunch in their beliefs. I can see you are one of them not only in appearance, but you have their dignity and courage. You, too, possess an inbred strength lesser men do not," Marietta noted, wiping a tear from her cheek with her fingertips. "You have no idea how much Lije had been anticipating this, how perfect he wanted the revelation and your induction into our family to be. Try as he might, he cannot control the reactions of others involved, and he forgot to take those reactions into account. I can't imagine any of this has been easy for you to bear, but I will tell you this: Like Lije, I don't need a signed document to see that you are Evan's son, which in turn makes you my grandson. You've inherited a temper from Evan, that much is plain to see, and when he simmers down, perhaps he'll realize how ludicrous his insistence on written proof is." Her voice became choked. "I know so little about you, but I dearly hope that will not always be the case. I want you to know, Jeremy, without a doubt, that you have my love from this day forward. You will continually be in my thoughts and prayers. If you ever have need of a place to call home, Lije and I hope you will remember us. We've more land than we know what to do with—Lije will see that some acreage is carved out for you; I know him that well. It pains me to see this situation unravel without a satisfactory conclusion."

"Ma'am?" Jeremy offered Marietta a clean handkerchief, which she gratefully accepted. If she had wanted him to feel bad, she was doing a good job of it.

Marietta used the handkerchief to dab her pale blue eyes, took a deep breath, and sighed. "I remember times when Lije and Evan quarreled so bitterly over the woman who was your mother. There was even one occasion when I thought they might actually come to blows—but they never did. This is probably a moot point now, more than twenty years later, but I do know that Evan had it in his heart to marry her—he loved her, even if he shouldn't have. He'd have loved you, too, had she told him about you. But Justine Prentiss disappeared, and after their final break, he never heard from her again. Evan married Ruth-Ellen out of a sense of duty, certainly not out of the abundance of the feelings in his heart. When she is told of your existence, she will see you as the profound personification of Evan's sin. She will be offended, she will resent him for what he's done, and she will grow to despise you, since you are his firstborn and that, potentially, can shift things for her own sons. I believe you are wise enough to understand that expecting instant forgiveness is impossible. And while forgetfulness might one day be cultivated, it will be a good long time before it's achieved." Concluding her soliloquy, Marietta stood on tiptoe to grace Jeremy's bearded cheek with a genuinely affectionate kiss. "God bless you, Jeremy. May He watch over and protect you until we meet again."

"Thank you, Mrs. Southerland," Jeremy commented, fidgeting. "You may rest assured your words have not fallen on deaf ears, and while I sincerely appreciate your kindness, I rather doubt there is much chance that we shall ever meet again."

"The Lord works in mysterious ways." Marietta mustered a wavering smile. "You don't yet know what He has planned, and neither do I—but we will in time. His time."

"I'll believe it when I see it," Jeremy muttered. "Good-bye, Mrs. Southerland."

"Good-bye, Jeremy," she waved and added prophetically, "good-bye for now."

☆☆☆☆☆☆☆

After inspecting a portion of the herd, Jeremy found he could not argue with Drake's assessment—the remounts were quality horseflesh. "What now?" he wanted to know. "We just take the horses and run?"

"That's about it," Drake confirmed. "The sooner the better."

"And when this particular shipment doesn't show up at the horse depot in Giesboro?" Jeremy pressed.

"The officials will be led to believe that the horses were lost to a band of Southern raiders," Drake replied. "Not a stretch for the imagination."

"Who paid for all these horses?" Jeremy asked. "A herd like this must've cost somebody somewhere a pretty penny."

"Don't worry about it," Drake brushed Jeremy's query aside. "The balance has been taken care of."

"By who? You?"

"Don't ask too many questions, friend. There may come a time when you're liable not to like the answers. The best advice I can offer is don't look a gift horse in the mouth."

"Interesting turn of phrase." Jeremy rolled his eyes at Drake's pun.

"Captain?" Weston Bentley fell into step beside Jeremy on his way to the second holding pen.

"Yeah?" Jeremy nodded to Kidd Carney and Curlie, both of whom stood guarding the paddock gate.

"I hate to be the bearer of bad tidings, sir," Bentley interrupted, shuffling his weight from one foot to the other. "But we got some serious trouble."

Jeremy did not like the sound of his fellow rider's tone. "What's the matter, Bentley?"

"Come with me." Bentley led Jeremy past the pens and behind the barn, where about forty horses were corralled. "Boone and I separated these from the rest—and that's not counting the dozen that have died already. Look at them."

Jeremy's stomach knotted. "A dozen *dead*?! What, are the horses sick? What's wrong with them?"

"Tristan doesn't think it's a disease, but more a case of moldy hay," Bentley reported. "I'm inclined to agree." The elder rider lowered his voice so that Jeremy almost had to strain to hear him. "I don't think they were well treated on the train. Somebody deliberately fed them horses bad provender—and the animals were hungry enough to eat it. I don't reckon they'd have gobbled it up if they weren't starving."

Following Bentley up and over the fence, Jeremy's ire increased tenfold. Everywhere he looked he saw the colicky horses pawning the ground, rolling from side to side, biting their flanks. A lack of fresh manure showed that there was certainly a blockage problem in the animals. Jeremy's hands clenched in impotent fists; there was absolutely nothing he could do for the crampy horses that had already broken out in a cold sweat.

"This is criminal!" Jeremy muttered angrily. "Why would someone intentionally harm them?" It made his skin crawl to think that the deed was done with premeditation. "Who'd deliberately make waste of good horseflesh!"

"Beggin' yer pardon, Captain," Bentley forced a cough to clear his throat. "Now keep in mind this is just speculation, but we heard that one of Southerland's sons is a former Union officer. Can't imagine that Southerland would want good horses to go to us Rebs knowing they was to be used by the side who permanently injured his own flesh and blood, can you?"

Jeremy shook his head. "Lije Southerland doesn't strike me as the vindictive type."

"It can't be proved that somebody deliberately did this," Boone pointed out.

"With your permission," Bentley continued, "I'll have the boys and the wranglers round up the healthy horses. We'll take as many as we've got left and head home."

Jeremy nodded in acquiescence, but his eye flitted over the wranglers Drake brought with him from South Union. He wondered whether any of them knew anything about moldy hay.

"And have you given any more thought as to how we're gonna get back?" Bentley pondered aloud.

"I reckon our best chance is probably to take them up the Valley and cross the Blue Ridge at Chester Gap. We'll have to keep a lookout for Jessie Scouts, but I suppose that's the lesser of the evils than having to fight off any number of Union patrols. Once we get south of Chester Gap, that ought to put us behind our own lines. From there we'll be able to find out where General Stuart has established winter quarters."

"Aye, sir," Bentley agreed. "We'll get some horses through, even if not all of them."

Drake, having learned of the dead and dying horses, went directly to the pens. Down on his knees, he rubbed his hands over one of the barrel-chested horses. He put his ear to the mare's flank, listening with abject disgust to the gurgling and strong rumbling within. Wasting no more time, he went in search of Jeremy. "I hope you don't think I had anything to do with all this."

In a detached monotone Jeremy answered, "I don't know what to think."

"Is that an accusation?"

"Take it for what you will."

"So, you're leaving, just like that?" Drake snapped his fingers.

"I told you before we left the Cobbs that I have a job to do," Jeremy said flatly. "There's still work to be done."

"Jeremy, wait. You're angry—and with reason—but let's take a step back for a minute and look at this in a rational manner." Drake unknowingly echoed Bentley's sentiments. "This looks to me like *sabotage*. We can get to the bottom of it if you'll just talk to me."

"The way I see it, we've still got a herd of about twelve dozen horses—horses that can be put to good use when we get back to Virginia. General Stuart will approve of their quality, I'm sure. Beyond that, I've got nothing more to say to you."

"Jeremy," Drake began again.

Jeremy held up his hand to cut Drake off. "Don't. Just shut up and let it go. It was a risk coming here, one that I was willing to take—but that's only the half of it. Just... Oh, just forget it." He stalked away.

"I'm trying to ensure that this isn't a botched mission," Drake called after him.

Jeremy spun around to face Drake. "Look, do me one last favor before you ever decide to do me another—and don't bother! I've had just about all the favors I can stomach right now." He avoided Drake's eyes when he added, "There's no call for you or any of your drovers to ride back with us. I've got enough men of my own to handle the decreased size of the herd. We appreciate your efforts on behalf of the Southern cavalry."

"And what about the Southerlands?"

"What about them?"

Drake shrugged. "Listen at least to what Ridge has to say."

"If you're so interested in what Ridge Southerland has to say, you listen to him. I'm not about to. I don't care anymore." Jeremy stood toe-to-toe with Drake and stared into his turquoise eyes. In a voice that was almost a strangled whisper he lamented, "You *knew* about my name, and you didn't even bother to tell me. My, what a great friend you've turned out to be!"

"Jeremy!"

The sandy-blond, square-shouldered Rebel captain refused to answer. Hurt was the mortar, anger the bricks. The invisible wall stood thick between them.

Drake was well acquainted with his friend's pride and stubbornness. "Fine," he muttered, angry himself. Arguing the point further would be fruitless—it had gone bad all the way around. Best to leave some thread to rebuild with later on. "Take care, friend." He used the same moniker for Jeremy as he always had, but even to his own ears there was a strangely hollow ring to the title.

Out of the corner of his eye, Drake saw one of the drovers from South Union hanging around the paddock where the sick horses had been isolated. Two more of them had died, and Drake didn't like the contemptuous demeanor of the man's stance. As Drake approached, the man momentarily faced him—then suddenly high-tailed it out of the paddock, headed toward the summer kitchen to have breakfast with the other drovers.

Drake recognized the drover: Clive Fairweather was Ruth-Ellen's brother. Had Clive somehow found out that the horses weren't going to Geisboro but were going to Jeremy instead? And had Clive discovered somehow that Jeremy was Evan's son, thereby viewing him as a threat to the inheritance of his sister's sons? Drake groaned, not wanting to believe his own speculations. Yet if Clive had acted on what could be construed as a weak motive at best, sabotage was *exactly* what had happened to the horses. Drake had no irrefutable evidence; unless something could be found to substantiate an outlandish accusation, he would not mention it to Lije Southerland. The old rancher had enough on his mind already without having to contend with more. Drake opted to keep his suspicions to himself, at least for now.

Chapter Ten

Point Lookout, Maryland

Standing on the fringe of a huddled mass guarded by rifle-toting colored soldiers, Ethan wanted very much to believe that the tears in his eyes—as well as those in the eyes of his comrades—were caused by the biting whip of the wind across the marshy peninsula. But he knew better. The dismal sight of his surroundings left an unswallowable lump in his throat. At first glance, Point Lookout—or Camp Hoffman as it was officially recorded—showed little potential for escape. The narrow tongue of sandy land was bordered by the Chesapeake Bay to the east and the Potomac River on the west. On a clear day the eastern shoreline of Virginia was probably visible, and that was a notion Ethan would rather not dwell on. It was easy enough to be home-sick without the ability to see his native state from where he was confined. *So close,* he mused, *and yet so far away...*

A dashing gust of wind barely stirred the translucent gray mist and low-hanging clouds shrouding the prison compound and hospital complex. The strong blasts sent the waves splashing against the rocks, showering the new inmates with salty sea spray. The dread and drear of the place was palpable. The lighthouse, poised on the southern-most tip of Maryland, sent a recurrent beam slicing through the murky gloom.

Ethan shivered, and he did so even more as black-faced guards prodded the Rebel prisoners along, walking from the landing at the wharf to the post headquarters for processing by the provost marshal. After registration and a thorough search, the prisoners were escorted into the prison pen.

Conical tents aligned in rows separated by "streets" housed sixteen men apiece. Ethan was assigned to a tent that had a single vacancy. The man before him had died of scurvy sometime during the previous night, and the body, destined for the Dead House, was carted out just as Ethan was ushered in.

Ethan curtly introduced himself to his dour-faced messmates, then spread his thin blanket on the vacant spot opposite the door and sat on it. Through the open tent fly he viewed the fourteen-foot-high walls bordering the stockade, complete with an exterior catwalk. From their elevated vantage point, guards rotated around the pen, always watching with an eager eye for a Confederate to approach the Dead Line. If that boundary was crossed—whether intentionally or inadvertently—the guards would shoot to kill.

Five crackers, a couple of ounces of meat, a half cup of watery carrot soup—Ethan's stomach rumbled long into the night after such meager rations. Within hours he learned that prisoners who had money didn't fare quite so badly here. Food, blankets, and items of clothing could be procured, for a price, if one had the right connections. The widely accepted mode of exchange was not currency. More often than not, bartering could be successfully accomplished with hard tack and tobacco. Thirst and cold were going to be Ethan's immediate concerns: The water was not fit to drink, and Ethan judged that his already shabby uniform would offer him little protection from the elements. A dismal thought, considering the winter months were yet ahead.

After three weeks, Ethan had saved up enough hard tack to "buy" a piece of stationery and an envelope. After four weeks he had enough tobacco stashed for the cost of postage. The postmaster read every word of Ethan's letter to Taylor Sue, deemed it passable without need for censorship, and put it with the other outbound mail.

Taking his time in returning to his tent, Ethan supposed the letter would never reach Taylor Sue by Christmas. He could only pray it would reach her at all.

☆☆☆☆☆☆☆

Carey Home in Linden Row
Richmond, Virginia

Salina curiously unfolded the coded pages written to her in a criss-cross style. What she read astounded her.

> *As you will soon see, I have entrusted to you more secrets than even your father knew. I have the utmost confidence that you are trustworthy and will not make the contents of this dossier public knowledge any more than you would disclose the plans I have for the powder works and California. You are clever enough to keep your mouth shut when the occasion calls for it. Guard my secrets, Salina. My life, among others, depends upon your ability to do so.*
>
> *If confession is good for the soul, then bear with me as I explain: I am not a Union colonel, which you have already guessed. I am a double agent for the Confederate Secret Service. I initially enlisted in this war as a common Billy Yank, but changed sides, which would make me, in the eyes of most, a traitor. A compound set of circumstances brought with them grave disillusion, and for reasons of my own, I learned to hate the "Grand Army of the Republic." The Confederacy bought me, and I have accepted my lot, knowing the measure of risk. I am the mole in the Federal government that Duncan Grant hunts so diligently. I am the one who devised a plot for the assassination of Lincoln that neither your father, nor you, would forward to the people who could have carried it out. I am the one who killed Malcolm Everett the day he was sniping at you, and I am the one who will cut down John Barnes as soon as I can find a plausible way to do so. I will see that Barnes pays for what he has done to my family. An eye for an eye.*

Assuming that you will read the enclosed pages in their entirety, you will discover that the identity of your husband's father is my oldest brother, Evan. You will also uncover the fact that Jeremy and Lance Colby are cousins, but that's another kettle of fish altogether. Back to the subject at hand, I need to inform you that Evan's death was a case of mistaken identity; miraculously Evan lives. He is presently at the Cobb farmstead. By the time you receive this, he will possess a copy of this same information you do.

With regard to Jeremy's surname, there is nothing I can do to set the record straight—it will fall to Evan as to whether or not he acknowledges Jeremy as his legitimate heir. Until formal recognition is granted, Southerland is not a name Jeremy can legally claim without my brother's consent.

Hearing and understanding are two vastly different things. I would not wish to be in the person's shoes who has the task of making Jeremy understand any of this— and I fear that task will fall to you, Salina. You are his helpmate, his solace. You must be his strength. I realize this is not a "nice" situation, there is no tidy way to sweep it under the carpet. Jeremy's tie to the Southerland family affects us all, including you and the child you have conceived. I know not what else to tell you. I have no advice to offer save this: Don't be deluded. This will not be easy—not when the pride and stubbornness of Southerland men are involved. I can say that because I'm one of them.

I regret having to parcel this assignment out to you, but I thought it only fair to warn you of the impending storm. You're intelligent; rely on your own good judgment. You have your father's comprehension, perception, and compassionate heart. Garrett was good to Jeremy, and I know that you love my nephew very much. You will need both wisdom and strength to deal with this situation.

Burn this letter, if you would. Incriminating is but a mild adjective, and I have no desire to have it inadvertantly fall into the wrong hands. I merely felt compelled to give you some sort of explanation; you're entitled to at least that. Repeat only what you feel necessary for

Jeremy's benefit. I do not know his exact whereabouts, but I do know he'll come back to you. He'll need you more than ever.

With sincerest regards,
Eldridge Southerland

Several hours later, Salina closed the dossier. Maybe she should have heeded Drake's warning about letting sleeping dogs lie. The dossier was a revelation, but she feared it might not be a welcome one in Jeremy's way of thinking.

With hands that shook, Salina fed Ridge's letter to the flames. She restlessly paced the floor in front of the fireplace. "I so wanted to give him a name. I just didn't *know* the investigation would uncover all *that*! Jeremy and Lance—*cousins!*"

Taylor Sue's knitting needles stopped clicking for a moment, a miniature bootie dangling between them. She had pieced together the implication contained in the package by stealing a glance over Salina's shoulder, reading while she was too engrossed to notice. Now Taylor Sue was glad she had done the reading, for her sister-in-law clearly assumed she knew what was going on. "Salina, you'll do yourself no good fretting over it. There is nothing you can do to change what's past, or who's related to whom. You'll have to let Jeremy deal with the knowledge of his family history in his own fashion."

Taylor Sue was right, yet Salina continued to pace the floor in the back parlour.

"We've been here a short time, but already I can see how restless you are," Taylor Sue whispered.

"Maybe I need some air. I'll take a walk, bring back a newspaper if there are any to be had." She fetched her cloak and buttoned it securely. "It's just that I don't like being idle. If there's something I can do to help out, I'd much rather pass the time that way."

"If you insist on going out, then by all means, please do pick up a newspaper. I'm sure Papa will want to hear if there is any news from the front."

Salina nodded, her net snood bobbing at the base of her neck. She put on her gloves and pulled her hood up over her dark head. "I'll be back in an hour, I promise." She walked away from the three-story brick townhouse, her mind far distant from the crowded streets of downtown Richmond. It wasn't until she came to the corner of First and Broad Streets that she realized she'd walked two blocks in the opposite direction from that which she'd intended.

"Silly me," she scolded herself for her absentmindedness, but as long as she was there, Salina caught up with a young boy hawking the latest edition of the *Richmond Enquirer*. Headlines still carried reports concerning the late-November battles at Chattanooga, Lookout Mountain, and Missionary Ridge. The campaign in Tennessee had ended in defeat for the Confederate forces under General Braxton Bragg by the Federals under the command of General Ulysses S. Grant, and by the end of the month, Bragg had tendered his resignation.

In Virginia, a new engagement flared along the Rapidan River between General Lee's Army of Northern Virginia and General Meade with the Army of the Potomac. Several preliminary casualty lists were printed as a result of the fighting near Mine Run. Neither Jeremy's name nor any belonging to his men was included, and for that Salina was grateful.

"Crazy Bet! Crazy Bet! Crazy Bet!"

The taunting chants of a handful of boys pulled Salina's attention from the newspaper to the object of the shouted ridicule. Across the street, an old woman shuffled with a partial limp. Her head was covered by an overlarge sunbonnet, her dress stained, cloak tattered and torn. She looked dirty, carried a battered basket over one arm, and seemed to be speaking to no one but herself in an off-key, singsongy voice.

The boys threw stones at the woman as their mantra resumed: *"Crazy Bet! Crazy Bet! Crazy Bet!"*

"What nasty little scoundrels," Salina commented to the paper seller. "Who is that poor woman?"

"Don't waste your sympathy on the likes of her, ma'am. That's Elizabeth Van Lew. She's always talking to herself, mumbling, singing. She's crazy as a loon—and she's no Confederate!" He spat into the gutter. "There're even rumors that she's a Yankee *spy!*"

Salina looked at the woman in a decidedly different light. "Then why hasn't she been taken into custody, locked up at Castle Thunder or Castle Lightning?"

"Cain't be proved," the paper seller shrugged. "Ain't nobody that seems to know enough about her for certain. They cain't pin anything on her to verify suspicions. I heard tell that she visits the Union prisoners at Libby—brings 'em food and books, but the commandant doesn't see any harm in her efforts. She's just crazy."

The very mention of Libby Prison sent a violent shudder through Salina. "Thank you for the paper," she told the seller. For a few minutes more, she watched the old woman continue to shuffle along, presumably toward the Broad Street train depot and away from the assault of the young scoundrels, until her slight frame melded into the crowds. Salina tucked the newspaper under her arm and walked toward Robertson Hospital on the corner of Third and Main.

Miss Sally Tompkins—or "Captain Sally," as she was called as a result of the military rank bestowed upon her by President Davis as a preventive measure to keep her hospital from being shut down—was delighted to renew Salina's acquaintance. "I most certainly could use another pair of experienced hands like yours, my dear, and I've no doubt that you are equally as willing to help now as you have been in the past. What concerns me, however, is your present condition. I've no wish to expose you to scenes that are too indelicate for you. I wouldn't want you to endure any hardship that might possibly have an adverse effect on the baby."

"But, Captain Sally, I simply can't abide not doing something useful," Salina told her. "Please, if you don't feel right about taking me back as a nurse, then may I beg your indulgence for permission to read to the men? I can write letters for them, or sing. Do a little mending..."

Captain Sally, a diminutive woman with a generous heart and outstanding reputation, considered Salina's request. "Agreed," she nodded. "Let's say twice a week, Tuesday and Sunday, at half-past two o'clock in the afternoon. You may sit with the men for two hours each day. Nothing strenuous, mind you."

"It's a start," Salina said, readily accepting the hospital director's terms. This was Wednesday. "I'll come again Sunday next."

"Very well. I'll look forward to seeing you then."

☆☆☆☆☆☆☆

A courier arrived at the Carey home in Linden Row with a message for Salina from General Stuart. The message was brief, obviously written in haste, but it contained a train ticket, a timetable, and a summons to Orange Court House, providing she felt well enough to travel. The instructions were simple: She was to take the Central Virginia Railroad to Gordonsville, change trains, and catch the Orange & Alexandria Railroad to Orange. By taking the morning train out of Richmond, she could be in Orange before dusk on Christmas Eve. A woman, Mrs. Isaac Gillette, would meet her and take her to a house in town where Jeremy would join her.

I've furloughed a large portion of the cavalry corps for the purpose of sending the men home to rest, recuperate, and procure horses wherever they may be found, Stuart wrote. *Captain Barnes will have his orders by the time you arrive.*

As Taylor Sue assisted Salina with her preparations for the impending journey, Jennilee interrupted them. "A crate's been delivered, Salina. Won't you come open it?"

Salina and Taylor Sue looked at each other and in unison proclaimed, "Drake!"

Indeed, the shipping address was listed as the city of Boston. Packed within the wooden crate were bottles of cider, jams and jellies, sugar, flour, canned vegetables and pickles, dress patterns and two bolts of cloth, needles, pins, thread, quinine, laudanum, flasks of whiskey, candles, peppermint candy canes, and a tin of fruitcake. One of the jelly jars was broken, but the sticky sweetness had not damaged the yard goods.

"What's that?" Jennilee pointed to the envelope Salina had nearly overlooked.

Salina plucked the letter from the envelope. Unfolding the page, she found a letter from Aurora Dallinger wrapped around one hundred dollars in Union greenbacks. She sat down at the kitchen table. "Let's see what Aurora has to say."

November 30, 1863
Mrs. Jeremy Barnes
Linden Row on Franklin Street
Richmond, Virginia

Dear Salina—

It is with good cheer that this crate is sent to you. Inside you will find things we hope will make your holidays a little more tolerable. Now that you are settled in one place, I have been charged by my brother that a crate should be delivered to you once a month. He will brook no argument on the subject.

To catch you up on the latest news, Ellie is still with me and we celebrated a lovely Thanksgiving here at Grandmamma's. We speak of you often and pray continually that you are well. It is my hope that Drake will return to Boston for Christmas. I believe the relationship that has been brewing between him and Ellie might yet end up with a proposal, but don't you dare say a word until it's official. We are already good friends, Ellie and I, and I would not object to gaining her as a sister. Drake says you and Taylor Sue were dear friends long before you became in-laws.

I don't know how you are fixed for material for dresses. I imagine that you're growing out of just about everything you have by now. I picked out the prints myself, and have included some patterns for you. You must promise to send us word through the lines when the baby comes.

This fall has been a whirl of parties and bazaars, and soon the New Year will be upon us. Amazing how time marches on. I still think of Mason, as he meant so very much to me. It has been more difficult than I ever would have imagined to get him out of my heart and my head. I have thrown myself into working with the U.S. Sanitary Commission and have had some success at raising funds and necessities for soldiers' aid and relief. It is hard to yearn for a new year when it is certain that come spring the armies will be campaigning again.

Forgive me for being glum. As I said, this is sent with the intent of bringing good cheer. Know that we think of you often. Relay our best wishes to Jeremy.

> *Your Yankee friends in Boston,*
> *Aurora Dallinger and Elinor Farnham*
> *(with Drake's compliments)*

Beacon Street
Boston, Massachusetts

"Well, bless her heart," Taylor Sue commented. "I would have liked to have had a chance to meet Aurora. I feel as if I should know her from what you've told us about her."

"She is very much like Drake in some ways—but in others they are in no way similar," Salina laughed. "Aurora is a character."

"Did you have any idea that Drake was so enamored of Elinor?" Taylor Sue queried.

Salina inclined her head. "I've seen them together, and they seem to get along well, but no, I really didn't know it had transpired into the proposal stages. Drake's not the kind of man to be rushed or pushed into anything. He'll have thought it all out, made sure it's what he wants before he takes any action. No one forces Drake into doing what he doesn't want to do."

Taylor Sue nodded. She eyed the dress patterns with interest. "With your permission, I'll set to making the dresses while you're away. I could have them completely done for you by the time you return from Orange."

"There's two bolts of fabric; pick one out for yourself, and I'll take the other. I don't know when I'll be back from Orange." There were no words Salina could think of to express her elation over the idea of spending Christmas with her husband and her agony over leaving her sister-in-law alone.

"You're stalling, Salina," Taylor Sue said briskly. "Your train leaves early tomorrow morning, and you're not half packed yet."

"Jennilee..." Salina turned to Taylor Sue's sister. "Would you mind sorting through the rest of this and storing it away?"

"I'll see to it," Jennilee assured her. "God bless Drake. We can have a ham for Christmas dinner now!"

"I'll take the extra medicine to Captain Sally this afternoon," Salina decided. "She can certainly use it."

☆☆☆☆☆☆☆

December 24, 1863
Orange Court House, Virginia

A blanket of snow whitened the ground, yet it had not deterred Mrs. Isaac Gillette from bundling up her daughters, Rosalynde and Salome, and bringing them along with her to the depot in time to meet one Mrs. Salina Barnes, who was due to arrive on the afternoon train up from Gordonsville.

"Hello! And Merry Christmas!" The two ladies hugged each other in greeting as if they had known each other for years rather than this being the first time they'd ever met. Compassion and caring shone brightly in Mrs. Gillette's eyes.

"Oh, Mrs. Gillette." Steam encircled Salina's hooded head as her breath met the cold air. "It is so kind of you to take me in for the holiday! General Stuart's telegram did not spare much in the way of notice," she lightly complained. "Well, here I am. You are an acquaintance of the general's, I take it?"

"He attends services at our church whenever duty and camp location allow him to do so. The general happened to be in Orange Sunday last. He inquired if I might have a room to let, and I told him I did, since one of my boarders has gone to Strasburg to stay with a sister until the New Year. The general indicated that he had an interest in securing temporary accommodations on behalf of one of his men, and then he filled me in on the rest of the particulars. A courier was out from camp earlier to confirm that your captain should put in an appearance sometime before supper." Mrs. Gillette led the way toward a parked wagon. "I've taken the liberty of doing a bit of decorating in the room with evergreen boughs and holly cuttings."

"I'm sure it's lovely. Thank you." Salina smiled warmly at this woman who was an instant friend. She looked down at the two Gillette girls, judging their ages to be about nine and eleven.

"I hope this journey wasn't too tedious for you," Mrs. Gillette said. "The general didn't make mention at all of your—condition."

"The trip was fine," Salina assured her. "I'm just happy to be here."

Mrs. Gillette grinned over Salina's obvious anticipation. "We'll take you home and have you settled in before the captain arrives with his 'orders.'"

It was a short distance to the gabled house where Mrs. Gillette and her daughters lived. In addition to the Gillettes, three boarders lived in the comfortable home: an older gentleman who was a retired professor from the University of Virginia, a widow who'd lost her husband in the Second Battle of Winchester, and the young woman who'd gone to Strasburg.

"I hope you don't mind the stairs—it's two flights up," Mrs. Gillette apologized, preceding Salina up the stairwell. "But you'll find the room charming. It faces the street and provides a lovely view, what with the snow."

It was indeed a delightful room—cozy and welcoming. Mrs. Gillette stirred the fire in the grate beneath a mantel laden with fragrant evergreen boughs. A tapestry dressing screen divided the living area from the sleeping quarters, and a small spirit lamp with a copper teakettle waited to be warmed by candle fire.

"I trust you'll be comfortable here during your stay," Mrs. Gillette said. "If you have need of anything, please don't hesitate to ask. My house is your house."

"How can I thank you, Mrs. Gillette?"

"You can start by calling me Nettie—everyone does." She paused to sniff the air. "Mmmmm. By the smell of it, Aunt Susey has already started to fix supper, so you just come on down when you get out of those traveling clothes. We're rather informal here— breakfast is usually between eight and nine, dinner before two, and supper by half-past eight, give or take a few minutes." Nettie took Rosalynde by one hand and Salome by the other. "Come along, girls. Let's give Mrs. Barnes a chance to settle in."

"If I'm to address you on a first-name basis, then you must call me Salina."

"Very well, Miss Salina," Salome piped up.

Rosalynde waved. "See you at supper, Miss Salina!"

Salina unpacked her satchel. She had a gift for Jeremy wrapped in brown butcher paper tied with gold, green, and red ribbons, which she put, along with some peppermint candy canes, on a marble-topped table near the hearth. From the window, she could see down the street only as far as the light from the windows penetrated into the darkness. It was the waiting that was the hardest part of all.

In the dining room Salina was introduced to Professor Bauer and the widow, Hester Carroll. Salina was on pins and needles anticipating Jeremy's arrival, and although they went ahead and started the meal without him, it wasn't long before a cavalryman knocked loudly at the front door.

Nettie instructed Aunt Susey to answer the door.

"Evenin', sir," the black woman greeted. "Won'tcha cum in?"

"Captain Jeremy Barnes reporting," the horse soldier announced, kicking the snow from the bottom of his boots and brushing cold flakes from the brim of his hat and sleeves of his gray coat. "I bear dispatches from headquarters with General Stuart's compliments."

"Who is it, Aunt Susey?" Nettie unnecessarily asked.

"It'd be a capt'n, Missus. From da gen'ral's headquartahs. Ya want ah should show 'im inta da dinin' room?"

"Please," Nettie said. "And bring another plate from the kitchen."

"Ya kin cum on, Capt'n. It'd be cold out dere, an' supper's on in here," Aunt Susey told Jeremy. "Ya kin brung dat dispatch right inta da dinin' room."

Salina's heart skidded against her ribs. She had the singular pleasure of watching Jeremy falter in midstep, halting when he saw her. *"Sallie?!"* he sputtered, the perplexity plainly showing on his bearded face. "What are you doing *here*?"

"I believe, if I'm not mistaken, that I'm the recipient of that dispatch." She nodded toward the envelope he held in his gloved hand.

Jeremy reexamined the unaddressed envelope, his whiskers split in a wry grin. "Well, I reckon the general's tricked me into a first-rate surprise this time!"

Entrapped in Jeremy's secure bear hug, Salina's mirthful giggle rippled. She gave Jeremy a saucy kiss. "There really ought be a dispatch, though, or some sort of orders at the very least. He indicated there would be. Here, let me see." She tore open the envelope and withdrew the page. Reading aloud, she mimicked Stuart's rich voice:

Cavalry Hdqtrs. at Camp Wigwam
Army of Northern Virginia
Christmas Eve, 1863

Mrs. Captain Barnes:

Commencing immediately, your husband, Captain Jeremy Barnes, is hereby granted leave of absence until the 26th instant, when his presence will be required back at headquarters in time to answer at roll call. Inform him that he is requested to remain in the vicinity of Orange Court House, however, so that he might be found, if need be. In the interim, the pair of you are duly ordered to have a Merry Christmas and to accept this commanding officer's best wishes for a most cheerful holiday.

I am most respectfully,
J.E.B. Stuart
Major General, Commanding

"Bless his heart!" Salina exclaimed, having dissolved into a fit of giggles halfway through the reading. She flashed a warm smile at Jeremy. "God bless General Stuart."

"Amen!" Jeremy tossed his plumed hat aside, unbuttoned his coat, and yanked off a worn pair of gloves. He occupied the empty chair next to his wife and with feigned somberness pronounced, "He'd court-martial me if I didn't follow orders, you know."

"Yes," Salina agreed. "I'm sure he would. Therefore, we *must* have a cheerful time—general's orders."

Salina introduced her husband to the others at the table. As supper resumed, she felt Jeremy's heavy gaze resting on her, drinking in the picture she made. She wished the meal over with so that they could slip up to their room to be alone, but out of courtesy to their hostess, they politely remained even after Aunt Susey had cleared the supper dishes away.

A freshly cut pine tree was hauled into the parlour, its crisp scent mingling with the aroma of candle fire and hot chocolate. Hester played Christmas carols on the piano during the tree trimming, and Jeremy was called upon to set the golden star on the highest point. Salina's sweet voice blended with the others in singing:

> *God rest ye merry gentlemen,*
> *let nothing you dismay;*
> *Remember Christ our Savior*
> *was born on Christmas Day;*
> *To save us all from Satan's power,*
> *lest we were gone astray.*
> *Oh, tidings of comfort and joy,*
> *comfort and joy;*
> *Oh, tidings of comfort and joy!*

The Gillette girls busied themselves with stringing popcorn and dried cranberries into garlands that were roped around the tree. Just before bedtime, Nettie hung their respective stockings at the mantel. Good-nights were spoken and Christmas wishes merrily exchanged. The professor and Hester went their separate ways, and Salina followed Jeremy to the cozy room on the third floor.

For a moment Jeremy was content to simply hold Salina close, her dark head tucked beneath his whiskered jaw. They warmly kissed each other, thankful for any time together, however brief. Being with Salina made the past few weeks seem very distant to Jeremy, almost as if the events that had transpired had happened to someone else. Salina was Jeremy's safe haven; he found refuge with her. "Oh, Sallie... look at you!"

"I'm fat and I'm starting to waddle."

"Prettiest thing I've seen in a long while." Jeremy grinned, banishing her feelings of self-consciousness concerning her present girth. "You're beautiful, and I love you." He shifted to stand behind her and rested his large hands on her swollen belly.

"Then you are happy with this surprise?" Salina tipped her head back to look up at him over her shoulder, searching his unpatched eye, caressing his thick black whiskers with her fingertips.

"Of course I am happy!" He kissed her again.

In Salina's observation, the furrows in Jeremy's brow made him appear older than his twenty years. Salina became determined to smooth away those lines of worry. Something undefinable in his demeanor was different. Something had happened—something that had changed him—and while Salina's curiosity yearned for satisfaction, she deemed it best not to pry. Talking would more quickly erase the uneasy distance between them brought on by long months of separation, but she knew him—he would not open up or confide in her until he was good and ready to do so. General Stuart had kindly granted them time for reunion, during which Salina planned to do whatever she could to help Jeremy put the war aside. These precious hours meant more to her than any tangible gift could have.

"I'm certainly happier with this surprise than I have been with some others as of late," Jeremy murmured near her ear. "My own sweet Sallie Rose." He held her, drawing comfort and strength and love from her.

Their quietude was fleeting, however, for over the top of Salina's head Jeremy spied a folder tied neatly with string lying on the drop-leaf table. The folder looked hauntingly familiar to him; the pleasant warmth he felt inside was suddenly usurped by a chilling numbness. "What is *that*?"

Salina hesitantly identified the object to which he pointed. "That is..." She took his hands in her own. "Well, Jeremy, that's your history. Your family tree." She looked up at him anxiously, remembering Ridge's written admonition. "Darlin', that folder contains the truth of your real name."

Jeremy abruptly set Salina at arm's length. He stalked across the room, snatched up the dossier, and without troubling to open it, dumped it into the crackling fire.

"Jeremy!" Salina cried, hastening toward the hearth.

He caught her in his arms, effectively preventing any rescue of the pages. "Let it burn," he ground out.

"But that's documentation of our baby's history as well!" She struggled against him.

He would not free her. "I said let it burn!"

The flames greedily licked over the pages, blackening the edges first, then spreading to consume the entire dossier. Only when the last shreds were charred beyond retrieval and reduced to ash did Jeremy turn to confront his wife. "How did *you* come by a copy of *that*?"

Salina's eyes blazed in a temper that matched his. "It was sent to me by a man named Eldridge Southerland. A man who is an uncle of yours—a flesh-and-blood relation, unlike John Barnes. Jeremy, that folder contained the findings of an investigation pertaining to *you*—to who you are. Ridge had started an inquest without knowing Drake had retained his attorney to do the same. You see," she confessed, "I asked Drake if he could somehow find out what the initials E.S. stood for..."

Jeremy retreated from her as though she had a contagious illness he had no desire to catch. *"You* put Drake up to conducting the investigation?" he stammered in disbelief.

"Drake's attorney did the detective work," Salina clarified. "Jeremy, I know how much you dislike bearing the same surname of Barnes. For that reason, I wanted to see if there was some way to find out what your name should be. I thought..." She nervously fingered the gold heart-shaped locket she wore. "I thought it might give you some peace."

"Oh, this is rich!" Jeremy shook his head. "You and Drake conspiring to find me a name!"

"Don't stand there and tell me that you weren't as curious as we were, Jeremy! You tried to find out from your Aunt Isabelle who your father was, but she didn't know his full identity. Based on the information that was in that folder, your father is a man named Evan Southerland. *Southerland* should be your name, too."

"But it's *not*!" Jeremy roared. "And it never will be!"

"It might be someday," Salina ventured. "Jeremy, Evan Southerland survived Shiloh—in spite of John Barnes's attempt to have him murdered. There must be a way to contact him, to advise him of your existence."

"Evan Southerland knows I exist," Jeremy said harshly.

Salina's emerald eyes widened, conveying the question of How? when her voice failed to raise it.

"I saw the man, Sallie. He told me himself he was my father."

"What?" Salina tentatively touched Jeremy's arm. "How did you meet him? Where?"

Jeremy shook off her hand.

"Jeremy," she persisted, "where have you been?"

"Humph..." he lowered his head, staring into the flames. Agitated, he kicked the hearth with the toe of one boot. "That's asking, isn't it?"

"All right." Salina took a deep breath and mentally counted to ten. "Let's start over for a minute. From the beginning this time: Come in! It's so good to see you! Won't you have a seat?"

Jeremy stubbornly declined to indulge her. "I've been riding all day; I'd prefer to stand."

"Suit yourself." Salina sauntered past him, settling into the leather-upholstered chair. "You can tell me your story later. I'll do the talking for now." She launched into an informative soliloquy, giving him a summary of the events during their weeks of separation, allowing him no room for either replies or inquiries. "I'd have written to tell you all this—but I had no idea where I should address your letters."

Jeremy remained mute throughout her monologue, biting his tongue, standing aloof in brooding silence.

The minutes ticked between them. Salina was not about to let him waste the time they had. "Where have you been?" she repeated her earlier question.

Jeremy leaned an elbow against the mantel shelf. "From camp to Cobbs, almost to Harpers Ferry, and back by way of the Valley of Virginia."

Salina was puzzled. "Why?"

"I was led to believe it was for horses—but there was much more to it than that," Jeremy answered cryptically. He pinched the bridge of his nose between his thumb and forefinger. "It wasn't just about horses."

Jeremy turned his back toward Salina, bracing his palms against the mantel. He angled his head to the side, his profile silhouetted by the flickering firelight. "Forgive me." His voice was a raw whisper. "I'm still trying to deal with this new knowledge of Evan Southerland—the way it makes me feel and the hurt it stirs here." He pointed to his heart. "I try not to care, try to convince myself to believe that it makes no difference—but I can't seem to talk myself out of it. It *does* matter." He sighed. "I've no business lashing out at you when all you wanted was to help me."

"If you don't want to talk about it, I won't force you," Salina whispered in return.

"No—I want to tell you."

"I should've consulted you before I set Drake and his attorney into action." Salina was remiss.

"In hindsight, yes, I'd say you should have. But at the time, you did what you thought was right." Jeremy shrugged. "In all honesty, Sallie, there is some satisfaction in learning for certain that my sire was *not* Campbell Barnes."

Salina laid her shawl over the side of the leather chair. She stood behind Jeremy, kneading the tension out of his taut neck muscles. Jeremy faced her then, taking her cold hands in his own, rubbing some warmth into them. Dropping to one knee, he placed a gentle kiss on the rounded curve of her protruding belly. He laid his ear against the outer wall of her abdomen and tightened his arms about her waist. He did not see Salina smiling down at him, though she did so with love shining in her eyes. She asked, "What do you hear?"

"A heartbeat, I think," Jeremy replied in a low murmur. "Probably yours, but I'm sure it's part of the baby's, too." He tipped his head back to look up at her. "This child of ours..."

"Yes?" Salina prodded.

"This child *will* know it is loved from the start. It will never be made to feel as if it weren't wanted."

Salina agreed with a confirming nod, sensing that his words were a result of his own brokenheartedness. "Darlin', I've told you before: I believe you are going to make a fine father."

A slow, wonder-filled smile spread over his mouth. "You're going to have to help me along the way."

"I'll do my best." Salina tugged on Jeremy's hand, leading him to the sleigh bed in the center of the room. "Lie down here beside me." She situated herself on her side and placed Jeremy's hand on her stomach. "Now be still."

Jeremy started to say something, but Salina was quick to shush him. "Sssshhhhh. Just be patient."

He waited, scarcely breathing, hand resting exactly where she'd set it. The anticipation sparkled in his eye. Then he felt it: a tiny ripple against his hand. It was enough to constrict his heart.

"Just think, Jeremy, you'll be able to hold it soon..." she murmured against his shoulder.

Jeremy bit his lip, a rush of salty tears blurring his vision. His mouth tarried near her brow as unchecked teardrops trickled down his cheeks and into his whiskers. "I..." He swallowed, but the lump in his throat remained. "Oh, Sallie Rose," his voice was ragged with wonder and emotion. "I love you so."

"We love you, too," Salina happily pronounced. "My own Horse Soldier."

Sometime later, Salina donned her dressing gown and went to stir the dying embers with the iron poker. She added three logs, coaxing the flames into warming the temperature in the room. She sat staring at the fire, entranced by the glowing orange light. *Lord, thank You for allowing Jeremy to be here with me. Comfort him, Lord; be the balm to his broken heart. Give me words that will ease his mind and soothe the pain he suffers. Be with Ethan—keep him warm on this Christmas Eve night, shield him from hunger and disease; be with Taylor Sue and the Careys; be with Mamma and Duncan and Yabel...be with all our friends and family who are too distant to share the joyous celebration of Jesus' birth. In a week's time we shall begin a new year, and I pray now for the wisdom and the strength to get through whatever it holds in store for us. Keep our child in Your protection; guide us according to Your will.*

"Sallie?" Jeremy propped himself up on his elbow, rubbing sleep from his eyes. "What are you doing?"

"Praying, stoking the fire."

"Come back to bed."

Salina smiled and snuggled back under the covers with him.

"Your feet are cold!" Jeremy grumbled.

She got out of bed and put on a pair of socks. "Better?"

He shivered, chuckling. "Yes."

With Salina securely in his arms, Jeremy told her of Drake's telegram and the proposition that was put before Stuart. Jeremy made a concerted effort to expound on his feelings concerning the night Evan appeared in the barn at the Cobbs and of his anger over the belief that Drake had lured him there for the Southerlands' benefit. But all that paled when he told Salina that the horses had been fed moldy hay.

"It gets worse," Jeremy continued. "We drove our depleted herd as far as Front Royal, then went up the Valley, using the mountains as a screen between us and the Yankees. We were almost at Chester Gap when Boone reported that a number of the horses were coughing and sweating. We examined them closely and found more than two dozen were afflicted with ulcerated nodules, enlarged glands beneath their jaws, and a bloody, gluey discharge coming from their noses. Since Tristan had lost a mount to Glanders before, he attested that our horses were indeed suffering from the disease."

Glanders was contagious. Salina knew enough to know the ailment could spread among horses—and in some cases to humans. The results of it, more often than not, were deadly.

"If a horse manages to live through the sickness," Jeremy explained, "it sometimes will be marked with a star-shaped scar on its hide. Once its system generates an immunity, it can become a carrier, passing the disease on even though it no longer displays the outward symptoms itself. We found a handful of scarred horses—and apparently, once they were introduced to the herd, they spread the infection."

"If the moldy hay was not deliberate, the diseased horses must have been," Salina said, arriving at the same conclusion Jeremy had. "What did you do?"

"All we could do was to separate the sick horses from the healthy ones as quickly as possible, but by then it was too late. The two-week incubation period probably started even before Drake left Kansas with the herd."

"And you believe someone did this maliciously?"

"It crossed my mind. Moldy hay might have been a legitimate oversight, a bad coincidence. The Glanders—well, that's different. It could easily foster the opinion that somebody purposely sabotaged the stock."

"But you know Drake—he'd never do something that despicable." Salina wondered why she felt as if their friend needed a defense. "Jeremy, Drake wouldn't deliberately harm horses!"

"No, he wouldn't," Jeremy conceded. "I'm convinced that Drake didn't have anything to do with either calamity. It just wasn't meant to be, evidently—the horses, I mean—which is a pity. We could've used them."

Jeremy was quiet, withdrawn. Salina thought he had drifted off to sleep, but then he said, "When Drake and I said our good-byes, they weren't exactly spoken on the best of terms."

"Did you fight him?"

"Not with my fists. Neither of us is as hot-headed as we used to be—but we had words that were not all pleasant," Jeremy murmured. "I was angry—with him and with the situation he put me in. He's worked at South Union for the better part of a year. He knew my name before I did, yet he didn't bother to tell me about it until *after* my confrontation with the Southerlands. Drake, you see, has always had the luxury of knowing who his father was—even if they were estranged for most of his life." Jeremy's exasperation and disappointment were tangible. "If Drake was such a *good* friend, he should've taken the trouble to warn me before setting me up! Between the way he acted and what he *didn't* say... He made me feel that he was standing up to be counted with *them*."

"And the man who is supposedly your father?"

"To see Evan Southerland was like looking into a mirror, Sallie—twenty years hence. His voice was so..." Jeremy shuddered involuntarily. "It still haunts me." Salina remained silent.

"I look just like him, yet I cannot take his name." Jeremy was mentally miles away from Orange Court House. "My very existence casts a disgraceful shadow of reproach upon the Southerland family. That's all I am to them, Sallie—a disgrace—pure and simple. Well, maybe not so pure. Evan sinned; I'm merely the unfortunate result— the consequence of his wrongdoing."

It broke Salina's heart to hear Jeremy's anguish, to feel the despondency in him. Even with her back to him, Salina could envision the grief that drew his black brows together in a frown, and she cringed at what he'd been through. "This is my fault," she breathed. "I am ashamed that I didn't foresee how much pain knowing your name would bring to you."

"It's not your fault, Sallie. How could you have possibly known that the *illustrious* Southerland clan would refuse to claim me?" Jeremy spoke harshly, more so than he intended. "They don't want any part of me—any more than John Barnes or my mother wanted me. I serve no other purpose in their eyes save to expose the dark family secrets."

Salina turned toward him, framing his bearded face with her hands. "*I* want you, Jeremy Barnes. You'd do well to never forget that! I want you, and I need you, because *I* love *you*!" She kissed him reassuringly. "If you can't take the name that is rightfully yours, then you may share mine. I've told you before: It matters not what your name is! Didn't Shakespeare write something about a rose smelling just as sweet even if it was called something other than a rose? Regardless of what name you choose as yours, it will not alter the way I care for you. You are my husband, the father of my child..." Her impassioned declaration changed into a fierce hug.

Jeremy rested his forehead against hers. Again words failed him as the means to express his jumbled thoughts, and unwanted tears stung his eyes. Salina held him close and whispered words of comfort. Jeremy was the shape of a man with a boy's bruised heart, insecure, frail of hope, and in need of strength.

"Let it out, Jeremy," Salina soothed. "Let it go." Her fingers deftly massaged the nape of his neck.

The stubborn fight drained out of Jeremy as his muscles began to relax. The quietude between them extended until at last he shuddered a heavy sigh, gnawed on his bottom lip, and wiped away the last of his tears. "You must think me weak."

"No," Salina instantly disagreed. "You have been strong for me on occasions when I needed a good cry—it's only fair that I return the favor."

Jeremy grumbled, "Not very manly of me."

Salina lifted his chin with her forefinger. "You feel better though, don't you?"

"Some," he reluctantly admitted.

"How many of the horses died of Glanders?"

"Mmmm..." Jeremy reluctantly returned to the topic of the lost horseflesh. "Roughly a hundred."

"And there were two hundred horses to start?" Salina dared ask, "How many did you come back with?"

"All total: twenty-eight." Jeremy answered flatly. "The trip was a complete debacle."

"So few!" Salina's exclamation sounded dejected even to her own ears.

"We lost about a quarter of the herd to moldy hay, half of it to Glanders. Fifty-two healthy horses remained when we reached Chester Gap. After we burned the carcasses, C.J. and Jake took care of destroying those marked with the star-shaped scars," Jeremy told her. "We judged it wiser to shoot the carriers rather than risk spreading the disease further. Unfortunately, their gunfire drew the attention of a detached Union patrol, and so we were forced to bargain with the Yankees to prevent certain capture: They required two dozen horses in trade for letting us make a most convenient 'escape.' There were six of them against the nine of us, but none of us on either side was eager to take any unnecessary chances. We eventually returned to camp without bodily injury but with hardly more than a tenth of the number we anticipated bagging when we set out. We considered ourselves lucky that none of our original horses became affected."

"And after all that, what did General Stuart say?"

"What could he say?" Jeremy shrugged. "At least we didn't get captured. He was grateful for that and chose to let the matter rest there. He arranged for us each to keep a mount of our choice as reward for our efforts—the spoils of our 'raid.' The rest were turned over to the quartermaster and probably ended up with the horse artillery. Stuart didn't even make me write an official report. I got the distinct impression that he has no intention of letting the caper be made known."

The matter was closed. There was no further discussion of either Jeremy's name or the horses.

☆☆☆☆☆☆☆

Christmas Day dawned with a bright yellow sun that sent slanting rays through the drapes even though they were closed. Jeremy blinked several times against the morning light, disappointed to find Salina's side of the bed empty. He found a note on her pillow and opened it, his eyes falling on the lines she had hastily jotted down:

My darling,

I came upon these words while reading the scriptures this morning, and I felt compelled to share them with you. They seem to have taken on new meaning, especially in light of our conversation last night. It is my hope that you will take them as an encouragement, as I did when I read them.

"For ye have not received the spirit of bondage again to fear; but ye have received the Spirit of adoption, whereby we cry, Abba, Father. The Spirit itself beareth witness with our spirit, that we are the children of God: And if children, then heirs; heirs of God, and joint-heirs with Christ; if so be that we suffer with him, that we may be also glorified together. For I reckon that the sufferings of this present time are not worthy to be compared with the glory which shall be revealed in us."
Romans, Ch. 8, vv. 15–18

I believe in my heart our Heavenly Father has His eye upon you, Jeremy, because you are one of His children. He will keep you in His righteous right hand. Along with His unconditional love, you have all of my love and devotion. Think on that, my darling Horse Soldier, so that you may put your anger to rest, or it will eat you from the inside out.

> *See you at breakfast.*
> *Your own,*
> *Sallie Rose*

No more than a quarter of an hour later, Jeremy found Salina outside. "You shouldn't be out here doing chores, Sallie," he admonished. "What about the baby?"

"Jeremy, I am not an invalid: I can still bring in water and collect eggs," Salina asserted but submissively relinquished the bucket to his helping hand. She kept hold of the egg basket herself. "It's the least I can do to help Nettie."

Jeremy nodded; it was typical behavior of Salina. Falling into step beside her, their boots made parallel tracks in the snow on their way back to the house. At the back stoop, he caught one of her gloved hands in his. "I read your note," Jeremy announced. "You're right, Sallie: An earthly father is nothing to be compared to our Heavenly Father. His love and grace for us are more than sufficient. I was born into circumstances beyond my control, and there is nothing I can do to change them. I've been praying, Sallie, trying to turn this tangled mess over to the Lord. He says in His Word that we can cast our cares upon Him and He will give us rest. I'm honestly trying to let it go and not dwell on it."

"Let Him deal with it; He's much bigger than our problems," Salina encouraged. "Though, admittedly, sometimes it's easier said than done."

"Ain't that the truth," Jeremy drawled. "Come on. Let's get you inside where it's warm. The Gillettes have invited us to attend service with them at St. Thomas's after breakfast, but before we leave, I want you to open your Christmas presents."

Salina's curiosity was piqued, and she hurriedly followed her husband back to their room.

Jeremy's gift to her was a knapsack filled with yarn, knitting needles and crochet hooks, along with several yards of flannel, gingham, and calico to be fashioned into small blankets and miniature clothing. Jeremy was in a very good mood this morning, Salina noted, very much like his old, teasing self. The hurt was gone from his eyes, and his infectious smiles were plentiful.

"Don't forget about this." Jeremy handed her a small wrapped package that was at the very bottom of the knapsack.

Salina pulled the string and unfolded the paper. Her green eyes grew round in surprise. "Jeremy, these are beautiful!" She fingered a garnet brooch and matching earbobs. "I shall wear them to church," she pronounced. "In fact, we need to hurry up."

She scurried to find the package she had wrapped for him.

Jeremy untied the green, red, and gold ribbons and impatiently discarded the brown paper wrapping. He was delighted to receive a pair of new gauntlets, four pair of woolen socks, a compact New Testament, and a small brass-edged photograph case containing a recently made likeness of Salina. "This treasure," he pressed his lips to the framed portrait, "will be kept in my vest pocket, right next to my heart."

After partaking of biscuits and hot cider, they went down to meet the Gillettes and Hester Carroll. Nettie complimented the young couple: Salina on the way her new brooch and earbobs graced her frock, and didn't Jeremy look most handsome in his uniform sporting his clean, new gloves?

"I've got new socks on, too," he teased, "but you just can't see them."

Prior to the service, the Barneses mingled briefly with some of the other men from nearby encampments who had come to town for Christmas service. General Lee was present, along with his adjutant, Major Taylor. General Stuart was there with Flora, and most of Jeremy's own men put in an appearance, too.

Festive carols were sung before and following the text read from the second chapter of Luke. The service focused primarily on the birth of Jesus Christ—a powerful message in its own right but one lacking in the usual patriotic zeal oftimes administered from Southern pulpits. The Christmas message extolled the great love God had for all mankind, so great that He sent His only begotten Son to fulfill the role of Savior. Christ was born so that He might die on a cross to atone for man's sin and rise again on the third day. His blood was the sacrifice, and in His name alone were forgiveness, salvation, and life everlasting.

After the service, Salina discovered that Nettie had hoarded her supplies in order to lay out a veritable Christmas feast. She, Hester, and Salina worked together in preparing a menu that boasted fluffy mashed potatoes, tender ham, a mix of peas and carrots, cranberry relish, hot cross buns with fresh butter, and sweet potato and mincemeat pies for dessert. Unbeknownst to her daughters, Nettie had baked a chocolate layer cake as an added treat.

Through the kitchen window, Salina watched Jeremy playing in the snow with Salome, Rosalynde, and three of the neighbor children. A snowman, which leaned precariously to one side, sported a gray felt hat with a black plume fluttering in the icy breeze, a carrot for a nose, and chunks of coal for the eyes and grinning mouth. Oddly enough, the grin was a shade lopsided...

Salome spied Salina at the window and waved gaily. Jeremy looked up and saw his wife, who smiled appreciatively and blew him a kiss. He caught it, pressed it against his heart, and tossed back a jaunty salute.

Salome and Rosalynde were disappointed that Jeremy declined their invitation to make snow angels outside after Christmas dinner. They contented themselves instead with playing their new games and reading books, grudgingly allowing him time alone with Salina.

☆☆☆☆☆☆☆

Jingling sleigh bells could be heard through the streets of Orange Court House that Christmas night. Salina drew the drapes aside to view the arrival of a boisterous party of serenading officers.

"That would be the Amateur Glee Club." Jeremy identified his fellow cavalrymen from headquarters: "Sam Sweeney with his banjo; his cousin Bob, the violinist; Major McClellan with his guitar; Willie Pegram on the flute, and Theodore Garnett with his triangle. They have a habit of assembling at General Stuart's tent in the evenings to play and sing—often mixing their programmes with jokes, charades, and other games. When General Stuart grows tried of the performance, he gathers his buffalo robe around him and bids everyone a fair good-night. Within five minutes of his signal," Jeremy held up his hand with fingers splayed, "the entire camp beds down for the night—all except for the videttes on duty, of course."

A loud pounding on the Gillettes' front door drew Jeremy's attention from the revelers below. Aunt Susey permitted the late-night callers entrance, and Jeremy opened the door of their room before C.J. and Curlie had a chance to knock.

"A Merry Christmas, Captain! And to you, too, Miss Salina!" C.J. grinned. "Will you come out with us? We're going caroling with the Glee Club."

"It promises to be quite a party afterwards," Curlie added with an entreating nod.

Salina's eyes danced. "Jeremy, please, may we go?"

"Only if you bundle up warmly. It's freezing out there," Jeremy tapped the end of her nose.

Salina was glad to see Bentley, Boone, Tristan, Cutter, Jake, and Kidd Carney again, all in seemingly good spirits. At their final destination, the generous hostesses circled the room with serving trays filled with cups of eggnog and spiced cider. Inevitably someone suggested the parlour floor be cleared to make way for a dance, and the horse soldiers accomplished the task with all due haste.

Salina was introduced to Captain John Esten Cooke as well as to several of the members of the Glee Club. Cooke was a cousin to Flora Stuart, and a published author. "I have read a sampling of your works, sir. I'm told you've been working on a biography of the late General Jackson."

"Indeed I am." Cooke smoothed his mustache and goatee. "'*You may be whatever you resolve to be*'—that was one of the great Stonewall's maxims."

Salina had heard the phrase before, from Ethan, who'd first learned it during his tenure as an assistant surgeon with Jackson's corps. "Will General Stuart be among the party this evening?"

"No, ma'am. He's spending some much deserved time with Flora, Jimmie, and little Virginia. They have few opportunities to be together anymore," Cooke commented.

Salina nodded in understanding, her eyes traveling until she located her husband. "The war creates more than its fair share of unwanted separations."

"No talk of war this evening," John Esten Cooke declared. "It's Christmas, after all, and we are here in an attempt to make it a merry one!"

"Indeed!" Salina smiled.

"Have you met Sweeney yet?" Cooke inquired.

"The banjoist? No, I have not yet had the privilege."

"You will," Cooke predicted, grinning all the while.

"Salina!" From across the parlour Clarice Carpenter waved a lacy handkerchief.

"It's been a pleasure to meet you, Captain Cooke," Salina curtsied politely. "I beg you will excuse me."

"By all means." Cooke bowed, then took his leave to find the young lady who'd promised him her first reel. The musicians were already tuning up for the dance.

The cousins greeted each other with a hug. "What brings you to Orange Court House, Clarice?"

Boone answered in Clarice's stead, "Me. I brought her to Orange."

"You went behind the lines to get her?" Salina quizzed.

Boone grinned sheepishly. "Some things are worth the risk—right, Captain?"

"Very much so." Jeremy moved into place at Salina's side and winked at Boone's sweetheart.

The petite young lady stood in the possessive hold of her cavalier's arm, and like him was blushing profusely. She extended her left hand for Salina's inspection. "Boone has asked me to marry him. Mama has given her consent." She looked up at Boone and smiled even though she was still talking to Salina. "I've accepted him."

"Congratulations!" Salina beamed happily at the betrothed couple.

Jeremy echoed Salina's sentiment. He nodded toward Kidd Carney, who was pleasantly occupied kissing a dark-haired young lady, since the window seat they shared was directly beneath a lofty sprig of ribboned mistletoe. "First you and Miss Clarice, Boone; but I wager there'll be wedding bells for Carney next."

The two couples chuckled as they spotted the other riders among the revelers, each of whom was dancing with all the gallant bravado he could muster. The ebullient atmosphere wasn't entirely a front, but there was a measure of pretense necessary to cover how depressing spending Christmas away from home and loved ones was.

Over cups of eggnog, Clarice and Salina whispered confidences in an out-of-the-way corner of the room. "Delia just up and ran off with him," Clarice apprised Salina of her sister's elopement. "Mama was fit to be tied, of course. That Yankee private just swept her off her feet."

"And you haven't heard from her since?"

"One letter came—from Philadelphia—to let us know she was happy." Clarice shrugged away her own pensiveness. "I guess we have to trust that all's well that ends well."

"Yes, I suppose so." But Salina was downcast by the news just the same.

A gray-clad horseman approached the ladies. "Pardon me, ma'am," he said to Salina, "but I've been informed that you are the wife of Captain Barnes."

"I am," Salina confirmed with a nod. "And you are?"

"Sam Sweeney, ma'am."

"You're the banjo player," Clarice remarked. "I've heard of you."

"Nothing but good, I trust," Sweeney grinned. "Mrs. Barnes, it has been suggested to me by Major McClellan that you might be game enough to accompany me in a song."

"Well, certainly, I'd be honored," Salina smiled. "Did you have a particular selection in mind?"

Sweeney's eyes held a mischievous glance.

"I'll detain Captain Barnes," Clarice assured the banjo player with a wink.

"What's this all about?" Salina wanted to know as Sweeney directed her to a separate sitting room away from the parlour.

"We need someplace quiet where I can teach you the melody and the words to the song I want you to sing with me. Once you hear it, ma'am, I think you'll clearly understand the jist."

"Who put you up to this?" Salina wanted to know. "His men?"

The banjoist chuckled. "You might say this song could be a tribute to your husband. Judge for yourself."

Sweeney played the song for her, and Salina laughed most heartily. It did not take her long to memorize the lyrics.

"I've been looking all over for you," Jeremy complained to Salina some twenty minutes later. He shot a curious glance at Sweeney. "What's going on?"

"It's just a song, Captain," Sweeney remarked blithely. "Your lady has graciously allowed me to borrow her voice for the next number."

"I'm just going to sing," Salina seconded Sweeney's statement. "Here, go sit down, right over there." She pointed to a specific chair near the center of the parlour.

Taking a break from the traditional Christmas tunes, Sweeney began to play songs that were favorites among the cavaliers. With the Glee Club providing the accompaniment to Sweeney's lively banjo, Salina sweetly sang the little ditty he had taught her:

> *As they marched through the town with their*
> *banners so gay*
> *I ran to the window just to hear the band play*
> *I peeked through the blinds very cautiously again*
> *Lest the neighbors should say that I was looking at*
> *the men*
> *Oh, I heard the drummer's beat and the music so*
> *sweet*
> *But my eyes at the time caught a much greater treat*
> *The troops were the finest I ever did see*
> *And the Captain with his whiskers took a sly glance*
> *at me.*

The present company clapped in time to the music. Jeremy's men hooted uproariously and stomped their boots against the wooden floor. Jeremy's initial embarrassment was short-lived; he appreciated the prank, knew it was meant in fun, and threw his head back in good-natured laughter. He couldn't mask his chuckles, try as he might, and Salina launched into the second verse with the same level of animation and enthusiasm as she had coquettishly rendered the first:

> *When we met at the ball I, of course, thought 'twas*
> > *right*
> *To pretend we had never met before that night*
> *But he knew me at once, I could see it by his glance*
> *And I hung down my head when he asked me to*
> > *dance*
> *Oh, he sat by my side at the end of the set*
> *And the sweet words he spoke I shall never forget*
> *For my heart was enlisted and could not get free*
> *As the Captain with his whiskers took a sly glance*
> > *at me.*

The song concluded with Salina sitting coyly on Jeremy's lap, *she* glancing rather slyly at *him.*

"You are somethin' else," Jeremy grinned broadly.

"So you keep telling me," Salina laughed, laying her head on his shoulder.

Tristan appeared, mistletoe in hand, holding it aloft over Jeremy and Salina's heads.

Jeremy obligingly shared a holiday kiss with his wife, regardless of the audience and their teasing applause.

"Well done, Miss Salina, well done indeed," Sweeney complimented her.

"Thank you." Salina stood and took her bows. "Thank you all."

Another of the tunes that piqued Salina's imagination was one that painted a humorous yarn concerning a regimental bugler:

> *The shades of night were falling fast*
> *(Tra-la-la, Tra-la-la)*
> *Bugler blew his well-known blast*
> *(Tra-la-la-la-la)*
> *No matter be there rain or snow*
> *The bugler still is bound to blow*
> *Upidee-ah-dee-ah-dah, Upidee, Upidah*
> *Upidee-ah-dee-ah-dah, Upidee-ah-dah*

He saw as in their bunks they lay
(Tra-la-la, Tra-la-la)
The soldiers spent the dawnin' day
(Tra-la-la-la-la)
"There's too much comfort there," said he
"And so I'll blow the Reveille"
In nice log huts he saw the light (Tra-la-la,
Tra-la-la)
Of cabin fires warm and bright
(Tra-la-la-la-la)
The sight afforded him no heat
And so he sounded the retreat
Upidee-ah-dee-ah-dah, Upidee, Upidah
Upidee-ah-dee-ah-dah, Upidee-ah-dah

Upon the fire he spied a pot
(Tra-la-la, Tra-la-la)
Choicest viands smokin' hot
(Tra-la-la-la-la)
Says he, "You shan't enjoy the stew"
So Boots and Saddles loudly blew
They scarce their half-cooked meal begin
(Tra-la-la, Tra-la-la)
'Ere orderly cries out, "Fall in!"
(Tra-la-la-la-la)
Then off they marched through mud and
rain
Only to march back again
Upidee-ah-dee-ah-dah, Upidee, Upidah
Upidee-ah-dee-ah-dah, Upidee-ah-dah

But soldiers you are made to fight
(Tra-la-la, Tra-la-la)
To starve all day and march all night
(Tra-la-la-la-la)
The chance that you'll get bread and meat
That bugler will not let you eat
Oh, hasten in that glorious day
(Tra-la-la, Tra-la-la)
When bugler shall no longer play
(Tra-la-la-la-la)

> *When we through peace shall be set free*
> *From Tattoo, Taps, and Reveille*
> *Upidee-ah-dee-ah-dah, Upidee, Upidah*
> *Upidee-ah-dee-ah-dah, Upidee-ah-dah*

The Glee Club played on, the dancing resumed, and the games continued. The hands on the grandfather clock in the foyer spun around all too quickly. Salina and Jeremy opted to desert the party and go back to the Gillettes to make the most of the last bit of time they had together.

Huddled together against the cold of the snowy night, they talked in earnest, unsure when they would be together again. As the dark of the night blanched into dawn's early light, they were stirred to wakefulness by the Glee Club's jovial rendition of a chorus from an old sailor's song. The singing resounded between the buildings and along the otherwise empty streets.

Reluctant farewells were exchanged early on the morning of December's twenty-sixth day. Salina cried, though she hadn't meant to. She'd rather Jeremy leave with the memory of her smiles and her laughter, not her selfish tears. Honor dictated that his responsibility was to the inevitable call of duty.

"I've paid Nettie for the use of the room," Jeremy told her somberly. "She's assured me that you will always have a place here. Chances are rather good that I could send for you again sometime before spring. Maybe, God willing, we'll see each other once more before the baby comes."

Salina hugged Jeremy tightly. "Please, be careful. I'd go crazy if you were locked away in prison somewhere. Absolutely stark raving mad."

"I'll be fine." Jeremy kissed her again, then rode away at a brisk canter. He didn't want to repay the general's goodwill by being late in reporting back. He returned to Camp Wigwam just as the chief trumpeter raised a bugle to his lips, blowing the call for Reveille.

Chapter Eleven

Richmond, Virginia

$\mathcal{T}$he evening darkness concealed the black mourning wreath on the door of the Carey home. It wasn't until Salina had crossed the cobbled walk and climbed the front steps to the porch that she discerned what it was, and it was a shock. She pounded insistently on the door until Jennilee came to answer. "Jennilee, what's happened?"

"Papa d-died in his sleep on Christmas Eve n-night," Jennilee sobbed without restraint. "We w-woke up on Ch-Christmas, and he w-was g-gone..."

Salina was well acquainted with the overwhelming sense of loss Taylor Sue's sister presently felt. "It hurts beyond words," Salina said compassionately, giving Jennilee a hug. Glancing over the girl's head into the parlour, Salina identified the sawhorses that had supported Colonel Carey's coffin.

"Welcome back." Taylor Sue appeared in the entryway. She had deep circles under her eyes. Biting her lip, she beckoned Salina to come in out of the cold. "Jennilee, would you please take Mama her tea?"

Jennilee departed to carry out her responsibilities.

"Oh, Taylor Sue, I'm so sorry!" Salina squeezed her sister-in-law's icy hand. "How is your mama?"

"She didn't attend the funeral this morning she was so prostrate with grief." Sinking into the nearest chair, Taylor Sue twisted her damp handkerchief in her hands. "Oh, Salina, what am I to do? Papa was always so sure there was hope for Ethan's exchange. I didn't even get a letter from Ethan for Christmas." A fresh wash of tears spilled down her wan cheeks. "I'm glad you're back. I'm simply not strong enough to deal with this alone."

"When's the last time you got some sleep?" Salina queried, pulling her bonnet strings loose and discarding her gloves.

"I've not slept since the morning you left for Orange," Taylor Sue answered in a dull monotone. "When I close my eyes, I see Ethan's face in place of Papa's in the casket."

"Sssssshhh," Salina comforted. "I'm here now; you can count on me."

Upstairs, Salina sat at the foot of Taylor Sue's bed, softly singing hymns that were intended to convey solace. When she thought her sister-in-law to be asleep, Salina extinguished the kerosene lamp and started to return to her own chamber. Taylor Sue's tired voice halted her. "We're not the only family with troubles this Christmas. The Lees, too, have suffered loss."

"Has something happened to Rooney?" Salina immediately thought of General Lee's imprisoned son.

"No, not to Rooney, but to his wife: Charlotte Lee is dead."

"I know she had been ill for quite some time," Salina began.

"Her health had been failing rapidly ever since the day Rooney was captured at Hickory Hill," Taylor Sue stated. "Custis Lee volunteered to take his brother's place in Fortress Monroe if they would just let Rooney out long enough to come home to see his wife. The petition was flatly denied. I heard one of the undertakers at Oakwood Cemetery say they'll lay her to rest alongside her little children who went on before. Poor Charlotte..."

"Poor Rooney," Salina murmured. The depth of the man's agony she could only imagine, and she quickly sent up a prayer requesting Rooney's speedy release—and Ethan's as well. A shiver stole down her spine; she could not readily shake the premonition that the New Year would be one fraught with tragedy.

☆☆☆☆☆☆☆

Several days later, Jeremy made an unexpected sojourn to the Confederate capital. Upon learning of the colonel's death, he extended his condolences to the Careys, but his words did not quite seem to register with the colonel's widow. Rachel Carey tended to occupy her hours in brooding, mutely staring at a photograph of her deceased husband while she held his unsheathed sword firmly in her stiff grasp.

"She sits there, saying nothing, doing nothing," Taylor Sue confided in a low whisper. "I know Papa had never fully recovered from his stroke, and now I suspect that he valiantly tried to hide the fact that he was in constant pain. The medicine Drake sent helped, yet it still wasn't enough." She willfully turned the subject in another direction, addressing her brother-in-law. "I assume you've heard the news circulating Richmond?"

"The accounts of General John Hunt Morgan?" Jeremy queried.

"Aye," Taylor Sue nodded. "He's been the talk of this town for days on end."

Morgan, who operated with his division of cavalry primarily in the Western Theatre, was renowned for leading bold raids in Kentucky and Tennessee and for meritorious conduct that had set the stage prior to the Battle of Stones River a year ago. He'd been apprehended near New Lisbon, Ohio, and subsequently incarcerated at the Ohio State Penitentiary. In November, Morgan and a number of his officers escaped the Federal stronghold and triumphantly made their way back to the Confederacy.

Jeremy coaxed Taylor Sue into coming along with him and Salina to the grand reception at the Ballard House, where Richmond was preparing to acknowledge the acclaimed Rebel hero's visitation. Jeremy felt she deserved a respite from the erratic behavior of her mother, if nothing else, and the only way to achieve that was to get her out of the house on Franklin Street.

At first Taylor Sue was hesitant to accept Jeremy's invitation. Proper adherence to traditional mourning rituals ought to have restricted her from attending the reception, but the war had conspicuously altered the once-rigid formalities. Almost everyone in Taylor Sue's acquaintance had lost someone to the fighting; consequently, it fell to those bereft families to memorialize their dearly departed while enduring as best they could in spite of the mounting absences. "I believe Papa would've encouraged me to attend as a way to show my Southern pride. He wouldn't have begrudged me for taking part in celebrating a hero's triumphant return." But Taylor Sue cast a worried glance at her mama. Intuitively she realized that in a sense, Rachel Carey had died along with her husband. The widow scarcely noticed her elder daughter's exit from the house on the night of the Morgan reception.

The Ballard House was aglow with candle and gaslight. It seemed all of Richmond society had turned out to catch a glimpse of the fabled cavalier.

General A.P. Hill had been asked to deliver a brief address, but a throat ailment had prevented him from doing so. In Hill's stead, General Stuart had been pressed into service as an extemporary speaker.

Salina didn't precisely recall all of the words General Stuart had spoken, but she did hear a man seated near her speculate as to whether Stuart's remarks had been meant to dispel rumors of a rivalry between the two cavalrymen. Before Stuart was halfway through his presentation, Salina's attention had shifted from the bewhiskered cavalry chief to the hauntingly familiar figure of a red-haired woman, resplendent in an exquisite velvet ball gown of a deep cobalt hue. The ermine-trimmed frock did not have the look of garb acquired from the local dressmakers' shops.

"Who is that?" Taylor Sue, too, had spotted the richly clad woman flanked by a number of Richmond's upper echelon.

"I'm not sure..." Salina was puzzled.

"I recognize Mrs. McCloud in that circle. She's an acquaintance of Mama's from the Soldiers' Relief Society. Shall I go pay my respects and see what the fuss is all about?"

"By all means," Salina encouraged, solicitously relieving Taylor Sue of her cup of punch. But as Taylor Sue engaged in conversation with Mrs. McCloud, it dawned on Salina who the woman in the velvet dress was. Immediately she scanned the room for Jeremy.

"You recognize her." It was not a question but a statement of fact.

The voice of Ridge Southerland startled Salina, who noted the *gray* of his uniform. "What brings you to Richmond?"

"I'm finishing a job." Ridge offered no details whatsoever. "Where's your husband?"

"I don't know—I was looking for him myself. I presume he was summoned into discussion with General Stuart, probably due to some pending military matter." Flippantly Salina added, "If the Yankees would just let us alone, we could commemorate the return of our heroes in peace."

Ridge reciprocated her impish grin, watching her face intently as her smile was replaced by solemnity.

"It didn't go well in Maryland." Salina silently willed Jeremy's uncle to give her his honest appraisal.

"No, it didn't," Ridge admitted. "Jeremy left hurt and angry— and I can't say as I blame him. I might've reacted in the same manner myself had I been thrust into the difficult position that he has been. In truth, I daresay he's handled it much better—I have a foul temper."

Salina's smile reappeared. She had witnessed supporting evidence of that firsthand.

"I reckon Evan is back in Kansas by now—stewing. We gave him quite a lot to think about. I take it you are in receipt of the package I sent?"

"I did receive the dossier, but Jeremy destroyed it. He wants no part of you or anything further to do with the Southerland clan," Salina warned. "So, with all due respect, I'm asking that you not stir up trouble here tonight. I've only got Jeremy for a short time; I want you to leave him be."

"I'm not here to stir up trouble, Salina," Ridge glowered. His sapphire glance rested on the red-haired woman across the room. "Tonight I've got a separate matter that requires my immediate attention."

"That woman?"

"You know her, don't you?" Ridge insisted.

"I...," Salina squinted, pondering. "I thought I recognized her..."

"I'm sure you did. Don't let the fur and trappings fool you— she's *exactly* who you think she is."

Salina blanched. Her wedding-ringed hand unconsciously pressed against her pounding heart. It was with some difficulty that she whispered the name: "Justine?"

"In the flesh. Our paths will cross again soon, Salina, but for now I beg you'll excuse me." Ridge politely touched the brim of his hat in deference. In the next instant he'd blended into the throng; the gray of his uniform provided the perfect concealment, what with so many officers and soldiers among the dense crowd.

Ridge's sudden retreat made Salina shiver. Something was going on—of that she felt keenly aware.

Taylor Sue reclaimed her cup, taking a sip of punch before she divulged what she had gleaned from her amiable chat with the old dowagers. "*She* is Lady Wentworth, wife of Lord Colin Wentworth, Earl of Chetenham. The pair arrived in this country several weeks ago by way of a British packet. The earl purportedly had some arcane dealings with a number of high-ranking officials in the Federal government—contacts with whom he was acquainted prior to the outbreak of war here in America. Upon concluding his business, Lord Chentenham and his wife sailed to New York, then to Boston, where he and his valet—who in truth is a Southern buying agent—set out on a substantial shopping spree. All purchases were loaded onto a private steamer bound for Bermuda, where the steamer took on additional goods and shortly thereafter made an attempt to run the Federal blockade off the coast of North Carolina. A Union gunboat opened fire on the steamer, but the earl's crew endeavored to outrun the Yankees. Had they been stopped as ordered, they would certainly have been searched and the contraband goods impounded—and the earl had no wish to be imprisoned on account of his cargo. The steamer successfully eluded the gunboat but failed in negotiating the shoals along the coast, and the steamer wrecked. Believing that the steamer would sink, the Federals abandoned their pursuit. Indeed, the steamer was imperiled, and it might well have been the end of the Wentworths—except that a Confederate privateer providentially came to their aid. Not only were the passengers and crew saved, but the swift rescue efforts netted more than half of the illegal cargo the steamer had been carrying. That privateer was captained by Randle Baxter..."

"Mary Edith's husband?!" Salina interjected.

Taylor Sue's glance surveyed a cluster of men standing but a few yards away in the reception hall, positively identifying the captain of the privateer. "Mary Edith is here tonight, too."

"My cousin's here—in Richmond?" Salina stood on her toes to see above the crowd, but to no avail.

"Just arrived," Taylor Sue confirmed. "Randle sent for her, since he's going to be in Virginia for a time. His ship took a powerful beating on his last voyage to Nassau—not to mention during the rescue of the earl's steamer—and is in severe need of repair before he can make another run to England. Randle's being touted as a hero in his own right for saving the Wentworths and their cargo."

"What is the earl's business with us?" Salina's *us* referred to the Confederacy in general.

Taylor Sue shrugged. "Mrs. McCloud told me the steamer's cargo included munitions, leather, meat, and other accouterments that General Lee's army is in want of, but what was even more valuable was the information the earl provided to the Confederate navy."

"What sort of information?" Salina raised an eyebrow in question.

"I don't know—in fact, no one seems to know." Again Taylor Sue shrugged. "And that is all I can tell you; Mrs. McCloud doesn't know any more beyond what I've just relayed."

"You did well," Salina commended. "Thank you, Taylor Sue." Casting another covert glance at Jeremy's mother, Salina acknowledged that Justine was still very beautiful—and Justine knew it. One might be hard-pressed to believe the woman had a soon-to-be-twenty-one-year-old man for a son. Salina doubted very much that Lady Wentworth had taken the trouble to admit to her husband that such a son had ever been born.

Salina tried to envision Justine soaked to the skin in a saturated Worth gown, a tangle of wet hair plastered to her skull after being fished out of the dark waters of the Atlantic. "Her ladyship seems to be taking great pleasure in regaling Richmond society with her harrowing tale of near-tragedy."

"Obviously," Taylor Sue concurred. "She probably doesn't even know who General Morgan is, or that this party was hosted in his honor, not hers."

Salina agreed, for it was true: Jeremy's mother had always had a penchant for being the center of attention; she considered it her due. Salina's curious glance was caught and held fast by the reciprocated look of surprise on the face of the countess. "Justine..." Salina murmured in a dry whisper.

Justine Newman Prentiss Barnes Wentworth wrenched her startled gaze from the face belonging to the daughter of Annelise and Garrett Hastings. Her shrewd eyes rested instead on the tall, lean man standing directly behind Salina. Justine didn't have to be told that the brawny Confederate cavalry officer was her son. *He looked so like his father...*

Salina felt the unmistakable tension in the hand Jeremy had placed at the small of her back. "Upon my word!" he muttered tightly. "What is *she* doing *here*?!" Once the shock ebbed, he tested his legs and found that his feet would indeed carry him. Without a second thought, he abandoned Salina where she stood and threaded his way through the crowd.

Incidentally, Randle Baxter crossed Jeremy's path and put out a hand to halt Jeremy's determined progress. "Barnes! Gracious, man, but it's good to see you again!" Randle made a quick evaluation of Jeremy and the patch covering his right eye. "How are you?"

"Well enough, Baxter. Well enough." Jeremy grimly shook the hand of his cousin by marriage. "Mary Edith," he acknowledged with a distracted nod. "If you'll excuse me for a moment, there's someone I must see. I'll be back shortly." But in that moment of inattention, the red-haired woman vanished from the party.

☆☆☆☆☆☆☆

From his post near a marble-mantled fireplace in a spacious side parlour, Ridge Southerland watched Justine's flight from the Morgan reception with no small degree of amusement. Justine's staccato steps retreated from the high-ceilinged ballroom to the nearly empty hallway. Ridge followed at a distance as Justine hastened across the upstairs passageway connecting the Ballard House with the Exchange Hotel located directly across Franklin Street. Ridge waited only until he was sure that Justine's husband had not taken notice of her departure. The Earl of Chetenham was, presumably, still involved in the miry debriefing process with the Confederate authorities; he was not likely to return to his suite anytime soon. Ridge saw this as a propitious chance, so he took it.

☆☆☆☆☆☆☆

"There's a gentleman to see you, Lady Wentworth—an *officer* gentleman, mum."

"I'm not expecting anyone, Flanna, so kindly tell whoever it is that I'm not accepting callers at this time of night. You may inform the man, whoever he is, that he may leave his card and call again tomorrow if he so chooses. Lord Wentworth has several appointments set for the afternoon already, but perhaps there might be time to arrange a brief meeting."

"Pardon, mum," the flustered Irish maid bobbed an apologetic curtsey, "but this officer gentleman ain't come to see Lord Wentworth. He's here to speak with *you*. He says I should tell you that it was a *Southerland* who was callin'. He seemed certain sure you'd see him on account of that, mum. He implied he knowed you, mum, and he just come into the sittin' room of his own accord. Said he'd be more'n happy to wait for you there."

"Oh, out of my way, girl!" Justine stormed past the hired help, vowing to dock the maid's pay for such an untrained blunder.

Hearing the rapid tattoo of clicking heels on the glossy wooden floor, Ridge stood braced to speak before the regal-looking redhead could utter a single syllable. "I thought you might come running, *Lady Wentworth*. I'll admit it took longer than I expected to track you down, but alas, I have succeeded at last, *milady*. That nice nurse at the Georgetown hospital you tried to bribe was quite helpful. She painted a crystal-clear picture of you, of how many times you visited my brother, and even what your name was when I paid her more for the information than you did for her silence."

Justine schooled her elegant features to reveal no expression save a manufactured smile. "My sincerest apologies, Mr. Southerland—that is what my maid told me your name was—but I haven't the foggiest notion as to why you would intimate that I should recognize your name, because I do not. Nor do I care a whit for who you think you might be—it makes no difference if you're first cousin to Jefferson Davis, I'll have you thrown out of this hotel in short order if you don't voluntarily remove yourself from my rooms, sir. At once."

Ridge grimaced. "You still don't lie very well, Justine, especially when you're backed into a corner. Otherwise, you're as smooth as silk, that's what you are." He stood with his hands clasped behind his back, assessing her. "It's hardly a surprise that you don't remember me—I was just a lad of fourteen when Evan brought me with him to New York in the spring of 1842. I was hardly worth your notice. You had eyes for no one save my brother. The fact remains, however, that *I* remember *you*."

"Are you, perhaps, hard-of-hearing, sir?" Justine Wentworth was falsely polite. "Let me say it again for you: If you elect to stay and make a nuisance of yourself, I'll have you forcefully removed. I'll give you another chance to depart, and then I'll put action to my words so you know I mean them."

"Let me rephrase what I mean, Justine: I'll stay put until you give me what I came for, or I'll expose your sordid past to the world. I'd wager your Lord Colin doesn't even know the half of your colorful history, does he? It'd be a shame to air your dirty laundry before the adoring and attentive social elite here in Richmond—just as it would be for the entire peerage in London, wouldn't it, *Lady* Wentworth?"

Recollection returned in a rush, but Justine wasn't about to give Eldridge Southerland the benefit of knowing it. She *did* remember him. She calmly seated herself in a wing-backed chair across from the one Evan's younger brother occupied. "I've nothing to hide from my husband," she lied.

Ridge called Justine's bluff. He settled back with ease, crossed his legs, and drummed his fingertips on the leather arm of the chair. "Very well. We'll wait until Lord Wentworth returns, and the three of us can discuss it then."

The uncomfortable stalemate lasted for a third of an hour before Justine finally broke the unbearable silence. She couldn't take that impertinent sapphire stare boring into her. "All right, Mr. Southerland, you win. How much will it cost to keep your mouth shut about whatever it is you think you know about me?"

"I'm hurt, Justine, that you think me criminal enough to stoop to blackmail," Ridge sulked. "You're quite mistaken—I don't want your money. I merely want the truth—*in writing*—but that can wait for the moment." Ridge leaned forward, resting his elbows on his knees. "You can start by explaining why you wouldn't marry my brother when he asked you to become his wife."

This time Justine did not pretend that she didn't know what Ridge Southerland meant. "Evan's idea of happily-ever-after did not coincide with mine. Your brother was a very handsome man, very kind to me when we met by chance after the death of my first husband. It was a time when I had need of a friend, but Evan became much more. I fell in love with him in New York; we had some very pleasant times in the city, but our dreams were never the same. He was rich to be sure, and a match between us would have been favorable, financially speaking, but Evan expected me to live there in *Kansas*, of all godforsaken places. I refused. We argued about the ranch, about his precious acreage—and all those beeves! In case you hadn't noticed, I was not cut out to be a cattle baron's wife. I was, and still am, far too fond of the comforts that dwelling in town and high society offer. I wanted him, but I wanted no part of the ranch. Evan offered an ultimatum, all or nothing—I could not have one without the other. Breaking my engagement to your brother was one of the bitterest things I'd ever done. It hurt me a great deal."

"Really? That's quite a declaration from a woman who reportedly has no heart in her," Ridge's tone was cutting. "Please—do go on."

"I had run out of money by the time I discovered my affair with Evan had blossomed into more than I counted upon, but I wasn't about to grovel to have your brother take me back. Evan would have married me to make an honest woman of me, if for no other reason; his sense of integrity wouldn't have allowed him to do otherwise. I didn't want to embroil him in a meaningless marriage; we would've grown to resent each other.

"I was without means to support myself, let alone an ill-conceived child. There was a man in Fairfax Court House who used to chase after me—Campbell Barnes. It was easy to dupe him into a proposal of marriage, but I found out quick enough what a dreadful mistake I'd made! Several weeks shy of nine months from the day Campbell and I were married, I gave birth to a 'premature' son who resembled his true father so much I hated him for it. Jeremy was a perpetual reminder that Evan loved that blasted land and livestock more than he did me. I could have been happy with Evan if it hadn't been for his devotion to that wretched ranch!

"My marriage to Campbell was a disaster," Justine continued. "He was more fond of his whiskey and his cards than pleasing me, and he gambled everything away before eventually drinking himself to death. Since I had no great affection for him, I kept company away from him as much as I could. Campbell's brother John swore I was to blame for Campbell's faults; he threatened me. The day after Campbell's funeral I acquired enough funds for passage and sailed for England straightaway. I wasn't about to wait and see if Campbell's mad brother would make good on his word."

"Marriage to Campbell Barnes was not your first taste of wedlock, though," Ridge pressed.

Justine didn't deny it. "I was married to Mitchell Prentiss and had two daughters by him. They live with his sister in Vicksburg. Mitch's family didn't like me very much, but Mitch and I loved each other, in our own way. He died of consumption and left me a widow, and his sister snatched his girls from me so fast it made my head spin. In the end, it turned out to be a blessing, for we hardly knew each other, and I doubt seriously that the girls missed me any more than I missed them. I'm not the mothering sort."

Ridge neither agreed nor disagreed with her statement. "Following the death of Mitchell Prentiss, you took a holiday in New York, where you met my brother, dallied with him, married yet again, and gave the other man's name to my brother's son. Why didn't you take the boy with you to England?"

Justine's laugh was brittle and taunting. "Do you honestly believe I could have caught myself an earl with a fifteen-year-old son dragging on my apron strings? Please, Mr. Southerland!"

Justine flashed a wicked grin. "Colin has grown children by his own previous marriage who will inherit his title and estates—my brat wouldn't have figured in with anyone's plans."

Ridge swallowed the bilious tasting anger rising in his throat. "That so-called brat is my nephew."

"Jeremy," Justine whispered hoarsely. "I named him Jeremy Evan Barnes."

Ridge's short-lived grin reflected his triumph: confirmation from the woman's own lips. He ground out, "And you completely abandoned the boy."

"As you pointed out, I am somewhat of a heartless creature. Some men have claimed that to be part of my charm," Justine added coyly.

"Where does Evan figure into this? Why did you go see him in Georgetown?" Ridge demanded.

"When I heard that he was there at the hospital—I mean, I'd heard first that he was dead from an acquaintance of mine living in Washington City. But to find Evan alive...after all that had happened... A part of me yearned to see him once more for myself. I never told him about the boy—in fact, I never told him anything. Evan was heavily sedated when I visited the ward, and I only stayed for a few minutes."

"You went to the hospital on *three* separate occasions—the nurse told me."

"And each time he was sleeping!" Justine wrung her milky-white, jewel-studded hands. "I honestly don't know what I could have said to him even if he had been awake! He wears a wedding band—I can only assume he married somewhere along the line, and that makes me happy to know that he went on with his life, as I went on with mine. It was enough for me to see him lying there, breathing. I don't care whether you believe me or not, but I did love your brother once."

Ridge still wasn't convinced of the depth of her long-ago feelings for Evan, but he nodded just the same. For several drawn-out moments, he studied her. Justine was certainly over forty, yet not a gray strand dimmed the fiery hue of her hair.

"My husband's business affairs will be settled by the end of the week," Justine said. "We'll sail for England as soon as possible. I hope never to see this desolate country again."

"Good." Ridge cracked his knuckles and stood.

"Is that all then?" Justine inquired haughtily.

Ridge looked down into her pensive face, one still fetching with very few telling lines. It was not difficult to understand how she'd bewitched Evan all those years ago. "Yes, you've told me what I wanted to know—but I need proof. Written, documented, *signed* proof."

Justine openly balked. "You're out of your mind if you think I'm going to sign..."

"You *will* sign a document, and you may be assured of my silence. You don't comply, and I'll have you trumped out of this town, maybe tarred and feathered. You wouldn't want me to ruin the image you have worked so hard to construct; it wouldn't do you any good to disgrace your husband."

"Why must you have it in writing?" she objected. "Isn't a verbal confession sufficient? It would do your family no credit to learn that there is a woods colt out there somewhere who is the spitting image of Evan! I know a bit about the stainless reputation of the Southerland family. Jeremy has no knowledge that Campbell Barnes is not his father, for I've never divulged the name of his true sire. Heaven knows if John Barnes ever found out the truth, he'd want to kill Jeremy."

"Barnes has already tried to kill Jeremy—more than once. No, a verbal confession is not sufficient. My family already knows of Jeremy's existence, and Evan has seen him, but I want Evan to *read* it so that he has no doubt whatsoever. Evan's entitled to the truth, Justine, and Jeremy is entitled to his rightful name. My brother will not acknowledge his son if you don't."

"It wasn't fair to bring him into such a life as the one I introduced him to. Many were the times I contemplated going to a local slave woman for something to rid myself of an unwanted complication, but I had neither the nerve nor the conviction—I wasn't strong enough to carry through with an alternative measure like that. Jeremy's mere existence was punishment enough for my sin!"

The two stared at each other again. Ridge adamantly refused to budge. At length Justine gave in to his demands. She unwillingly composed the requested affidavit, signing her name with a flustered flourish at the bottom of the page. "Now, sir, I believe this discussion is concluded, and mark this: We have no further need to *ever* conduct business between us again. I'd be obliged if you'd find your own way out." She lifted her chin, tossed her head, and removed herself to the adjoining room.

Tucking the affidavit into his vest pocket, Ridge watched Justine go. Shutting the suite door behind him, he muttered, "Heartless creature, indeed!"

☆☆☆☆☆☆☆

Jeremy lingered in town for an entire week after the reception for General Morgan. It took every ounce of effort Salina had to keep her husband from brooding overmuch on the lost chance to confront his mother. Three mornings in a row Jeremy'd gone out scouring hotel registers in an attempt to find her, but from each establishment he had come away empty. There was simply no trace of her. Either Justine was no longer in the Confederate capital, or she was savvy enough to have gone into hiding until her imminent return to England. Salina harbored the suspicion that had Jeremy had his way, Justine would've been found out—and Salina had a feeling *that* was a predicament his mother could ill afford. So yet again Justine had turned her back on her son.

Taylor Sue respectfully declined to accompany Jeremy and Salina to the handful of gatherings they were invited to, firmly insisting they had no need of a third wheel. "Your time with Jeremy is scarce enough as it is." She would brook no argument from her sister-in-law. "Go, Salina; have a good time while you may."

At one of the assemblages—termed a "starvation party," as there was no food served and only water was offered to drink— Flora Stuart and Salina sat together in the audience while the general, Jeremy, and several other officers had been selected to partake in the charades.

An incident backstage, the result of a mishap with the props, sent one of the actresses tumbling from her elevated perch on a ladder. No injury was incurred, but amid the peals of laughter came the implication that General Stuart, whose responsibility it was to hold the ladder steady, had been derelict in his duty. Stuart was banished to the audience, and General Fitzhugh Lee, nephew of Robert E. Lee, replaced him as holder of the ladder.

Salina voluntarily moved into a vacant chair; Flora then slid over so the general could have the seat beside her. Salina heard Stuart whisper to his wife: "What's the matter, dear? Have I grown two heads? Why are you looking at me like that?"

"What happened back there?" Flora's concern was plain.

"I was distracted. It was too stuffy, too confined," Stuart answered offhandedly, "and for all I know the stile wasn't properly set. There's no call for such a fuss." He smiled down at his wife in a reassuring manner.

Salina sensed that while Flora said nothing more aloud, her disquiet had not diminished by half. One of the guests asserted that Stuart had been talking with Hetty Cary instead of paying attention to the business at hand; others whispered he had dozed off backstage—and sleeping on duty was a cardinal sin for any rank of soldier.

Stuart looked tired and war-weary to Salina's discerning eyes. A burden of responsibility rode on his shoulders, and Salina knew enough about the man to ascertain that he did not take his obligations lightly. Underneath the outward show of good nature, the fate of his family, country, and men pressed heavily. If the stories Salina heard were true, it was little wonder that the general slept so infrequently in camp or on the march.

Not long after the mishap on stage, a staff officer arrived to fetch Stuart on official military business, and Flora, relieved to be away, left with him. Salina was still thinking, after Jeremy had performed his part in the tableaux, how much she admired Flora Stuart. Salina absently wondered if she were in position like Flora's, would she be able to handle with an equal measure of dignity the knowledge that her husband was adored by the masses, as Stuart was? Flora stood behind her husband without fail, and the general's looks openly betrayed how he loved her. Stuart was a national hero to the Confederate population, and yet, when not viewed upon the pedestal that his widespread fame and sensational accomplishments had placed him, he was an ordinary man—a husband to his wife and a father to his children.

Salina abruptly squeezed Jeremy's hand, causing the flash of a lopsided grin. She responded with a reciprocal smile. Selfish as it might be, she was content that Jeremy was only a captain in the Confederate cavalry and that his name was relatively anonymous. He was her man, her own Horse Soldier, and she decided that sharing him with the Cause was trial enough without having to share him with notoriety or fame!

☆☆☆☆☆☆☆

The eve of Jeremy's twenty-first birthday coincided with his last night in Richmond. To celebrate, the pair made an event of it, going out on the town. Salina had Jeremy open her gift of books first, and because of the delay, they didn't arrive at the Richmond Theatre until half-past eight, therefore missing the start of the first show. During intermission, they mingled with other patrons in the reception room of the dress circle, helping themselves to ice water from a silver cooler set out for refreshment. They found the second play, Shakespeare's *Taming of the Shrew*, wholly entertaining.

The horse soldier took pleasure in "courting" his wife, considering they hadn't had time for a customary wooing prior to their marriage. He escorted his wife to a first-rate supper at the Spottswood Hotel following the play. The romantic evening was one of those special occasions that Salina would cherish long after he left her.

Knowing that Jeremy was bound to leave at the break of day, Salina had hoped to share their last few hours together quiet and content in each other's arms. But quiet was not what they found upon their return to the townhouse on Franklin Street.

Pansy had run off for good. Disturbing as that was to the residents, the desertion of the Careys' housekeeper paled in comparison to the unexpected arrival of Ridge Southerland.

"Go away," Jeremy commanded. "You ought to know you're not welcome here."

"I didn't come to discuss family issues," Ridge said dryly. "I came on official business." He held a set of sealed documents specifically addressed to Captain Jeremy Barnes.

It didn't matter that they shared a common bloodline, Jeremy didn't trust Ridge in the least. "What's all this?"

"I was hoping you'd tell me," Ridge hedged.

"Why don't the two of you adjoin to the sitting room?" Salina pointedly suggested, her eyes imploring Jeremy to cooperate peaceably. "I'm sure it's warmer upstairs than it is down here. I'll put on a pot of coffee."

Shortly, Ridge was savoring the rich, aromatic brew. "How did you manage to get ahold of real coffee?" he asked as Salina poured from the silver coffeepot to refill his cup.

"The same place I got the material for my gown," Salina evaded, unwilling to reveal her source. Homespun was the fashionable mode of dress in the Confederate capital—it was quite nearly perceived as a badge of honor among Southern ladies—but Salina had wanted to look her best tonight for Jeremy's sake.

Setting the shiny, footed pot back on the serving tray, Salina noted that Jeremy had broken the seal and already read his orders. "What is going on?" she inquired directly, electing to occupy the empty chair between the two men. "Come now—you both know I can keep a secret."

Ridge shot a look of grudging admiration at Garrett Hastings' daughter. He looked to his nephew. "Are you going to brief her, or shall I?"

"Have you heard of anything pertaining to a woman named Elizabeth Van Lew?" Jeremy queried.

"Yes," Salina nodded instantly. "I've seen her, in fact. Strange old woman...perhaps. In truth, I'd venture that she's as sane as any of us." She told Jeremy and Ridge about the boys who'd pelted the shabbily dressed woman with stones, chanting after her, *"Crazy Bet!"* "She shuffles as she walks, hums or talks to herself regularly—but the supposed craziness could be an act she portrays extremely well. I know she usually goes out in the company of one of her colored employees—Van Lew is an ardent abolitionist and has freed all her family's slaves. Most folks despise her for her views; they won't have anything to do with her."

"Which allows her the freedom to conduct traitorous activities on behalf of the Union with little interference," Ridge deducted.

As an afterthought Salina added, "Her house is on Grace Street, which runs the next block over between Franklin and Broad, on the hill between 23rd and 24th Street on the way out to Chimborazo. It's a big, columned mansion with curving wrought-iron staircases in front."

"Ridge has orders to see if he can make some headway into discovering her ring of Northern contacts, if not the participating spies themselves," Jeremy stated.

This sudden change of assignment didn't make any sense to Salina. "But what of the plans for California? Have the operations concerning the Powder Works been called off?"

"Not entirely, just postponed," Ridge attested. "Dr. Nichols and Hank Warner have returned to the West. They're laying the groundwork. When the time is right, I'll be joining them in California."

"And until then you've been reassigned to monitor alleged Union spies?" Salina inclined her head. There was something more he wasn't telling them, she was sure of it.

"The plan entails some undercover work," Ridge began.

Salina's green eyes snapped. "Exchanging gray and butternut for blue wool again?"

"Aye, Salina," Ridge nodded. "I'm to infiltrate Libby Prison; I'll be masquerading as a Union prisoner."

Jeremy stared at the floor, unable to meet Salina's incredulous expression.

"No!" She shook her head. "Jeremy, we can't let him do this— it's too dangerous!" She didn't hear the agreement from her husband she hoped for. Adamantly she continued, "Ridge, you could *die* in Libby Prison!"

"We all take chances, Sallie," Jeremy replied coolly. "Ridge feels this is one it's his duty to undertake."

"Why?" she insisted. "What can be gained from posing as an imprisoned Federal officer? You cannot be ignorant of the horrendous stories that concern that hideous place! They say it's akin to a living hell."

"Elizabeth Van Lew has obtained permission to visit Federal prisoners, purportedly giving them food, books, and clothing. I've been assigned to find out the methods she employs to relay intelligence to and from the inmates—to discover how her operations work inside the prison and how she gets her information forwarded to the authorities in Washington."

"And then?"

"And then I'll report the findings. No one in Richmond has been able to pinpoint her tactics. Van Lew is suspect, but she doesn't leave a visible trail. Think about it: She would make a prime candidate for harboring Union escapees should plans for a breakout ever come to fruition."

Salina shivered at the incomprehensible thought. "How do you propose to get into the prison?"

"Jeremy has orders to 'capture' me and bring me in. He'll then turn me over to Ross, the clerk."

"And that will appear plausible enough because he's done that sort of thing before." Salina swallowed. "How will you get back out?"

"That's my affair," Ridge said enigmatically. "Once I've done my job, they'll remove me from the prison."

"They?" she pounced on the ambiguous pronoun.

"Don't fret, Salina. There are government and military authorities involved with this, but confidentiality is key. I've said all I'm going to about it." Ridge turned to Jeremy. "I need your help, Captain. You've deposited prisoners at Libby before. That alone should be a convincing start."

"I brought *one* prisoner to Libby," Jeremy qualified. "I delivered John Barnes there."

"Yes," Ridge nodded. "I'm well aware of that."

Salina shivered at Ridge's ominous tone. "You're not in this for the sake of Elizabeth Van Lew—you're in it for revenge against John Barnes."

"I've said all I'm going to say," Ridge repeated coldly.

Jeremy sensed that Salina's perception of the situation was more accurate than his uncle was willing to admit. "And if I don't cooperate?"

"I reckon I'll have to devise an alternative plan," Ridge shrugged. "Garrett trusted you, Jeremy. He trained you to operate within and at the direction of the Secret Service. I was hoping to tap that knowledge—and I want a description of Barnes himself." He paused, trying to read Jeremy's reaction. "I know all about what Garrett used to do; we had a mutual understanding and a high regard for each other's abilities. Was I wrong in believing that you possessed the same brand of necessary daring? Forgive me if I'm asking too much. I'll try to understand if you don't have the nerve to get involved again—though you scarcely have the same justification as Salina for not wanting to continue active participation."

The underlying implication of cowardice was not lost on Jeremy. "I'll offer no excuses, Ridge. I'll play along. But you'd better have a sound plan, or I'm afraid my wife might be quite right: You could die in there."

"I'm not ready to die." Ridge's wolfish grin appeared. "Not by a long shot. I've too much to do yet, too many things left to accomplish."

Salina looked askance at both of them. "Fine. You two make your plans for this *ridiculous* mission. I'm going to start praying now—you're both going to need it."

Jeremy slipped into bed an hour later. Salina stiffened at his touch. "Sallie, don't be angry."

Salina sighed raggedly, allowing Jeremy to draw her into the circle of his arms. "I'm not angry," she whispered against the column of his neck. "But I am afraid, Jeremy; afraid that somebody's going to get seriously hurt in a prank like this. *Vengeance is mine, saith the Lord.* It is not up to you or to Ridge to murder John Barnes. God will punish him for what he has done. You almost killed him once—"

"That was in self-defense, Sallie. You know that."

"Yes, I do know that. You had a prime opportunity for a second attempt, yet you didn't follow through. Why are you agreeing to do this thing now when you must know that you're only helping Ridge conspire to commit murder?"

"What Ridge does on his own time during his confinement behind those walls is his business," Jeremy emphatically declared. "He'll answer for his own actions; I will answer for mine. I am bound by my orders, and they are specific: I'm to play out the charade that will lead any witnesses to think that Ridge is indeed a captured Yankee officer. Once I've turned him over to Ross at the commandant's office, my job is done."

"Believe that if you will," Salina whispered forlornly. She did not ask any more questions, and he did not offer any additional answers.

When Salina awoke, Jeremy was gone.

Chapter Twelve

*J*anuary seemed endless. The configuration on the calendar showed five Saturdays paired with five Sundays, and in the long days in between, the new routine established in the wake of Pansy's flight became commonplace.

While Mrs. Carey remained secluded in her upstairs room, Salina, Taylor Sue, and Jennilee continued living out a normal existence to the best of their abilities. They divided the chores among themselves: the cooking, marketing, and cleaning. For the sake of added income, Taylor Sue enlisted the aid of one of Colonel Carey's former acquaintances. With that gentleman's endorsement, she was able to obtain a position within the Treasury Department, signing Confederate notes. It was not a demanding job, but a tedious one; she never complained. Jennilee resumed her classes at Mrs. Pegram's on a part-time basis while Salina continued to work at Robertson Hospital twice weekly.

Sometimes Salina would take an afternoon off to see Flora Stuart on the occasions when the general's wife visited her sister

Maria and brother-in-law, Dr. Charles Brewer, at their house a few blocks away on Grace Street. Flora took Salina along with her to meet the Lees, who had moved into a brick townhouse of the same style as the Carey residence but situated on the opposite side of Franklin Street and closer to Capitol Square. Mrs. Lee, confined by arthritis to a wheelchair, and her daughters Mildred, Mary, and Agnes had taken on the duty of knitting socks for the Army of Northern Virginia. Salina was invited to take part in the industrious calling whenever she had the inclination to join them. She was forewarned, however, that she must learn to make a double heel. Marching had a tendency to wear quick holes otherwise.

With increasing frequency, Taylor Sue and Jennilee looked to Salina for guidance. Though it was Taylor Sue's mother's household, the overseeing of routine matters fell to Salina, who was gradually left with the bulk of responsibility for the day-to-day operations.

Donning a shawl over her crocheted cape and then her cloak on top of the shawl, Salina made an effort to keep warm, thus stretching the wood supply as far as she could. While writing a letter to her mamma, sitting sideways to be closer to the writing desk, she paused at intervals to blow on her fingertips. Her fingers and feet were equally as cold, even though her toes were nestled in two pair of socks and her hands were gloved with knitted fingerless mittens. The shiver that ran the length of her spine was not entirely due to the low temperature of the room; to her it seemed as if this interminable lull might be the proverbial calm before a storm.

She completed the letter to Mamma, intending to post it along with another she had written to Clarice, Aunt Tessa, and Aunt Ruby. Her walk to the post office was postponed, however, when a courier came to the door with a hand-delivered epistle from Jeremy. Salina eagerly opened the envelope, naturally resting a hand on her enlarged abdomen as she read.

Camp Wigwam
January 29, 1864

My Darling Salina—

I have read Les Miserables, which I have lent to Kidd Carney, and have begun Great Expectations. Reading fills my time between hours of drill and picket duty. With the new recruits and new horses, we have mounted drill and foot drill daily. Free time is a luxury which is spent, if not reading or writing, with the horses. They are well—their waking hours directed by the bugler's calls, just as ours are—but an isolated incident of Glanders recently claimed one of Genl. Stuart's mounts. None of the other horses seemed to be affected by it. It was disturbing, for it brought back too many memories of that ill-fated venture to Maryland.

Theodore Garnett has recently been made an aide-de-camp, and he recently accompanied Stuart to Richmond. A number of the scouts Stuart has employed behind enemy lines came in to report the happenings in Genl. Meade's encampment. Mosby has been promoted to Lt. Col.; by now you might have learned that he and his men suffered a defeat earlier this month at Loudoun Heights, near Harpers Ferry. Genl. Rosser has never approved of the partisans, and has written to Genl. Lee, with the agreement of Generals Early and Fitz Lee, that the partisan command should be abolished. Mosby's men have been harassing the Union outposts and collecting prisoners and always-needed horses, but Genl. Rosser evidently does not take these merits into account. In the fight at Loudoun Heights Mosby lost two of the leading officers of the 43rd Battalion, Lt. Turner and Capt. Smith. It was a sad affair, that.

Sad, too, that I write to inform you that Sam Sweeney died on the 13th instant of smallpox. Though he is gone, I fancy I can sometimes still hear the echoes of his banjo, and I will always remember him with fondness for that song he taught you. His music played a vital part in helping alleviate the dull routine of camp. He is sorely missed at headquarters.

I had the pleasure of seeing Mrs. Nettie Gillette in church on Sunday last, and dined with her, Rosalynde, and Salome. She and the girls are faring well and send their best regards. Nettie informed me that the room upstairs will remain vacant, as the previous boarder has opted to remain in Strasburg indefinitely. The room, she says, is at your disposal. She has kindly issued an open invitation for you to come whenever you are able and *willing. You know I have no objections to having you near, Sallie, but my conscience won't allow me to pressure you into leaving Taylor Sue and Jennilee alone there in Richmond. They depend on you, are sustained by the strength you bolster them with. You are a comfort and faithful companion to her in her time of need, as she has been to you in times past. It is just something to keep in mind: you have a place if and when you should deem it time to sneak away for a visit. I do trust you will come for a few days at least when the weather warms up.*

I have been back and forth between our headquarters and those of General Lee, about two miles distant. I had the occasion to carry dispatches to Gordonsville a few days ago and ran into a friend of Ethan's there. You remember Dr. Shields, I'm sure. He is no longer in service with the Second Corps under Genl. Ewell's command. He has been reassigned to the collection hospital at Gordonsville located at the Exchange Hotel. He had been deeply concerned over Ethan's "disappearance" after Gettysburg, but had only heard uncorroborated rumors of Ethan's imprisonment. Dr. Shields is going to write to Duncan. I supplied him with the information that should ensure a delivery directly to him if the message can be gotten through the lines. Dr. Shields, once learning the particulars, vehemently insisted that Ethan should not be held at all. After the first battle at Winchester, during the Valley campaign, Dr. Hunter McGuire—who served as Stonewall Jackson's medical director—devised an agreement that supposedly was accepted by the Federals declaring that medical personnel should not be retained as prisoners of war. Dr. Shields is going to apply to Dr. McGuire for assistance in seeking measures to obtain Ethan's release. I hope that this bit of news will give you some cheer and I pray, as I know you do, that your brother is soon exchanged.

Take care, my darling, of yourself and of our little one. Kisses to you.

Your own,
Captain Jeremy Barnes
Stuart's Cavalry, C.S.A.

Ethan released! Salina couldn't keep her hopes from soaring. *Wouldn't that be some pumpkins!* Just yesterday Taylor Sue had brought home a tale of a Southern prisoner who had escaped the confines of the Old Capitol Prison in Washington using a set of civilian clothes that had been smuggled to him. The Southern soldier had slipped past his guards and enlisted the aid of sympathetic friends he had in the city. If Dr. Shields had success in making Dr. McGuire aware of Ethan's plight, perhaps something could truly be done to help free him. If they would validate Ethan's identity to Duncan's government's satisfaction, they could get him out of Point Lookout and he could return home!

☆☆☆☆☆☆☆

February 9, 1864

As Ridge shivered on the damp wooden floor of Libby Prison, his teeth chattered. He felt nauseated from breathing contaminated air; the hunger in his stomach rumbled loudly enough for nearby prisoners to hear. His blue uniform, clean when he'd entered on the first day of his voluntary incarceration, was becoming as filthy as those worn by the other officers.

Libby had lived up to—no, it had *exceeded*—the horrendous reports given by souls fortunate enough to have survived the rotten, stinking pit. Disease, lice, lack of proper clothing and food, all ran as rampant as the vermin that infested the place. Twice since his arrival, Ridge had secretly ventured to a section in the basement known as Rat Hell, finding it to be aptly named. There was no denying the conditions were utterly deplorable. The South, with all its braggadocio in insisting that each Rebel could whip ten Yankees, had been ill-prepared as far as hospitals and prisons were concerned. It was an afterthought that warehouses had been commandeered for service of this nature. It seemed that no one on either side of the conflict had planned ahead as to what to do with captured or wounded enemy soldiers. Therefore, the suffering abounded.

Ridge now understood why Northerners were in such an outrage when they heard the accounts of committed atrocities as told by exchanged parolees. Yet, were the conditions at Libby any different from what Southern prisoners endured at Elmira, Point Lookout, or Johnson's Island? He thought not. The South was not intentionally starving the Federal prisoners, as the Union claimed. As it was, the Confederate commissary could scarcely feed the soldiers in its own ranks, let alone acquire adequate provisions for incarcerated foes. The Rebels had limited resources, which were not wasted on the prison system. They needed to keep their fighting forces alive if they had any hope of continued campaigning come spring.

The oppressive silence was punctuated by occasional snores and habitual coughing. Ridge rolled onto his side, drawing his jacket closer around him. He had no blanket. His only source of warmth was that which emanated from the men sleeping on either side of him. Behind his tightly closed lids, familiar faces appeared. Salina's came first, her concerned emerald eyes filled with a mingling of tears and pity for his wretched soul. Salina believed him to be a blackguard of the first order, and essentially he was just that. He'd always had a dark side to him, though he'd tried to emulate the goodness of his father and eldest brother throughout his life; he just hadn't come yet to the point in believing in all that his father did.

The next face was Damaris Cobb's. If her pale beauty haunted Ridge, the memory of her kisses surely taunted him. Ridge banished Brisco's sister from his mind. He had more pressing matters to worry about than whether or not he would ever have a chance for reconciliation with her.

Ridge thought instead about the things he'd learned since the day Jeremy had most effectually played out the charade required of him and the cold detachment with which he had turned Ridge over to the prison clerk. The performance, very likely, was not much of a stretch for Jeremy's acting abilities. In light of their dealings with each other, Ridge couldn't blame Jeremy for not liking him, and he didn't hold it against his nephew.

Like every other prisoner processed through the commandant's office, Ridge had been searched upon arrival, and anything remotely valuable was confiscated. He'd taken a hit from the blunt end of a walking stick for intentional impertinence to a guard, and tonight he'd again been denied his "supper" for failing to answer promptly at roll call.

The snarling reproach of the commandant had effectively served to gain John Barnes's notice, causing him to seek Ridge out at a later time. That sorry excuse for a man had, ironically, confessed that he'd learned from other inmates that Ridge, too, had been deposited at Libby's gates by none other than Jeremy Barnes.

Ridge had acted coolly aloof to the major, yet he offered a willing ear into which Barnes poured a litany of curses heaped upon Jeremy's head. Barnes's hatred of Ridge's nephew shone like a feverish sickness in his bloodshot, glassy eyes. Barnes recounted in perfect detail the objections he had for Jeremy's very existence while swearing that he would kill Jeremy if it was the last thing he ever did.

Biting his tongue raw to keep from lashing out in defense of his newly found though estranged nephew, Ridge willingly let Barnes ramble on. Barnes had even gone so far as to share a book with Ridge to help while away the hours. "Miss Van Lew doesn't forget us," Barnes had said. "She knows how we suffer in here."

The book had been a miraculous find for Ridge, yet he could only suspect that the tiny pinpricks in some of the pages were some sort of secret device employed for relaying messages through the printed letters. Regrettably, Barnes retrieved the book sooner than Ridge had wanted to return it. Ridge hadn't had enough time to analyze the code, if one indeed existed. Among whispers between the prisoners, always out of earshot of the guards, it seemed that there was much more to the supposedly crazy Miss Van Lew than met the eye. As far as Ridge could tell, the Union officers esteemed her with admiration and respect.

Another telling sign had come in the form of an innocent-looking egg carried into the prison in Elizabeth Van Lew's basket. Hollowed out, the shell was a container for a minuscule scrap of paper that was secretly delivered and eventually brought to the attention of General Neal Dow. Ridge hadn't yet been able to glean what the scrap of paper said, but he hadn't given up trying. Whatever covert operations were going on, he was convinced Van Lew was tied directly to them. Pity that the Confederate guards didn't do a better job of paying closer attention to the crafty little woman of Northern sympathies.

A stealthy footstep and a pair of muffled whispers summoned Ridge's attention. Even in the darkness, Ridge's keen sapphire eyes distinguished the shadowed forms belonging to Major Barnes and a second lieutenant from an Illinois cavalry company named Heggy. Ridge didn't need light to imagine the rodent-like eyes of John Barnes or his tangled beard, greasy hair, tobacco-stained teeth, dirty fingernails, and bony joints. Barnes's tattered uniform hung loosely on his thinning frame, a testimony to the amount of weight he'd lost during his captivity. Heggy, Barnes's disinterested partner in crime, was so nondescript in appearance that Ridge could almost believe him invisible.

Following at a cautious distance, Ridge descended through the kitchen and into the bowels of the prison, down into the cellar by way of a secret passage near the fireplace. *Ingenious—and surely not the work of Barnes alone.* Ridge had heard rumors of an escape route in the making and pondered now whether there was more truth than fiction to the alleged tunnel. An audible scrambling in the east cellar was followed by near-perfect stillness. Taking a bold step into Rat Hell, Ridge attributed the scurrying under the stale hay to the rats who made their homes in the dark and dankness. *Maybe there was no one human here at all...*

A driving fist to his midsection proved otherwise. Ridge was roughly thrown up against one of the wooden posts that supported the floor of the level above. His breath streamed out of his body, his left shoulder burned like fire. As his attacker pinned him to the post, a protruding metal spike punctured Ridge's skin and scraped against the bone of his shoulder blade.

"Aaahhhh!" Ridge ground out, the searing pain of his torn flesh almost more than he could stand. His left hand dangled uselessly at his side.

Major John Barnes's diabolical face leered before Ridge's fluttering eyelids. "Blast yer blue eyes, Colonel, and yer nosy ways! Curiosity killed the cat, ain't ya heard?"

You could die in Libby Prison... Ridge made no reply as his dark head lolled to one side.

"Heggy!" Barnes called to his accomplice. "Go tell Rose there ain't nothing but *rats* down here! Tell him to stick with the plan. Tell 'em to get going while there's still time."

Rose? Ridge's mind cleared just long enough for him to put the name with the face he knew belonged to the colonel of the 77th Pennsylvania Volunteer Infantry. *Colonel Thomas E. Rose.* Ridge had on more than one occasion seen the man talking with Van Lew. Ridge sucked in his breath as the pain consumed him.

John Barnes cast a hate-filled glance at the man pinned to the support post. There was a look about this so-called colonel that reminded him of his so-called nephew, Jeremy Barnes. The unbalanced major suddenly snapped. In his twisted mind, the man before him *became* Jeremy, and Barnes pummeled him with a repeated series of undefended blows. As his victim's awareness and his own irrational anger abated, Barnes unmercifully pulled Ridge off the spike and dumped him headfirst into a rancid mound of hay. The offended rats squealed in protest at the intruder, clamping their sharp teeth into Ridge's skin. Had Ridge not already passed out, he'd have felt every sting of the knife-like bites. Reality, however, already eluded him.

The angered rodents didn't stop with biting Ridge. They made a run at Barnes as well, and several inflicted injury in spite of his efforts to kick the vermin away. Swearing profusely, Barnes fended off the attacking vermin and rejoined the group at the entrance to the completed tunnel. Heggy had secured for them a place in the second batch of officers who would make their way out in their turn. They were to wait an hour before following after the first group got out. Secrecy was crucial; otherwise the guards would be alerted and the escape would be foiled. Word could not be suppressed, however; it spread faster than wildfire among the Yankee prisoners. Before the Confederates knew what had happened, more than a hundred Federals had gained their freedom by crawling the length of the tunnel.

☆☆☆☆☆☆☆

From the direction of Capitol Square, the portentous sound of the tolling tocsin pervaded Richmond. Salina, under her four quilts and not wanting to face the morning just yet, listened with curiosity. The bell tower chimed whenever there was some imminent danger lurking on the outskirts of the city. Immediately Salina pushed the blankets aside and rubbed the sleep from her eyes. *The capital surely wasn't being invaded by the Yankees— or was it?*

Jennilee threw open the door of Salina's room, panting and holding her side.

"What is it, Jennilee? What's happening?" Salina pulled on her flannel wrap and knit slippers.

Taylor Sue and Mrs. Carey arrived at Salina's door as Jennilee replied, "It's an escape! Last night, better than a hundred Union officers tunneled out of Libby!"

Salina raised a trembling hand to her brow, trying in vain to force her groggy brain into a coherent pattern of thought. Her eyes locked with Taylor Sue's, each viewing the unmistakable terror in the other's expression. Salina spoke with discernment according to the intuitive churning within her. "John Barnes might well be at large in this city."

"Dear God, have mercy!" Taylor Sue heaved a rushed prayer heavenward. "Salina, do you really believe that?" But the rhetorical query did not require a reply. If Salina felt strongly enough to say it aloud in the first place, there was reason to believe that she wasn't merely making an idle guess.

Prompted by fear, the women gatherered their weapons and ammunition, unanimously agreeing that it would be far better to be prepared for the worst and not have it happen than to be caught unawares. Salina took inventory of their provisions and supplies, gauging how long they might be able to survive without leaving the townhouse.

"But the militia will recapture the escaped prisoners and punish them accordingly," Jennilee asserted. "Won't they?"

"There is a reasonable chance that some of them will make good on their getaway," Salina cautioned. "Better to be safe than sorry."

Along with the pealing bells, incessantly barking dogs could be heard growling and yipping more fiercely than hounds on a fox hunt. Search parties marched through Richmond's streets in pursuit of the self-liberated enemy soldiers. The town was paralyzed by disbelief that such a dastardly thing could have happened at all.

"Our militia won't find much, I reckon," Salina confided to Taylor Sue, who was staring listlessly out the window. "If those Yankees were smart, they'd head directly for their own lines."

"If they had any sense at all, they'd hide out to wait for darkness to fall and *then* do their running," Taylor Sue remarked, wringing her hands.

Once the sun did set, apprehension and unease alternately crashed like waves against a sandy beach. The girls convinced Mrs. Carey to go to bed, and Jennilee reluctantly turned in as well. Salina sat alone, rocking to and fro with only a small tallow candle to illuminate her own room. The eerie sounds of the dogs and the ongoing quest outside pressed in through the pores of the brick walls and the cracks of the securely bolted doors. Salina didn't cotton to being made an unwilling prisoner in the Carey house, and her mind wandered far too freely for her own liking. When she could stand no more solitude, she poked her head into her sister-in-law's room but found it empty.

"What are you doing down here?" Salina queried, having located Taylor Sue in the front parlour—revolver in hand.

"This is serious, Salina," Taylor Sue whispered. "What if...?"

"Hush!" Salina inadvertently snapped. She sat down next to Taylor Sue on the horsehair sofa. She held out her hands. "When two or more are gathered, the Lord is in their midst. We need to pray."

With joined hands, the young ladies bowed their heads to pray, their hearts concurrently petitioning for calm and for strength.

☆☆☆☆☆☆☆

In an empty shed, Heggy awaited the lighting of the gas lamps. There were but a few people on the streets during the cold night, and he presumed that news of the prison escape had permeated the Rebels' capital city. "The secesh folks ought to be utterly terrified that we're out here lurking in their shadows!" he sneered. "Serves them right to be scared, shaking in their beds. They ought to be made to pay for the way we've been treated in that despicable hellhole, eh, Major?" Heggy looked over his shoulder. "Major?"

"Uhhhhh," groaned Barnes.

Heggy didn't like the reddened, puffy look of the rat bites on both of the Major's exposed calves and on the hand he'd used to swat the vermin away. The major's eyes were more glassy than normal, his bottom lip a bluish-gray. Heggy was unable to view Barnes's top lip for the overgrowth of a greasy mustache. He repeatedly slapped the major's cheek, trying to keep him awake. "No time to sleep, sir. We've got to keep moving. Dark only lasts for so long."

"Uhhhhh," came the repeated reply.

Heggy pulled stolen fruit and a loaf of bread from beneath his shirt. From his pocket he withdrew a pilfered bottle of ale. He scratched his head to drive away the lice that infested his long, scraggly hair while he tried to piece together what they should do next. "Sir, I think we'd do well to head toward the river. I heard some of the other prisoners mention a Union encampment near Yorktown. We've got to make it at least that far before our own people will take care of us."

In addition to stealing food and finding a place to hide, Heggy had acquired a discarded coat and a soggy blanket, which he spread out on the shed floor to dry. His own shoes had holes clean through the soles; the major's boots had only a fraction of an inch of tread left. The cold and ice could be treacherous if the men didn't take care. Heggy contemplated other details he'd heard from the other escapees concerning sympathetic Union families in the Southern capital, but he could not for the life of him remember names or addresses. Then he recalled hearing that Elizabeth Van Lew, the Union-loving woman who frequented Libby, lived somewhere on Grace Street. He decided to try there first, hoping that the woman would be able and willing to take them in.

Church bells indicated the hour with eleven strokes, and Heggy deemed it time to get moving. Major Barnes was only slightly aware since eating and having something to drink; he still appeared quite unwell.

The men walked and walked, ducking into shadows at every sound of a passerby. Major Barnes was getting impatient—they'd traveled for blocks on Grace Street and not come across any homes that matched the description of the Van Lew mansion.

"Ya ain't smart as no steel trap, ere ya, Lieu-ten-ant?" Major Barnes barked the insult. "Ya prob'ly got us headed in the wrong di-rection all together."

Heggy's faced turned a mottled red. "Maybe my bearings are a little off, sir," the junior officer admitted. "I'm in no way familiar with the layout of this cursed city! Shall we about-face and go back?" He didn't relish the idea of traversing up and down any more of Richmond's hills, especially when he was more than half supporting the weight of the major. Heggy wasn't a strong man anymore, thanks to his prison tenure, and taking deep breaths in the cold night air gave him chest pains.

"Don't go back down Grace Street," Major Barnes wheezed. "Go over another block so's we won't pass anyone we might've just done. Hear?"

"Yes, sir," Heggy ground out. He didn't care much for the bad-tempered major, but they were comrades-in-arms and could be of use to each other—for as long as it took to get themselves out of hostile territory.

Heggy didn't even know the name of the street they were currently on, save that it was one block removed from Grace Street. It was a residential district and seemingly dead-ended at Capitol Square.

The steady cadence of horses' hooves prompted Heggy to hustle the major off the sidewalk and into a darkened alley behind a row of brick townhouses. The alley offered more hiding places than did the street if they should need them.

A flash of lantern light appeared at the mouth of the alley. Heggy pulled the major through a winter-dead garden and down a short flight of stairs to wait in the shadows until the lantern carrier passed. He reached for the carving knife concealed in his boot—a token he'd filched from the prison kitchen once when it had been his turn to cook for his messmates. It was the only source of protection he and the major had.

The lantern came nearer. Barnes and Heggy watched between the stairs, pressing themselves flat against the wall under the stairwell. The lantern carrier did not halt his steps. With a relieved sigh, both Union men waited in stillness for a few minutes longer to ensure that the searching Rebel had truly moved on.

The major's consciousness was waning, and Heggy hadn't the strength to carry him to either Elizabeth Van Lew's house or the James River, whichever might happen to be the closer destination. Heggy tried the handle of the nearest door and found it to be locked against him. "Like they knew we were coming," he muttered in irritation. He wrapped his hand with a portion of the blanket and punched his fist through the window next to the rear door of the building. Clearing the remaining glass from the sash, he stuck his hand through the opening and unbolted the door to gain entrance. Most likely, the residents were Rebels, Heggy assumed, but perhaps he could force a little Southern hospitality out of them on behalf of the ailing major.

☆☆☆☆☆☆☆

"Did you hear that?" Alarm danced in Taylor Sue's eyes.

"Sounded like a broken window," Salina whispered lowly.

"Someone's downstairs," Taylor Sue accurately determined.

"My pistol is in the drawer of the sideboard. Get it. I'll go fetch the Spencer from my room." Salina mentally chided herself for not thinking to bring the rifle with her in the first place.

Taylor Sue positioned herself in the dining room with her revolver. Her sister followed Salina back down. Salina stationed Jennilee on the opposite side of the central hallway, holding a long piece of firewood to be used as a club. The three waited.

The instant Jennilee heard the shuffling footsteps at the top of the stairs, she bravely slammed her cudgel down hard on the shadowed form that had ascended from the kitchen below. The man's body fell into a crumpled heap on the floor. Salina lit the wick of a hurricane lamp to illuminate the face of the intruder.

"He's a Yankee!" Taylor Sue exclaimed with distaste, her revolver trained on him lest the blow hadn't completely knocked him out.

"An escaped lieutenant," Salina clarified, using her foot to roll him over. "Nice work, Jennilee. Now, all we need is some rope to tie him up until we can get the provost guard to come for him."

"There's a coil stored under the pie safe," Taylor Sue remembered. "I'll go—you two keep an eye on him."

Inadvertently, Taylor Sue walked into the clutches of a second, unseen escapee. Bony fingers dug into her shoulders, backed her up and into the light. The odiferous, bearded man knocked the gun from her hand, then reached down to retrieve the carving knife that had fallen from Heggy's hand.

"Back off." Salina pointed the muzzle of the Spencer at the man. "Do you hear me? I said back off!"

The blue-clad officer lifted his head, his face revealed. The knifepoint hovered precariously close to the side of Taylor Sue's throat. "We-ell, well, if it ain't Salina Hastings," Major Barnes growled with maniacal malevolence. "Out of all the houses in Richmond, Heggy blindly leads us to yours. I'd call that destiny!" Barnes's demonic laugh sent chills of dread racing down the spine of each of the young ladies. "Imagine that! Maybe I cain't curse him for his poor sense of di-rection after all, seein' as how we've wound up here!"

Salina's finger twitched on the trigger of the rifle, but she held her fire. With Taylor Sue between herself and the major, she didn't have a clear shot. "John Barnes!" Anger replaced her fear as she spat the depraved Yankee major's name.

"Put the gun down, Missie," Barnes wheezed, "or I swear I'll kill her. Don't think I won't!"

Taylor Sue's tawny eyes brimmed with tears. Without words, she implored Salina to do whatever she must, whatever she thought right.

"Let my daughter go!" Mrs. Carey shrieked from the landing, aiming her dead husband's rifle at the intruder.

Barnes squeezed Taylor Sue's arm until she gasped from the pain, the knife blade pressing just a hair closer to cutting her skin. "You sassy wenches had better get used to doing what I say, or I mean it, I will kill her!" His glassy eyes fastened on Salina. "And then...then I'll finally deal with you, Missie. Once and for all." He swore and shouted loudly, "Drop the guns!"

Mrs. Carey and Salina reluctantly did as they were told.

"That's better." Barnes momentarily relaxed his grip on Taylor Sue, but the knife remained at her throat. "Now, you!" he snarled at Mrs. Carey. "Get down here. Sit right over there and don't move an inch!"

Rachel Carey complied with the gruff order, her eyes still locked on the firm grip the major retained on her daughter's arm.

Heggy groaned, putting a hand to his throbbing head. He felt blood, and staring at his hand, gawked open-mouthed at the shiny red ooze coating his fingers. Raising his head made the room spin.

Barnes kicked Taylor Sue's discarded revolver to his companion. "Heggy! Keep watch on those two!"

"Aye, sir." Heggy slowly retrieved the gun.

"Who else is here?" John Barnes's eyes scanned the hallway and the dining room.

Jennilee, seeing that Heggy's faculties had been dulled by the blow she had delivered, gave Heggy a swift kick in the shin. The revolver went off, launching a bullet into the glossy wood floor. Heggy slapped Jennilee so hard her lip split open and began to bleed. "Impudent little wretch. Do you want all the neighbors to hear?"

The split second of distraction was all Taylor Sue needed to dodge the knife in Major Barnes's hand, twist his arm down, and plunge the blade deep between his ribs. Air seeped from the major's punctured lung. Barnes lashed out at Taylor Sue, shoving her hard into the wall, cursing under what little breath he had left. "Ya'll pay...for...that!" He strained to pull the bloody knife free from the stab wound and waved it toward Taylor Sue, who sidestepped him, though he kept coming after her.

"You want me to kill this one, Major?" Heggy abruptly pulled Salina toward him, twisting her arm behind her back, yanking her into the center of the room. Salina squirmed; the bruising pressure of the lieutenant's hold on her intensified.

"No, ya fool!" Major Barnes rasped. Holding the bloody knife pointed toward Taylor Sue, he picked up the Spencer repeater and aimed it at Salina's heart. "That pleasure'll be all mine! So help me, I'll kill her myself if it's the last thing I do!" His lips curled in a malevolent grin when he saw how very pregnant Garrett Hastings' daughter had grown. His itchy finger caressed the trigger. "Tonight I will have the pleasure of seeing the next generation of the Hastings wiped out *and* the extinction of Justine's treacherous deceit!"

"*NO!*" Taylor Sue pitched herself between the rifle and Salina just as the major fired his shot. The bullet slammed into her back, wrenching her body, piercing her shoulder blade. Taylor Sue stumbled forward into Salina's outstretched arms, grabbing on to her for support. "Sa-lee-na..." Taylor Sue's eyelids fluttered before she swooned to the floor, consciousness deserting her.

"Taylor Sue!" Salina was instantly on her knees beside her sister-in-law's prone form. *"Taylor Sue!"*

Jennilee used surprise to her advantage and wrestled the revolver away from Heggy. Turning the weapon on him, she closed her eyes and squeezed the trigger. The single shot plowed straight through the Union lieutenant's skull; the man was dead before he hit the floor.

Barnes lurched into action, holding his bleeding wound, advancing on Salina again. Through tear-filled eyes, Jennilee saw him moving. She blinked several times to clear her vision, the gun held steady in both hands. "Take another step, and I'll pull this trigger again," she vowed in a shaky voice.

"And if she doesn't get you," Mrs. Carey again had the rifle in hand, the major in her sights, "I will."

John Barnes halted, weighing the situation to determine whether either of the Careys really meant it. He decided Jennilee was the weaker link. "Yer scared, girlie. An'...ya should be. Ya done...murdered a man...in cold blood. Murderers...hang...for their...crimes...in this country...just like they do up...North. Ya got blood...on...your hands...girlie. Ya...done...spilt...Yankee...blood..."

Jennilee dropped her gun, dissolving into another rush of terrified tears. Barnes targeted Salina again. Mrs. Carey took a shot, but her aim was wide.

Salina backed away as Barnes took an unhampered step toward her. A shot came from the floor with a deadly upward trajectory. The bullet hole in Barnes's breast could be seen for a mere instant before a surge of blood filled the opening, gushing from the gaping wound.

Taylor Sue stirred herself into awareness just long enough to finish what the stabbing had not. "Pray for me, Salina," she begged through her pained tears. "The commandments say 'Thou shalt not kill.' Please pray...the Lord will...spare me...for taking...Barnes's miserable life..." She wrenched her gaze from the sickening sight of the felled major. "He...can't..." she swallowed and tried to speak again. "Salina, he can't...hurt us...anymore..."

"You acted in self-defense, Taylor Sue!" As Salina cradled her sister-in-law in her arms, the blood from Taylor Sue's wound absorbed into her wrapper and nightgown. "Jennilee, you both did what you had to!"

"We killed them." Jennilee stared down at her trembling hands, her cheeks wet with streaming tears. "We killed them!"

Salina's own salty tears rained down on Taylor Sue's pale face. Salina lifted her head. Rachel Carey stood mute in shock and disbelief. "Mrs. Carey," Salina cried, "please—you've got to go fetch Dr. Brewer right away! If she... If Taylor Sue..." Her words faltered, and her breath was ragged. "We have to think of the baby. She needs help desperately!"

Jennilee saw that her mother stood rooted on the landing, showing no signs of hearing or inclination to obey Salina's directive. "I'll go for Dr. Brewer," she volunteered.

"Fine, Jennilee. That's fine; you go—quickly! I'll make your sister as comfortable as I can."

Jennilee gave the bodies littering the floor a wide berth. Their blood was already absorbing into the wood, making indelible stains.

"Just go on, Jennilee," Salina encouraged. "We'll deal with them later."

☆☆☆☆☆☆☆

Jennilee ran as fast as her wobbly legs would carry her. She nearly collided with a small detachment of gray-clad militia men, and she sobbed out the gist of what had happened at the Carey house, begging that they go immediately to Linden Row. By the time she returned to the house on Franklin Street with Dr. Brewer in tow, the home guard soldiers had evacuated the lifeless bodies of the Union officers and were assisting a neighbor lady with cleaning up the residual mess. The soldier in charge attempted to collect the facts of the matter for his report from Jennilee, but her breathless replies were piecemeal and vague at best. He would have to sort the answers out later to gain some semblance of order.

Dr. Brewer, toting his medical kit, nodded to the neighbor lady, persuading her to keep on with calming Mrs. Carey.

"Thank you for coming," Salina murmured. She apprised Dr. Brewer of the situation to the best of her ability, including the fact that Taylor Sue had roughly a month left in her term before her expected confinement. "I beg of you: What can I do to help you help her?"

"We'll need sheets and blankets, Miss Salina. More wood for the fire. We've got to keep her warm," the surgeon insisted as he conducted a preliminary examination. "She's lost a lot of blood and has already gone into shock."

"I'll see to the firewood." Jennilee was glad for something to occupy her.

Salina arranged the blankets on the dining room table, and Dr. Brewer lifted Taylor Sue, settling her on the makeshift operating table.

"What about the baby?" With fresh tears stinging her eyes, Salina declared emphatically, "She can't die, Dr. Brewer. She just can't!"

Dr. Brewer usually dealt with medical situations in a forthright manner. Tonight, he attempted to tone down his customary candor but found he could not do so and still make Salina understand the grave peril involved. "Your sister-in-law's condition is unstable. I believe she is strong, but there is much at stake. If she weren't carrying a child, this might be a little less complicated."

"I have faith that you will do all in your power to save her, Doctor." Salina's hope and reliance on his skills sparkled through her tears.

Charles Brewer laid out his instruments with practiced deliberation. "I appreciate your confidence, but you must be realistic. If it should come to making a choice between Taylor Sue's life and that of her child, I will have better luck in helping the baby live. Do you understand me?"

Salina's emerald eyes clouded, but she nodded. She recognized the tell-tale signs of dilemma in the draw of Dr. Brewer's brow and grasped the difficulty of his position. "Just do what you can for her, that's all I'm asking. God will take care of the rest, according to His will."

Without further delay, Dr. Brewer proceeded with the operation necessary to remove the bullet from Taylor Sue's shoulder. Salina resolutely stood at his side, ready to assist. "This is not my first experience in an operating room." The surgeon was thankful to have someone with some experience with medical procedures, even if it was limited. It was better than nothing.

The neighbor lady, Mrs. Hoffman, rounded up a ball of twine, a pair of scissors, and a stack of towels. She tended the fire while Jennilee found the baby clothes Taylor Sue had so lovingly knit.

All through the surgery, Salina's lips moved in a constant stream of silent prayer. She did exactly what she was told when called upon and lent her hands when they were most needed. Dr. Brewer rolled Taylor Sue onto her side. He probed the bloody wound with his fingers until he located the spent projectile, then with precision plucked it from the wound. Salina shuddered when Dr. Brewer dropped the lead bullet into a pan with a resounding metallic *clank*.

At length the operation was satisfactorily completed. Dr. Brewer discarded his blood-speckled apron and cleansed his reddened hands. Later on, assured that Taylor Sue rested comfortably, he took the time to give Salina a thorough examination. Bruises were already forming where Heggy had had his rough hands on her. Thankfully, Salina had felt her baby move since the attack, and the surgeon determined that the incident had not traumatized the little life within her.

Jennilee's cut lip did not require stitches; Mrs. Carey downed the sleeping draught Dr. Brewer prescribed without the slightest hint of argument.

The following afternoon, Dr. Brewer, along with his wife, Maria, came to inquire after the patients at the Carey home. He was in no way surprised to see Salina keeping vigil in the chair at Taylor Sue's bedside. She had been in the very same position when he'd left in the early hours before dawn.

Fever and delirium had set in. Taylor Sue writhed beneath the blankets, tossing her head from side to side, murmuring Ethan's name.

"She sometimes clutches her belly," Salina nervously reported. "That pulls at the shoulder wound and sets it to bleeding again. Isn't there anything else that can be done for her relief?"

Dr. Brewer wasn't overly pleased with the prognosis. Checking Taylor Sue's status for himself, he nodded to his wife. Maria withdrew to the kitchen downstairs to concoct a foul-smelling, vile-tasting herbal brew that would induce the labor of Taylor Sue's baby.

"But why?" Salina pulled on the doctor's elbow. "Tell me why must you bring on the birthing early?"

"Taylor Sue's strength is ebbing, Salina," Dr. Brewer gently explained. "If she delivers her baby at this stage, there is a greater chance that the child, though premature, will survive. If we wait, she may not have the fortitude to endure hard labor, and both mother and child could perish."

Salina's eyes fell slowly from Dr. Brewer's grave expression to the floor as the full meaning of his words registered. Her mind raced. *What would Ethan do if he were here?* But Ethan, away and imprisoned, was not on hand to consult. With no alternative than to agree with what the surgeon believed to be the best course of action, Salina quietly nodded her acquiescence.

Taylor Sue grimaced and gagged as the potent, horrid-tasting potion was administered by Maria's hand. Soon the onset of cramps and contractions stirred her from semiconsciousness to agonizing lucidity.

The hurt Salina was feeling in her heart was almost beyond bearing. She had no earthly idea how Taylor Sue was able to withstand the wrenching pains without shrieking at the top of her lungs. By the next morning, the baby finally came. In a dreamy, singsong whisper, Taylor Sue declared her son's name to be Ethan Jeremy, as her husband had wished.

☆☆☆☆☆☆☆

Thirty-six hours following the birth, Taylor Sue opened her amber eyes. She was neither groggy nor feverish, and she seemed to have clear knowledge of what was happening around her. She even took a little cornbread softened with chicken broth and drank half a mug of lukewarm cider.

Settling deep into her pillows, Taylor Sue asked, "Have you ever seen an angel, Salina?"

"Yes, I think I have—two of them to be precise."

"When?"

"Oh... It was in Maryland. Jeremy and I were headed toward Virginia and Shadowcreek after leaving the Grants in Pennsylvania. We crossed a creek not far from the Cobbs' place and ran into a bit of trouble."

Taylor Sue shifted on her side to try to get comfortable. "You've never made mention of angels before. Where were they?"

"When we crossed that creek near the Cobbs, the wagon stuck in the streambed. The right front wheel had broken," Salina recounted. "Two men dressed in Yankee blue came to our rescue, knowing full well that we were Southern. Jeremy was ill then, sacked out in the back of the wagon, unable to be of any usefulness. Those Yankees had me get up in the driver's seat and guide the team of mules forward. They both pushed the wagon from the rear, rocking the submerged wheels out of the muck. But in truth, it almost seemed as if they had *lifted* the wagon from where it was stuck, and when it was back on solid ground, I saw that the wheel was in no way damaged. It was *whole* again, not broken. I bawled myself silly through the entire episode, so afraid yet so thankful. They would take nothing in compensation; they didn't even tell me their names. And then, they up and disappeared, Taylor Sue, just as sure as I'm sitting here next to you. One minute they were with me;

the next, there was no tangible sign of either them *or* the horses they'd been riding. I didn't question it at the time. I just wanted to believe that their assistance was attributed to providential intervention. Yet now, looking back on the incident, I'm convinced that they *must* have been angels."

"Mmmmm..." A small smile flickered at the corners of Taylor Sue's mouth. "I'm sure they were."

"Have you ever seen an angel?" Salina turned the question back on Taylor Sue.

The smile on Taylor Sue's face broadened. "Oh yes, Salina, I have; hundreds of them. They all bowed down around the glassy sea at the foot of the crystal throne of God, just like it tells in the book of Revelation. I saw the Lord, Salina, our Saviour Himself." The light grip she had on Salina's hand became crushing. "He was clothed in a bright, white robe, and He held out His hands to me—hands that bore scars from the nails that held Him to the cross. A glorious rainbow light showed all around Him, silhouetting His features from view. In His voice were love and peace, encouragement and strength. 'In a little while,' He told me, 'You'll have no more pain, no more tears, no more sorrow, no more sadness. You will have life everlasting, for I have seen your name written in the Book of Life.'" Taylor Sue's intense eyes riveted on Salina. "I'm not going to live, Salina. We must face that. I am not afraid to die, for absence from this body is to be present with the Lord. Promise me something?"

"What?" Salina swallowed with difficulty.

Taylor Sue took a labored breath. "I want your word of honor that you will look after Ethan Jeremy for me. I'm giving my son into your care, for I cannot be a mother to him." Her golden-brown eyes entreated Salina to be sensible, to accept reality. She licked her dry lips. "Tell your brother how very sorry I am..." The tears streaked her face. "You will raise our son as your own, won't you? Jeremy won't object, I'm sure."

"Of course Jeremy won't object, and of course we'll look after him," Salina vowed. "But, Taylor Sue..."

"No, Salina," Taylor Sue shook her matted head. "I'm not getting any better. You know it, and I know it. It's better to be prepared. I am at peace with knowing that the Lord will come for me in His own time."

Tears fell down Salina's cheeks. "But, Taylor Sue..."

"Don't cry anymore, Salina. You're the strong one. You *must* be strong and courageous. You *must* have faith—and trust. Ethan... He will not understand." She let out a shuddering sigh. "Please, Salina..."

"What else, Taylor Sue? Anything." If Salina could have traded places with her sister-in-law, she would have. Her anguished mind wrestled with the knowledge that Taylor Sue had taken the bullet meant specifically for her. "What can I do?"

"Bring my boy to me. I should like to hold my son," Taylor Sue requested weakly.

Salina hastened to retrieve little Ethan Jeremy from his bassinet and wrapped him in a crocheted blanket. She gingerly placed the baby boy in the protective crook of his mother's arm.

"I want you to tell him—when the time comes—how very much he meant to me," Taylor Sue implored.

"I'll not let him forget you, Taylor Sue. I'll love him and I'll care for him, but he'll not lose your memory as long as I am here to see that it flourishes."

A serene smile molded Taylor Sue's pale lips. "Thank you, Salina," she whispered hoarsely. "My good friend and sister—I love you dearly. May God help you...and continue to supply you with His unfailing strength."

Little Ethan Jeremy, who favored his father with his dark hair and deep blue eyes, made a contented gurgling sound. His tiny fingers caught and held a fistful of his mother's tangled russet tresses. Taylor Sue's tremulous smile was one filled with adoration. She placed a kiss on her son's soft cheek and closed her weary eyes.

"He sounds hungry." Salina was already learning how to translate the various noises he made. Her eyes traveled the scant distance from the face of the baby to the face of her sister-in-law. "Taylor Sue?"

Silence.

"Taylor Sue?!" Salina cried out, a rush of tears blurring her vision. She buried her face in her hands, and her shoulders shook uncontrollably. She bit her lip hard. "Father God, she is surely with You now..." Her throat ached with words unspoken. The devastating blow of losing her dear friend was more than she thought she could stand. She put her forehead to Taylor Sue's brow and wept bitterly. "How shall I get along without you?"

☆☆☆☆☆☆☆

As Salina, Mrs. Carey, and Jennilee were leaving for the church for Taylor Sue's funeral, a uniformed soldier came to pay an unexpected call. "I realize this is not the best of times," the orderly deducted from the grief-stricken faces of the ladies descending the porch stairs, "but I must be allowed to speak with Mrs. Jeremy Barnes. It is a matter of grave importance."

Salina's blood ran cold. *If lightning can strike twice*, she thought pessimistically, *so can disaster*. Her heart raced; the fear that the man brought bad tidings of Jeremy threatened to steal her breath away. "I... I am Mrs. Jeremy Barnes."

"Ma'am," the orderly doffed his kepi. "If I may speak plainly."

"Please do." She hugged the baby, E.J. as she'd begun to call him, close to her breast.

The orderly shot an apprehensive glance at the other ladies.

"We are on our way to St. James, sir," Salina explained, "for a funeral."

"This will only take a minute, ma'am," he assured her.

"Jennilee, take E.J. and your mamma to the carriage. Tell Mrs. Hoffman I'll be there directly."

Jennilee obediently took her sister's baby and led her mother next door to the neighbor's waiting carriage, granting Salina and the butternut-clad orderly privacy to talk between themselves.

"Please, sir, if this is about my husband..."

"No, ma'am. This hasn't got anything to do with your husband."

A relieved sigh rippled through Salina. "I thought...well, no matter. Why have you come?"

"Captain Sally Tompkins sent me from Robertson Hospital. A man was brought to her for care early this morning—a Yankee officer. He was half-dead, yet so far, he's been responding favorably to the treatments the chief surgeon has administered. He's not out of danger, however, not by a long shot."

Salina blanched. "Are you at liberty to tell me this man's name?"

"Colonel E.S. Ridgeford."

"Ridge?" she breathed.

"You are acquainted with him, then." It was not so much a question as it was a confirmation. "Your name and address were handwritten on a slip of paper Captain Sally found in one of his pockets."

"Will he live?" Salina queried.

"Don't honestly know," the orderly answered. "As I said, he's not out of danger yet. And he's delirious."

"What's happened? What's wrong with him?"

"Dr. Garret said something about *pyaemia*—that's blood poisoning, ma'am. I've only ever heard of it. I've never seen a case myself, but I read something in a medical book about it once. I'll tell you plain, ma'am, seems to me that's usually fatal. Not too many who contract it ever live to tell the tale, sorry to say."

So Jeremy wasn't dead, but Ridge might soon be. Dilemma tugged at Salina.

"Sir, I am on my way to bury my sister-in-law, and since it is impossible for me to be in two places at once, I must deal with one tragedy at a time. I beg you to please thank Captain Sally for sending you to me with this news, but I cannot come this instant. Please tell her that I will come to the hospital as soon as I am able—my presence alone will not sway whether the man in question lives or dies."

"Aye, ma'am," the orderly nodded. "My condolences, ma'am."

Salina felt a stone's weight pressing against her heart as the orderly departed. "When it rains, it pours," she lamented. *I cannot do this on my own, Lord. Please—please send me some comfort in these dark hours. An old adage teaches that every back is fitted for the burden; Your Word tells me that You will not give us more than we can bear. I must trust, as Taylor Sue faithfully reminded me, that all things still work together for good somehow.*

The raw, icy wind blew unfelt by the small cluster of mourners who weathered the elements to gather at Hollywood Cemetery for the burial. The shock of Taylor Sue's passing numbed them all. Bouncing her brother's son in her arms, Salina hushed the boy and held him close to keep him warm. Jennilee stood next to Salina, supporting the grieving Mrs. Carey; Mrs. Hoffman and her little girl stood opposite, along with a trio of ladies Taylor Sue had worked with at the Treasury Department. The selfsame reverend who'd married Ethan and Taylor Sue the year before at St. James Church now read the funeral service over Taylor Sue's flower-bedecked casket. Salina retained only snatches of the phrases the minister spoke in an effort to comfort:

...I am the resurrection, and the life, saith the Lord: he that believeth in me, though he were dead, yet shall he live: and whoso-ever liveth and believeth in me shall never die...

...We brought nothing into this world, and it is certain that we can carry nothing out. The LORD gave, and the LORD hath taken away; blessed be the name of the LORD...

"...Hear my prayer, O Lord, and with thine ears consider my calling; hold not thy peace at my tears," the reverend quoted, later adding, "...Lord, thou hast been our refuge from one generation to another."

Salina glanced down at little Ethan Jeremy, the first of the next generation of the Hastings family. The child within her would join him as part of that next generation. They would *never* have cause to look over their shoulder for any harm dealt against them by John Barnes, not ever again.

"...So teach us to number our days," the reverend went on, "that we may apply our hearts unto wisdom. Glory be to the Father, and to the Son, and to the Holy Ghost; as it was in the beginning is now and ever shall be, world without end. Amen."

"Amen," Salina's voice echoed with the others present.

The pine coffin containing Taylor Sue's remains was lowered into the freshly dug grave. Salina jerked involuntarily as each shovelful of earth landed to cover it up. In a wavering voice, she sang a song of faith that had been a favorite of Taylor Sue's:

> *Oh, when shall I see Jesus and reign with*
> *   Him above*
> *And shall hear the trumpet sound in that*
> *   morning*
> *And from the flowing fountain drink everlast-*
> *ing   love*
> *And shall hear the trumpet sound in that*
> *   morning.*
>
> *Shout, Oh Glory! For I shall mount above the*
> *   skies*
> *When I hear the trumpet sound in that morning.*
>
> *His promises are faithful, a righteous crown*
> *   He'll give*
> *And shall hear the trumpet sound in that*
> *   morning*
> *And all His valiant soldiers eternally shall live*
> *And shall hear the trumpet sound in that*
> *   morning.*

Shout, Oh Glory! For I shall mount above the
     skies
When I hear the trumpet sound in that morning.

The mourners turned to walk back up the hill toward the iron gates at the cemetery entrance, but Salina lingered at Taylor Sue's graveside. She held E.J., bundled warmly in his blankets. With firm resolve she repeated her vows to love and care for him.

"He'll be a fine boy, Taylor Sue," Salina whispered fervently as the undertaker worked to refill the six-foot-deep hole. "A very fine boy." She dabbed her cheeks with her handkerchief. No words could convey what she felt knowing that Taylor Sue had courageously died in her place. "I don't clearly understand why God has taken you from us, why your son has been robbed of his mother, and your husband of his beloved wife. I know in my heart that His ways are higher than ours, and I know that from where we stand, we do not see the entirety of His perfect will. I have yet to send a telegram to Ethan, and I don't pretend to know what I can say to ease the blow. I can only hope it will reach him at all at Point Lookout. I fear you spoke the truth when you said he will not understand any better than I, but I will continue to pray that neither of us shall grow resentful, that we will have the capacity to accept that which we cannot comprehend. We are weak, but He is strong. We have need to rely on Him and the strength He provides more than ever."

Salina wiped away another tear, sniffing to keep her nose from running. "Good-bye, my friend."

Chapter Thirteen

*R*idge looked awful, almost as if he were already a corpse. The slight rise and fall of his chest indicated that he was still breathing of his own accord.

Salina covered her nose and mouth with a handkerchief to avoid breathing the tainted air in the quarantine tent. Her eyes filled with compassion for her husband's uncle, whose sickly pallor glistened with fever-induced sweat. The bite marks on his arms were inflamed and oozing with pus; Salina correctly speculated that Ridge's legs bore similar lacerations, equally discolored.

"Rose..." The name was emitted in a strangled voice from Ridge's dry and cracked lips. "Rose..."

Salina squeezed Ridge's hand, then exited the tent, clearly distressed.

"There, there, Miss Salina," Captain Sally Tompkins offered compassionately. "Come to my office. I imagine this must be quite a shock to you."

Salina obediently followed the hospital administrator to the small room where her meticulous records and files were kept. Captain Sally had a good measure of success here. With just fewer than two dozen beds, the limited number of patients allowed exceptional care and reduced the death rate dramatically. It was encouraging to know that Ridge would receive the best possible treatment, and Salina's hope in his living through this quandary increased, albeit remotely.

Captain Sally dispensed a drink of cool water to revive Salina. "The orderly I sent over came back with the news of the death in your family. I was most sorry to learn of it."

Salina nodded, returning the glass empty. "The mourning wreath on the front door now represents two lives lost." Her glance traveled out the office window and fixed on the quarantine tent. "I pray it will not serve to represent a third."

"Dr. Garret will do all he can," Captain Sally assured Salina, "but you have seen how it is with him."

"Please, Captain Sally. How did Ridge come to be here?" Salina inquired. "Who brought him?"

"Two of the new guards and one of the medics from Libby Prison delivered him to us," Captain Sally answered. "Do you know this man well? This Colonel E.S. Ridgeford?"

"I don't claim to know him well, but I know of him," Salina admitted. "We are acquainted."

"You were aware he was a prisoner at Libby."

Salina weighed the plausibility of confiding in Captain Sally. In the end she concluded that the little lady would prove trustworthy and would honor a patient's confidentiality. "His name is not E.S. Ridgeford, nor is he a Federal officer. His true name is Eldridge Southerland. I am related to him by marriage on my husband's side. Ridge was not actually a prisoner at Libby—he was inside on an undercover mission for the Confederate Secret Service. The project was a gamble from the start, but apparently he had sufficient reason to believe that by infiltrating in the guise of a prisoner, he might entrap a contact involved with a Union-based spy ring operating here in Richmond."

Captain Sally's expression disclosed her initial surprise, but it faded quickly. "No wonder..."

"No wonder what?"

"Let me go back to the beginning and tell you what I know of the situation," Captain Sally offered. "The morning following the prison break, Colonel Ridgeford, as he was known, missed roll call.

He was missed again the next day. It was thought by some that he had made a successful escape—until the prison authorities were making a thorough search of the cellars. Shortly before they happened upon the entrance to the tunnel dug by the Union prisoners, they discovered your colonel unconscious. He'd been lying in the filth in one of the cellars for a good long while, certainly long enough for the infection to pervade his system. He's most fortunate that they found him when they did. Exposure might have finished him off for good if the blood poisoning didn't.

"Your colonel apparently had a Rebel contact of his own inside the prison, someone who knew he was *not* the Federal officer he was posing as. When the situation was fully revealed to Captain Turner, he deemed it appropriate to have Mr. Southerland sent here to see if any help could be given, or at the very least make him as comfortable as possible until..."

"He's not going to die," Salina declared with determination. "I have witnessed his stubborn nature. If he's got any fight left in him, he'll lick this."

Captain Sally did not contradict Salina's statement. She continued instead with her narrative. "Captain Turner, to maintain the guise, made it appear as if Colonel E.S. Ridgeford had died there in prison. The colonel was taken out through the dead house in a ventilated coffin, put on a wagon, and secretly brought here before first light this morning. Thankfully, Dr. Garret was here at that time, and he took charge of the situation. The medic explained to Dr. Garret and me that while the man was clothed in Union garb, he was in fact a Rebel and required immediate attention. The medic also mentioned that all his mumblings were wholly unintelligible except for the name of Rose, which he repeats over and over. Do you know who Rose is? A sister? A sweetheart? Or his mother, perhaps?"

Salina shook her dark head, calling to memory the destroyed pages of the Southerland dossier: To the best of her recollection his sisters, both deceased, were *Martha* and *Maida*; his mother, *Marietta*. Damaris Cobb was probably the nearest thing Ridge might have had to a sweetheart. "I have no idea who Rose might be—but I heard him call the name myself, even in the few minutes I stood at his bedside. Odd..."

"Yes, very odd," Captain Sally agreed. "Delirium can do strange things to a man's mind."

"That's the truth," Salina nodded. "Dr. Garret has quarantined him—is Ridge contagious?"

"Dr. Garret feels it best to keep him away from the other patients in the event that he is, but a clear diagnosis has not yet been determined. Fresh air will probably be beneficial for him. We needed you to make a positive identification, but in the event that he is contagious, I would advise you not to stay too long near him, not in your condition."

Salina nodded reluctantly. "You will keep me posted as to his progress?"

"But of course," Captain Sally assured Salina. "You've had a difficult day, my dear. Go home and rest if you can. We'll see to your Ridge Southerland."

As Salina was leaving the hospital, she passed A.Y.P. Garret, Robertson Hospital's chief surgeon. "Thank you for coming, Miss Salina. Your verification of who our latest patient is has been noted. We will do all in our power to care for him as best we can and leave the rest to Providence."

Salina appreciated the surgeon's optimism, even if it was restrained.

"When he was found, he was clutching this." Dr. Garret handed a bent *carte-de-visite* to Salina.

Salina stared at a sepia-toned portrait of none other than Damaris Cobb. "If you're going to ask me if this is the mysterious *Rose*, I'm sorry to disappoint you. I know this lady; her name is not Rose."

If Dr. Garret viewed it peculiar that the man would carry a picture of one lady yet call out for another, he was discreet enough not to make an issue of it. The surgeon scratched his head. "Well, again, I thank you for coming to identify him. I'm sure Captain Sally has already guaranteed that we will keep you apprised of his case."

After bidding the doctor good day, Salina made a decision: She still had to compose a message to Ethan—and she would send one on to the Cobbs as well.

☆☆☆☆☆☆☆

"Twenty-six, twenty-seven, twenty-eight, twenty-nine, thirty." Salina checked her count twice over. There were indeed sixty double-heeled socks in the batch. She wrapped the socks in brown paper and dispatched Jennilee to deliver them to Mildred Lee so that they could be sent to General Lee's encampment. "Please convey my compliments to Miss Mildred and let her know that I will forward another batch as soon as I can finish them."

"I'll be sure to tell her," Jennilee nodded. "Are you going to the hospital today?"

"Yes, but not until you return," Salina assured her. By mutual consent, they had endeavored not to leave Mrs. Carey at home alone. Since the day of Taylor Sue's funeral, Mrs. Carey adamantly refused to leave her room, and she had been insistent that E.J.'s cradle and layette be transferred into her chamber. She hardly let the boy out of her sight, though she often forgot to do things like change his diaper or feed him.

Jennilee brought back to Salina Mildred Lee's sincere thanks, an invitation to call and knit whenever she felt up to socializing, and a report of a new occupant in the home the Lees called "The Mess."

"Mildred decided a pet was needed for diversion, and she found a squirrel, which they've named Custis Morgan—*Custis* for her brother, and *Morgan* for the general," Jennilee explained. "He's usually into all sorts of mischief, and if he doesn't stop biting at strangers, he's quite liable to end up in squirrel stew!"

Salina could well appreciate the longed-for respite that any distraction could supply. Even the most minute details could make the war and the mourning retreat for a few cherished moments.

"We're to have a new occupant here, too, Jennilee," Salina informed her. "Come to the sitting room. I want you to meet Damaris Cobb and her brother Brisco."

Jennilee performed a perfect curtsey and gave a pleasant showing of the manners she diligently studied at Mrs. Pegram's. She made no objection whatsoever to taking Damaris in. "The more the merrier, isn't that what they say?"

"I issued the invitation without consulting you first, Jennilee, but I shouldn't have. This is your home, and I am a guest of your family," Salina amended.

"But you're the responsible one, Salina," Jennilee acknowledged. "You keep us all in line. I trust your judgment. You are more than welcome to stay here in Richmond with us, Miss Cobb."

"Thank you," Damaris nodded to Jennilee.

"My sister and I are indebted to you for your kindness, Miss Carey," Brisco bowed.

Jennilee flushed under Brisco's courteous attention. "Goodness, but doesn't that make me sound all grown up! Miss Carey, indeed."

For a brief instant the room was filled with long-absent laughter, music to their weary souls.

"I'm going to take Damaris and Brisco with me to the hospital so they can see Ridge," Salina told Jennilee. "That's why they've come, in response to the telegram I sent."

Jennilee nodded. "I do hope he's faring better today." She swallowed, for she had heard from Salina how bad off the undercover colonel was. "I'll get supper started while you're gone."

"E.J. is with your mama," Salina mentioned, slipping her arms into the coat Brisco held for her. "He's probably due for a diaper change."

"I'll check on him," Jennilee smiled, heading toward the staircase.

"E.J.?" Brisco inquired.

"Ethan Jeremy—my brother's son. Taylor Sue gave birth to him shortly before she died." Salina took a deep breath and added, "He's another of my responsibilities, though quite an adorable one. Looking after him is giving me practice for when my own child is delivered."

"I should say so," Damaris smiled empathetically. "I know all about seeing to the little ones. I've helped Mum look after all of my younger siblings for years. Count me willing to assist in any way you see fit."

"I'm glad you've both come," Salina nodded to each of the Cobbs. "I didn't know what else to do, and I know that you both are his friends. If there was ever a time that Ridge needed help from anyone in his life, now would be it."

"You say the doctor is doing all he can," Brisco affirmed.

"Is he any better?" Damaris wanted to know. "Your telegram didn't sound altogether encouraging."

Salina lowered her eyes. "Well, he's no worse."

"Which means he's no better either," Brisco determined. "What else can you tell us? What should we expect when we get there?"

On the walk to Robertson Hospital, Salina briefed the Cobbs. She led them through the indoor wards and out the rear door to the quarantine tent. Ridge was still delirious, and he still repeatedly called the name of Rose.

Damaris visibly bristled, a spark of jealousy indicative of the fact that she had *some* feeling for this self-proclaimed scoundrel— though she'd tried unsuccessfully to banish him from her heart. "Oh, Ridge..."

"If it's any consolation to you, Damaris, they found him clutching your likeness in his hand." Salina returned the photograph to its original owner.

"Then who is Rose?" Brisco wondered aloud.

Salina shrugged. "That would seem to be the mystery. Until he fully wakes up and can tell us, we may never learn who Rose is or what happened to him there in Libby."

Brisco shook his head. He couldn't imagine what Ridge had been thinking when he pulled a stunt like this. Whatever it was, it had to have been important to him. Ridge had performed a number of Secret Service–related deeds for money, but he never went through with them without conviction to back him up. "We'll stay with him for a bit," Brisco told Salina. "You don't have to wait on us. We'll be back in time for supper."

"I'll go read to the men while I wait for you," Salina suggested.

"Very well," Brisco agreed.

In spite of the dread that traveled the length of her spine, Salina kept reading the newspaper: The report claimed that over half of the prison break escapees had been rounded up and returned to confinement, but the remainder—save for two who had drowned—had managed to clear the sentries and get through to the safety of the Union lines. The man responsible for coordinating the planning and digging of the route out of Libby was Colonel Thomas E. Rose of the 77th Pennsylvania Volunteers. Colonel Rose hadn't been among those to reach refuge after crawling through the tunnel to freedom. He'd been recaptured and was once more incarcerated at Libby.

Then it dawned on Salina. "Colonel *Rose!*" She muttered the name aloud, engulfed by a sickening wash of realization. She headed directly for the quarantine tent. "Brisco!" She shoved the newspaper at him. "It's right here—I know what he's saying: Ridge knew who dug the tunnel. He was trying to tell someone that Colonel Rose was the instigator."

Brisco scanned the article. "So he'd found what he went in for. And he'll pay for it with his life."

"Don't say that!" Damaris adamantly countered. She couldn't deny that the understanding of Ridge's cryptic message came too late to be of use to anyone, but she wouldn't write him off just yet. She had paid attention to the way Salina had poured her heart and soul into Jeremy's convalescence when he was shaking his dependency to laudanum, and Damaris silently vowed to apply the same passionate devotion to seeing Ridge through his immediate troubles.

Further articles stated that Captain Turner, the prison commandant, had accused his own guards of taking bribes from the incarcerated Yankee officers. As punishment for allowing one hundred nine Union men to gain their freedom in the very heart of the Confederate capital, Turner had ordered the Rebel guardsmen thrown into Castle Thunder without the benefit of a court-martial. One of the lower rooms in the basement of the prison was reportedly filled with blasting powder. If another escape was attempted by the Northern inmates, the Rebels swore they'd blow them all to kingdom come.

The liberated Federal officers, men who considered themselves miraculously fortunate in having made good on their escape, went back to their people and spun horrific tales of the horrendous conditions they'd been subject to. The North, in a cry of outrage, demanded that some sort of action be taken.

If the indignance produced by the outrage were enough to reestablish a more organized rate of prisoner exchange, Salina mused, *perhaps there would be a viable hope that Ethan would be included in the cartel. If... Perhaps... Hope...* Nothing was certain, and there had been no word from Dr. Shields to convey any results of Dr. McGuire's efforts on Ethan's behalf.

☆☆☆☆☆☆☆

Every evening of the following week was spent in revived discussions of the plans still being constructed with regard to the Powder Works in California. Brisco had assumed responsibility for the campaign himself, as he was unsure as to whether or not Ridge would be able to pick up where he'd left off.

Brisco wasn't particularly fond of the idea, but somewhere along the line, he realized that his sister would make a suitable replacement to fill the hole Salina created when she had abdicated her role in the Remnant. Mum had agreed with him, for they both knew another link was imperative to the forthcoming operations, what with Ridge out of action—and so Brisco decided it was time to broach the subject with the ladies.

Salina readily agreed to tutor Damaris in ciphering and codes. She labored to recall everything she'd been taught, every scrap of detail she could from the failed campaign of November 1862 that might assist Brisco in his endeavors at another attempt. "Dr. Nichols and Hank Warner are personally acquainted with some of the Western contacts," Salina reconfirmed. "Jeremy was involved to a degree, but Reverend Yates, at Fairfax Court House, might have more extensive knowledge of the operations than either Jeremy or I have. Reverend Yates, as well as Tabitha Wheeler, worked with my daddy before either of us was brought into the Network."

"I'll be sure to stop off and see them before I head west, then." Brisco made a mental note of it.

"And when are you going to take me with you?" Damaris wanted to know.

"Not this time, Damaris. There's still too much groundwork to be laid. You stay here: Look after Ridge until... Look after him and learn all you can from Salina."

"When will you be leaving?" Salina inquired.

"Right now."

"But..." Damaris and Salina objected.

"There's no point in my staying around here doing nothing. It's time for me to move on." Brisco scribbled an address of where to send word to him should Ridge's condition change. He pulled Salina aside. "I need you to do something for me. This was found in Ridge's coat pocket; Captain Sally gave it to me." Brisco handed Salina Justine's signed affidavit, the written proof that Jeremy was Evan Southerland's son. "You hold on to that. There may come a time when you'll need it."

☆☆☆☆☆☆☆

Not only had January seemed to take forever, but February of 1864 had *twenty-nine* days in it—and the elongated month came to an end much like it had begun: with the ominous toll resounding from the bell tower in Capitol Square.

March came in like the proverbial lion, the beastly roar attributed to an unexpected and virtually unchecked raid of Union cavalry with the city of Richmond as its target, bent on liberating prisoners held at Libby and on Belle Isle in the James River.

Telegraph wires were cut, demonstrations and maneuvers enacted to detain the forces on General Lee's left and to occupy the Southern cavalry away from the capital. Four thousand Union horsemen under Brigadier General Judson Kilpatrick had ridden southward for over twelve hours before the Rebels were aware that the Federals were on the attack. Twenty-one-year-old Colonel Ulric Dahlgren, with five hundred horsemen, split off from the main body and crossed the James, swinging downstream to destroy railroad tracks, burn buildings, and lay waste to acre upon acre in Goochland County.

At one point, an ex-slave guided Dahlgren's detachment to a little-used ford on the James where they had intended to cross and summarily rejoin Kilpatrick's column. The heavy rains, however, had swelled the river so that the ford was impassable. Dahlgren believed the former slave had deceived him, and in his wrath ordered the black man hung.

Pressing on without crossing the swollen river, Dahlgren still hoped to use speed and surprise to his advantage. Hearing cannon fire led him to incorrectly assume that Kilpatrick and his force had attacked ahead of schedule. Communication between the two Union commanders was considerably lacking, especially since the Rebels had captured Dahlgren's couriers, and Dahlgren had no way to know if the sounds of battle meant Kilpatrick's force was having any measure of success. Kilpatrick himself did not know that the defenders of Richmond were either boys too young or men too old to enlist with the regulars; furloughed officers; and home guard units consisting of workers from the armory, the arsenal, and Tredegar Iron Works. The stouthearted militia put up such a brave fight that they had the Yankees convinced they had run into nothing less than veteran infantry reinforcements. Without verification as to Kilpatrick's progress or position, Dahlgren elected to wait until dark before launching his attack on the outer ring of Richmond's defenses.

Using that same darkness to move the limited numbers of his gray cavalry, General Wade Hampton descended on Kilpatrick's troops, scattering them from warm bivouacs into the biting cold of a stinging snowstorm. Kilpatrick's cavalry fled down the peninsula to their own lines around Williamsburg and Yorktown.

Colonel Dahlgren had more distance to cover than Kilpatrick did to reach safety. He divided his detachment into even smaller segments, riding forward in the company of fewer than two hundred men. In King and Queen County, near Mantapike, the Confederates laid a trap. The ambush of Dahlgren's depleted force was swift: Dahlgren, an easy target at the front of his column, was killed almost immediately. The remaining Yankees under the dead colonel's command were surrounded and duly captured.

A thirteen-year-old boy found in the inner pockets of Dahlgren's overcoat a cigar case, some folded papers, and a memorandum notebook. On the second of March, the contents of the papers taken from Dahlgren's body were made known. Dahlgren had carried schedules, orders, and a disturbing address to his men:

> *You have been selected from brigades and regiments as a picked command to attempt a desperate undertaking—an undertaking which, if successful, will write your names on the hearts of your countrymen that can never be erased... Many of you may fall; but if there is any man here not willing to sacrifice his life in such*

> *a great and glorious undertaking, or who does not feel capable of meeting the enemy in such a desperate fight as will follow, let him step out, and he may go hence to the arms of his sweetheart, and read of the braves who swept through the city of Richmond... We hope to release the prisoners from Belle Isle first, and, having seen them fairly started, we will cross the James River into Richmond, destroying the bridges after us, and exhorting the released prisoners to destroy and burn the hateful city, and do not allow the Rebel leader, Davis, and his traitorous crew to escape... The bridges once secured, and the prisoners loose and over the river, the bridges will be secured and the city will be destroyed. The men must keep together and well in hand, and once in the city it must be destroyed, and Jeff Davis and his Cabinet killed.*

President Davis released the incendiary documents to the press for publication, stirring public opinion to a feverish peak. Dahlgren's orders, had they been achieved, would have been considered a violation of the laws governing civilized warfare. Once news of the Yankee plans were read by the residents of Richmond, a cry of outrage rose up demanding the execution of the captured Union raiders. High-ranking Confederate officials initially agreed with the suggestion, adamant about sending a clear message to the North. President Davis resisted these measures, however, and cooler heads, backed by General Lee, prevailed. The general's son Rooney was still a prisoner at Fort Lafayette; any retaliatory acts on the part of the Rebels might incite Northerners to harm Southern men incarcerated in Union prisons. The Union raiders were not put to death but were instead locked away in Libby—alongside the men they had set out to free.

The raid on the Confederate capital was a sobering affair that soured any hope of a remote chance that peace might come in the spring. The Dahlgren papers became a topic of bitter controversy. Union officials, of course, denied their validity, claiming them to be forgeries. Incensed Southerners elected to believe otherwise. When the dust settled, what truth remained was that the Dahlgren-Kilpatrick mission had failed and Richmond had again been preserved.

Chapter Fourteen

March 8, 1864
Washington, D.C.

"*A*unt Annelise?"

"In here, Lottie." Annelise Grant sat at the vanity mirror while Jubilee wove her auburn tresses into a loose braid, tucking the ribboned end underneath at the nape of her neck. A topaz necklace and matching earbobs sparkled in the gaslight. The dark-gold brocade gown trimmed with velvet accents was stunning in its simplicity— off the shoulder, narrow at the waist, supported by stiff petticoats and a wide hoop skirt. As Jubilee put the finishing touches on her coiffure, Annelise tugged on a pair of long gold satin gloves. "Don't you look nice," Annelise complimented her niece.

"It's a Worth design—Lance picked it out himself." Lottie held out the skirt of her gown. "Can you imagine? Had we been invited to a reception in Richmond instead of here in Washington, I wager we'd be wearing our best homespun instead of glorious frocks like these!"

Guilt pricked Annelise's poise; she felt chagrined for decking herself out in such finery, and as they often did, her thoughts centered on her daughter behind Rebel lines and her son in a Northern prison camp. Tonight, however, was an important occasion for her husband, and she could not shame him by looking anything less than her loveliest. As the wife of Major Duncan Grant, Annelise would inevitably be introduced to a number of notable personages in Washington at the Lincolns' reception, and therefore she once again banished her inherent Southern nature to the bottom of her heart.

If the rumors were to be believed, one of the attendees at the reception might well be General Ulysses S. Grant, who had come to the Northern capital for the express purpose of accepting his promotion to the newly reinstated rank of lieutenant general of all Union forces. No officer since George Washington had held so high a command. Grant would now report to the President directly.

Morning, noon, and night Annelise prayed that God would find a way to end this hateful war. With a shudder, she pondered as to whether or not the answer to those prayers had taken the shape of General Grant. Grant was a hero, what with his most recent victories at Vicksburg and Chattanooga. His tenacity in the Western Theatre of operations had merited the attention of the President. In the wake of the Battle of Shiloh, Lincoln had stated, "I can't spare this man; he fights."

And the fighting was what Annelise feared most of all. She prayed daily that the Lord would spare Duncan's life, for she did not want to be made a widow a second time.

"Mmm-mmmmm," the low appreciative sound came from over Annelise's bare left shoulder. Annelise looked up, startled. Duncan's eyes traveled over every inch of the fetching picture she made in the looking glass. "I daresay, in that getup, you'll be the belle of the ball, Mrs. Grant."

A smile formed on her lips, but it didn't reach her eyes. Duncan's phrasing again made her think of Salina, and of balls, barbecues, and parties past. "You're kind to say so, sir."

Duncan was spit shined and polished, pressed and starched in his dress uniform. His wife's gown was complement to his formal military attire. "What's the matter, dear?"

Annelise made a better effort at a genuine smile. "I've merely been thinking about a hundred things, some more melancholy than merry."

Duncan paused. Perhaps now was not the right time to tell her of the latest word he'd received from Point Lookout. No, he decided. After the reception would be soon enough to break her heart.

☆☆☆☆☆☆☆

The congealed crowd in the East Room of the White House was thicker than usual. Speculation buzzed amid the circles of attendees who waited to see whether U.S. Grant would make an appearance. The man was a bit late in showing up for the festivities, but he did eventually arrive, flanked by two of his staff officers.

General Grant's presence halted the flurry of whispers, and an expectant silence flooded the reception hall.

"Why, here is General Grant! Well, this is a great pleasure!" President Lincoln greeted the celebrated warrior.

Annelise, like everyone else in the room, strained to catch a glimpse of General Grant, who was invariably swallowed up by the pressing throng eager to get a look at him. The general was not a tall man, rather nondescript, with his short brown hair and beard. Listening to those gossiping around her, Annelise had heard Grant called everything from a drunk to a savior, that he habitually smoked cigars, and that his wife, Julia, traveled in the company of a female slave whenever she joined Grant in headquarters or camp.

Everyone wanted to laud the "new Caesar" with praise and hail his exploits, and the curious stares of the overbearing masses became intense. Proper decorum was suspended when the general allowed himself to be persuaded to step up on a wobbly red velvet couch so that all could gawk at him.

A thunderous cheer erupted. Grant seemed to be embarrassed by the adulation, and he was soon standing on his own two feet again. The veritable parade of handshakes and introductions commenced, lasting for more than an hour. It was during that time that Annelise, at Duncan's side, was presented to the man. Annelise smiled politely, meeting General Grant's light-blue eyes without flinching, and laughed appropriately in response to some comment made about his and Duncan's sharing the same surname, though no relative connection could be determined.

Confidence exuded from him. Annelise thought with a shudder, *Here is a man who will not run from the challenge that has been laid at his door.* Was Grant the physical symbol of the beginning of the end?

☆☆☆☆☆☆☆

Duncan left the flat early, his presence required at the White House. Annelise was still upset: The combination of last evening's reception and Ethan's letter bearing the tragic news of Taylor Sue's death was the cause. Duncan was powerless to do anything but let her weep it out. Losing her daughter-in-law hit her hard, and her grief was not merely for her own loss but for her eldest son as well. Taylor Sue's demise overshadowed any rejoicing Annelise might have done upon learning that John Barnes was no longer a threat.

Abraham Lincoln officially bestowed the commission of lieutenant general upon U.S. Grant, but Duncan was so preoccupied with what was going on at home that he only half heard what Grant read—something he'd had the foresight to put down on paper prior to his arrival:

"With the aid of the noble armies that have fought in so many fields for our common country, it will be my earnest endeavor not to disappoint your expectations. I feel the full weight of the responsibilities now devolving on me..."

Following the brief acceptance speech, Duncan again shook the commanding general's hand and offered his services if they should ever be of some use to him.

"I'll keep that in mind, Major," Grant assured Duncan.

After the presentation, Duncan went back in his office at the War Department. A new idea had come across his desk, one that was still in the planning stages.

Secretary of War Edwin Stanton had been in correspondence with General Ben Butler, commander of the Department of Virginia and North Carolina. There had been discussion concerning the enlistment of prisoners from places such as Point Lookout—providing those prisoners would take the Oath of Allegiance to the Union.

Early in January, Lincoln's secretary, John Hay, had met with Butler, and they had devised a questionnaire. Duncan reread each inquiry point by point:

1. *Do you desire to be sent South as a prisoner of war for exchange?*
2. *Do you desire to take the oath of allegiance and parole and enlist in the Army or Navy of the U.S., and if so which?*
3. *Do you desire to take the oath and parole and be sent North to work on public works, under penalty of death if found in the South before the end of the war?*
4. *Do you desire to take the oath of allegiance and go to your home within the lines of the U.S. Army, under like penalty if found South beyond those lines during the war?*

Butler had since received permission to conduct an interrogation of eight thousand prisoners; the process would no doubt take some time.

Duncan reviewed the questions again. He shook his head and closed his eyes. He knew Garrett's son well enough to guess that he would not be an eager volunteer for such duty as this. Ethan would stubbornly remain incarcerated if he couldn't be properly exchanged; he would likely brave the hardships, the lack of food, clothing, and shelter, even the degrading and cruel conduct of the guards, before he'd sign his name to the Oath.

Balancing his elbows on his desk, Duncan lowered his head. His shoulders sagged as he sighed, "Garrett, old friend, I'm at my wit's end. I don't rightly know how to help your son anymore. I just don't know."

☆☆☆☆☆☆☆

March 13, 1864
Richmond, Virginia

"You're sure you wouldn't like me to go with you?" Damaris Cobb held a wicker basket packed with sandwiches, oranges, cookies, and a bottle of sarsaparilla.

Salina securely tucked E.J. into the pram, snug and warm beneath his blankets. She placed the basket of food along with her reticule in one corner, out of the baby boy's way.

"I appreciate the offer of your company, Damaris, but I'd really rather go myself," Salina answered with typical Hastings determination and a fair amount of optimism. She'd had no notification of whether Ethan would be among the exchanged prisoners to arrive in Richmond today, but she could hope. "If... *when* Ethan steps off that flag-of-truce boat, I want a chance to be alone with him. I am well aware that nothing I can say or do will ease his loss, but my hope is that seeing his son for the first time will be a tonic to alleviate some of his pain." She smiled at Damaris. "Time is the ultimate healer, they say—but it takes so very long to dull the heartache."

Damaris nodded her understanding. "I'll look forward to meeting your illustrious brother when you bring him home. Just you be careful. There's liable to be all sorts down at Rocketts Landing today."

Damaris's prediction had been accurate. It appeared that half of Richmond's population had trekked outside the city limits to gather at the Landing on the James River. Even before Salina reached Rocketts she heard the armory band playing Southern favorites like *The Bonnie Blue Flag, The Virginia Marsellaise,* and *Dixie.* Hers was by no means a solo voice singing the war-inspired lyrics set to the familiar minstrel tune:

> *Southrons, hear your country call you!*
> *Up, lest worse than death befall you!*
> *To arms! To arms! To arms! In Dixie!*
> *Lo! all the beacon fires are lighted—*
> *Let all hearts be now united!*
> *To arms! To arms! To arms! In Dixie!*
>
> *Here the Northern thunders mutter!*
> *Northern flags in South winds flutter!*
> *To arms! To arms! To arms! In Dixie!*
> *Send them back your fierce defiance!*
> *Stamp upon the cursed alliance!*
> *To arms! To arms! To arms! In Dixie!*
>
> *Halt not till our Federation*
> *Secures among earth's powers its station!*
> *To arms! To arms! To arms! In Dixie!*
> *Then at peace, and crowned with glory,*
> *Hear your children tell the story!*
> *To arms! To arms! To arms! In Dixie!*
>
> *Advance the flag of Dixie!*
> *Hurrah! Hurrah!*
> *For Dixie's Land we'll take our stand,*
> *And live or die for Dixie!*
> *To arms! To arms!*
> *And conquer peace for Dixie!*
> *To arms! To arms!*
> *And conquer peace for Dixie!*

The multitude gathered at the Landing did so in anticipation of the arrival of Confederate prisoners coming home from Fortress Lafayette, Monroe, and Point Lookout in exchange for Federals who had been held at Libby and Belle Isle. The City Guard had turned out. Ladies by the hundreds, like Salina, toted baskets and hampers of food and drink for the returning warriors. Salina steered the pram to a place where she would be able to see the steamer's approach.

The boat was very small on the river at first, growing larger by degrees until it became clear that there were *two* flag-of-truce boats, not just one. Salina's optimism soared—the chance that Ethan would be one of the men onboard increased a hundredfold. Male voices rang out over the water: *"Hurrah, hurrah, for Southern rights, hurrah!"* Salina's heart swelled with Virginia-bred Southern pride. These were the men who'd fought gallantly for the sake of duty, honor, and country—and had paid a hard price for independence. Patriotism flowed strong in her veins, and her hopes were buoyed.

Hats, handkerchiefs, and unfurled Confederate flags waved and fluttered. The returning prisoners lifted up three cheers for the good ladies of Richmond. Their faces, however, were still too distant to be recognizable.

Salina suddenly felt as if she were looking at the scene through a stereoscope and were not actually a part of the jubilation around her. In a vague way, the pageantry was reflective of the festivities prior to the Grand Review at Brandy Station last year. Hearty shouts sounded from the decks of the *William Allison* and the *A.H. Schultz*, and the crowd replied with resounding gusto.

"Miss Salina!"

Upon hearing her name, Salina turned away from the shore. "Hello, Mary, Mildred, Agnes!" She greeted each of General Lee's daughters.

"Is your brother coming home, too, then?" Agnes inquired.

"I received no official indication—but I can hope!" Salina's smile was timorous. "And yours?"

"Yes. Rooney is definitely supposed to be among the prisoners. He was formally exchanged for their General Neal Dow," Mildred explained.

Mary leaned over the side of the pram and tickled E.J.'s chin. "By the time we get Rooney home to The Mess with us, our father should be there, too."

The steamers were close enough now for the anxious Richmonders to identify the faces of the men onboard, and they to recognize those who had come to the docks to herald their return. A complete stillness fell as the first boat anchored; the crowd held its collective breath, consumed with palpable expectancy.

"There's Father!" A child's elated voice punctured the lull. "Mama, look! I see him! Father!"

Others along the riverside began pointing and waving to their own beloved ones. The soldiers disembarked down the gangplank, and the throng parted to make a lane for them.

Salina scrutinized the decks of the ships again, but by now they were emptied and the exchanged prisoners had been swallowed up by the waiting masses. Overwhelming disappointment descended, tightening like an iron band around her heart. Ethan had *not* been among the men returned from Point Lookout. Bitter tears collected in her emerald eyes, but she held them in check when she realized that there were others amid the assemblage whose countenances mirrored her own forlorn expression.

"Oh, Salina, I'm *so* sorry for you!" It was Mary Lee who noticed that Salina stood alone save for the baby in the pram. "He didn't come?"

"No." Salina forced herself to remain stoic. "But I'm pleased on behalf of your family today."

"May I present my brother to you?" Mary inquired.

Salina mustered her brightest smile. "I'd be honored to meet another General Lee."

Mary tugged on Rooney's gray sleeve and brought him over to where Salina stood.

"Ah, so you're Captain Barnes's wife." Rooney Lee, a large, bearded fellow, bowed over her hand. "It is a pleasure to make your acquaintance. The last time I saw your husband was during the fight at Brandy. He was crisscrossing that field with messages from one commander to another," the brigadier recalled. "Is he well?"

"Aye, he is by last report. Thank you for asking," Salina nodded. "Now that your wounds have healed and your freedom has been restored, will you be reporting back to General Stuart soon?"

Rooney's eyes contained an expression that reminded Salina profoundly of his father. "I don't know what I'm going to do just yet," he admitted candidly. "I'm not quite certain what options lie before me. All I know is that I would dearly enjoy a good meal, maybe a week in bed, and a clean change of clothes."

"I'm positive that your family has that and more in store for you," Salina replied. "Good day to you, General. And again, welcome home."

E.J. began to demonstrate his discontent, and Salina picked him up, blanket and all. She held him to her shoulder and firmly patted his back. "You're all right, darlin'. I'm sure you've just got a bubble." Her eyes continued to scan the crowd of faces. A hearty little burp sounded, but thankfully E.J. hadn't spit up on her.

The multitude at Rocketts thinned, then dwindled away. At last Salina abandoned the notion that Ethan had come but just hadn't found her yet. Settling E.J. back into the pram, she straightened and put a hand to the back of her waist, rubbing the momentary twinge away.

"Excuse me, ma'am?"

A bearded Confederate approached her with a battered kepi in his hand.

"Sir?"

"Forgive my boldness, ma'am, but you have a look about you," the Rebel soldier began. "You look a bit like Dr. Hastings, ma'am. Are you kin by chance?"

"Dr. Ethan Hastings?" Salina's hope was rekindled. "Is he here? Do you know where I might find him? I'm his sister; this baby is his son. Where is he?"

"Oh, he ain't here, ma'am, I'm sorry to say."

"He didn't come?"

"Not 'cause he didn't want to," the bearded man quickly replied. "The fact of the matter was that he was in the guard house when they went through the ranks to pick prisoners to be exchanged. You see, he got word saying as how his wife had passed on, and he just about went berserk. He'd already tried to escape once and got caught—this was his second offense. One night, I thought he might run right over the dead line, but something held him back, for none of us would have been able to talk him out of it had he really set his mind to go that way. Instead, he tried to swim out of the lagoon, but the guards caught him halfway to St. Mary's City. And that's the truth. I heard tell, just before we was put aboard the ship bound for City Point, that his punishment was to be sentenced to duty at the smallpox hospital. They say he didn't care a whit that he had to go work among the sick men; they say he didn't care about anything anymore, not after that letter came."

Salina couldn't keep the torrent of tears from spilling. "Smallpox hospital?" Her brother could get infected from the men he was supposed to treat. She thought of Sam Sweeney, Stuart's banjo player, dead of smallpox. "Dear God!"

The bearded soldier rubbed his jaw. "I'm terrible sorry to bring such bad news to you, ma'am, but when I saw you standing here, well, I thought you might be better off knowing for sure rather than wait in wonder."

Silently Salina nodded, fishing in her pocket for a handkerchief with which to dry her eyes and blow her nose.

"Ma'am?"

"Yes?"

"I can't say that I'd have done any different had I been in the doc's shoes," the bearded man admitted. "Trying to escape, I mean. He's not without courage, I'll say that for him." For a few minutes the Confederate said nothing, as if considering whether or not he should say any more, but finally he decided to go ahead. "This might be a small hope for you: I've heard of men getting out by faking their deaths and being carried out in coffins with holes in them. A good portion of the population in southern Maryland is pro-Confederate. If the doc did manage to somehow get free and get away, he'd find folks willing enough to help him."

"Sir, I do thank you for relaying this news to me." Salina's voice faltered for a moment, and she bit her lip. "I do thank you."

"You're most welcome, ma'am. I just wish it had been gladder tidings, that's all." The man replaced his kepi and was about to take his leave when Salina noticed that no one had welcomed him at the Landing.

"You haven't told me your name, sir," Salina pointed out. "To whom am I indebted for this information concerning my brother?"

"I'm Sergeant Andrew Lennox, ma'am. At your service."

"Mrs. Jeremy Barnes," she identified herself. "Have you no kin in town?"

"No, ma'am," the sergeant shook his head. "I don't hail from Virginia; I'm a North Carolinian by birth. I plan to get myself home to Charlotte on furlough to visit my sisters and my fiancée before I report back for duty. If you wouldn't mind pointing me toward the train depot in town, I'd be much obliged."

"All right," Salina agreed, "but only if you'll accept an invitation to have dinner with us. I live with Ethan's mother- and sister-in-law. I'm sure they, too, would want to hear whatever you could tell them of my brother. Would you do me the honor?"

Sergeant Lennox's stomach grumbled, as if on cue. A grateful grin brightened his features. "Don't mind if I do, ma'am."

Jennilee returned from church shortly after Salina had arrived home with Sergeant Lennox in tow. "There were *fourteen* generals at St. Paul's this morning!" the girl exclaimed. "They all came to give thanks for the hundreds of prisoners who've come home and to offer petitions of protection and provisions for the thousands still in the field. You missed a mighty powerful sermon, Salina. Where's Ethan?"

Sergeant Lennox stepped forward, relieving Salina from the duty of having to break the news to Ethan's sister-in-law. Then he filled the rest of the afternoon with embroidered tales of his association with a man he considered most brave.

True to her word, Salina provided the sergeant with directions to the depot along with a snack wrapped in a red bandanna. She pressed a half-eagle coin into the palm of his hand.

Sergeant Lennox stared incredulously at the five-dollar gold piece with its classic head and coronet imprint. "Mrs. Barnes, I cannot deprive you of such when you obviously got your own expenses to look after. Times is hard, and they're gonna get worse before they get better."

"It's a small token to make sure you get home." Salina would brook no further argument. "See that it's used for such, and give thanks to the Lord for it. He is faithful, and He continually provides."

"Amen," Sergeant Lennox replied.

At dusk Salina stood on the stoop and watched the sergeant depart, his gray uniform quickly dissolving into the lengthening shadows. She would have liked to persuade him to stay to supper so they could hear more of his stories—which, of course, were whitewashed for their "delicate sensibilities." But Andrew Lennox was eager to travel on to Charlotte, and Salina couldn't blame him for wanting to be on his way. Silently she prayed: *Lord God, my dear, dashing brother seemingly has landed himself in quite a fix. Please, rescue him, by whatever means You see fit. I know You can work in ways beyond our limited comprehension. I'm not pretending to understand the whys   begging for answers that do not come is pointless. I am in want of the strength to accept what I can do nothing about. Be with Ethan. Let him know without doubt You are continually with him and will not forsake him. Don't allow his determination to wane, or it will become his undoing. I couldn't bear that—I just couldn't!*

☆☆☆☆☆☆☆

Cavalry Headquarters
Near Orange Court House, Virginia

"Isn't she here?"

"No, Captain," Kidd Carney shook his head. "But this message came for you. It's from her."

Jeremy almost snatched the missive from Carney's hand. Fear that something dreadful had happened to Salina gripped him as his anxious eyes scanned the lines.

> *My darling,*
>
> *I regret that I am not already with you in camp, but I've had a little accident and Flora Stuart has insisted that the Fontaines would not mind putting me up for the night at their home near Beaver Dam Station. I feel embarrassed, really, over such a silly thing as a fall. I've been so awkward lately, clumsy and quite absent-minded. Flora tells me that this is not unusual for women in my condition, but there are days when I simply don't feel like myself. She assures me it will pass. I missed a stair while climbing aboard the train at the Beaver Dam Station. I just didn't see it, or wasn't paying close enough attention. My foot got tangled in the hem of my skirt, and... well, I won't elaborate. I'm sure you possess enough imagination to conclude that in that moment I certainly wasn't a picture of grace or refinement. Rest assured, I've done no harm to myself, save for bruising my pride, and I will continue the journey to Orange in the morning. In the meantime, dream of me—in the shape and form I used to be—and I will be with you shortly.*
>
> *All my love to my own Horse Soldier,*
>
> > > *Your darling,*
> > > *Salina*

Carney looked askance at Jeremy's furrowed brow. "Everything in order?"

"She's safe, with the general's wife at the home of Dr. Fontaine's family." Jeremy exhaled the pent-up breath he'd been holding. "She'll be here in the morning." Relief and disappointment played a duel across his rugged features. Then his face brightened. "I'll make you a deal, Carney: I'll take your picket duty tonight if you'll cover for me tomorrow night."

"Consider it done," Kidd Carney instantly agreed to the terms.

Jeremy wheeled Tucker away from the depot platform, directing the war horse back to cavalry headquarters. He knew precicely why

Kidd Carney had resolved to swap picket duty assignments: Miss Hollis was still quartered in Orange. Jeremy rode out of town whistling *Jine the Cavalry.*

☆☆☆☆☆☆☆

Colonel and Mrs. Edmund Fontaine, owners of Beaver Dam, were kind and gracious hosts, and Flora Stuart was an attentive companion to Salina, who spent nearly an hour after supper entertaining little Virginia Pelham Stuart. Salina even offered her assistance in changing the little girl's diaper when needed.

"Seems to me like you've got that drill down," Flora commented lightly.

"You forget, I have a little brother not yet a year old, and since E.J.'s arrival, I've been getting all the rehearsal I need for my motherly responsibilities." She paused, only then realizing how much she missed the dark-haired, blue-eyed little boy. "It really tore at me when it came time to leave my brother's son in Richmond," Salina confessed. "But Mrs. Carey, Taylor Sue's mama, wouldn't allow me to bring him to meet Jeremy."

Flora had heard of E.J.'s birth and Taylor Sue's death from Maria Brewer, her sister. She said somberly, "These past few weeks haven't been easy ones for you."

"No, they haven't," Salina answered honestly. "The Lord has promised that He will not give us more than we can bear. He knew I needed a respite, a chance to renew my strength. Mrs. Gillette's invitation to visit Orange couldn't have come at a more welcome time."

Flora's son Jimmie, a lad not yet four, entreated Salina to read him a story, and Salina happily complied. Jimmie was the type of boy with more energy than his body knew what to do with, and it was almost as though he feared falling asleep lest he should miss the slightest bit of action around him.

"He wears me out some days," Flora admitted when she finally had her sleepy little son tucked into bed. "He can be a handful." She settled herself into the rocking chair with five-month-old Virginia in her arms.

The two ladies talked well into the night. Salina put some delicate questions to Flora concerning childbirth and child rearing— things she might have discussed with Mamma had she been on hand for the approach of Salina's forthcoming confinement. Flora was gracious and compassionate in sharing of her experiences, especially since she'd given birth to three children of her own.

Salina listened intently to the words of General Stuart's wife, making mental notes and gleaning wisdom. Salina had already assisted Dr. Brewer with E.J.'s delivery and had witnessed the birthing firsthand. Fear often stems from that which is unknown, and Salina was determined to be prepared instead of unaware concerning the ordeal ahead.

"Unfortunately, my husband has never been with me when his children have been born. When Little Flora came, he was off fighting Indians in Kansas; same with Jimmie. When Virginia was born, he was off fighting then as well. She came shortly before the action at Bristoe," Flora added wistfully. "It was Yankees he was fighting this time, though, not frontier Indians. And duty prevented him from coming to me when Little Flora took ill in Lynchburg. That's where she died and is buried."

Salina murmured a soft condolence.

"I'm sorry," Flora hastened to apologize, dismissing her reminiscences. "I'm turning into poor company, forgive me."

"On the contrary," Salina argued. "You've taught me a good deal."

Flora smiled at her young friend. "I secured the invitation for you to stay here at Beaver Dam so that you might get some rest after your fall, yet here I am keeping you from obtaining a decent night's sleep. It is refreshing, however, to talk with someone like you who has an understanding."

"I do appreciate your kindness on my behalf," Salina smiled in return, "as well as that of the Fontaines."

Flora ushered Salina to a spare guest room. Salina found the room lovely, with a clear view of the lane leading up to the main house. "Good night, sleep tight."

Moments after Flora had taken her leave, a sharp stab of pain struck Salina, low and across her back, very nearly robbing her of breath. Salina sat down quickly in the nearest chair to combat the sudden rush of dizziness. When the pain dissipated, a drink of cool water from the pitcher at the commode made her feel somewhat better.

Unable to sleep, Salina lingered near the window. The moonlight pierced through the trees, and she could almost imagine the lone figure of a man with a plumed hat astride a horse trotting toward the columned porch of the two-story brick mansion. The image then blended into the night, disappearing. The gooseflesh prickled Salina's forearms as she hastily drew the drapes closed. Shivering unexpectedly, Salina was unable to discern as to whether the figure in her vision had been that of Stuart—or of Jeremy.

Chapter Fifteen

$\mathcal{A}$s the train came to a halt at the depot platform, Jeremy craned his neck to catch a glimpse of each passing window. He couldn't see Salina's face in any of them. This was the first train of the morning, though, he inwardly mused. The next was not due in from Gordonsville for hours. Passengers disembarked, cluttering the platform, and Jeremy could not locate his wife in the bustling crowd.

He felt a slight jab at his ribcage. He looked down to check on what he'd made contact with, but there was nothing, no one, there. When he turned back around, Salina stood before him, grinning impishly. "Good day to you, Captain."

Jeremy shook his sandy head. "Aye, Mrs. Barnes, it is indeed a good day!" He enveloped her in his arms and planted a quick kiss on her forehead. "You all right?"

"Yes," she answered, flushing under his close scrutiny.

"Come on, then." He took her gloved hand within his and led her through the crush of people. Tucker stood at the ready, and another mount was tethered at the hitching post beside him. "This is Josephine," Jeremy made the introductions. "Gentlest mare I've ever ridden. She'll take good care of you," he told Salina as he assisted her up into the sidesaddle. "Comfortable?"

"Yes, quite," Salina assured her husband. "Please don't forget my satchel."

"I'll see to it." Jeremy arranged with a porter to have her bag delivered to the home of Mrs. Isaac Gillette. He then explained to Salina, "We're having supper this evening at Mrs. Gillette's—and I've promised Rosalynde and Salome each a game of checkers—but the day is ours, and I've a surprise for you."

The pair of horses left Orange Court House at a leisurely walk. "Where are you taking me?" Salina wondered.

"You'll see," Jeremy grinned, but the expression was short-lived. He hadn't wanted to begin their time together with bad news, but he'd rather get it said and done. "Dr. McGuire drafted a letter of endorsement on your brother's behalf. Dr. Shields detailed a courier to take that endorsement through the lines under a flag of truce. The courier, however, was later found shot dead by the Yankees, having never made it to the lines, let alone through them. The McGuire letter was among the effects reported missing; it never made it to Duncan. Ethan is still a prisoner."

"I know," Salina nodded sadly. She shared what Sergeant Lennox had told her of her brother's ill-fated attempts to escape the confines of Point Lookout. "Lennox implied that Taylor Sue's death has left Ethan without a care for himself."

Jeremy's heart ached, for he'd loved his sister-in-law dearly. Taylor Sue had been a friend to him as well as to Salina, and her steady influence in their lives would be missed. But the ache was for Ethan, too. Jeremy couldn't imagine how he would feel himself if something happened to rob him of Salina. She was so much a part of him.

"What? Why are you looking at me like that?" she asked, trying to read the turbulent thoughts behind the leather patch and the intense expression in his sapphire eye.

"I love you, Sallie," he blurted out. "More than you know."

"I do know, though. You show me with your deeds; you wax poetic in the lines of your letters. Your descriptions and impressions of the things around you are vividly moving—your words describe the spirit of your feelings for me," she whispered. "I love you, too, Jeremy." She smiled brightly. "Now, what's my surprise?"

His lopsided grin reappeared. "Ah, that would be telling." A playful light shone in his good eye. "Come on. We've got another mile to go before we reach camp."

"Is General Stuart at headquarters?" Salina queried as they continued down the Old Plank Road, away from Orange, through the open, rolling fields toward a narrow valley studded with cedar and pine trees.

"Nope," Jeremy answered. "He's been away to Fredericksburg these past days on military business. Just a few of the staff went with him. He left me with orders to stay here."

"I've got a letter for him from Flora." Salina patted her pocket.

"Then upon his return, we'll see that the general gets his mail. He's due back tomorrow, I think."

The winter quarters belonging to the Cavalry branch of the Army of Northern Virginia were smaller than Salina had envisioned, until she recalled that a good portion of the troopers had been disbanded to go home and acquire fresh horses. "Jeremy?"

"Yeah, darlin'?"

Leaning forward slightly to caress the horse's neck, Salina's curiosity got the better of her. "Is Josephine one of the horses you brought back from Maryland?"

"Aye," he answered briskly, but he said no more. Instead he raised an arm with a sweeping gesture that encompassed the entire encampment and quipped, "Welcome to Camp Wigwam."

Before her was a neat, well laid-out collection of canvas tents and semipermanent structures. "Over there," Jeremy pointed, "are the couriers and escorts. My men and I have ours tucked back a little farther, in a nice cozy niche among the trees, near enough to be found when needed. That one up front belongs to Lieutenant Hagan. He's in command of the corps of Stuart's couriers."

"Do you report to him?" Salina asked.

"I report to Stuart," Jeremy clarified. "And over there," he nodded toward a pair of large stacks of hay and accompanying piles of corn, "is the forage sergeant's. He's got the chore of making sure we have enough to feed the horses we've already got stabled here."

A hundred yards farther on were the tents of Major Henry B. McClellan, Stuart's adjutant, and Major Andrew Reid Venable. And pitched near a pine tree was the grandest tent, where General Stuart dwelled. "His place is equipped with a brick chimney, plank flooring, and a framed, hinged door, even. Quite comfortable, for a general," Jeremy commented.

"A sight more comfortable than the quarters of a mere captain?" Salina grinned.

"Quite," Jeremy chuckled, "but we've managed to create a homey atmosphere, so to speak. None of us has frozen to death—yet."

Boone Hunter was on hand to assist Salina in dismounting. "A pleasure to see you again, Miss Salina."

"I'm glad to be here," Salina said. "How've you been, Boone?"

"As well as can be expected." Boone grinned sheepishly. "I caught a bit of a cold on our last expedition, but I'm feeling much better now."

Jeremy caught the eye of his subordinate and shook his head. Salina caught the motion. "What aren't you telling me?"

Boone bit his lower lip and stared down at his large feet.

Jeremy brushed Salina's inquiry aside. "We'll discuss it later. Is everything arranged, Boone?"

"Aye, sir."

"You go on ahead, then. Salina and I will be there shortly."

Salina would not let the matter rest. When they entered Jeremy's tent—a space Jeremy shared with Bentley, Kidd Carney, and Boone—she repeated her inquiry: "What aren't you telling me, Jeremy? That you've been someplace dangerous and have lived through a close call that you don't think I need to know about?"

Jeremy's eye focused hard on his wife. She was too perceptive. "I just don't want you to worry so much about me. I'll be fine. You've got to concentrate on the well-being of our baby."

Even as he mentioned it, she felt another twitch of a back spasm. She, in her turn, refrained from saying anything, for she didn't want to alarm him. They stood staring at each other, locked in a silent battle of wills. Jeremy ended the standoff by taking her in his arms, kissing her soundly. Sighing in resignation, Jeremy held her as close as he possibly could and told her of the action more than two weeks ago on the blustery night of March first.

"It was miserable: cold, ice, and sleet. We were with Stuart, on the trail of Custer..."

"You all were on your way toward Charlottesville," Salina interjected, understanding dawning, "while Dahlgren and Kilpatrick were closing in on Richmond."

Jeremy nodded. "We didn't know until it was all said and done that Custer's demonstration was a feint—and we bit." He gave her an abbreviated version of February the twenty-ninth and the dreadfully cold night of March the first: "We heard the concussion of Custer's artillery at Charlottesville; shortly thereafter General Stuart received word that those people had retired from their position. With that in mind, Stuart marched us northward in an attempt to cut off their retreat near Stannardsville. Our orders were to await Custer's main column and launch a surprise attack. But that night the rain froze before it hit the ground. For more than two hours, maybe three, we waited; we got wetter, more exhausted; we were freezing. We lit no fires, had no food. To no one's great astonishment, a detachment of Custer's force slipped past us en route to Madison Court House—probably using the sleet as a screen on their way back to their cozy encampments. I don't care how brave a soldier is, Sallie Rose, those were not conditions in which anyone could efficiently fight."

"I should think not." Salina reached up to smooth the deep furrow in Jeremy's brow.

"Custer discovered our position in his front and ordered a charge. His troops—considerably warmer than we were out shivering in our saddles—brushed us aside as if we were no more a threat than a pesky fly at a summer barbecue. Those people reached Madison with little resistance," Jeremy concluded.

Salina studied Jeremy's face. It was easy to discern that the taste of defeat was still bitter in his mouth.

"If Stuart had had all his men rather than only a quarter of Wilcox's brigade, I daresay we could have done some damage." A plaintive sigh escaped him. "It was several hours before we learned that Kilpatrick and Dahlgren were attempting to sack the capital. Theirs was the real mission, Custer's merely a ploy to keep us from joining Hampton in Richmond's defense. Curlie's fingers thawed in three days, Boone suffered a beastly cold, and Jake's horse froze to death. It was a memorable night," Jeremy quipped disdainfully, "but not for the right reasons."

"The newspapers were in an uproar over those documents that were found on Dahlgren's body," Salina remarked. "If General Hampton's troops hadn't stopped the raiders and they succeeded in carrying out their orders to burn the city and..."

"Sssshhh," Jeremy put his fingers to her lips. "They didn't succeed, Sallie. God preserved us, put a hedge around our capital, and we live to fight another day. This thing isn't over yet—we've still got an ordeal ahead of us, guaranteed."

Salina hugged him tightly. She so dreaded the coming of the spring campaign ahead.

Jeremy shook off the pensiveness brought on by the failed outcome of the recent raid and tried to invoke a more cheery outlook. "Are you up to taking another little ride?"

"What about Boone? You said we'd follow in a bit," Salina reminded him.

"Aye, that's where the riding comes in," Jeremy grinned.

Josephine stood docile and still while Salina mounted the sidesaddle. Jeremy stuck his foot into a covered stirrup and pulled himself into his saddle. He clucked to Tucker to walk on. "Let's not keep Boone waiting."

Though the mare's gait was smooth, Salina nearly fell off Josephine when two more pains struck, stronger than any of the previous ones she'd had to date. The spasms came quickly and left quickly. Breathing easier, Salina determined that the pain was not going to put a damper on this day with her husband. Besides, it was too soon for her to be going into labor. She had another month to go to complete her full term.

Their destination was an abandoned estate near the Rapidan River. Boone awaited them at the falling-down gate. He and Jeremy exchanged glances that signaled that all was well.

"Is this my surprise?" Salina asked as Jeremy helped her dismount.

"Wait and see," Jeremy admonished, grinning at her impatience.

They followed Boone and took their three horses to the barn, where a fourth horse was already chomping on a luncheon of oats.

A young lady stepped from the interior shadows.

"Clarice?!" Salina exclaimed.

"Hello, cousin!" Clarice grinned mischievously and gave Salina a welcoming hug. "It took you long enough to get here. The food is still warm, but just barely. So sit down."

Salina started to laugh. In the center of the barn floor a pair of rough wooden benches were aligned on either side of a makeshift table consisting of two wide planks balanced atop a pair of three-foot-high barrels. A checkered cloth covered the planks, and the table was set with silver, china, a glowing candelabra, and a vase choked with wildflowers.

Grace was pronounced over the indoor picnic, and the two couples engaged in conversation alternately punctuated with rippling giggles and heartier chuckles. Life in Culpeper, as well as the conditions in Richmond, was discussed at length. Eventually, Salina confronted Clarice and her beau. "I take it you two have done this sort of thing before."

"Aye," Boone admitted, squeezing his sweetheart's hand. "Indeed we have."

Salina's cousin nodded. "I have a validated traveling pass from the colonel who is billeted at our house. It makes it much easier for me to get through the lines. Boone and I meet here whenever we can."

The usually shy private brought his intended's fingers to his lips for a kiss. "And with reason."

"No doubt a very good one, if I'm reading this situation correctly: You're using your romantic rendezvous as a cover for an ulterior motive," Salina surmised. She asked her cousin directly: "How long have you been spying in Culpeper? Has Aunt Ruby ushered you into the Remnant?"

Clarice nodded in the affirmative. "Someone had to take your place, Salina. I'm proud to do my part."

"Then this picnic is, for all intents and purposes, an informational exchange." Salina saw the object of the gathering for what it truly was. So *two* ladies had been added to the circle of spies to fill the vacancy she left, and both would carry out their assignments well. Clarice and Damaris were very capable and, like Salina, could be relied upon to do what they were told with no questions asked. Neither Jeremy nor Boone offered any argument to Salina's correct assessment of the situation.

"What is this place? Who lives here?" Salina queried.

Clarice shrugged. "The former owners must've refugeed south or west, or at least that's what we suspect. The house is in a sad state of disrepair, and no one has ever come near the barn, to the best of our knowledge. This is just a no-man's-land, between the lines."

Salina glanced at Jeremy. *No-man's-land.* She didn't have to have it spelled out for her that it wasn't entirely safe for them to be here. Jeremy squeezed her hand reassuringly, wordlessly conveying that there was no need for her to fret.

A poetry reading followed the meal, then a game of dominoes. Boone recounted the humorous story of an *aide-de-camp* from General Rosser's staff and his most unlucky encounter with a skunk. "We could smell the stench a couple of miles *before* we even reached Hanover Junction," Boone told the ladies. "That poor fellow was issued a week's leave to rid himself of the highly offensive *perfume.*"

"Some of the cavalrymen got to feeling a little nauseous because of it," Jeremy added. "Bad lot, that."

Another cramp overtook Salina—this one powerful enough to make her cry out. Jeremy administered a massaging touch as treatment, and Boone tactfully took the opportunity to whisk Clarice away for a moment completely to themselves. "If you'll excuse us, we'll leave you to take care of your wife's needs in private," Boone grinned.

"Aren't you just the soul of discretion?" Jeremy gibed.

Yet Jeremy and Salina were left alone for five or six minutes at most before Boone came bursting back through the barn door dragging Clarice in tow. "Yankees!" Boone reported. "Five hundred yards and closing in awfully fast!"

Jeremy's mind raced. Salina made the decision for him: "Get out of here, both of you! Clarice and I can manage the Yankees."

The cousins revealed their respective revolvers. "She has an authorized traveling pass, and I'm pregnant. What can they possibly do to us?" Salina asked sweetly. "You two, on the other hand, could be taken. I don't want that." She gave Jeremy a quick kiss and swatted him on the behind. "Now, git!"

"We'll see you back at camp," Clarice echoed her cousin's sense of urgency. Boone and Jeremy needed to put distance between themselves and this place in a hurry.

The men were barely out the back of the barn when the Yankees entered from the front.

Two blue-clad riders with sidearms drawn crashed through the barn door. Expecting to find anything other than two well-dressed, proper Southern ladies, they stopped short. "What on earth is all this nonsense?!"

Clarice had intentionally spilled the contents of her haversack out onto the plank tabletop: miniature sweaters, nightshirts, caps, tiny socks, a small cream-colored afghan. "We're taking inventory of some things for my cousin's baby." She nodded to Salina, drawing their attention to her obvious condition.

Salina instantly picked up her cue and played along. She held up a little sweater of soft woolen yarn. "Quite adorable, aren't they?"

The Yankee rolled his eyes. "Adorable," he repeated, muttering something unintelligible about the silliness of females.

The second Yankee searched the stalls, then ascended the stairs to the loft. "There's no one else here. Just their horses."

"Leave them be," the first Federal said. "Never let it be said that we Yankees were unchivalrous enough to leave two ladies stranded without their mounts to return back to their lines."

"You're very kind, sir." Salina demurely lowered her eyes.

"I don't suppose you two gave any thought to the fact that you've selected a precarious part of the neighborhood in which to have your little *tea party*," he said with barbed sarcasm.

"Is there a problem?" Clarice asked with feigned innocence.

"Come on, be quick," the Yankee instructed. "Pack this stuff up and get yourselves gone. The next patrol might not look at this with the same forgiving nature."

Clarice consented. "We'll gather our things and clear out directly."

"And I wouldn't advise coming here again," the second Federal cautioned. "Never can tell who one might encounter. Rebs might come out this way, trying to scout our position—some of us might be out trying to scout theirs. If we were to run into each other, well, we'd be left with little choice but to shoot them on sight."

The cautionary inference was not lost on the girls. "We'll not stray this way again," Salina remarked.

Clarice bobbed a pretty curtsey. "Indeed, we'll certainly remember your kind warning."

Both Yankees tipped their hats out of reluctant respect and departed, but both Salina and Clarice were aware that the barn would be under surveillance until their departure.

An excruciating pain ripped across Salina's back as she settled herself onto Josephine. Salina held the reins tightly, watching her knuckles drain of color until the pain subsided. "Clarice, I... I'm not feeling quite right."

Clarice looked askance at her cousin. "Let's make haste."

They halted once on the way back to the cavalry camp, long enough to let the horses drink from the river near the ford. Salina used a tree stump as a boost to remount. As she placed her foot to the stirrup, a leg cramp and a back spasm hit simultaneously. She lost her balance and fell sprawling into the dirt.

"Salina!" Clarice exclaimed, horrified.

Scrambling to regain her feet, brushing the dusty red clay from her gown, Salina felt a surge of water soil her pantalets and petticoats.

Clarice stared open-mouthed at the puddle collecting at Salina's feet. "Oh, dear! This is not good!"

Salina's emerald eyes were wide as saucers; her mind went blank. What was it that she and Flora had discussed only last night?

"You can't ride," Clarice judged, "not like this."

"It can't be that much farther to the encampment." A strong contraction made Salina groan in agony.

Clarice took charge of the situation. "You're going to have to stay here. I'll ride to camp and get help. Will you be all right by yourself?"

"I have no choice," Salina gritted her teeth. "Go, Clarice. But please—please hurry."

Jeremy practically pitched a conniption fit when Clarice returned to Camp Wigwam without Salina. "Where is she?!"

Clarice hastily relayed to Jeremy everything from the arrival of the Yankee patrol to leaving Salina near the ford. "Her water's broken already. I think..." Clarice glanced up to meet Jeremy's worried eye. "I think she's having premature labor and may be delivering her child early."

Consternation gnawed at Jeremy. "I'm going after her."

No one attempted to stop him. Boone volunteered to accompany Jeremy, as did Bentley and Tristan. "There is safety in numbers, Captain," Bentley reminded him.

"I'll get the Spencers," Tristan offered.

"Should I request the use of one of the quartermaster's wagons?" Boone inquired.

"Aye." Jeremy was glad Boone was thinking clearly, for he certainly wasn't. "If Sallie's in no condition to ride, at least we'll have a way to transport her back here." He glanced at Salina's cousin. "Lead on, Miss Clarice."

Salina had propped herself up against a tree, hidden from view from the road. Her eyes flew open at the sound of approaching riders, her hands splayed across her belly. "Jeremy..." she breathed his name as he hunkered down next to her.

"I'm here," he crooned. "It's going to be all right, Sallie. Put your arms around my neck."

Salina did as she was told. Jeremy laid her in the back of the wagon bed, covered her with a blanket, then climbed up beside her and used his lap to pillow her head. She was indeed soaked through.

Boone started the wagon in motion while Bentley and Tristan watched for any sign of the enemy soldiers patrolling the sector.

Bentley's nod to Jeremy was one of encouragement. "She'll do all right. She's a fighter."

"Aye," Jeremy agreed. "Fight, Sallie. For yourself and for our child."

The next hours were a blur to both Salina and Jeremy. The tent was cleared to give Salina some privacy during her travail, but Jeremy remained by her, steadfast. He helped her out of her damp clothes and into one of his flannel shirts. He administered cool cloths—wiping her brow, her neck, her arms. Bentley stoked the fire to keep the tent warm; Jake rode into town to fetch Mrs. Gillette and Salina's satchel.

Each of Salina's contractions convulsed Jeremy's heart. "There must be *something* to do to make her more comfortable," he whispered to Mrs. Gillette.

"She's refused the whiskey I brought." Nettie shook her head. "It's all part of the curse, Jeremy. '...in sorrow thou shalt bring forth children.' But He has not forsaken us in our time of need. Trust in Him, Jeremy. And pray."

Jeremy couldn't remember at which point he climbed onto the cot, holding Salina loosely in his arms on his lap. It seemed to bring her a little relief to be propped up against him, but no real progress was being made. The hours of labor continued with little change, and long about midnight, Salina's strength began to wane.

Nettie conducted a rudimentary exam, feeling Salina's swollen abdomen with gently probing fingers. Her eyes locked with Jeremy's. "Unless I miss my guess, the baby hasn't turned. It's not in the proper position to be born because it's before its time."

"Bentley?" Jeremy turned to his friend, a man whose wife had borne him half a dozen children over the years. "Any suggestions?"

"Sorry, sir. They never let me near the birthing room." He kicked at the dirt floor. "The midwife usually came to tell me when I could come in and see my new baby, announcing whether it be a boy or girl child. My only experience is foaling and calving."

Jeremy's depth of experience ran along those same lines. "Mine, too." He had no idea how much different a human birth would, could, or should be.

"Let's get her up and walk her around a bit," Nettie suggested. "Maybe that will help speed up the contractions. Sometimes the pressure in the womb is enough to prod the baby to get into position."

"But not always," Jeremy jumped at the deduction.

"No," Nettie lowly admitted. "Not always."

After a bit of walking, clinging all the while to Jeremy's strong arm for support, Salina still hadn't made any significant change. "I'm not ready yet," Salina sensed that much herself. It was difficult to stay focused when all she wanted to do was sleep. And to some extent she did when she was back in the cot, resting once more in Jeremy's embrace. She dozed, only to be rudely jolted awake when the next contraction hit.

All through the night and into morning of the next day Salina's labor advanced. Clarice gathered diapers, blankets, clothes for when the baby would finally arrive.

"Captain Barnes, General Stuart has returned and wishes you to report to him at his tent at once," a cavalryman said, his loud words heard through the canvas wall.

Reciprocally, Salina's anguished cries were heard by the cavalrymen outside. "Captain Barnes?"

Jeremy extricated himself from Salina's grasp. He nodded to Clarice and Nettie. "I'll be back."

General Stuart listened to Jeremy's relatively calm explanation as to why he was currently unavailable for service. Stuart was on Jeremy's heels all the way back to the courier's tent. A quick peek through the fly showed him where Salina lay, writhing in pain. "I'll get another courier," the general nodded, his eyes grave. "Why didn't you send for Fontaine, man?"

Jeremy faltered. "I... I didn't want to bother him until..."

"I'll send him at once." Stuart's tone was clipped. The concerned general squeezed Jeremy's shoulder in mute solace. There were no words to say.

Surgeon John Fontaine brought his medical kit with him to the tent of Captain Barnes. Nettie gave an accounting to the cavalry medical director, who listened intently.

Mention of the word *breech* sent a wave of apprehension through Jeremy. He remembered how frightened Salina had been when she first found out she was pregnant. Had it been premonition that she might die? "What can be done?" he asked the doctor. "Tell me what to do."

"Go ahead and prop her up like you have been. Perhaps we can use gravity to our advantage." Fontaine's statement was starkly devoid of any guarantee.

Four interminable hours later, Fontaine quit attempting to coax Salina into drawing deep breaths. Instead he ordered her to begin pushing on command—but neither did that produce any results. Realizing that the protracted labor was creating a hazardous set of circumstances for both mother and child, the surgeon readjusted his rolled-up sleeves, washed his hands thoroughly, and reached for a blunt hook and pair of forceps. Jeremy shot an anxious glance in Fontaine's direction. The obvious agony Salina suffered was uncomfortably disturbing, and outside, the rest of Jeremy's men vigilantly prayed for a miracle.

Jeremy's Adam's apple bobbed in his throat as Fontaine carried the shiny silver tools to Salina's bedside. "Wh-what do you need those for?" he stammered.

"Your wife must have some assistance with the birthing, Captain; she won't be able to bring the baby on her own. Believe me, I'm doing what I can—for her and for your baby. Hold on to her, now—hold on tight."

Fontaine smoothed the raven curls plastered to Salina's head. He gently explained, without trying to terrify her, the procedures of what he must do. Her bloodshot eyes appealed to him to hurry up about it.

Grinding her teeth to combat the pain, Salina let her head loll back against the wall of Jeremy's chest. "Please, proceed, Doctor..." She groaned in desperation, "Please help me." Absently, she was thinking that she now understood what was meant by the phrase "bite the bullet." Salina was positive she could have severed a minié ball in half had she had one between her teeth. Off in the distance, obliterated by fog and haze, she thought the surgeon was whispering continued encouragement, but she wasn't sure. *Oh, God, please let it be over soon!*

Finally, at a quarter past the hour of eleven o'clock on the night of March seventeenth, Salina's baby entered the world—but the little daughter had a bluish cast to her skin; she was not breathing of her own accord. Dr. Fontaine slapped the baby's backside. No one present in Jeremy's tent breathed until at last the baby did.

Jeremy's eyes flooded with tears when Dr. Fontaine placed the child, barely sixteen inches in length, into Jeremy's large hands. The baby was tiny, weighing no more than five and a half pounds at best.

Nettie snatched up a towel while Dr. Fontaine continued to assist Salina in the last stage of her labor. "Here, Jeremy, rub the baby down, clean her off. It will get her circulation going."

Afterwards, Jeremy gingerly laid the baby on Salina's bosom. Sheer exhaustion, however, prevented Salina from lifting her head to view the little girl. Salina's eyes fluttered closed, and she heaved a fatigued sigh.

"Stay with me, Sallie Rose, stay with me!" After a few more anxious minutes, Jeremy noticed that his little girl was breathing successfully on her own with an increasingly steady pattern of inhalation and exhalation. Before his eyes, the baby's skin gradually changed from a sickly purplish gray to a healthy pink. At last the infant screwed up her little face and belted out a wail of a cry.

Dr. Fontaine, too, was vastly relieved. He wiped his brow with a rolled shirt sleeve. "Well, there's a sign that her lungs are functioning as they should!"

"Amen!" Nettie smiled, her eyes wet with remnants of her own tears.

Jeremy wept freely. "Glory, glory!" he marveled, shaking his head. He lightly kissed Salina's sweaty temple, and Salina smiled tiredly.

The new mother's voice was a hoarse, raspy whisper. "Is that what you're going to name her? Glory?"

"I ought to," Jeremy squeezed Salina's hand. "To God be the glory for sparing her—and you, my love. You came through like the trooper that you are!" Jeremy held the precious little bundle in his arms, adoring her with unmitigated awe. "Glory Stuart Barnes. That's what she'll be called." He looked askance at Dr. Fontaine. "Think the general will mind?"

"Mind?" Fontaine chuckled, cleaning his instruments and repacking his kit. "Knowing him, he'll be honored. After all, she was born in his camp."

Jeremy's heart overflowed with a mixture of love, joy, and pride. No words could convey how he felt in that moment. He was the proud father of a tiny little girl named Glory Stuart, and he vowed she would never doubt his love for her. Ever.

☆☆☆☆☆☆☆

When Glory was all of three days old, General Stuart came to pay an official visit. He stayed only a few minutes to offer his congratulations, compliments, and well-wishes. Salina belatedly reminded Jeremy to give the general Flora's letter, which he eagerly received.

The general flashed a smile. "I appreciate your playing courier, Miss Salina."

"My pleasure, sir." Salina smiled back at the cavalry chief.

Stuart's blue eyes rested on the tiny baby nestled in Salina's arm. "Might I be so bold as to ask if I may hold her, just for a moment?"

Salina readily turned the infant over to the general. Glory's small, delicate fingers immediately latched on to Stuart's long cinnamon whiskers. The general's convivial chuckle rumbled through the tent. "My little Virginia does the very same thing." The concern in his eyes, however, was aimed directly at Captain Barnes's wife. "How are you feeling?"

"Much better," Salina replied with an honest nod. "Dr. Fontaine has been most kind in his attention."

"Good." Stuart's keen glance took in every detail of the little child in his arms: her expressions, her eyes, ears, mouth, fingers. "She looks healthy enough, even if she did come a bit sooner than expected."

"Dr. Fontaine says she'll be fine in time," Jeremy remarked. "It might just take a while for her to gain her strength."

Stuart was delighted to learn that.

"I hope, General, that we haven't caused an imposition here. I'm moving into town later this afternoon," Salina told him. "I'll be staying at Mrs. Gillette's for a while before I return to Richmond." She met Stuart's eyes squarely. "I can't tell you how much I value your understanding, sir. I realize that as one of your junior officers, Jeremy should rightfully have been on duty. I deeply appreciate your leniency and willful distribution of his orders to other riders. I know it has meant the world to him to have been allowed to be by me at this time, and I assure you, it has meant that much and more to me."

Stuart cleared his throat. "I am going to have to send him out tonight."

"Duty calls," Salina nodded. "My husband will never bring dishonor to you or your command, General. He will do what is required of him."

"No argument there," Stuart agreed. "He's very good at his job, and I consider it a bit of good fortune that he serves so loyally. One day, your little Glory will be proud of him for the gallant service he has rendered in his country's defense."

"You're kind to say so."

Stuart could not prolong his visit, as he, too, had other matters that required his attention. He returned the baby girl into her mother's keeping and gave a congratulatory nod to Jeremy. "Godspeed your way, Miss Salina." He touched the brim of his plumed hat in salute and flashed a grin at her. "And again, many thanks for the letter. Kind of you to remember to deliver it in the midst of all this."

As the general exited the tent, Salina felt a stab of regret, a bleak feeling that this brief exchange might be their last. "General Stuart," she called after him.

He stuck his head back through the tent fly. "Miss Salina?"

"Please take care of yourself," she encouraged.

"I always do." His swagger led him toward his mount, and once in the saddle, he again tossed a jaunty salute at her. "Good-bye to you, Miss Salina, and to little Miss Glory. May God grant good health to you both."

"Good-bye, General," Salina smiled and waved with her free hand.

Shortly after a shared dinner of bean soup and day-old bread, Jeremy took Salina back into Orange. They bade each other farewell, and as she watched him ride out, flanked by Jake, Boone, Cutter, and Tristan, Salina shivered. Duty and honor were cold comfort at times like these.

☆☆☆☆☆☆☆

Almost three weeks had passed when, back in her room at the Carey house in Linden Row, Salina mentally reviewed the poignant scene of General Stuart's visit to Glory. It had taken this long for her to finally put her finger on what had been bothering her: Stuart had said *good-bye*—not "good day," not "see you soon." *Good-bye*. Was it her imagination, or had it had an ominously final-sounding ring to it?

In her best copperplate hand, Salina registered her daughter's name, place, and date of birth in the proper branch of the family tree at the front of her Bible: *Glory Stuart Barnes; born in Cavalry Headquarters at Camp Wigwam near Orange Court House, Virginia; March 17th, Eighteen-Hundred Sixty-Four.* Her daughter, Salina was not remiss in noting, had made her appearance in this world on the anniversary of the Battle of Kelly's Ford—a year to the day when the brave young commander of Stuart's horse artillery, the "Gallant Pelham," had met his untimely end.

Salina set the Bible, quill, and inkstand aside. She scooped Glory up and held her close. "Your coming, little lady, will give us a much happier occasion for which to remember the day."

Chapter Sixteen

Mrs. Salina Barnes
Linden Row, Franklin Street
Richmond, Virginia

My Darling Salina—

We've been skirmishing on a daily basis since your return to Richmond. No major entanglements, but the oft-quoted phrase "No rest for the wicked" has been circulating through the encampment. We aren't letting those people rest at all—we're merely giving back as good as we get, for they haven't allowed us any rest either.

I know it's been but a matter of weeks since you were at Orange, but I implore you, Sallie, please come back and stay with Nettie for a time. I need you, and I would love to hold our little Glory again. I leave the decision in your hands, as you're the one who must manage the procedure of bringing both babies with you. Glory was a month old yesterday, and I dearly want to see her again, as well as little E.J.

Is there still no word from your brother at all? He sent no message concerning his son, even by way of Duncan? I can't imagine that he would delay a reply if your message had reached him.

Clarice was at the Grand Tournament that Genl. A.P. Hill's corps put on last week. It was a fantastic spectacle which afforded quite a unique break from our regular duties. No cavalrymen were allowed to participate—the entire show was staged strictly by the infantry. There was a joust and a grand parade, most certainly a scene out of some medieval pageant, and not wholly unlike some of Genl. Stuart's past reviews. The Tournament boasted a Queen of Love and Beauty, crowned from among the maidens in attendance, and all in all it was a marvelous diversion. Didn't know those foot-soldiers had it in them, but maybe they do have a secret romantic side to their nature after all. You'd have loved the sights, Sallie, had you been here to witness them. I hàdn't much hankering to go to the dance that evening, and I voluntarily took on extra rounds of picket duty so that Carney, Boone, C.J., and Tristan might go and partake of the festivities. You'll have to get Clarice to tell you more about it next time you come out to visit.

Sources confirm Genl. Ulysses S. Grant has made his headquarters at the hotel across the street from the Court House in Culpeper. He hasn't replaced Genl. Meade, but Meade now reports to Grant, that has been affirmed. Clarice has been keeping herself busy as of late—she knows when to play the charade and when not to. So far, it's proven very beneficial. She has made several acquaintances, shall we say, since the Federal occupation began, and she passes information to Boone whenever she deems it prudent to do so. Some of her recent intelligence was so accurate, Genl. Stuart cited us for meritorious effort on behalf of the cavalry corps. She does an exceptional job, your cousin—every bit as good as you used to do. We've grown to rely on her.

We captured a pair of the Yankee videttes night before last. Their horses were superb—they made our mounts look raw-boned by comparison. We also took some rifles, and Boone, as usual, was thrilled to have procured another pair of boots big enough for those feet of his. We got it out of them that Pleasanton is soon to be replaced with a new commander for their cavalry. Grant is going to give the blue horsemen over to Brig. Genl. Phil Sheridan. It makes me uneasy, and I'm sure it doesn't sit well with Genl. Stuart either, knowing that the Federals' horses are vastly superior to ours, that their troops are far better equipped than we, and that they have been conducting drills through the winter using Stuart's brazen tactics as a pattern. It stirs a bleak foreboding.

I love you dearly, Sallie Rose. Kiss the babies for me. Let me know if you think you can manage a visit— I'll even meet you in Gordonsville if you'd like. If you are reluctant to travel with them, I'm sure Damaris and Jennilee would look after them for you, but I'd rather see all three of you for myself.

Your own Horse Soldier and devoted husband,

Captain Jeremy Barnes
Stuart's Cavalry, C.S.A.

☆☆☆☆☆☆☆

Point Lookout
Southern Maryland

One of Ethan's messmates held out a battered tin plate. "It's better if you eat it hot, sir. Go ahead. It's fresh. Nate killed it just this mornin'."

"No offense to your culinary skills, Henry, but I'm just not hungry for rat stew tonight," Ethan politely declined. He scratched his head, unsettling a couple dozen unseen lice. "I just need some sleep, that's all."

Ethan's stomach revolted at the idea of ingesting any portion of a rodent, smothered in stew or otherwise. The protrusion of his ribs was evidence enough of his discriminating taste, but he didn't mind going without. He'd had a few crackers at the hospital earlier and had been allowed to take part in the afternoon meal fed to the small-pox patients. Food was not foremost on his mind as it was with some of the inmates—getting out was.

Nate, Henry, and the others dug into their meal with gusto, savoring each mouthful as if they were sampling the finest fare. Ethan's glance touched each haggard face; Tim Gage's was missing from the group collected around the stewpot.

"Where's Gage?" Ethan inquired.

The others got real quiet, and no one dared meet another's eyes.

For a brief instant Ethan thought Gage might have died as a result of the severe chest cold he had; the man was too stubborn to go to the infirmary. Ethan had offered to make a mustard plaster for him, even if it meant "procuring" the ingredients from the hospital stores.

Henry was the one who finally answered. "They got to him, Doc. He couldn't handle it anymore, and he took the Oath. He left this morning along with five hundred others who signed up to wear blue and fight for the Yankees."

"He wasn't well. Surely they could see that. Why did he...?" Ethan was at a loss.

"Gage got a letter from his wife," Nate elaborated. "She begged him to give up and get free. They told him they'd get him decent treatment, that he'd get well and regain his strength by the time they reached Norfolk. They'll be kept there until they ship them west to fight the Indians."

Ethan might have expected it from any one of the others, but he didn't see it coming in Gage. It was a common enough occurrence, though. Ethan shouldn't have been surprised. In the past few weeks, hundreds of Southern prisoners had taken the Oath of Allegiance to the Union in exchange for their freedom. Ethan couldn't honestly say that he hadn't toyed with the idea himself, but the last shreds of his pride held him back.

In truth, Ethan had nothing left to go home to. The dark depression that overpowered him upon receiving word of Taylor Sue's death by way of Salina's letter still bent his shoulders and plagued his thoughts during every waking hour, as well as in those hours when he tried in vain to get some rest.

A blast of cold air penetrated the thin wall of the tent. Ethan curled up in his space, pulled his threadbare quilt up over his head, and blanked out the ongoing conversation between his messmates. He didn't want to hear about who had died from scurvy today or who'd been shot by the guards or how many pieces of hardtack it had cost to get a chaw of tobacco. Ethan wanted to cry in peace, but there was none of that to be had.

☆☆☆☆☆☆☆

May 3, 1864

Jeremy sauntered up the sawdust walk. He straightened his jacket, removed his hat, ran a hand through his sandy mane, and then settled the hat back on his head. Knocking on the door frame of General Stuart's tent, he said, "Captain Barnes reporting, sir, as ordered."

"Barnes." Stuart opened the door. "Good of you to come so soon. Major McClellan is on his way out."

Jeremy studied his commander for a moment after the adjutant departed. The general seemed troubled and contemplative at the same time. Clearing his throat, Jeremy inquired, "What are the orders, sir?"

"Orders?" Stuart arched an eyebrow. He shook his head, clearing whatever cobwebs had been cluttering his mind. "Yes, orders." Stuart was no longer distant but was crisply businesslike as he unrolled a map of the area known as the Wilderness. A year ago, almost to the day, Stuart had taken over for the injured Stonewall Jackson during the Battle of Chancellorsville and had led the infantry in the action at Hazel Grove that won the day for the Army of Northern Virginia. Jeremy was familiar with the lay of the land depicted on the map because he had scouted a good portion of the territory before. "Are we going back there again, sir?"

"We fought at Manassas twice, we circled George B. McClellan's army twice, and now it seems as if we will indeed do a second tour of duty in the Wilderness," Stuart replied philosophically. "And soon. I want you to go see what you can learn by taking a ride along here." He pointed to the place that demanded attention. "It may take you all night. I want all the details you can get for me. Accurate stuff."

Jeremy saluted. "You shall have it, sir." He was told to take his men with him and two days' worth of rations just in case they were cut off from their base. The men were not to return until they had the intelligence required of them, and they were to leave at nightfall.

☆☆☆☆☆☆☆

All through dinner at the Gillettes, Jeremy's demeanor was glum. Salina suspected the reason, but she waited for him to tell her what was on his mind. His distraction unintentionally sent Rosalynde and Salome away from the dining room as soon as they finished eating; Nettie had the tact to leave the young couple to themselves.

Jeremy held a child in each of his arms, committing to memory every detail of their winsome little faces, while Salina absently picked at the hem of her linen napkin. Jeremy didn't look up from Glory and E.J. "In my jacket pocket is a train ticket. You're going back to Richmond this afternoon."

"I figured," Salina nodded somberly. "I'm already packed."

The frenzy at the train depot was added indication that the winter's inaction was at a close. Camps had broken. The armies were preparing to move out. The spring campaign was started.

"ALL A-BOOAAARRDDD!" the porter bellowed in the tone of a foghorn.

Salina looked up at Jeremy's pensive face. Jeremy kissed each of the babies good-bye, then held Salina close to him before bestowing upon her a kiss of her own. "Do me a favor," he requested of her. Jeremy pressed a folded square of paper into her gloved hand. "Keep this for Glory. I want her to have it one day."

Understanding shone in Salina's eyes. "Did you write a poem for her?"

"Aye," Jeremy nodded, a smile teasing the corners of his lips. "You can read it if you've a mind to, but only after you're away."

Salina nodded, clutching the paper tightly.

"ALL A-BOOAAARRDDD!" The porter's second call urged the young lovers to say their farewells.

A liveried conductor came to Salina's aid in getting her, Glory, and E.J. settled for the ride to Gordonsville. Salina blew Jeremy a kiss through the window, waving to him until she couldn't see him any longer. Resting her shoulders against the seatback, she unfolded the paper square and eagerly read the lines scrawled in Jeremy's handwriting:

> *In weeks prior to the day of her birth*
> *I oft dreamed of a sweet little girl*
> *Whose wide-eyed expression, abounding with*
> > *mirth*
> *Is to me more precious than any pearl.*

The night I married her mamma was indeed
The very night she was in love conceived.
I never imagined or dared to believe
What a blessing to my soul she'd come to be.

My darling daughter—the product of
A strong and deep abiding love—
Quite effortlessly stole the key to my heart;
She is both her mamma and me, in part.

Her bright smiles melt my troubles away
For her life I give God the glory all.
How eagerly I anticipate the day
When "Daddy" she will call.

"Oh, Jeremy..." Salina breathed, deeply touched by her husband's tenderly inspired words. She lovingly caressed her little girl's cheek and said, "Glory Stuart, your Daddy's a poet!"

☆☆☆☆☆☆☆

Salina would have liked to disembark at Gordonsville just to stretch her legs. Even though the babies had both been rocked to sleep by the motion of the chugging train, she couldn't leave them by themselves. On the platform she recognized General Stuart's former medical director, Dr. Talcott Eliason. The doctor was in earnest conversation with a lady, and that lady was Flora Stuart. Dejection sagged Flora's shoulders as she concluded her discussion with Eliason and boarded the train. In spite of her attempt to bury her disappointment, great tears balanced on Flora's lashes as she, with Virginia and Jimmie in tow, searched for a vacant row. Regaining her composure, Flora focused on Salina's familiar face. "Did your husband send someone to intercept you, too?"

"I'm sorry, Flora, I don't know what you mean." With an inviting hand, Salina pointed to the empty seat across the aisle from her.

"Did you make it as far as Orange before Jeremy sent you back?" Flora restated her query. "I traveled up from Richmond in the company of Major Henry Kyd Douglas, formerly of General Jackson's staff. I was coming to visit Stuart, but he sent Dr. Eliason to tell me I must return to either Ashland or Richmond. I've sent word back to him that I will go stay with the Fontaines at Beaver

Dam." Her bottom lip quivered. "He has ordered camp broken; the cavalry will be on the move as soon as tomorrow."

"You didn't get to see him at all?" Salina lamented sadly. Flora shook her head. "Well, I've been in Orange these past few days. Jeremy bundled me off when he got orders from the general for a scouting mission. Perhaps Jeremy and his men are to reconnoiter the route by which the cavalry will move out."

The sullen miles of the journey went quicker with Flora to talk with. Young Jimmie was lively and active, to say the least. Salina could see where chasing after one such as he could wear a body out. Glancing at E.J., Salina was all too aware that his sire was none other than her own brother—and given that, she had ample reason to believe that when E.J. grew to be Jimmie's age, there would be an equal measure of rambunctiousness in him.

"Beaver Dam Station!" the conductor announced the next stop. Flora offered to obtain permission from the Fontaines for Salina to visit again, but Salina declined the invitation. "I'd better do as Jeremy said and return to Richmond. That's where he'll expect to find me."

Flora nodded her understanding. "I trust we shall meet again soon under better circumstances."

☆☆☆☆☆☆☆

Union War Department
Washington, D.C.

Major Duncan Grant sat with his head bowed low over his desk. With the fingers of his left hand he kneaded the taut muscles in his neck. The fingers of his right hand simultaneously drummed the desktop. It had not been a good two weeks. Duncan had been to Maryland to see Ethan in prison and been given that one's flat refusal to take the Oath to get himself out of that hell-hole.

"I don't care if you've got special dispensation from old Abe himself," Ethan had practically spat in his face. "I *won't* go south to fight against my own kind. I didn't enlist in the Confederate Army to fight—I joined it to heal those in need. Why would I now join a corps of bluebellies your own government doesn't even trust?!"

Duncan had failed to invent a viable answer. What Ethan said was true. The Federal government wasn't yet convinced that this experiment of recruiting ex-Confederates was a sound course of action. Speculation was such that those who'd signed the Oath would in all likelihood desert given the first opportunity.

Ethan had looked awful. In fact, Duncan hadn't recognized the man when he was brought to the post commander's office for the interview. He'd heard reports that local Maryland women had come to "see the show" inside the stockade pen. If Ethan's appearance was anything to judge by, it must have been a horrific show at that. Garrett's son was painfully thin. The dark circles under his eyes gave him the haunted look of a skeleton. So lean was he that he made a picture of skin over bone with little meat in between. Ethan's hair and beard were greasy for lack of proper washing, and the cough with which his conversation was punctuated caused Duncan no small concern.

Duncan had made mention of Ethan's new son, trying to spark some, *any* response—but there was none. He spoke of Yabel, telling how fast Ethan's little brother was growing, and of how much Annelise wanted to come out and see him for herself.

"You'd let her come and see me like this?" Ethan cocked an eyebrow. "And break her heart? You've got to know as well as I that she wouldn't recognize me any easier than you did—even though she is my mother."

It wasn't until Duncan made reference to the 1st U.S. Volunteers again that a fire shone in Ethan's eyes at all. The Yankee major had been thankful for the vehemence; Ethan's strong reaction lent promise that though he was close, he had not yet completely reached the pit of despair.

Exhaling deeply, Duncan ran both hands through his thick, chestnut-colored hair. Annelise had been teasing him about the streaks of gray salting the hair near his temples, a hint telling his age. "And I'll be in a wheelchair before my son's fifth birthday if this war continues much longer," he said dismally, glancing at the recent newspapers strewn across his desktop.

General Grant had crossed the Rapidan unopposed at the beginning of May. He'd had his first taste of battle against Robert E. Lee in the horrendous tangle of woods, shrubs, vines, and underbrush collectively known as the Wilderness. Shot and shell had set fire to the thick, oppressive growth, and wounded men from both sides had burned to death in the inferno before help could reach them.

Duncan retched at the mental pictures that he could conjure of the miserable scenes filled with choking smoke, the heat of flame, and the maniacal screams mingled with pleading prayers, beseeching God for a speedy end to the hellish torture.

General Grant was beaten back. In light of the defeat, the Army of the Potomac had expected him to retreat—as every other in the long line of commanders preceding him had done. Grant, however, had done the unexpected: He'd moved *forward* instead of back.

Lee and the Army of Northern Virginia had won the race to the next point of contest—Spotsylvania Court House. The fighting there was no less brutal, no less costly to Grant. At a place called the Mule Shoe, the bullets had flown so thick that a twenty-two-inch tree had been sawed down, and if the casualty reports were to be believed, Grant had lost two men for every one of Lee's who fell.

Part of the reason Grant was suffering such heavy losses was that his cavalry, commanded by General Phil Sheridan, was not attached to the main body. Sheridan had adamantly stood his ground against Meade, railing the victor of Gettysburg for limiting the mounted Federal force to guarding supply wagons and providing escorts for the army brass. Jeb Stuart and his cavalry were doing as they always did: wreaking perfect havoc. Sheridan reportedly bellowed at Meade that if he were cut loose, he'd go after Stuart, through to the Confederate rear, and whip him out of his boots. Grant sided with Sheridan in this instance, telling Meade that if Sheridan had said that, he probably knew what he was talking about. The Union cavalry was summarily cut loose.

Duncan knew his wife's son-in-law well enough to know that where Stuart was, Jeremy was sure to follow.

☆☆☆☆☆☆☆

May 10, 1864

"Anything else, sir?" Jeremy pulled himself into his saddle with his latest set of orders.

"Deliver that dispatch, probe that sector, and meet up with us as quickly as you can," Stuart reiterated. "I'll join up with the columns shortly. Sheridan cannot be allowed to get to Richmond. The capital must be defended at all costs."

"Yes, sir!" Jeremy saluted, but he hesitated to wheel away. "Sir, would you rather I go with you?"

General Stuart flashed a smile. "You've already guessed where I'm going, and I appreciate your concern, Barnes, but I'll take Venable with me. You go on and get your work done. I'll be along."

"Very well, sir," Jeremy again saluted. "Godspeed, sir, and give my best to your wife."

Stuart waved Captain Barnes off. He found Major Reid Venable, and the two rode in haste toward Beaver Dam Station. Sheridan's cavalry had inflicted an injurious strike there at the Confederate's advance supply base on the Virginia Central Railroad. It was said that the fires had not yet been contained. Flora and the children were at the Fontaines—scarcely a mile from where the depot had been laid to waste.

The ruins made Stuart's stomach churn. The scent of sizzling bacon was still heavy on the morning breeze. Much-needed meat rations, bread, medical supplies—all burnt up. The depot guards had evidently done what they could to keep the stores from the hands of the advancing raiders. The Yankees had added to the damage, destroying more than a hundred railroad cars and two locomotives. The Federals liberated prisoners taken during the fighting at the Wilderness and Spotsylvania, then cut telegraph wires and wrecked track for a good ten miles. Stuart turned his back to the blackened destruction. At a gallop he rode up the lane to the Fontaines.

From an upper-story window, Flora Stuart saw her husband approach, and her heart leapt. She was out the front door, across the white-columned porch, and down the steps of the red brick manor house before he reined his gray horse to a halt.

Major Venable dipped his head in polite deference to the general's wife but kept a respectful distance, giving his commander and Mrs. Stuart a moment alone. She was obviously safe, which would ease Stuart's mind. He'd unsuccessfully tried to hide the apprehension he felt concerning his family's well-being.

Stuart didn't dismount, as there simply wasn't time. He spoke a few whispered words to his wife, then glanced toward the porch, satisfied to see that his children, too, were all right. Leaning down from his saddle, he gave Flora a lingering kiss before he and Venable took their leave. The men rode hard over the miles between themselves and the Confederate cavalry, rejoining them on the march to confront Sheridan.

☆☆☆☆☆☆☆

May 11, 1864
Yellow Tavern
Six Miles North of Richmond

In eight days there had been no break in the fighting between the Army of the Potomac and the Army of Northern Virginia. Jeremy's little band had suffered. Jake Landon was wounded in the

Wilderness, and both Cutter and Curlie had gone down in the action around Spotsylvania Court House. The three of them were not expected to live, and Jeremy knew that as he watched them loaded onto a transport train bound for the receiving hospital at Gordonsville. But there was always hope, and he firmly believed the Lord still had a plentiful supply of miracles.

Jeremy looked into the dust-streaked, worn faces of the five left with him. The gray cavalry had ridden hell-bent-for-leather to get between Sheridan's oncoming troopers and the Confederate capital. Men and horses were bone weary. "This is it." Jeremy told his men what in their hearts they already knew. "Today is going to tell—one way or the other."

"Aye," Bentley groaned, adjusting himself in the saddle.

"It seems we've beat Sheridan here," Boone observed.

Kidd Carney muttered ominously, "Maybe because he wanted us to."

None of them had to be reminded how outnumbered they were against a blue force that boasted some twelve thousand troopers. The Rebels had started out with eighty-five hundred, or thereabouts, but three of Stuart's brigades had been left behind with General Lee.

"Give me another go at those Wolverines," Tristan grated, a menacing light in his tired eyes. He was still smarting over the fact that his brother Archer had been felled by a bullet from Custer's command.

"Be careful what you wish for," Jeremy cautioned, rubbing his bearded jaw in contemplation. He reckoned they were about forty-five hundred strong, and Sheridan would have the luxury of a three-to-one advantage.

Jeremy's mind momentarily relived a scene from the the fighting around Spotsylvania. Stuart had sat on his horse for hours on end, with only Major Henry McClellan at his side. The general had sent the rest of them away to fight dismounted, and the Horse Artillery had done a commendable job on the Federals. The main portion of the battle evolved around the line Fitz Lee's troopers had established early on. Stuart had been drawing enemy fire, and he kept sending McClellan off with dispatches to subordinate commanders. Either Stuart had had a lot to say during the heat of the battle, or he was trying to keep his adjutant out of harm's way, just as Jeremy believed he had intentionally done for them. It was told that General Lee's troops twice had halted in mid-march, insisting that General Lee himself make for the rear or they would not advance a step farther. There was a greater desperateness to the fight than Jeremy had ever seen before.

Grant was not the retreating type; Sheridan's cavalry was bearing down. Horses that had been ridden beyond the breaking point were almost too weary to endure the unsavory confrontation that was coming.

Near the intersection of Mountain and Telegraph Roads stood an abandoned tavern once painted yellow. Not far distant was the junction of two other roads that formed the Brook Turnpike. From this point, it seemed that all roads led to Richmond, Jeremy mused. Stuart had chosen this ground and decided the course of action he must take. Major McClellan was sent into the capital bearing a dispatch addressed to General Braxton Bragg invoking the aid of the available infantry to put a halt to Sheridan's advance. Somewhere in the back of his mind, Stuart reckoned that Grant's objective was taking Richmond—but that Sheridan's was Stuart himself.

A blistering fight ensued from midmorning to noon, yet the blue cavalry was unable to penetrate Stuart's right. General Fitz Lee and his brigade repeatedly threw back the invaders. A disturbing lull commenced around two that afternoon—a chance for both sides to catch their collective breaths and redeploy or reinforce. The guns of the Horse Artillery and the fighting, both mounted and dismounted, had thus far gone the Rebels' way.

About four, the terrible, deadly thunder roared again. Sheridan pitched in with all that he had, striking hard at the left and breaking through the front, capturing guns and gaining ground.

Jeremy's eyes blurred with gunsmoke. The tangy taste of sulfur powder coated his lips. The enemy's repeating rifles spewed forth ceaseless fire. The combat disintegrated into a hand-to-hand affair in some places along the line: Sabres clanked with a chilling metallic ring; pistols barked, discharged at short range. The 1st Virginia staved off the Michigan troops thrown upon them, beating them back. The bluebellies ebbed, returning in the same direction from which they'd come. As Jeremy paused to reload, he watched, almost transfixed, while Stuart fired off round after round into the receding foe. Yelling to be heard above the din and clamor, the general encouraged his men to stand steady. "Give it to them!"

Tucker had been wounded by a shot, and Jeremy took possession of the nearest riderless horse he could find. A ricochet glanced him, but he ascertained no wound, felt no blood, only a sharp pain smarting near his ribs. Hours later he would find that the silver-backed cover of the New Testament Salina had given him for his birthday was what had stopped the errant bullet. The projectile smashed into the silver cover but had not torn through the pages of God's Word. Not only had the Gospel saved his soul, but it had, for that day, preserved his life.

Between the charges and countercharges, Jeremy emptied and reloaded his pistol more times than he could tally. He caught a glimpse of Stuart through the bluish-gray haze just as a dismounted Yankee horseman fired a deadly shot—one that inflicted a mortal blow—aimed directly at the cavalry chief's abdomen. General Stuart reeled forward in his saddle. His head dropped; his plumed hat fell to the ground. As General Stuart put a hand to his side, his usually controllable mount threatened to unseat him.

Jeremy struggled to fight through the Yankees impeding his path.

Captain Dorsey helped the general down from his saddle and settled him to rest against a tree trunk. The blood oozed from the wound in Stuart's midsection, saturating his blouse, sash, and jacket and seeping through his gloved fingers.

Dorsey doggedly refused to leave, intent on protecting Stuart from the very real threat of capture. Another horse soldier set off to procure an ambulance. By the time Jeremy got to the scene, a number of staff had gathered, Dr. Fontaine among them, circling around their commander. A handful of couriers waited at the general's side.

General Fitz Lee was summoned. Stuart told the nephew of Robert E. Lee essentially the same thing he'd been told by Jackson when command devolved to him at Chancellorsville: "Go ahead, Fitz, old fellow. I know you'll do what is right."

The gray troops fell back disorganized. "Go back!" Stuart shouted as best he could, urging his men to keep on. "Go back and do your duty as I have done mine, and our country will be safe!"

Jeremy's glance meshed with Stuart's. The severity of the hurt was plainly reflected on the general's face.

"I'd rather die than be whipped!" Stuart's ringing voice was choked with a mix of pain and passion.

Another whizzing bullet prodded Jeremy from inaction. A fixed position could get one killed. Jeremy snapped a respectful salute toward the downed cavalry chief. Stuart received Jeremy's respect with an imperceptible nod, wordlessly ordering him to resume pursuit of the Federals. With a last glance back over his shoulder, Jeremy watched Stuart loaded into an ambulance to be taken, presumably, into Richmond for care.

☆☆☆☆☆☆☆

Once out of range of enemy fire, Dr. Fontaine halted the mule-drawn ambulance wagon so that he could give the general's wound a more thorough examination. Stuart was in shock. He looked bad, but no one would admit it to him, even when he asked. He blinked several times in an attempt to stay focused, but the savage heat caused by the wound in his belly burned him. Stuart was too familiar with battle and corresponding wounds not to know that a gut-shot man had little chance to live. "Well, I don't know how this will turn out," he said to those around him, "but if it is God's will that I shall die, I am ready."

Fontaine ordered the ambulance to proceed. Additional medical treatment could be obtained for him in the capital. The mules ran along at an unmerciful pace, jostling the ambulance wagon the entire way. As Stuart lay on his back, his arms crossed over his chest, his pain was all-consuming. The general couldn't rightly distinguish cannon fire from thunder. He wanted Flora.

☆☆☆☆☆☆☆

The fighting just north of Yellow Tavern lasted but an hour after Stuart's removal from the field. The day was growing old, the rain poured down, and the damp gloom hampered visibility. Sheridan reached the outer works of Richmond's defenses—a mere three miles from the capital. He'd come close enough to hear the alarm bells in the city pealing out warning of the impending threat of grave danger but was repulsed. If Sheridan had had the manpower, he could've gone in and captured the Rebel stronghold, having taken the almost identical path Kilpatrick had ventured not three months ago. It might have been a grand coup and would have made Sheridan a vaunted Northern hero for sure. If he hadn't checked his impulsive instincts, the war might have been over that night.

☆☆☆☆☆☆☆

The murky night of May eleventh was a dark one for the Confederacy. Reports of General Stuart's wounding went out and spread as rapidly as the fires in the Wilderness had done. If Stuart were to die, there would be no replacing him.

In spite of the rain, a crowd of soldiers and concerned civilians held a somber vigil outside the Brewer house on Grace Street. Salina left Jennilee tending to the babies while she went out among the watchful ones, awaiting any scrap of news on Stuart's condition. "He can't die," she muttered under her breath. "Oh, God, why him? Why, when we need him so badly?" Her petitions on behalf of her country gave way to prayers for her friend, the general's wife. Salina wondered whether Flora was still at Beaver Dam, whether she'd heard the tragic news that her husband had been shot.

The crowd abated, and it was late when Salina decided to return home.

Jeremy reined his replacement horse up when he spied Salina's slump-shouldered form shuffling dejectedly along the sidewalk. He pulled Salina up behind him, and she clung to him tightly for the duration of the short ride.

"He's there then, with the Brewers?" Jeremy queried as he assisted her down from the horse's back. He could tell that she was relieved to see him unharmed, and her grief for Stuart was plain.

"Aye." She was vaguely aware of his wet, mud-splattered uniform. "Where have you been?"

"I went clear out to Beaver Dam to see if Mrs. Stuart had been notified or if she had need of an escort into the city. They told me that she was already on her way."

"She's not here," Salina shook her head sadly. "I stood out in front of Brewers for more than three hours after they brought him in, and she didn't come."

"You've been out in this downpour for three hours?!" Jeremy latched on to his wife's shoulders. Salina apparently hadn't given a clear thought to the prospect of pneumonia—which she'd had before and was susceptible to, since her lungs had been weakened by the illness. "Sallie?"

Salina shrugged forlornly, searching her husband's face. "Do you suppose Flora is all right?"

"She's probably had to detour and go the long way around. The Federals are everywhere," Jeremy remarked bitterly.

"The bell tower has been tolling nonstop for two days," Salina whispered. Suddenly her knees buckled, and she clutched Jeremy's arm for support.

Jeremy swept his wife off her feet, carrying her up the steps and into the brick townhouse. With Jennilee's able assistance, he made sure Salina was dry and warm, snugly tucked under the comforter to ward off any chill. Assured that things were well and Jennilee all right, Jeremy paused to look in on E.J. and Glory before he returned to the house on Grace Street. He was allowed in out of the rain, but the room where Stuart lay was already full of people.

The doctors offered nothing encouraging. It was only a matter of time, and in the morning, Stuart accepted his fate. He set about putting his affairs in order.

☆☆☆☆☆☆☆

On the morning of May twelfth, a telegram brought the disastrous tidings to General Lee. It was a severe blow. Lee informed his staff: "Gentlemen, we have very bad news; General Stuart has been mortally wounded. A most valuable and able officer..." Lee's composure broke. After a moment, he added in a shaky voice, "He never brought me a piece of false information."

☆☆☆☆☆☆☆

The Brewer house had a constant stream of notable visitors. Major McClellan, having reported to General Bragg, came. Von Borcke, the mighty Prussian, came. President Davis came. Theodore Garnett came. Reverend Joshua Peterkin from St. James Episcopal Church came. But Flora hadn't come.

Stuart asked for his wife repeatedly. He alternated between lucidity and delirium. He gave orders to his men as if he were still at the front lines of battle, and he seemingly spoke to his dead daughter, Little Flora, perhaps realizing that he would soon be with her. Ice was applied to his side to give him some relief from the intense pain. Stuart eventually broke a promise he'd made to his mother as a boy of thirteen: He drank of the whiskey offered to mitigate his hurt. He didn't have much to leave in a will; the meager contents of his earthly possessions were distributed: his horses, his personal belongings, a pair of spurs... His sword went to his son.

The general wanted to sing *Rock of Ages*, but it hurt too much. He was fading fast, and he knew it.

Jeremy stood unobtrusively in a corner of the room where Stuart lay, silently observing, an unswallowable lump in his throat. "...but I would like to see my wife," he heard Stuart murmur. "But God's will be done."

A third of an hour before the clock chimed eight times that night, General James Ewell Brown Stuart died.

☆☆☆☆☆☆☆

General Lee buried his white-bearded face in his hands when word reached him of Stuart's passing. Thirty-one years was, by Lee's definition, a young man. Lee went to his tent alone to bear his grief in private, but one of Stuart's staff officers arrived and gave the commanding general a full report of the events that had transpired from the time Stuart had been shot until he'd been pronounced dead. It was too much for Lee, who had loved Stuart like a son. "I can scarcely think of him without weeping."

Lee eventually drafted General Orders, No. 44:

> The commanding general announces to the army with heartfelt sorrow the death of Maj Genl J.E.B. Stuart, late commander of the Cavalry Corps of the Army of Northern Virginia. Among the gallant soldiers who have fallen in this war General Stuart was second to none in valor, in zeal, and in unfaltering devotion to this country. His achievements form a conspicuous part of the history of this army, with which his name and services will be forever associated. To military capacity of a high order and all the nobler virtues of the soldier he added brighter graces of a pure life, guided and sustained by the Christian's faith and hope. The mysterious hand of an all wise God has removed him from the scene of his usefulness and fame. His grateful countrymen will mourn his loss and cherish his memory. To his comrades in arms he has left the proud recollection of his deeds, and the inspiring influence of his example.

Chapter Seventeen

*T*he line of hushed mourners outside the Brewer house was long. Jeremy and Salina were with those waiting their turn to pay their respects to a man who had been to them both friend and compatriot in the fight for Southern independence. Step-by-step they inched their way forward. Salina rested her head against her husband's solid shoulder, gripping his hand tightly, but Jeremy would not be comforted. His abject silence betrayed his devastation more eloquently than any words might have done. Salina knew how much Jeremy had looked up to Stuart, admired him, and strove to emulate him every bit as much as he'd tried to live out the examples Garrett Hastings had taught him. Now both of the men who had been the closest representation of a father to Jeremy had been wrenched from him by Yankee bullets; they'd paid with their lives the costly price of their convictions.

A scant moment before entering the house, Salina caught a whiff of roses in the air. Had it been another occasion, she might have smiled, deeming it only right and fitting that the buds flowering outside the door should be yellow—the very color the army associated with the cavalry branch of service. On this joyless day, however, the ironically appropriate tribute could not lift her spirits. From that time on, she would forever associate the image of the late Confederate Cavalry Chief with the sight or scent of a yellow rose.

Dabbing at her tears, Salina saw that Jeremy wept unashamedly. In their turn, they filed slowly past the inert form laid out on the billiard table. A pristine white sheet covered the body, tucked under the long, cinnamon beard. Salina exited the room with echoes of departed laughter and the lyrics of *Jine the Cavalry* ringing in her ears.

Flora was in another chamber. "You made it." Salina greeted the young widow with a consoling hug.

"I didn't arrive until last night," Flora shook her head. "He'd been dead for going on three hours by the time we finally got here. Oh, Salina..." Her forlorn eyes brimmed with tears.

"I'm so very sorry," Salina offered. "What can I do for you? Is there some way I can be of service?"

"I don't know," Flora shrugged, undecided and uncertain. "I haven't thought much further ahead than to the funeral later on."

"We'll be there," Salina squeezed Flora's cold hand. "You just call on me if there is anything I can do for you. You know where to find me."

Flora nodded, wiping away her tears. "Thank you."

Salina started for the door, but Flora stopped her. "The pair of you were special to him; there was a distinct fondness in his tone whenever he mentioned either of you. You honored him immeasurably by bestowing the name of Stuart on your little girl."

"Much like you honored Pelham by giving his name to your daughter. Glory will bear her name just as proudly as Virginia will hers." She cleared her throat. "And, if you'll permit me to say, the general was special to us as well—so are you. We'll be praying for you."

Again, Flora nodded, plying her damp handkerchief to her mournful eyes.

☆☆☆☆☆☆☆

Jeb Stuart's funeral was read by Reverend Peterkin. A number of staff officers in their battle-stained uniforms showed up at the service at St. James, Jeremy and his men with them. Many city officials attended, too, but Stuart's fellow commanding officers were noticeably absent, still engaged in fighting to save Richmond from the attacking Yankee forces.

The metal coffin was adorned with a cross of white roses and a simple green crown of woven bay leaves. There were no dry eyes, for all partook of suffering the sorrow of so deep a loss.

At the conclusion of the service, Stuart's coffin was taken by hearse to Hollywood Cemetery. The four white horses leading the rig were bedecked with black plumes, symbolizing the renowned feather Stuart had worn.

The usual pomp and circumstance was lacking as the lethargic procession moved from the church to the gates of Hollywood. The pallbearers transferred the coffin from the hearse to its resting place without the accompaniment of martial airs; the thunderous roar from the cannon defending the city limits furnished the death knell. At the grave site, Dr. Minnegerode, the reverend from St. Paul's, spoke in eulogy.

Under a shared umbrella beneath the steady rain, Salina shuddered. Jeremy's arm stole around her shaking shoulders. She was tired of death. A parade of departed friends, relatives, and acquaintances marched behind her closed eyelids: Daddy, Taylor Sue, Colonel Carey, Browne Williams, Harrison Claibourne, Pepper Markham, Archer Scarborough; soldiers she'd nursed in field hospitals; men like Jackson, Stuart, Pelham—and too many others. The heavy press of despondency against her heart was almost enough to undermine Salina's hope.

Hours later, after Jeremy slipped into a fitful sleep and the babies were nestled in their cradles, Salina painstakingly cut a printed poem out of one of the Richmond newspapers. She pasted the piece into her much-neglected journal, noting again the closing stanzas:

> *And thus our Stuart at this moment seems*
> *To ride out of our dark and troubled story,*
> *Into the region of romance and dreams*
> *A realm of light and glory.*
>
> *And sometimes when the silver bugles blow,*
> *That radiant form in battle reappearing,*
> *Shall lead his horsemen headlong on the foe,*
> *In victory careering.*

☆☆☆☆☆☆☆

A day or two following the funeral, Salina returned home tired after dutifully working her shift at Robertson Hospital. The normal occupancy had been temporarily increased to accommodate new wounded. With more to be done than hands to do it, Captain Sally Tompkins kept a cool head, her directions administered with all the discipline of a competent field general. Her rules, regulations, and routine were strictly adhered to and enforced.

The reports of the fighting at Spotsylvania Court House continued to appear in newspaper print and were passed along in the telling. Once again Grant had taken a beating but had refused to retreat. He tenaciously proposed that he would "fight it out on this line if it takes all summer..." For the Army of the Potomac under his command, there was no going back. General Lee had his work cut out for him. Speculation was rife: If Grant kept maneuvering to the right in his attempts to flank the Army of Northern Virginia, he would eventually reach the James River—and if that happened, Grant's tactics would dictate the onset of a siege. His performance at Vicksburg now appeared as a foreshadowing...

No need to dwell on what hasn't happened yet, Salina scolded herself. She went upstairs to her room and found Jeremy sprawled across their bed, fast asleep, with E.J. and Glory snuggled atop his broad chest. She leaned against the doorjamb, arms crossed, and savored the precious scene. The little ones, she noted, were growing satisfactorily. When she took them out in the pram, people often stopped her on the street to admire and compliment her on her handsome "twins," who in truth did favor each other in appearance, since both of the children had Hastings blood. Salina would usually pause to explain that Glory was her daughter but that E.J. was the son of her imprisoned brother.

The open letter at Jeremy's side was about to change the tune of her story. Salina picked up the pages that Jeremy had obviously read for himself. The letter was written in Ethan's hand, and as she read it, Salina found its contents difficult to stomach.

> *...I am giving you my son, you and Salina jointly, in the hope that you will take the boy and raise him as your own. I cannot be a father to him from this distance, from behind the walls of a stockade pen, and God only knows if or when I will ever see him with my own eyes. I don't want him deprived of any measure of the boundless love which is your gift, and I beg you to give him equally as much as you surely bestow upon your daughter. Please, my friend, do this for me. I would be much obliged if you would consent and arrange for a formal adoption at your*

convenience. It would be a great load off my mind to know that you will accept E.J. as a son and a brother for Glory. You are too well acquainted with the experience of what it is like to be fatherless, and I pray that you will step in and take my place on E.J.'s behalf. I'm relying on you to make my little sister see that this is my sincere wish; she will comply once you have explained that this is the best course of action I can devise. Make her understand...

The dejection and demoralization seeped through each of Ethan's written lines. It was so uncharacteristic of him to give up without a fight, but then Salina realized that the horrors of prison could change a man as surely as the terrors of battle could—and did. The tragedy of Ethan's experiences had left an indelible mark on his mind, spirit, and soul.

Salina left the letter where she found it. This was a discussion that would take place in due time, she was sure. For now, however, Salina let Jeremy sleep in peace. She placed a tender kiss on his brow and did the same to the heads of the infants in their repose.

Downstairs, Damaris was sewing, pumping away on the treadle that operated the machine. Jennilee sat nearby working buttonholes on the uniform shirts that Damaris had sewn together. The pair of them were quite skilled, and the quickly assembed uniforms they turned out resulted in needed extra income. Mrs. Carey had finally started to leave her room from time to time, but she was still uncommunicative and never the left the house. She stared sightlessly out the window, looking at the scenes along the street without actually seeing them. Jennilee had become resigned to the fact that her mother had been unbalanced ever since the awful night of John Barnes's attack and might never recover from the sudden loss of her husband and eldest daughter.

"Are you going out again, Salina?" Jennilee inquired.

"I'm going to call on Flora." Salina tied her bonnet strings beneath her chin. "If Jeremy wakes up, please tell him I'll be back soon."

"Will do," Jennilee nodded.

"Give our condolences to General Stuart's wife," Damaris requested.

Salina promised she would. On her way out, she passed the marble-topped table that had become a place of remembrance. The assorted frames displayed portraits of Garrett Hastings, Stonewall Jackson, Colonel Carey, Taylor Sue—and most recently a *carte-de-visite* of Jeb Stuart had been added to the collection. A small palmetto star and black mourning ribbons garnished each frame. A photograph of Ethan was there as well but was set aside from the others, separated by a blue-glass vase filled with fresh forget-me-nots. *Ethan...*

The request in Ethan's letter, Salina reasoned as she shut the front door behind her, was basically a moot point. E.J. was already installed in the circle of her family; the legality was merely a formality.

After Glory was born, Salina found she was able to play wet nurse for E.J., and she could decidedly mark his thriving progress from that point. She loved the little boy wholly and completely; Ethan's letter was only belated permission for something she'd already promised Taylor Sue she would do. Salina didn't believe for an instant that Jeremy would deny her brother's wish; Jeremy would never turn his back on E.J. She rather believed that her husband would welcome a son with open arms. Certainly Jeremy loved Glory like no other, but he had so much to give.

The only impediment Salina could see to a speedy adoption proceeding would be Mrs. Carey. Salina feared that Jennilee's mother would challenge Ethan's directive concerning E.J. and cling tenaciously to custody of the boy because he was her last link to Taylor Sue. Mentally, Mrs. Carey had gone over the brink. She was by no means fit to care for E.J. *Well,* Salina determined, *that was a bridge they would have to cross if and when they came to it.*

"It's good of you to call." Maria Brewer answered Salina's knock with a tremulous smile. "My sister will be pleased that you took the trouble to visit."

"It is no trouble," Salina assured Maria. "No trouble at all." She couldn't help but notice the stacks upon stacks of mail piled high atop the sideboard. Every other available space was taken up with vases full of vibrantly hued spring flowers.

"People have been generous in their outpouring of condolences," Maria commented. "My brother-in-law was well-known, well-respected, and, by a good many, well-loved. Word reached us that one of Stuart's former comrades from the old days out in Kansas and on the frontier, John Sedgwick, was killed by a Confederate sharpshooter two days before Stuart fell. A murderous business this," she breathed. Swallowing, she absently queried, "Do you know what Sedgwick said about Stuart once?"

Salina shook her head. "What?"

"He said that Stuart was the best cavalryman ever foaled in America," Maria prattled.

They might've shared a laugh over the play on words if they hadn't been so close to shedding tears.

Salina inquired after Flora. "Is your sister accepting visitors?"

"A few; it's been difficult," Maria replied.

Salina sympathetically shook her head. "I can't even begin to imagine."

Flora appeared, her eyes red-rimmed and tired. "Salina. I thought I heard your voice." There was no trace of a smile, but neither was there any indicator that she wished for Salina's quick departure.

"What have you been doing besides crying?" Salina gently asked.

"Reading letters." Flora included her sister in the conversation. "This was delivered this morning." She read the opening paragraph addressed to her by Mrs. Mary Custis Randolph Lee:

> *How little I thought my dear friend when I received a letter from you some weeks since asking me to write to you, that my first epistle should be penned under circumstances like the present. I will not attempt to console you. In God above can you now find help, but I will freely mingle my tears with yours, for one whom we both loved, I need not tell you how sincerely. Ever since I first knew him at West Point he attached himself to me and mine with an affection which was warmly reciprocated. I have followed his glorious career in our arduous struggle with a mother's pride. He has truly "borne the burden and heat of the day" from the commencement of this cruel war, and how he would have rejoiced to see its triumphant close, for I feel that such it will be, but God's ways are not our ways. Like the young oak torn up by the storm in all its vigor and greenness he has been wrenched from us. Perhaps God wills that we should cease our trust in man and look only to Him.*

Flora took a shuddering breath. "She goes on to say that I should call on her soon so that we may speak of things she is unable to write. Mrs. Lee and her daughters have been very kind in their concern."

"What are you going to do?" Salina dared wonder.

"Our father has written." It was Maria who answered. "He is trying to convince Flora to go North. He's even arranged for guaranteed transportation and safe conduct through the lines."

Flora's eyes blazed. "I've refused to go North. Jeb wants his children raised in the South, where they belong. It was his sincere wish..." She faced Salina and continued with less vehemence: "I've been thinking I'll go to Lynchburg, or to Saltville. William Alexander Stuart, my brother-in-law, is in charge of the army's interest in the salt works. The Stuart family have always taken me in with open arms, never made me feel anything less than most welcome among them. It is my duty to honor my husband's wish in that."

Once more Salina extended an offer of assistance to Flora, be it watching Virginia and Jimmie for an hour or two, sharing a cup of tea, or providing a sympathetic shoulder to cry on. Flora appreciated Salina's friendship in these dark hours. "Rest assured," she said, "I'll make it a point to see you before I leave Richmond."

"You must take care of yourself as best you can," Salina admonished. "I can say this now, as I too am a mother and understand more clearly what it means as I couldn't have done before: You must think of the children now. You have to go on for their sake; they have only you to rely on."

"Aye." Flora's children would never grow up intimately knowing their father, a man who had been more absent than present during their short lives. Jeb Stuart would forever be a name to them, a face in a photograph, a legendary hero of the Southern people immortalized in verse and in song. It was Flora's responsibility to see that they knew how much he loved them even if they were too young now to remember that love in the years to come. As for Flora, she would treasure in her heart the vibrant and poignant memories of Jeb Stuart until her dying day.

☆☆☆☆☆☆☆

While watching Salina feed Glory and E.J., Jeremy gave serious contemplation to what his own immediate future held. Two weeks had passed since Stuart's death, and Richmond had not fallen to the hands of the enemy. Fitz Lee's tough resistance had been a match for those people, who'd eventually withdrawn to the relative safety of their own lines. Sheridan had moved slowly in joining Ben Butler's Union force down on the peninsula, as if to prove that the Yankee cavalry was not running away.

"Have you given any further consideration to E.J.'s adoption?" Salina questioned.

"I have," he admitted. "And the only thing that makes me hesitant in proceeding is that I can't bear the thought of giving the name of Barnes to Ethan's son. I *hate* this name, Sallie. I didn't want to give it to you, and I didn't want to give it to Glory. I don't want to saddle E.J. with it, either."

"It might only be temporary," Salina said cryptically. "You never know, Jeremy. The Southerland name may yet be an option."

Jeremy scowled at her. "You've been talking to Ridge again."

"I talk to Ridge every day," she pointed out. "He's a guest in our home here." The recovering man had been installed in one of the spare rooms since being discharged from Robertson Hospital.

"He's filling your head with notions that aren't going to happen," Jeremy grumbled. He and Ridge had managed to keep out of each other's way. They were polite enough on the surface, but they did not intentionally seek out each other's company. "Jennilee told me he's leaving soon."

"Tomorrow, as a matter of fact. Jeremy, you ought to know that Drake will be here come morning. I know that you two have not spoken or been in touch since the episode with the horses, but maybe now is as good a time as any to put your differences behind you."

There was no censure in Salina's tone, merely suggestion, but Jeremy stubbornly declined to answer. He knew about the monthly boxes that were delivered. He knew that Drake, in spite of their rift, continued to share his abundant resources without grudge. If he had been honest with himself, Jeremy might have admitted that he regretted the rift, that he missed Drake's friendship.

Salina placed E.J. in his cradle while she changed Glory's soiled diaper, then reversed the procedure. Both babies cooed, happy, clean, and full.

Jeremy sat cross-legged on the floor between the cradles. He rested his elbows on the side of each cradle and held out his pinkie fingers so that each child could grasp one. E.J. kept up a steady stream of gurgling, as if he were giving orders, while Glory's wide eyes fixed on Jeremy's face, watching his every move. Jeremy pursed his lips in a kiss, and Glory smiled at him, waving her free hand and kicking her legs. She was the apple of his eye, without a doubt.

"When I go back, I'll have no official rank, Sallie," Jeremy said at length.

"But your captaincy..."

"Was Stuart's doing, and Stuart is no more. He arranged the rank as reward for devoted service to him. I fought under his command because he rescued me from the scrape I was in by including me in that prisoner exchange after Sharpsburg. I volunteered my service to him. Now, I'm not sure what to do or where I fit into the scheme of things from a military point of view."

It was on the tip of her tongue to impulsively tell Jeremy not to go back at all, but Salina wisely kept her own counsel.

"I reckon I could report to Fitz Lee or Wade Hampton—but maybe now the time is right for me to go back to Northern Virginia. I could ride with Mosby."

"And your remaining men? What about them?"

"They've already said they're willing to go with me, if that's the choice I make."

"They're as loyal to you as you were to Stuart," she commented.

"Comrades-in-arms," Jeremy acquiesced. "We've become close because facing death on a regular basis does that to you."

"True friends." Salina hunkered down in front of him, resting her elbows in a like manner on each of the cradle edges. "As for me, I'm bound to stay here in Richmond, Jeremy. Jennilee needs me—her mother's situation is so questionable, I wouldn't feel right to leave her on her own. Damaris could go back to her home, behind the lines, but I suspect she would rather stay here until Ridge takes her with him and Brisco to California. Essentially, there is no place else for me to go: Shadowcreek is gone; I don't particularly fancy Ivywood, though the Armstrongs would take me in; Fairfax is occupied; Culpeper is occupied."

Jeremy's lips pressed together in a firm line. He didn't relish the idea of being separated from Salina for any length of time; he never did. And now Glory and E.J. had carved their respective places in his heart, making his imminent departure even more difficult. He saw the practicality in what Salina was saying: Richmond was where she would remain. At least here she had a roof over her head and food to eat. She and babies would be safe enough here as anywhere. And if she stayed in one place, he'd know where to find her whenever he might have a chance to visit—he just didn't know when that would be.

"Duty calls," they both chimed in unison.

On her knees, Salina leaned forward to kiss Jeremy. "Be strong and courageous, my Horse Soldier. We three will faithfully await your return."

☆☆☆☆☆☆☆

Cobb was with Drake when he arrived at Linden Row. Damaris was delighted to see her brother and to get caught up on all the news from home. Ridge could see in Brisco's eyes that he must look bad to his partner's way of thinking. "I'm getting stronger every day," he insisted. "I'll be ready when the time comes to go to California again."

"I'll take you home and let Mum tend you some more before you even think of making the journey west. You're not ready, Ridge, but we'll discuss all that later." Brisco momentarily set the matter aside. "Duncan Grant is on your trail again. No, let me rephrase that: Duncan is still looking for Evan."

"What makes you think that?" Ridge queried.

"Last time I visited his office, I found a file of information he has collected on your brother. He's reopened an investigation that he thought would lead him nowhere. It is an eventuality that he will uncover the fact that Evan is still among the living and that technically E.S. Ridgeford is dead."

"As long as Duncan doesn't make the connection to you as the mole, that's all we have to worry about," Ridge asserted. He asked for an update on the plans for the new Western Campaign.

"We're ready to move ahead with California," Brisco declared. He spent the next few hours going over the progression of the plans. Damaris added her input while Salina and Jeremy listened in uninterfering silence.

Ridge was duly impressed with the reports. "I don't know if I should be proud or hurt that none of you have seemed to miss a beat since I've been laid up. Maybe you should continue on without me."

"But we can't take *all* the praise for your hard work and inspiration," Damaris remarked sarcastically. "Do come along with us anyway."

"Maybe. I'll think about it," Ridge muttered, folding his arms across his chest. "I wouldn't want to be in your way, or anything."

Damaris shot Ridge Southerland an eloquent look, which Brisco deciphered in a flash. Brisco clamped a heavy hand on Ridge's shoulder. "Have you kissed my sister again?"

Highly amused, Ridge's lips twitched. Damaris blushed hotly. "Once or twice," he answered truthfully, but with a rogue's smile.

Brisco eyed his sister with a bit of hesitant reserve. "No broom handles this time, Damaris?"

"Not a one," she assured him.

Salina and Jeremy chuckled knowingly: They'd heard the tale of Damaris stalking Ridge with a broom stick in hand after he'd blatantly stolen a kiss.

Downstairs, another guest was admitted to the Carey home. Jennilee directed Drake to Ridge's room.

Drake spoke into the chilled awkwardness first, even before the pretense of an exchange of polite greetings could be committed. His words deftly cut through the discord between him and Jeremy: "It *was* a case of sabotage," he stated emphatically. "I've found out that Ruth-Ellen's brother, one of the South Union drovers, deliberately mingled diseased horses into the herd prior to our leaving the ranch for St. Louis—it was just time enough for the incubation period to play out. Once I was sure, I confronted him, and he confessed. Clive admitted to listening at keyholes and to knowing who you are, Jeremy. It was an attempt to strike out on behalf of his sister's tarnished honor. He thought he could make Evan pay somehow by robbing you of the horseflesh. He didn't understand that because Evan sees you as his enemy, he was equally as pleased that the horses didn't make it into the Confederate cavalry service."

Ridge whistled lowly. "Clive? I can see where he believed he was acting as Ruth-Ellen's champion."

"In a manner of speaking he was," Drake agreed. "At first Ruth-Ellen was glad to have Evan home alive instead of dead, to have her title of 'widow' revoked. But her acceptance of his return has been tempered with the bitter resentment over the known fact that he fathered a child with another woman. Ruth-Ellen has denounced Evan—won't have anything to do with him. She's taken to living in one part of thc manor, Evan another." After a long, deafening silence, Drake sized Jeremy up. "So—am I acquitted?"

Jeremy swallowed his Southerland pride. "Aye, friend." The two men shook hands in earnest.

Later on, the arrival of Tristan, Bentley, Kidd Carney, C.J., and Boone ensured a full house. The men camped out on the floor of the parlour after supper, and the remaining occupants turned in to their rooms.

Salina lay awake under the muslin sheets. Jeremy and Drake lingered in the sitting room discussing something. Salina could hear tone but not words. The conversation sounded amiable enough.

When Jeremy did enter the room, he went to the cradles straightaway. He stood for a long time watching the children sleep while the moonbeams slanted over them, rememorizing their faces, their forms, and the soft sound of their breathing. He added these details to the smiles and bright eyes of the cherished memories he would take with him. For all he knew, those precious little smiles might well have teeth in them the next time he was able to visit.

When he finally came to Salina, it was with a sense of urgency. She wrapped her arms around him, pinning him close. "I'll miss you when you leave in the morning."

Jeremy's eyes found his wife's in the dimness. "Perceptive as always."

"And don't you forget it," she quipped.

The remainder of the wee morning hours was not wasted on sleep. Each put on a stoic front for the benefit of the other, understanding there were no guarantees as to when or where they would be together the next time. Or even whether there would be a next time. Salina was much more aware of mortality than ever in the wake of General Stuart's death, and in light of the uncertain future she was determined to assure Jeremy of her love and loyalty.

As he dressed at dawn's light, Jeremy confided in her. "It has been brought to my attention that you were in possession, for a time, of a document that proved Evan's paternity beyond reasonable doubt."

"I was." Salina did not deny it. "I forwarded that particular piece of evidence to Marietta Southerland. I asked her to safeguard it for you."

"I would have liked to have seen that," he confessed.

Salina looked askance at him. "How could I have possibly known? I sent it away because I didn't want to take the risk of your destroying it had you found it among my things."

He couldn't argue with her—not after he'd fed Micah's dossier to the flame. "I don't suppose you had the foresight to make a copy, did you?"

"Do you accept that you are the son of Evan Southerland?" she challenged in lieu of answering. "Even if Evan hasn't yet come around to formally admitting it himself?"

"Ridge made a point: I may not share the man's surname, but I have his face and his blood. Justine signed over the last shred of proof. I believe the evidence— my father will have to come to his own conclusions."

Salina nodded. "Very well. So be it."

"Well? Did you make a copy?" Jeremy reiterated.

His wife's eyes twinkled mischievously. "No, darling, I didn't make *a* copy. I made *two*."

☆☆☆☆☆☆☆

The morning meal was hurried. Ridge and Brisco were already prepared to leave. Damaris would travel back to Maryland with them.

Half an hour later, Bentley approached Jeremy's wife as she stood in the garden observing the riders while they saddled, loaded, and mounted their steeds. "Miss Salina, ma'am?"

"Bentley." She spoke his name with an accompanying smile as bright as the blossoms around her. "What can I do for you?"

Bentley held a small, battered, and worn sketchbook in his hand. "I was with Curlie at the dressing station on the Spotsylvania battlefield a little before he died. He wanted you to have this especially, and he bade me tell you what an adventure it had been to serve under your husband's command."

Salina's eyes misted as she viewed the bloodstain marring the cover and edges of several of the pages. Opening the sketchbook, she found pages filled with drawings, sketches, and portraits. She was astonished to find among the penciled works scenes rendered of the Richmond Theatre, the ball following the Grand Review at Brandy Station, a haphazard dance at Shadowcreek, her wedding in camp at Gettysburg, and the Christmas party in Orange. The portrait of Stuart holding Glory in Jeremy's tent at Camp Wigwam took Salina's breath away. There was a recreated scene of the tournament joust of Hill's Third Corps, and a veritable collection of vignettes portrayed Jeremy and each of the riders, sometimes alone, other times in groups, during moments of camp duty or conducting reconnaissance. There were two sketches of Salina herself, one of Clarice with Boone, and another depicting Carney's sweetheart, Miss Hollis. Salina's favorite rendering, next to the one of Stuart and Glory, was of Orion dining on oats from a feed sack that Jeremy held in his hands. "When did he make these?" Salina wondered in amazement, her fingers tracing the penciled form of her husband. "Curlie captured all of us here, and look—here he is in a self-portrait as vidette."

"Aye, it seems none of us escaped Curlie's artistic eye. And in answer to your question, Miss, none of us is quite sure when Curlie drew them. None of us recall ever seeing him with the sketchbook. We figure he fixed the pictures in his mind, then played them out on paper to pass time off duty." Bentley nodded, conveying the supposition the riders collectively agreed upon. "Didn't know he had it in him."

"They are beautiful works of art." Salina again leafed through the pages, halting at a drawing of Stuart at a campfire with Jeremy and a map, both men holding a mug of coffee while they presumably discussed reported enemy positions and movements of their troops.

A torn page fell from the sketchbook. Bentley retrieved it, and Salina peeked round his shoulder to view a scene of the pastoral landscape at the Cobbs blend into a picture of dozens of horses.

"Bentley?"

"Aye, Miss?"

"Did you ever see Evan Southerland?"

"No, Miss Salina, ma'am, I didn't. But I reckon he saw us plain enough." Bentley gave her a wink. "Don't fret, Miss. I'm sure it will all work out in the end."

"Thank you for this." Salina put the picture of the horses back into the sketchbook. "I will treasure it."

"I believe that was Curlie's intent." Bentley touched the brim of his hat in salute. "You take care of those sweet little young'uns, now, hear?"

"I will. Take care of my husband," Salina requested.

"We'll take real good care of him, never you mind about that, Miss," the cavalryman smiled.

Salina smiled, too.

Jeremy leaned from his saddle and kissed his wife good-bye. Salina shivered in the warm morning light. She remembered Flora telling her that Stuart had bade her his last farewell in the very same manner.

☆☆☆☆☆☆☆

Grant and the Army of the Potomac had taken a pounding at Spotsylvania, but Lee again stalled those people at the North Anna River. The newspapers recorded skirmishes at Totopotomoy Creek, Haw's Shop, Hanover Court House, and Old Church. Cold Harbor—the area so named not for a body of water but because the old stage stop at the crossroads did not serve hot food to travelers who sought rest there—was the next point of a major-scale clash.

From the last day in May to the twelfth of June the two enemy armies engaged in continuous warfare with barely a handful of days to rest, bury their dead, and determine what to do next. On the third of June, in an attack against entrenched Confederate lines, seven thousand Federals were lost in under an hour's time, the bloody carnage strewn in gory piles between the battle lines. Grant was said to have told his staff that he regretted that assault more than any other he had ever ordered. In a letter home, one of Grant's subordinate generals wrote to the effect that Grant had finally learned that he was not in the West, and certainly not facing Rebels under Braxton Bragg in Tennessee. This was Robert E. Lee and his Army of Northern Virginia.

Lee's army had been taught a harsh lesson in Pickett's Charge eleven months prior: It was not invincible. But the seasoned

Southerners were a determined lot nonetheless. The gray army was not as easily demolished as Grant would have liked it to be. The Northern press called the Federal lieutenant general a "butcher" for leading his troops like lambs to the slaughter. The North had the resources to keep on filling the holes created by the fifty-five thousand dead. Potential candidates for the upcoming presidential race sowed seeds for negotiated peace with the Confederacy. Lincoln was aware of all the political ramifications in this election year, and he continued to back his chosen general. "The man fights," the Union President had noted of Grant on more than one occasion. Lincoln had at last found someone to match the tenacity of Lee, and he needed Grant to continue his strategy if this war was to come to its end.

The Army of Northern Virginia had suffered unspeakably through the past forty days of fighting, though its losses had not been as great as those it had inflicted on Grant's troops.

After Cold Harbor, one thing became incontestably clear to the Southern commanding general: There was nowhere else for Grant to carry out another flanking maneuver—Richmond lay squarely in his path. It was up to Lee to see that Grant didn't steal a march on him. General Lee spoke plainly to General Jubal Early: "We must destroy this army of Grant's before he gets to the James River. If he gets there, it will become a siege, and then it will be a mere matter of time."

☆☆☆☆☆☆☆

Gossip ran amuck along the overcrowded streets of Richmond. Salina and Jennilee did their best to ignore the rampant rumors of an impending siege. Reports had it that General Lee was sending for reinforcements from as far away as Florida. The citizens of Richmond had not forgotten that Grant had starved Vicksburg into submission and surrender; they feared he would employ the same tactics against the Rebel capital. People knew that Richmond would starve more quickly than Vicksburg had, and in light of this, many hundreds packed up all their belongings to leave the city limits. Jennilee took Mrs. Carey out of the commotion, opting to travel to Bristol, where relatives on her mother's side of the family would take them in.

Thus, Salina remained alone in the house in Linden Row. She had no place else to go. This was where Jeremy had left her along with their two children, and this was where he would return to look for them.

☆☆☆☆☆☆☆

By the fifteenth of June, an all-out attack on Petersburg had commenced. Grant's latest strategy was to take and hold fast the railroads south of Richmond that were the major supply lines to the Rebel capital.

Within the week, President Lincoln visited Grant's headquarters and City Point, where the James and Appomattox Rivers melded.

Major Duncan Grant was among the entourage that accompanied the Union leader, and while Lincoln met privately with Generals Grant and Sherman and Admiral Porter, Duncan took the opportunity to have a thorough look at the place.

The Appomattox House, former residence of the Eppes family, had been taken over by the quartermaster general, Rufus Ingalls. Grant evidently preferred a tent on the lawn to the manor house for his own headquarters.

Up until recently, City Point had been employed as a trading point for the exchange of prisoners. The Bermuda Hundred campaign had made extensive use of the landing, and Grant's arrival had ensured that the newly constructed wharves would make up a portion of one of the busiest ports in the world.

The City Point railway was expanded. Practically overnight warehouses appeared, shops were constructed, and hospitals established. One hundred thousand Union soldiers would draw their rations, clothing, ordnance, fodder, and orders from this massive supply base.

Off duty on the night before he was scheduled to return to Washington with Lincoln, Duncan put on an old disguise. Dressed like an old man in a black broadcloth suit, he infiltrated the city of Richmond under the cover of darkness. He paid a hasty call to the Union spymaster who resided in the Grace Street mansion located halfway between 23rd and 24th Streets. After his interview with Miss Van Lew, Duncan went farther into town, successfully locating the red brick townhouse on Franklin Street where Salina lived.

Duncan saw that the gaslight in a room on the second floor was lit, and through the open shutters he heard Salina's melodious voice singing to either her own daughter or Ethan's son. Unexpectedly, a hand drew the curtain aside, and Duncan quickly moved farther into the shadows along the nearest wall to avoid detection. From his position, he could not see the face of the young lady peering down from the window into the street below, but he did recognize the glint of light winking off the barrel of a pistol. Knowing Salina, she probably *felt* someone watching her. Her instincts, he knew, were that good. Satisfied that his stepdaughter was faring well enough on her own, Duncan disappeared into the night and was back through the lines to City Point before dawn.

☆☆☆☆☆☆☆

July 2, 1864
Mrs. Salina Barnes
Linden Row, Franklin Street
Richmond, Virginia

My Darling Salina—

A Happy Anniversary to you, Sallie Rose!
It is hollow compensation for me to write and tell you how very much I wish we were together to intimately celebrate the mark of being married for our first year. It is a year's time by the calendar's standard only, for in all we have barely spent a quarter of that time together in the same place since the night I took you to wife. But when I do see you again, Sallie, we will honor the occasion with all the mirth it deserves, even if it is a bit belated.
I have been retained as courier—though with things having reached such a frenetic pace of late, no one has bothered to check my "official" status. Kidd Carney and C.J. have recently gone over to the 43rd Battalion, leaving Bentley, Boone, and me as the orphans, so to speak. We've been riding between Hampton, Fitz Lee, Rosser (before he was wounded), Lomax, Wickham, and etc., literally zigzagging back and forth across Virginia. We report to no specific commander and are attached to no particular headquarters. We go wherever, whenever we are ordered to do so. I am still considered "Captain" Barnes, apparently since that is how I was known to Stuart. There are instances when organization is at a premium and clarity does not run rampant. My prior service to the General has seemingly been received as nonverbal endorsement bearing out my reliability and trustworthiness—which they continue to put to the test,

*over and over. In just a little while we will ride out
again, this time with dispatches for General Early. I have
another mount in addition to Tucker now, which I will
tell you of in due time, and though I try not to ride them
into the ground, I've been pressing them hard and wearing out their horseshoes with all the galloping I do over
countless miles.*

*After we left Richmond, we were immediately
thrown back into the fray against the Federal cavalry. We
were engaged in battle at Trevilian Station, near Louisa
Court House—outnumbered, as usual, and they better
equipped than we. This scenario is commonplace anymore, standard procedure. We hadn't eaten much in three
days, and our horses had only had a few hours' worth of
grazing before the conflict erupted. The advantage shifted
from side to side several times on June 11 and the contest
was hot. We lost guns, we recaptured them. Prisoners
were taken and liberated. All weapons on both sides of the
firing lines—repeating rifles, carbines, pistols, revolvers,
and sabres—were deliberately utilized with pernicious
intent. By ten o'clock on the night of the 12th the fighting
came to a close, and in the end we had carried the day.
Brandy was quite a cavalry clash, but there had been
infantry support there. At Trevilian, the fighting was
strictly between horse soldiers, both mounted and dismounted, and batteries of the Horse Artillery. Robert
Preston Chew did a commendable job with his Howitzers,
and Wade Hampton, considering what he had to work
with, displayed admirable leadership throughout the desperate circumstances. By comparison, I suppose Stuart
was more wont to strike with a rush, quick and deadly;
Hampton is steadfastly deliberate, he takes his time to cal-
culate the planning and he had a measure of success with
such tactics.*

*Sheridan's motive was to join their General Hunter
at Charlottesville. Hunter was in the Shenandoah Valley
with 18,000 men. Sheridan's orders were also to demol-
ish the Virginia Central Railroad—which would have
badly crippled our supply lines. As it was, they wrecked
miles of track by setting fire to the ties, laying the rails
over the top, and letting the heat of flame bend the iron
out of shape and usefulness. Ultimately, though, their*

mission failed: Sheridan did not reach Charlottesville, did not make contact with Hunter, and the railroad has been repaired. We didn't allow him achieve what he'd set out to do and he was forced to retreat with regrets over his failure to carry out Grant's instructions. We were in pursuit for a hundred miles afterwards, following a direct path of two thousand dead horses, their stench pervading all the way to the White House on the Pamunkey River. It was a criminal case of sheer waste: the horses, due to extreme fatigue from the fight, were unable to keep up with the Yankee retreat. Sheridan hadn't the time to stop and wait—he had the horses shot through the head rather than let them fall into our hands.

Tristan Scarborough was lost to us. The last intelligence I could get concerning his whereabouts was prisoner status. I am guessing that they took him to the Ogg House, where a temporary field hospital had been set up, but I am unsure as to where they might have taken him for further medical treatment.

The fight at Trevilian was almost commemorative—Stuart has been dead for but a month. It holds one remarkable instance, however. At a full gallop, I was on my way to Fitz Lee from Hampton when I was jumped by a lone Federal apparently separated from his platoon. I was knocked from my saddle, and Tucker kept right on going. I was left on foot in between the lines. The Federal cavalryman aimed his sidearm at me, and at that point I thought for sure I was going to be carted away a prisoner. But as it happened, it was not to be so. Sallie, I found myself face-to-face with Lance Colby. He was every bit as astonished as I by our incredulous predicament. The fury of battle waned in each of us upon recognition, cautious wariness replaced the rage and ire. He politely requested my revolver, which I naturally refused to hand over. I raised my gun level with his—there was but a scant yard of ground in between—but neither of us could bring ourselves to squeeze the trigger. We stood glaring at each other for a hazy moment in which time around us seemed to stand still. "Well, cousin," I said to him. "What are we to do now?" Colby blinked, having no idea what I meant, utterly unaware of our connection. Duncan must be withholding information from his trusted lieutenant, for I am certain your stepfather has drawn the connection between me and Colby. Boone and Bentley rode up, each having his sights trained directly on Colby. I ordered them not to shoot, and for him to drop his aim. Colby was relieved of his weapon. We could have captured him outright, but I couldn't do it, Sallie. I couldn't give the go-ahead to my men to carry out the order. I was tortured with thoughts of Lottie and of the baby they have—and I thought of you, and of ours. I am so grateful for the time when Colby stood up to admit his guilt and thereby acquitted me of Lottie's unfounded claim of dallying with her. I remembered occasions when Colby was kind to you and Taylor Sue and he didn't have to be. I couldn't maliciously repay him either with a prison sentence or by taking his life when I had it in my power to do so. Instead I let him go. It's his horse I took as my alternate mount and left him to walk back to wherever it was he'd come from. Colby held his head high—it must have been the gunsmoke that made his eyes water. "How is that you call me cousin?" he demanded of me. I told him my father was his mother's brother, but I don't think he believed me. I don't know what he was doing there, when usually he is with Duncan, but I didn't waste time in finding out. I told him to hurry up and go before I had a change of heart—he didn't need to know that I wouldn't have; I let him believe what he wants to believe. I reckon by now he's forced Duncan into telling him all that he knows about the Southerlands—and Duncan will no doubt begin to ponder over how I came to know. To think, Sallie, that there was a time when I was envious of my own cousin and didn't even know it. It is almost amusing if viewed in the right light. It certainly gave Colby something to think about on his way back to his own lines, without a mount, but nonetheless free. That was the last I saw of him. Our "family reunion" was short-lived because the fighting wasn't.

Boone has just arrived, and Bentley will soon follow. I must close for now so I can post this on our way. Hugs and kisses for the babies. I will always love you.

> Your own,
> Capt. Jeremy Barnes
> C.S. Cavalry

Chapter Eighteen

August 9, 1864
Union Supply Depot
City Point, Virginia

*S*alina didn't dare question Drake on what measures he'd had to take to acquire a traveling pass for her from the provost guard—in truth, she didn't *want* to know. She knew him, and she would rather just consider it another in a lengthening list of instances when extensive probing was better left undone. Instead, she made up her mind to graciously go along with whatever arrangements Drake had magnanimously worked out on her behalf. Quite evidently, it made little difference as to which side of the Mason-Dixon line Drake elected to conduct his business on, for he operated shrewdly, using his chary connections to full advantage in *both* countries.

Mrs. Hoffman had generously agreed to watch E.J. and Glory for the day, just as she did on the afternoons when Salina worked at Robertson Hospital or went to market. Mrs. Hoffman's four-year-old daughter loved the babies, and she mothered them as if they were her own living dolls. To Salina, it felt odd to be completely free of responsibility, for free time was an indulgence she had not had in many a month.

Drake had greeted her at Rocketts Landing outside of Richmond, reintroduced her to his ship's captain—a swarthy Spaniard named Rafe Montoya—and calmly given the command to set out for the Federal base of operations. Salina shivered under the August morning sun. Though Drake had yet to divulge the purpose of the outing, she knew that he wouldn't do anything to endanger her.

Joining Salina on deck beneath the shade of the awning, Drake seated himself in the vacant chair to her right. He handed her a glass of sweetened tea and ice chips garnished with a mint leaf.

"Well, Little One, don't you want to know where we're going?" he prodded, wondering at her uncustomary lack of curiosity.

"I reckoned you'd tell me what I need to know when I need to know it." Salina demurely sipped her tea.

Drake grinned, his white teeth flashing brightly against his copper face. "I'm taking you to see Rorie and Ellie."

Salina's curiosity was indeed piqued. "They're at City Point?"

"Aye," Drake confirmed. "They came down with the U.S. Sanitary Commission and are working in one of the hospitals."

Salina's emerald eyes shot a knowing glance at her companion. She knew of the strong feelings he had for his sister as well as for their friend. "So does this mean you'll be in Virginia more often? If you were to take a more active role in the Dallinger shipping lines that carry freight and supplies to the Yankee army, it would provide you with a plausible reason to be near, wouldn't it?"

Drake shook his head. "Good try, Little One, but you know me: I can't stay away from the ranch for long. I have periodically scheduled meetings with Micah in Boston to ensure the family fortunes are on an even keel, but no, I don't plan to stay in Virginia. Rorie and Ellie independently orchestrated their relocation. In fact, I'd only found out that they'd left Boston when I got a telegram from Grandmamma informing me that she holds me entirely responsible for disrupting the peace and tranquillity of her life since the day of my inglorious induction into the Dallinger household."

Laughing softly, Salina deduced, "In other words, she's blaming you for Rorie's desertion."

"As if she thinks that's any skin off my nose." Drake shook his head. "My sister is no simpleton. She's been well-educated—at Grandmamma's insistence—only now to be criticized for exercising her ability to think for herself. Rorie's got a sharp mind under those burnished curls of hers, and she uses it. She also has a giving heart and feels called to help in whatever way is available to her." He playfully poked at Salina's shoulder. "Not terribly unlike *some* I know."

"And Ellie?" Salina queried, a brow arched. "How do you really feel about her? Are you engaged?"

Drake shifted in his seat. "Apparently the letters my sister sends with the crates are chock full of information, aren't they?"

"Surely you weren't going to keep it a secret from me?"

"No, I just didn't want to hear you say 'I told you so.'"

"Now, why would I say that?" Salina inclined her dark head.

Drake shrugged his broad shoulders. "The real reason I brought you down here, Little One, is that Ellie and I are going to get married this afternoon, and since Jeremy isn't here to stand up for me, I was wondering if you'd do the honors."

"Oh, Drake! I shall be proud to!" Although she hugged him sincerely, there was a perplexed expression when she pulled back. "And you're going to let Ellie stay here, to continue her work with the Commission at the hospital?"

"Little One, if I tried to make Ellie go back to Boston, a place which she isn't any more fond of than I am, she'd flatly object. I thought about taking her west to the ranch, but I've got some business that is going to keep me traveling for a few months. I didn't want to leave her alone at South Union. She can be just as stubborn as you are, and she can fend for herself. She and Rorie are much like you and Taylor Sue used to be. They're close friends, and they lean on each other through the good times and the bad. They'll be fine as long as they're together, I'm sure."

Salina smiled. "You might have business which requires your attention elsewhere, Drake, but if you love Ellie half as much as I think you do, you'll be back here at every chance you get—in spite of the ranch or Boston."

Drake grinned, knowing it was pointless to argue. "We'll see you back to Richmond late tonight, and then I'm taking her to England for a honeymoon."

"England?"

"I have to go to a business meeting," Drake sighed. "Something to do with the shipping lines and the freight company I inherited. Micah will meet us there."

"And does Micah know you will have married the lady he had an interest in?"

"Well, according to Rorie, he and Ellie never entertained any serious intentions. Micah made a scene and put on a show for my benefit."

Salina nodded sagely. "It wasn't a case of your fear of my saying 'I told you so,' Drake. You didn't want me to expound on the extreme thickness of your skull—isn't that more accurate?"

"That's was it," Drake admitted with a grin. "That was it indeed."

A singular light Salina had never seen before shone in Drake's turquoise eyes. "You must love her very much—probably more than you know yourself."

"You know full well I wouldn't go through with marrying her if I didn't. I don't do what I don't want to, and I don't say things I don't mean," Drake unnecessarily reminded her.

"I truly hope you're both very happy together," Salina declared. "Jeremy will be sorry he missed it."

☆☆☆☆☆☆☆

It was nearly quarter-past eleven that morning when Rafe Montoya maneuvered the Dallinger yacht toward an available slip and lowered the anchor. "Welcome to City Point, *amigos*," he said offhandedly.

Salina's jaw dropped, weighted by sheer incredulity, as she observed the scene. A virtual forest of masts protruded from scores of ships moored at the maze of piers jutting into the water from the shoreline. The bustling wharves crawled with teamsters, dockworkers, military personnel, and assorted civilians. Unloaded goods were transported from dozens of barges to numerous storehouses. The vast quantities of ammunition, weapons, clothing, foot gear, accouterments, and food—along with anything else required to keep a well-supplied army marching, drilling, eating, armed, outfitted, mounted, and fighting—were purely astronomical. "My word..." she breathed.

The expression on Salina's pretty face needed no translation. Drake could see in her eyes what she was thinking: *If only we Rebs had such unlimited resources at our disposal...* But the Confederate Commissary Department and quartermaster general were not so fortunate.

Salina's look changed from a mixture of stark disbelief and envy to childlike bewilderment. On the breeze, the smell of fresh-baked bread wafted from the post bakery.

Drake explained before she could ask: "A hundred and twenty-five thousand loaves produced each day. They bake it, load it onto the cars, and move it out by rail to the entrenchments around

Petersburg. The bread is still warm from the ovens when it's delivered to the soldiers manning the Union front, about seven miles away."

Salina's heart thudded with impotent fury. "Don't tell me any more," she muttered despondently, blinking back a sharp sting of unshed tears. "I don't care to know about all the things those people have got in their favor!" The panorama of abundance that spread before her caused agony as she mulled over how the Federal Army ever got such a foothold on Virginia soil. The numbing realization that those people had become so comfortably settled, and with seemingly little regard that this was enemy territory to them, made Salina's heart hurt. It was painfully evident that they would not soon be abandoning the uncontested ground they had gained.

The ship's captain would necessarily remain on board with the crew while Drake escorted Salina to shore. Since Rafe was uncomfortable being so close to Union authorities, Drake instructed him to keep out of sight, on the outer fringes if that would make him feel better. "We'll be back no later than ten p.m. Bring the yacht up again by then."

"*Sí, amigo.* I will do as you say and meet you back at the appointed time," Rafe saluted.

An ambulance wagon awaited Drake and Salina. The orderly expertly guided the horse-drawn conveyance up Pecan Avenue, past the stables, row upon row of sutlers' stores, and tents pitched in neat, U-shaped lines across the lawn of Appomattox Manor. Roughly a mile west of army headquarters, Depot General Hospital extended across two hundred acres. During the summer months of 1864, the Federal medics treated ten thousand soldiers who had been wounded in the spring campaign and, most recently, at the Battle of the Crater. Their destination, however, was not the hospital itself but a boarding house nearer Commission headquarters. Elinor Farnham and Aurora Dallinger were on the front porch, waiting anxiously. They each hugged Salina in a warm greeting.

"Can you believe it's been almost a year since we've seen each other?" Aurora questioned.

"We're so glad you could come!" Elinor exclaimed with a bright smile. She had the same telling look in her eyes that Drake had in his.

But before Salina could open her mouth to say how honored she was to be with them, a tremendous explosion rocked the earth so violently she was literally knocked off her feet. The ear-splitting blast was deafening. A thunderous quiet immediately fell, and in the next moment, hurled bits of debris rained down over a wide-spread area on the Point. Initial shock gave way to confusion, screams, shouts, and an aftermath of disorderly mayhem.

Drake quickly had his sister, his bride-to-be, and his best friend's wife back on their feet. The ladies brushed dirt—and splinters of wood—from their skirts.

"What?!" Aurora shaded her eyes with her hands. "Have the Rebels landed?"

Elinor looked to Salina, who took no offense at Aurora's spontaneously blurted query. Her own inquiry was tongue-in-cheek. "Did you bring your army with you, Salina?"

"If only," she muttered with a wistful grin, adding forlornly, "but I seriously doubt that." Salina gazed back toward the direction from which the ambulance had brought them up from the wharves. The air was filled with ashen particles drifting down like snowflakes. "Drake, look!" Salina pointed to a column of thick smoke rising from the water. "Do you suppose Rafe and the yacht are safe?"

"I don't know, but I'm going to find out," Drake said with marked determination. "You go along with Ellie and Rorie. I'll be back as soon as I can."

"Drake—we'll be at the hospital," Aurora told him. "There must be wounded from a conflagration like that. We might be needed."

"I'll find you," he assured them, hurrying off, but not before he placed a chaste kiss on each of their brows.

"Drake told me that General Grant keeps his headquarters here," Salina mused.

"Aye," Elinor nodded.

Salina lowered her eyes. "Then they're sure to blame us for it now—whether it's our fault or not."

☆☆☆☆☆☆☆

At Depot General Hospital, Aurora led Salina to a cot and pointed to a camp stool. "Stay put. Ellie and I will see what's to be done. In the meantime, it's probably best if you stay here."

"Good day to you, Miss Salina," the occupant of the cot drawled.

"Tristan Scarborough!" Salina's eyes expressed sorrow over the pitiful sight of Jeremy's missing rider.

"Aye, it's me," he smiled at her. "You're about the last person I'd ever have expected to see here."

"And I could say the same for you!"

The pair of fellow Rebels wiled away their fortuitously allotted time talking, speculating as to the cause of the explosion, catching up on old news. One of Tristan's arms was casted, and he had bandages encircling his brow and ribcage. On his opposite arm, Salina saw a six-inch line where the flesh of his forearm had been laid open, bare to the bone, by a Yankee sabre cut. "How many stitches did it take to keep that wound closed?" Salina asked.

"I lost count. Have you heard from the captain at all?"

Salina nodded. "A letter came a few days ago." Jeremy's brief missive had been sketchy, obviously written in haste. It had given a threadbare glimpse of "Jubal's Raid," which she relayed to Tristan: In the first weeks of July, the Union capital had been given a rude scare, and the occupants, including their President, had tasted the worrisome fear that accompanied the very real threat of invasion. General Jubal Early's force of fourteen thousand Rebels had routed Federal lines under the command of Lew Wallace in battle near the Monocacy River in Maryland, but they had not been able to make good their attempt to capture Washington. Chambersburg, Pennsylvania, had been sacked and put to the torch in retaliation for Federal destruction of private property in Lynchburg. Two-thirds of the town was destroyed. The Confederates had wanted to pull forces away from Grant and Richmond, and to a degree they had done so, but not enough. "Jeremy didn't mention where he was writing from," Salina added, "so I really am not sure where he is, but apparently Kidd Carney and C.J. have been with them. That would lead me to believe either they are with Jeremy again, or Jeremy, Bentley, and Boone have gone over to Mosby's command."

Tristan seemed quite sure of himself when he whispered to Jeremy's wife, "They'll be back this way eventually." But he did not elaborate. It wasn't that Tristan didn't trust Salina, but cold caution prevented him from telling her that he was in no hurry to convalesce. Tent walls could have ears...and he didn't need it known that he'd been secretly contacted by a member of the 2nd South Carolina Cavalry who worked with Hampton's chief of scouts—a sergeant named George Shadburne. This select band operated not far from City Point itself from a yet undetected base in the Black Water Swamp. The Federals would eventually christen them the "Iron Scouts," as over time they would collectively prove their intrepid skill in avoiding capture once their nocuous deeds were done.

When Drake came to Tristan's cot, it was with news that Rafe and the yacht were unharmed and that he was taking personal responsibility for Tristan for the day, having wheedled permission and a pass from the surgeon in charge of the ward. The recovering invalid was allowed to attend the wedding and reception, with strict instructions as to when he was to be returned to the confines of the hospital.

The ceremony that joined Drake and Elinor in holy matrimony was solemnly performed at candle-lighting by an obliging hospital chaplain. Upon the exchange of vows, rings, and a kiss to seal the agreement, Drake and his bride were officially pronounced man and wife. The nuptial festivities that followed, however, were tinged with talk of the earlier explosion.

"Any theories about that?" Salina earnestly queried out of earshot of the other invited wedding guests.

"No," Tristan answered honestly.

Salina furtively whispered, "Do you want me to talk to either of my friends about the possibility of getting you out of here?"

"No!" Tristan shook his head quickly and emphatically. "Miss Salina, I'm unable to go into the details with you, but please, do not be concerned for me here. Miss Aurora, she keeps an eye out for me, but I am where I need to be for the moment. Do you *understand?"* his eyes implored.

Suddenly Salina did understand what it was that he wasn't telling her: Tristan was taking a long time to heal *on purpose.* She whispered, "Fine. But if you should change your mind, remember it was Ellie who helped me spring Kidd Carney from Camp Letterman."

"Aye." Tristan already knew that. "But even if I did," he laughed, "I'd have no hankering to slip through the lines decked out in female fashion's latest style, thank you just the same!"

Salina laughed, too, but remarked in all seriousness, "Don't be so sure, Tristan. You know there are occasions when one will go to great lengths to do whatever one must—and that includes resorting to disguise if need be."

"Point taken," Tristan tempered his rebuttal, for Jeremy's wife knew what she was talking about.

Drake and his new wife joined Salina and Tristan. "I hate to break up this reunion, Little One, but the time has come for us to go."

Tristan was summarily returned to his ward, convincingly feigning exhaustion as he said his good-byes. Aurora saw him settled comfortably on his cot and dutifully made sure he stayed there. Tristan's parting glance to Salina encouraged her, wordlessly telling her not to worry.

"Good-bye, Tristan," Salina nodded to the rider. "And God bless you."

"He will," Tristan grinned.

Darkness did not completely hide the horrendous scene at the docks. The destruction couldn't have been plainer had it been full noon. It went without saying that Rafe's insightful choice to move the yacht out away from the wharves had been a miraculously sound decision. Standing at the railing while the steamer sailed toward Richmond, Salina and Elinor attentively listened to what Drake had been able to learn: The initial explosion had been traced to an ordnance barge. Immense damage had been inflicted on a nearby boat, the *Kendrick*, which reportedly carried a combustible cargo of artillery ammunition, small arms, and cartridges. A newly constructed warehouse had been completely razed, and almost two hundred feet of the wharf along the waterfront had been reduced to splinters. Broken timbers, along with wreckage of all description, and the gruesome remains of men and animals had been strewn over a broad portion of the encampment. Murmurs increased in volume and portent concerning a torpedo deliberately launched by Confederate saboteurs, but there was far too much evidence to sift through as yet, and conclusive declarations were postponed until more convincing facts could be compiled. A measure of doubt obscured any clear-cut assumption; there was the consideration that accidents had happened before.

☆☆☆☆☆☆☆

A week before Salina's eighteenth birthday, Mosby's rangers attacked a Federal wagon train near Berryville along the Winchester Turnpike. The plunder included musical instruments, supplies, equipment, and a good many other items the Confederates could put to use. The spanking new blue uniforms were a case in point: A number of the raiders swapped their old, worn gray or butternut uniforms, turning the jackets inside out to display the lining rather than the navy-colored wool.

The strike might have produced an even richer payoff had the partisans not overlooked the strongbox that accompanied the Union paymaster en route to the Yankee garrison at Winchester. The box had contained a bankroll in excess of one hundred thousand dollars.

Yet even without the money, the partisans made out tolerably well. They acquired a small quantity of valuables from their prisoners and captured more than five hundred mules, not quite three dozen horses, and roughly two hundred head of beef cattle. The raid proved beneficial for the occupants of Berryville, too, as they took full advantage of nabbing their share of the plunder after the rangers were through collecting their own spoils.

The return of the raiding party to Fauquier County was an unforgettable sight to those who witnessed it: Mosby's men sported their new blue uniforms, played the untuned instruments, and sang merrily while they herded the captured cattle along. At Rectortown, the haul was divvied up. Most of the cattle and mules were sent on to Gordonsville, but several steers were bestowed as a token of thanks upon families in Fauquier and Loudoun Counties who willfully overlooked the risk involved in providing shelter for the rangers when they needed it.

Sheridan was forced to pull out of Winchester, redeploying his troops to a point north of Berryville. The Northern cavalry commander learned the hard way that he could not effectively protect such protracted lines of communication. His scouts brought word that reinforcements were being sent to Early in the form of Kershaw's division and Fitz Lee's brigade of Confederate horsemen. General Grant was outraged when reports of the Berryville Raid reached his headquarters at City Point. His wired message to Sheridan bespoke his ire:

> *If you can possibly spare a division of cavalry, send them through Loudoun County to destroy and carry off crops, animals, negroes, and all men under fifty years of age capable of bearing arms. In this manner you will get rid of Mosby's men.*

The mordant reply Sheridan sent back to his commander on the seventeeth of August set in motion a grim and irrepressible chain of events soon to follow in the wake of his actions: "Mosby has annoyed me and captured a few wagons. We hung one and shot six of his men yesterday."

☆☆☆☆☆☆☆

August 20, 1864
Richmond, Virginia

Duncan Grant had been with President Lincoln in the telegraph office in Washington eleven days earlier, on the morning of August ninth, when General Grant's telegram of 11:45 had arrived from City Point. Duncan had been briefed on the particulars of the explosion at the ordnance wharf, and shortly thereafter, Lincoln had confidently put Duncan's name in the hat as the one who would depart post haste to serve on the board of inquiry, which would be convened and presided over by Lieutenant Colonel Horace Porter.

Duncan despised himself for what he was about to do, the things he would be forced to say; but he had been left with little choice. During his portion of the investigation, he'd come across the record of a pass that had been issued with Salina's name on it, and he was bound to find out what on earth she had been doing in City Point in general, let alone on that specific day. Ironically, his morning devotional had included the fifth verse of the nineteenth chapter of Proverbs: *A false witness shall not be unpunished, and he that speaketh lies shall not escape.* Duncan resolutely set his jaw. He was determined to get the truth from his stepdaughter, even if it meant having to shake it out of her!

☆☆☆☆☆☆☆

With a critical eye, Salina picked over the meager selection of fruits and vegetables, not overly impressed with any of the available spun truck on display at the poorly stocked market stalls. She had reluctantly purchased two pounds of fresh shad for a steep price, along with some scallions, a lemon, and four cans of condensed milk. As she added a half-pound of bacon to the basket slung over her arm, she felt the hairs on the back of her neck stand up. The sudden urge to drop everything, gather her skirts, and run was almost overwhelming. Careful to make no quick or unnatural movements that would draw undue attention, Salina hastily separated herself from the crowd at the marketplace and made her way toward Linden Row.

All the way home, Salina sensed the unrelenting presence of an unseen follower. Twice she unnecessarily crossed the cobbled streets at a diagonal, hoping to catch a glimpse of someone in a store window reflection, but all she saw was a hunched old man in a suit of ebon broadcloth. Prudence dictated that she not go to her own doorstep—she went instead to Mrs. Hoffman's.

"What ails you, Salina? You look right peaked," her next-door neighbor proclaimed.

Salina answered only when she had assured herself that Glory and E.J. were safe. "I have reason to believe someone is following me. Do you mind if I slip out your back door?"

"And go into that empty house alone?" Mrs. Hoffman queried. "Stay here instead," she insisted, inferring that there was safety in numbers.

Salina stayed on for an hour, but eventually she did sneak out the back door with her grocery basket and a baby in either arm. Convinced that no one had broken in, she lit only one hurricane lamp when darkness fell. By its light she fed the children, tucked them into their cradles, and sat between them with her back against the wall—Spencer repeater, pearl-handled pistol, and spare ammunition within easy reach. She waited, a prayer on her lips.

At length the back door of the townhouse opened and closed again. Stealthy steps cautiously ascended the stairwell. Salina was not as surprised as she thought she should have been when the familiar face of her stepfather appeared at the door.

"Now, I'm *sure* you didn't come all this way—in *that* getup—just to wish me a happy eighteenth birthday!" Salina bit out sarcastically.

Face-to-face with Garrett Hastings' daughter, Duncan's resolve melted like ice cream on the Fourth of July. Duncan relieved Salina of the gun she had trained on him, putting it out of her immediate reach, and enfolded her in a protective embrace.

"It's good to see you too, Duncan, I think..." Salina could not guess what had prompted him to seek her out—here in the Confederate capital. "What are *you* doing *here* of all places?"

"I came to prove something to myself," Duncan answered raggedly. His storm-gray eyes shifted from Salina's puzzled countenance to the cradles and their occupants—his grandchildren.

"And you've been here before," she softly charged. "This is *not* the first time you've spied on me."

Duncan shook his chestnut head. "No, it's not."

"How did you...?"

He cut her off, reinstating an attitude of belligerence as a means to instill a healthy dose of fear in her. "This is *not* your interrogation, it's mine! Sit down—over there," he commanded, brooking no argument.

Salina immediately obeyed, then waited in uncomfortable silence.

The little sigh that escaped Glory was followed by a big yawn. E.J. squealed, waving his clenched fists to underscore his good humor. Peering over the sides of the cradles, Duncan could not remain unaffected after both pair of eyes latched on to his face, looking up at him in wonder. His line of questioning did not begin as his stepdaughter obviously anticipated.

"So your husband agreed to the adoption, I take it?"

"Aye," Salina answered softly. "I suspect Ethan knew from the start Jeremy would raise no objection."

"May I hold them?" Duncan wanted be sure that Salina wouldn't fly at him in a mother's protective rage if he dared touch either of the wee ones without permission.

Slowly Salina nodded, granting his unexpected request. She was confused by the complete disappearance of his anger from a moment before.

Duncan picked up the little girl first. Glory Stuart was a darling miniature of Salina but with the sandy-blond hair and vivid blue eyes of her father. E.J., on the other hand, had eyes every bit as green as Salina's and hair of raven black—definitive Hastings traits. Duncan covered the babies in their beds as both children returned to sucking their drool-drenched fists. He complimented his stepdaughter. "They are beautiful children, Salina. I'm sure you and Jeremy must be very proud of them both."

"We are indeed." Salina was still a bit skittish of him, a shade distrusting. "You know all about what goes on with us, don't you?"

"To a large extent I do," Duncan acknowledged, his eyes filled with crimination. "I also know about the Southerlands, that Jeremy and Lance could've killed each other at Trevilian if they'd a mind to, and that you were at City Point the morning of the explosion. Tell me you didn't have anything to do with *that*, Salina! Make me believe beyond a shadow of a doubt you had no hand in, or any prior knowledge of, the time bomb that blew up two million dollars' worth of property, killed forty-three people, and wounded a hundred and twenty-six others! Reassure me that that *wasn't* an assassination attempt on the lieutenant general!"

Agitated, Salina twisted her wedding ring around her finger. "Is that what you think? That I somehow contributed to that?" It would have made her laugh if the gravity of his accusation weren't so condemning. "But then, given my past history, what other conclusion could you have drawn?"

"Convince me that I've drawn the *wrong* conclusion," Duncan ground out between his clenched teeth.

Salina didn't bother explaining about Drake and Elinor's wedding—he'd find that out eventually anyway, when his investigation led him further on. "You've got the wrong conclusion," Salina rebutted. "Honestly, Duncan, that's the truth—I'm not just saying it because that's what you want to hear. I had just as much of a chance at winding up a victim as anyone else on the Point that day—General Grant included!" She shook her head, flippantly adding, "I might've been a good agent once, Duncan, but I was never *that* good. I suppose I ought to be flattered by your confidence in my sorely underused skills. Not only have I adhered to the conditions Lincoln set forth in my pardon to *behave*, but you need to remember I'm a mother to two small children. Do you think I'd do anything foolhardy enough to orphan them—especially when there is no telling if or when their father will ever return home? They need me; their well-being is my foremost concern! If I could care less about this war, I would, but I can't. Survival is what counts."

Duncan swallowed hard, properly chagrined. He couldn't blame her in the least if she thought he had completely lost his mind. An apology should have been forthcoming, something to make her understand that the war was eating away at simple logic and cold reason. Garrett's daughter, however, demonstrated a commendable graciousness in not requiring him to explain himself further. She was disinclined to make a precarious situation worse by forcing him to outwardly confess how utterly ludicrous his presumptions actually were. Instead, she found a forgiving smile and charitably invited him downstairs for whatever she could offer in the way of refreshment.

It wasn't long at all before she put the inevitable query to him: "Have you any word from my brother?"

Duncan took a deep breath. He could not lie to her; he answered without beating around the bush. "Ethan was lately released from Point Lookout."

Salina's beringed hand flew to her bosom to quell the pounding of her heart. "Released?" Salina noted his uncompromising stance, sensing the other shoe was about to drop. "But?"

"But five days ago your brother boarded the transport ship *Continental*, dressed in a *blue* uniform, Salina. Of his own accord, Ethan signed the Oath of Allegiance and freely enlisted with the 1st U.S. Volunteers. He's part of a regiment that was recruited from prison inmates. The 1st has drawn the assignment to a post in Dakota Territory. They will be stationed at Fort Rice, on the Missouri River, to help subdue the Indians who might have intentions of disrupting the relative peace along the emigrant trails."

Salina blanched beyond pale and gripped the edge of the table to steady herself, unable to catch her breath. It was *impossible* to fathom that her proud, determined brother would have renounced his convictions or turned his back on everything he stood for without influence or coercion. "Does..." She bit her lip. "Does my mamma know of this?"

Duncan nodded. "She saw your brother before he departed Point Lookout."

Salina's throat constricted. "Dear God..." She put a hand over her mouth to stifle the sob that shook her shoulders uncontrollably and choked off the rest of her prayer. "Ethan doesn't care about anything anymore."

"That's not true, Salina. He must've cared enough to want to *live*. He might've died in that prison had he elected to stubbornly remain in captivity. His health, had his condition worsened, might've deteriorated irreparably." Duncan gently rationalized the situation for her just as he had done for her mother. "I suppose Ethan finally began to see the handwriting on the wall. You know him, Salina: Unless Ethan viewed making this choice as his last hope for recourse, he wouldn't have done it. And if it makes you feel any better, you may rest assured that he protested with an honorable measure of fury when I initially approached him with the idea. He wanted no part of it then, none whatsoever. But since that time, things have changed for him..."

"Since then, she whom Ethan loved best no longer graces the face of this earth!" Salina pinpointed her sister-in-law's death as being the last straw that had broken her brother's will. She shut her eyes tightly only to see Ethan's gaunt and bearded face. For months she had prayed for his discharge, but with the assumption that he would come home to where he belonged. Salina would never have believed that abandoning Virginia in her hour of need was what would be demanded of Ethan in exchange for an illusory freedom.

With a great effort, Salina managed to collect herself. "I reckon I ought be grateful that you followed me, for if you hadn't come, I wouldn't have known... At least now I do." She licked her dry lips. "I believe both of us have said all that can be said, for now at any rate. If you will please excuse me..."

"Salina," Duncan began.

"I'm sorry I can offer you no more for the sake of hospitality. You are free to stay until you determine the streets are safe enough for you to move about." Salina drew a shaky breath and let it out. "And watch your back, Duncan. Don't give my mamma any further reason to grieve."

With that parting shot, she ran up the stairs and threw herself down on the bed, where she proceeded to cry without consolation.

Duncan let himself out the back door. This meeting had gone scarcely better than the last time they'd seen each other in Washington. As he worked his way through the Rebel capital undercover and back to his own lines, he couldn't help but think that if Ethan *had* died, Salina might've taken the news better than learning of what she mistakenly perceived to be a case of turncoat defection. One day, she might see that Ethan had not made a choice between blue and gray; he'd chosen life over death—period.

☆☆☆☆☆☆☆

Mildred Lee shook her head in wonder, her hands momentarily stilled in their work during a sewing bee at The Mess. The grapevine of the gossipmongers told of a clash that had occurred between a portion of Mosby's men and a Federal patrol comprising half a dozen Yankees in the vicinity of Charles Town. Only one of the Federals escaped death and got away. He carried back to Sheridan the dismal story of what had happened. It proved to be added fuel to an already kindled fire. Then another instance of note transpired near Kernstown: Mosby's rangers had "gobbled up" a twenty-man Union detachment—without firing a single shot.

"How do you suppose the regimental commander responded to news that the detail he'd sent out had vanished without trace?" Mildred asked the other ladies present.

Neither Salina nor Mildred's sister Agnes ventured to guess, and the ladies kept on sewing.

"Whatever happened to Custis Morgan?" Salina inquired after the noticeably absent squirrel that had for a time been the Lees' pet. If the other ladies inferred that she was seeking another direction for the conversation, they didn't make mention of it. The recounting of the 43rd Battalion's dangerous exploits was dropped from discussion.

"A few weeks ago, Custis Morgan slipped out," Agnes answered, "and he is now missing in action." She herself wasn't overly fond of talking about the vindictive atrocities exchanged between the Rebel partisans and Sheridan's men either. It brought to mind the harshness and cruelty that war inflicted. Her former beau, Orton Williams, had been captured by the Yankees near Franklin, Tennessee, and was condemned to execution for reportedly spying behind the lines. All this scuttle of hangings and blatant shootings served to remind her of the mysterious circumstances surrounding Orton's death. Agnes shivered, withdrawing into herself.

"Custis Morgan's escape was for the best, though," Mrs. Lee put in, knitting needles clicking rapidly. "He had a bad habit of biting our friends, and he was always underfoot." The wife of the commanding general inquired of Salina: "Have you by chance heard from Flora Stuart at all?"

Regrettably, Salina had not, but she expressed her hope that Flora and General Stuart's children were faring well in southwest Virginia with her in-laws.

The next afternoon, while Salina worked her shift at Robertson Hospital, she was more convinced than ever that impending disaster was imminent. She couldn't help but overhear the dire, worrisome tales the convalescents relayed concerning the disposition of the factions grappling in the Shenandoah Valley. Sheridan's blue cavalry and the roaming Jessie Scouts—Union raiders dressed in Rebel uniforms—pitted themselves against the partisans of both Mosby and a band led by Colonel E. V. White known as the Comanches. Events escalated, each instance more drastic in measure than the last. Homes and property had been maliciously burned with the intent of drawing Mosby's men out into the open for capture. Farm animals were slaughtered, silver and jewelry stolen, women and children turned out without shelter or food. Rage fed an increasing desire for revenge.

The brutal savagery progressed for another month, and still Salina had no word at all from Jeremy. She had no clue as to his whereabouts, and much as she tried not to worry about him, she couldn't stop herself from doing so. Mosby was wounded on September fourteenth, but by then Sheridan had already received a fatal order from General Grant:

> *Where any of Mosby's men are caught, hang them without trial.*

☆☆☆☆☆☆☆

E.J.'s "ba-ba-ba-ba" lifted Salina's forehead from where it rested on her crossed arms. Salina stood for a moment, having again been on her knees in prayer for the safety of her long-absent husband, and then lay down beside the happy-sounding boy. Since Jeremy's last epistle in early August she'd received no additional letters, no hasty telegrams, no word-of-mouth messages. It was almost as if Jeremy himself had been gobbled up.

"Ba-ba-ba-ba," Salina cooed back at E.J., nibbling at his neck and tickling his tummy until he giggled uncontrollably. His open-mouthed expression gave her a chance to see that he'd finally cut the latest tooth that had been plaguing him the past couple of days. "Well, there it is. I do see it!" She grinned at him, swiping the bottom half of his round little face with a spare diaper. "You and that drooly chin!"

E.J. gurgled and wriggled. He had no comprehension of how his dimpled smile revived Salina's heart.

Later, while the boy was napping and Glory was in full possession of her mamma's undivided attention, Salina groaned as a knock on the front door interrupted their play.

"I'm coming!" Salina called, carrying her daughter into the entry hall with her. "Oh, hello, Mrs. Hoffman. Won't you come in?"

"I can't stay long, dear. I just came to tell you..."

"Tell me what?" Salina prodded.

The neighbor lady hesitated.

"Have you seen the papers today?"

"No," Salina replied. "I've not been out yet. Has... has something of import happened?"

"It's all so distressing..." Mrs. Hoffman shook her head.

Last week, when Mrs. Hoffman had come to tell Salina of the fall and occupation of Atlanta, she had employed the same phrasing. It *was* distressing that since Atlanta had succumbed to Union control, the South had lost valuable rail lines and raw materials from Georgia—cut off with the compliments of William Tecumseh Sherman. Salina seated herself on the horsehair sofa, inviting Mrs. Hoffman to do likewise. She was almost afraid to ask, "What is it this time?"

"This might hit a little closer to home, dear, since it is believed that your husband does ride with the partisan rangers..." she sought to kindly warn the young matron.

"Mrs. Hoffman, please!" Salina was getting impatient. "What have you heard?"

The neighbor lady launched into a tale that was not told in chronological order or with any great accuracy, but was salted with hearsay. Salina pieced together, from the jumbled rush of explanation, the events that led up to the *distressing* part: The latest tangle at Front Royal between a detachment of Mosby's men and soldiers from the 2nd U.S. Cavalry had ended in a most brutal display of action—six captured rangers had been mercilessly executed by the Union troopers, four shot and two hanged. A note was found pinned to one of the misfortunate: *This will be the fate of Mosby and all his men.*

Salina's sharp gasp for breath completely startled little Glory. As Salina bounced the baby girl on her lap to quiet the cries, she managed to ask, "Who...who were the rangers? Did the paper not give their names?"

Mrs. Hoffman was sure that if the names had been listed, none of them was Jeremy's... She was sure she would've remembered if it was...

The fear in Salina's bosom clutched her heart like an icy hand squeezing unmercifully. Uncertainty threatened to steal her breath, but a niggling of intuitive reason arrested her wayward thoughts. In her heart, if something had happened to Jeremy, she was sure she would feel it.

Before the week was out, the old man in the black broadcloth suit appeared across the street from the townhouse in Linden Row. Salina trimmed the gas lamps, and when she looked for him a second time, he was gone. In the morning, she discovered an unmarked envelope that had been slid under the back door.

> *The board of inquiry has adjourned. After days of testimony, there is still no absolute accounting for the explosion; the evidence is inconclusive. Whoever the perpetrator was could not be precisely determined, as anyone who would have had corroborating firsthand evidence was killed in the blast. The incident has been ruled an accident. Security has been tightened, to say the least.*
>
> *I am off to Washington to take care of matters before I return to headquarters for the winter. I plan to bring your mamma and little brother back with me to camp. Your cousin and her husband will probably follow as a matter of course.*
>
> *Assuming you have heard of the appalling ruthlessness up in Front Royal, allow me to put your mind at ease. Having seen the official report myself, I can vouch that your husband—nor any of his band—were the victims. In fact, I doubt they were anywhere near Front Royal at the time of the executions. I strongly believe that Hampton—who had probably learned of their cowboy background and experiences and hand-picked them because of it—took them along with him on the recent foray to Coggins Point and back. They never give up, do they? Had Stuart been alive to see it through, I'm sure he'd have laughed in our faces. If you ask me, it was far too reminiscent of those impudent exploits the late cavalry commander incorporated as his trademark. I often wonder how it is that our side has arrived at where we*

are when we can't seem to do anything to stop three thousand gray horsemen from penetrating our lines, shamelessly stealing twenty-five hundred head of cattle, and returning with beeves in tow virtually unimpeded from whence they came!

Enough said; there is little to be gained by crying over spilt milk. I will be in touch when I can.

It was no surprise that when her eyes arrived at the bottom of the page, Salina found it devoid of a signature. It had no need of one, for to her it was plain as to who had authored the informative note.

"God bless Duncan." Her heart felt a good deal lighter than it had in weeks, and Salina pondered the triumphant raid Duncan had mentioned and impulsively sang a verse from an old Stuart-inspired song:

> *There's a man in the white house with*
> > *blood on his mouth!*
> *If there's Knaves in the North, there are*
> > *Braves in the South.*
> *We are three thousand horses and not one*
> > *afraid;*
> *We are three thousand sabres and not a*
> > *dull blade.*
>
> *Come tighten your girth and slacken your*
> > *rein;*
> *Come buckle your blanket and holster*
> > *again;*
> *Try the click of your trigger and balance*
> > *your blade,*
> *For he must ride sure that goes Riding a*
> > *Raid!*

Chapter Nineteen

*W*hile Mosby was recovering from his September wounding, he paid a visit to the environs of Richmond and had a meeting with Generals Lee and Longstreet at their headquarters around Petersburg. When Mosby returned to Northern Virginia, a new target had made itself manifest: The Federals were going to rebuild the Manassas Gap Railroad, and Mosby had no intention of letting that happen. He was determined to disrupt the Union's attempts at restoring both communication and supply lines between Washington and the Shenandoah Valley. Sixty miles of track became the new theatre of operations for the partisan rangers, where the lightning-quick raids were frequent and rendered with ferocity. In a short time, more than seven hundred Yankee prisoners were forwarded to Richmond for confinement.

The "Greenback Raid" on the Baltimore & Ohio Railroad on October thirteenth—where a Union payroll of more than $170,000 was the seized prize—was followed by yet another coup: the capture of Brigadier General Alfred Duffié while he was out for a buggy ride within ten miles of his own headquarters. Salina had little doubt as to whether or not the arrest of General Duffié had been carried off as brazenly as the capture of General Edwin Stoughton from Fairfax Court House nearly two years ago. The rangers, she was sure, would have performed their duty with matchless zeal and aplomb.

Five weeks passed with no effort made to retaliate for the disparaging executions in Front Royal, even after a seventh ranger was hung in Rappahannock County. On November sixth, however, Mosby held a lottery drawing among twenty-seven Union prisoners. Those who drew slips of paper marked with the numbers one through seven were to be hung in reprisal for those rangers whose lives had been taken by the Federals. One of those Yankee prisoners was a drummer boy, whom Mosby and the other rangers deemed too young for participation in the punishment. The drummer was summarily let go, and another was made to draw in his place. Mosby did not stay to oversee the retribution enacted, as General Custer had reportedly done in Front Royal. Three of the Federals were hanged near Berryville, the remaining three were shot but not necessarily killed, for along with one of the wounded, the seventh man escaped—and when Mosby heard that, he was glad of it. It meant that Sheridan would receive, from the lips of his own men, the report of their experiences.

A trusted scout bore a letter to Winchester written by Mosby to Sheridan. The closing paragraph read:

> *Hereafter any prisoners falling into my hands will be treated with the kindness due to their condition, unless some new act of barbarity shall compel me reluctantly to adopt a line of policy repugnant to humanity.*

Sheridan complied. No additional "acts of barbarity" were committed directly against Mosby's men. By the end of November, Sheridan was instead bent on inflicting havoc directly on the population and the lands of Mosby's Confederacy. By noon on the twenty-eighth, Federal forces under Sheridan's command arrived at Ashby's Gap in the Blue Ridge Mountains. Riding through to Upperville, Middleburg, and Aldie, the blue invaders enacted the orders to burn everything useful to either Mosby's men or their horses. Sheridan's intent was to dislodge the irksome partisans from their hiding places, and while the destruction was utterly devastating, the Federals still failed in their mission to run Mosby to ground. Though the blue cavalry hunted high and low while scouting Loudoun County for any trace of him, they were able to discover only that Mosby and all his men seemingly had disappeared into the landscape.

☆☆☆☆☆☆☆

December 1864
Richmond, Virginia

The skinny bay horse tethered just inside the front gate was not a mount Salina recognized—but the man in the butternut uniform resting his back against the columned porch post was dearly familiar.

"Oh, my darling!" Salina exclaimed.

At the sound of his wife's voice, Jeremy Barnes raised his head, peering from beneath the brim of his felt slouch hat. Salina abandoned the pram on the cobbled sidewalk and flung herself headlong into his welcoming arms.

Having nearly knocked Jeremy's hat askew, Salina framed his lean, bearded face in her hands and kissed him. "Thank God!" It had been almost six months since she'd seen him.

"The neighbors will talk, Sallie," Jeremy grinned. "Let's go on in and celebrate." He lifted the pram up the stairs with both babies in it, setting it down in the entryway. Closing the beveled-glass door behind him, Jeremy's unpatched eye fixed on each of the cherubic faces belonging to the dear little ones. E.J. seemed wary of him, uncertain at best, but Glory Stuart showed no such reservations. Jeremy's daughter lifted her arms, entirely unafraid of him, wanting to be picked up and cuddled.

"She knows her daddy," Salina affirmed as she shrugged out of her cloak. She was pleased beyond words to have Jeremy home safe, but she almost envied her daughter the attention Jeremy was lavishing on her.

"They've grown so," Jeremy stated the obvious, holding the little girl close. Glory reached up, her little fingers targeting his eyepatch. One abrupt tug broke the tie that secured the eyepatch in place. Jeremy pried the patch from Glory's fist and kissed her hand, setting the damaged patch aside.

"Maybe she thinks you don't need that anymore," Salina laughed softly.

"Maybe," Jeremy agreed. "I suppose wearing it's just gotten to be a habit more than a necessity anyway."

"Can you see well enough without it, or will you need me to fix that for you?" Salina asked.

Jeremy squinted, forcing the usually covered eye to focus on several points about the parlour. It had been quite some time since he'd given his vision any thought at all, and it surprised him that he could plainly see more than he realized he could. "Let's just leave it for now."

E.J., sensing that Jeremy must be all right if Glory wasn't shy of him, sounded a request for attention.

"He's feeling left out," Salina nodded toward the boy. "These two are a pair. They share everything, and one can't have something the other hasn't got."

Jeremy grinned, lifting E.J. with his free arm. "Come here, son."

The endearment warmed Salina's heart. She couldn't get her fill of looking at Jeremy, from the top of his sandy-blond head to his broad shoulders and lanky frame, and back to his sapphire eyes. The scar near his eye, once such a dark purplish-red, had indeed faded.

"Have you missed me?" Jeremy teased her, basking in her unmitigated regard.

"Have I ever!" Salina nodded emphatically.

Momentarily setting Glory and E.J. down, Jeremy finally enfolded his wife in his arms and kissed her. Salina reciprocated his fervid kiss. Upon its conclusion, she buried her face in his chest, content to be held in the circle of his loving embrace. Suddenly her nose wrinkled in weak protest. "Mmmm," she shook her dark head. The pungent mixture of stale sweat, worn leather, and lathered horses assaulted her sense of smell. "When's the last time you had a proper bath?"

Jeremy tossed his head back and laughed. "I haven't seen you in months, and rather than being glad to have me here in one piece, your foremost concern is that I smell bad?"

Salina brushed away the horsehair that had transferred itself from his jacket to the front of her bodice. "That's not true. I *am* glad you're home, and I'm *extremely* thankful that you're all in one piece—but you do smell rank. I'll go start a fire and put some water on to boil. Are you hungry?"

"Aye, but I'll eat later. I've got to feed my horse first." Jeremy kissed Salina's brow and leaned down to tousle the hair on the children's heads before going out the door. Salina put the kettles on to boil and then got busy laying out a simple feast of cheese, crackers, cold fried chicken, and bread pudding with brandy sauce. She touched a match to the candles to increase the light and added a jug of cider to the fare on the table.

While Jeremy ate, Salina filled the copper hip bath in the pantry with steaming water. The babies were snuggly strapped into their chairs, and Jeremy kept them occupied, feeding them crackers and letting them sip from his cup in turns. Afterwards, he took the little ones upstairs and laid them in their respective cradles.

When Jeremy returned, the tub awaited him. In short order, he peeled off his butternut jacket and trousers.

"What happened to the jacket I sent you out in?" Salina asked curiously.

"It got torn...I mean, it got *worn* out," Jeremy hedged, knowing it was only a matter of time before she would discover his newest scar. "Though this one is looking a little ragged at the seams, too, isn't it?"

Salina gathered up the jean-cloth trousers with their braces and a glass-buttoned blouse of checked brown osnaburg, emptying all the pockets of their collected treasures. She put his clothes into a separate kettle of water for washing while her husband settled himself into the hot, soothing, sudsy water, resting his blond head against the edge of the tub.

"You going to scrub my back?" Jeremy invited.

"I suppose," Salina grinned impudently. She fetched a bar of soap and a washrag. "Lean forward."

Jeremy's head lolled forward, his bearded chin resting against his chest. Salina's soapy fingers eased the tension from the muscles across his shoulders and along the back of his neck. "What's this?" She traced a nearly healed laceration on his upper left arm, silently assuming that was the spot in which the old gray jacket had been *worn out.* "And these?" She indicated the greenish-blue bruises on his left knee.

"Just a scratch." He was again evasive, not wanting to upset her by recounting his narrow escape from capture during a recent foray behind enemy lines. "That and a few bruises are nothing to worry your pretty little head over." The implication was that there were other things to worry about.

"Tell me about the Beefsteak Raid," she requested, letting the matter of his injuries pass without further question. "You were with Hampton before you went back to Mosby's command, weren't you?"

"Aye. Driving cattle—there's a job. Where was Drake when we needed him?"

"Probably in England, still on his honeymoon," Salina replied saucily.

Jeremy's head snapped up, and his eyes grew round in surprise. He insisted she tell him all about Drake and Elinor's wedding before he would satisfy her curiosity about the daring escapade that led to the capture of nearly twenty-five hundred beeves.

"Stuart would've loved it—and looking back, it was quite the lark. One of the Northern newspaper correspondents wrote 'As a piece of raiding rascality it was perfect.' And Lincoln himself was quoted as saying it was the 'slickest piece of cattle stealing he'd ever heard of.'" Jeremy's tense muscles were finally relaxing. "A scout named Shadburne infiltrated City Point on a number of occasions. During one such adventure, he learned of the herd and got ahold of information bearing out that Grant was going to be away from the Point—paying a visit to Sheridan in the Valley. It was our chance to strike. We weren't informed of where we were going at first; we were only ordered to collect rations and mount up. The endeavor, however, had all the classic earmarks of a raid, so we knew that something was going on. At three o'clock on the morning of September fourteenth, we jumped off from Gravelly Run near Boydon Plank Road. Hampton assigned other cavalry and some of General Mahone's infantry to stage a diversion, which they effectively did for the three days it took us to get the job done. In the first day, we went twenty miles and stopped for the night at Wilkinson's Creek. We were beyond the Union pickets, with strict orders for no fires and no whispers other than what was necessary to convey commands. The next day we crossed Rowanty Creek, passed Ebenezer Church and Belshes Mill. Captain Belsh himself volunteered to lead a scout, since he was familiar with the swamps and roads surrounding his home. By midday we were across the Norfolk & Petersburg Railroad and all the way to the Blackwater River and the ruins of Cook's bridge. The engineers rebuilt the bridge on its old pilings, and none of us envied them their task. Their tall boots were all the protection they had from the water moccasins that infest the Blackwater."

Salina shivered, waiting anxiously for him to go on with his storytelling.

"General Hampton had purposely taken us by that route to confuse the Federals, since they knew that the bridge was out. While the engineers worked to put the bridge back together, Hampton finally outlined the plans for his subordinates. It was a three-pronged attack, if you could see it on a map. Rooney Lee, along with Colonel Chew's Horse Artillery, made up the left column. They went down the Lawyer's Road with instructions to block the Union forces at Prince George Court House and keep them from getting to Sycamore Church—that's where the 1st District of Columbia cavalry was posted, just two miles from where the beeves were being guarded at Coggin's Point. They say the 1st D.C. companies were some pumpkins: outfitted with 16-shot Henry repeating rifles and the finest horses money can buy." Jeremy sighed wistfully. Good horseflesh was as hard to come by as ever, and he considered himself blessed with the mount he had, even though the Morgan had certainly seen better days and was in want of new shoes.

"General Dearing took his force down Hincs Road to Cocke's Mill on Stage Road," Jeremy continued. "It was theirs to eliminate the Union pickets at Fleur de Hundred Road and to protect General Rosser's brigade from any threat that might've come from Fort Powhattan, just east of Sycamore Church. The middle prong, the main body, was commanded by General Rosser, and General Hampton accompanied him. Shadburne stayed with Hampton, and so did we."

"You, Bentley, Boone, C.J., and Kidd Carney?" She wanted to clarify who his *we* entailed.

Jeremy grinned. "Aye—and Tristan Scarborough."

"Tristan?! But of course!" Salina snapped her fingers. "No wonder he was taking so long to heal from his wounds. He was working with Shadburne. But how did he get out of the hospital at City Point?"

"Hmmm," Jeremy toyed with his whiskers. "If I'm not mistaken, he made some mention of owing a favor to Aurora Dallinger, I believe."

"Rorie and Tristan?" Salina arched an eyebrow. "Well... stranger things have happened, I suppose."

"Indeed," Jeremy readily agreed. "Where was I?"

"You stayed with Hampton," Salina reminded him.

"Yeah," Jeremy remembered, "we stayed with Hampton. We rode up Wells Road to Sycamore Church. The 1st D.C. held a strong position behind a wall of cut trees. Shadburne had initially reported the road open, but in the time between his reconnaissance and the proposed attack, the D.C. boys had thrown up a barricade that we had to fight our way through to get to the cattle. It was dark when the attack started, and the first charge was repulsed by the fire flying out of those repeaters. Casualties were heavy. Colonel Dulaney took some of his dismounted men in to remove the barricades. The 7th Virginia exploited the breach in the D.C.'s defenses. Once we were through the opening, White's Comanches disposed of the Pennsylvania troops guarding the herd. Their drovers tried to stampede them, but we got the beeves rounded up and headed back to our lines. A number of their drovers were—coerced—into riding along and moving the cattle with us; in truth, they weren't left any other choice but to comply. Fortunately, somebody had the foresight to bring along herd dogs, so between them, the drovers, and cavalrymen who quickly learned what to do to prod the cattle onward, we got those beeves moving toward the Blackwater River. The engineers reinforced Cook's Bridge to make it strong enough to hold the weight of the beeves. The herd was divided into four sections and tallied as they crossed the span—it took a while to get them all over the bridge to the other side. Afterward, the bridge was destroyed so the Federals couldn't make use of it in their pursuit.

"Rosser's brigade did their share of fighting if they hadn't, the raid wouldn't have succeeded. My men and I were ordered to go along with Major Venable and the detachment Hampton put in his charge. It was our job to drive that herd onward, keeping them ahead of any threat of Union repossession. At Neblitt's Mill Dam, we tried to move the steers past the water, but they practically stampeded to get to it. The roads were dusty and hot, and the whole lot of us, men and animals alike, were thirsty. The key was to keep them moving, though. We didn't bed down for the night until after we got across the Nottoway River at Freeman's Ford. Before sunup on the morning of the seventeenth, we drove them across the Weldon Railroad, and before noon they were confined in pens within the Confederate lines at Petersburg."

"And once again, the Yankees reacted too slowly to stop you," Salina rejoiced. She poured a pitcherful of water over Jeremy's head to rinse the shampoo out. "I reckon the troops in the trenches at Petersburg deemed the arrival of the cattle a most welcome sight."

"Sure they did—it meant they wouldn't be hungry for a while. The butchered herd fed General Lee's army for a month, staving off starvation for another day." Jeremy wiped the water from his face. "It all worked," he recalled, closing his eyes and reliving the adventure. "The conditions were in our favor, the Yankees were adequately confused, and the Lord was with us. Though General Lee had stringently cautioned Hampton against engagement with the enemy, the fighting we did was unavoidable. We did what we had to in order to succeed in our objective: Capturing the beef was satisfactorily accomplished."

Salina couldn't help but smile at the retelling of the gray cavalry's impudent antics. "You know, I got a letter from Mamma a few weeks back. In it she mentioned a dinner that Duncan had attended shortly after the raid. General Grant had invited his subordinates to a fine meal that was distinctly lacking in *meat*. One of the general officers inquired as to how long General Grant thought it would take to starve out Lee and take Richmond, and Grant reportedly replied, 'Forever, General, if you keep feeding Lee's army with beef.'" She and Jeremy both laughed, and then she went on to say, "According to what Duncan told Mamma, General Grant was relatively good-natured about the affair, but those people found it unnerving nonetheless. Between the explosion at the ordnance wharf and the raid on the cattle, the picket lines around the Point have been reinforced considerably. I am not sure at all whether or not an attempt will be made to sneak me through the lines for Christmas."

"You would go back there?" Jeremy queried. "If given the opportunity?"

"Only out of my desire to see Mamma," Salina qualified. "It's been more than a year since I've seen her or Yabel, Jeremy. She hasn't even seen Glory or E.J., except in the photographs I've sent to her. Yes, if Duncan provides a way, I will go."

For a moment Jeremy was silent. He couldn't forbid her the opportunity to see her family. "Just you be careful, Sallie." He trusted her judgment, knowing she wouldn't do anything she didn't think was right.

"Where are your men now?" Salina wondered.

"They'll be here tomorrow," Jeremy answered, lacing his fingers between hers. "We've got tonight, darlin', but then I'm leaving again in the morning, or as soon as they get here. The armies have gone into their winter encampments, but we of Mosby's battalion aren't having time to rest. We've got work to do."

"It seems to me that the cavalry always rides," Salina said wistfully, knowing that the horsemen were relied upon to continue their duty regardless of circumstances. She was determined to make the best of the little time they had to share and be thankful for it.

Studying Jeremy's large hand, she noted that his fingertips had shriveled and appeared like wrinkled, pale raisins. "The water's getting cold." She started to reach for a towel for him.

He caught her fingers with one hand and motioned for her to lean toward him with the other.

"What?" She eyed him with a skeptical look.

"I love you," he said simply, flashing a disarming grin.

"I love you, too." Salina complied with his unspoken request for a kiss.

The instant their lips touched, Jeremy pulled Salina into the tub with him, sending tepid water sloshing over the sides.

"Jere-me-ee!" Salina's plaintive protest was met with a succession of kisses.

Jeremy retained a stone-faced expression. "I do love you, Sallie," he repeated with uncontrived solemnity, "very much."

"I know." The intensity of her gaze was meant to convince him of the depth of her assurance.

"Now let me go," she wriggled, uselessly attempting to free herself. She could feel the bathwater saturating her skirt and petticoats. "Jeremy," she laughed, "we're making a frightful mess!"

From upstairs, E.J.'s vociferous wail reined both their attention. "Did you change their diapers before you put them to bed?" Salina queried.

Jeremy shook his head and shrugged. "They seemed fine when I laid them down."

"Well, he can't be hungry, so he probably needs a changing. Will you let me go, please?" Salina was prompted to action, and Jeremy reluctantly released her. With a smirk, he watched his wife head upstairs, regardless of the fact that, with every step, water dripped from the hem of her skirt.

By the time Jeremy joined Salina on the second floor, he found the hurricane lamp burning brightly and both babies wide awake. "Apparently they weren't quite as tired as I thought they were."

Salina smiled at him. "Like me, they want your attention." As she exchanged E.J.'s wet nightdress for a dry one, Salina told Jeremy of their son's recent accomplishment. "He'd pulled himself up using a corner of the dining room tablecloth as leverage, but the fabric gave way. A crystal vase was knocked over, but thankfully did not break, and he scared himself more than anything. He's much more selective in what he lays hold of now before getting to his feet. He's taken a few steps, but then he reverts to crawling. I'm certainly going to have my hands full when they're both walking!"

A lump of regret lodged in Jeremy's throat. If the war ever ended, he'd be able to spend time with his family, and he wouldn't miss out on the little things, the everyday things, that were important in their own right. But for the warm welcome and loving reception each of these three precious ones accorded him, he might've felt like an outsider looking in on his own family.

Glory, on hands and knees, scooted over to where Salina stood and used her mamma's skirts to pull herself to her feet.

"I've no doubt Glory will be following his suit soon enough, for whatever E.J. does, she feels compelled to try it, too." Salina nodded at her daughter. "Don't you?"

A bright-eyed grin and a gurgle of laughter was the reply.

Salina gladly let Jeremy have a second chance at putting their little ones down for the night. He held them both on his lap, rocking and singing softly until Glory's and E.J.'s eyelids drooped in contented repose.

☆☆☆☆☆☆☆

Over breakfast in the kitchen, Salina plied a hundred questions at least, and Jeremy answered them all to the best of his ability and knowledge. He ate two bowls of oatmeal with brown sugar while he told Salina what he knew of John Hunt Morgan's death, of the devastation Sherman was meting out across a sixty-mile-wide swath of Georgia, and of the raid General George Stoneman had led against Saltville and Wytheville. Salina hadn't touched a bite, and she wrung her hands nervously when Jeremy finished telling her of the demolition the Federal cavalry had inflicted on the salt and lead mines in southwest Virginia.

"I pray Flora and her children are all right," Salina whispered, shaking her head in disbelief. "Poor, poor Flora! To have left Richmond in hopes of getting away from the conflict that robbed her of her husband's life... only to be at the center of the fury again!"

"The loss of the lead mines, well, that goes without saying as to how greatly that affects us. And the saltworks were vital," Jeremy mused. "The Confederacy will be hard-pressed to preserve meat at all now, even if another such endeavor as the Beefsteak Raid should be an option in the future."

"I'll write to her again," Salina decided. "I've not heard from her for several months, and I'm not sure at all that she got my last letter."

"Speaking of letters." Jeremy recalled that he had a collection of unsent letters for her in his valise. "I've been writing regularly. I just wasn't sure that if I sent them they would reach you. So I didn't send them."

Salina accepted the stack of envelopes. "I shall read each word with relish once you've gone again."

"The events are mostly old news now, but the sentiments are no less emphatic than when I penned them."

E.J. again pulled himself up to a standing position, this time clutching one of the chairs until his wobbly legs became steady. Jeremy held out both hands to the boy. "Come on," he practically dared. E.J. took his first steps directly into Jeremy's arms. "Sallie, did you see that? He's walking!"

Salina smiled, immensely proud of the boy—but realizing, too, that before long she'd be running herself ragged trying to keep up with him.

All too soon, Bentley's tentative knock sounded at the front door. "Good mornin', Miss Salina, ma'am."

"Hello, Bentley." Salina welcomed him into the warmth from the cold outside.

"Everything ready to go?" Jeremy asked his fellow rider.

"Aye, Captain. We're ready when you are."

"It won't take me ten minutes to get the Morgan saddled," Jeremy rejoined.

Salina kept her eyes downcast, but that didn't prevent her husband from detecting her disappointment. The scant hours had passed so quickly, and there was no telling when the next time they would see each other would be.

Bentley offered to look after the children while Salina followed Jeremy out to the small stable behind the row of brick townhouses. There was too little time left to say all the things she wanted to tell him, so she kept quiet, deciding to fill the letters she would write him with the thoughts and feelings abounding in her head and heart. She watched him as he swiftly brushed the Morgan's back and sides with deft strokes. Jeremy folded two saddle blankets lengthwise and in thirds, sliding them down from the horse's neck to avoid wrinkles. On top of the blankets went the rawhide-covered Jenifer-style saddle, and then came the bridle and bit. Jeremy's nimble fingers worked the buckles as he fastened both valise and bedroll to his saddle. He then secured his saddlebags along with a nosebag two-thirds full of grain.

Salina handed Jeremy his replenished canteen, followed by his rifle. He put both items over his head, adjusting the shoulder straps in an X across his chest. He'd already donned his belt with his cap pouch and cartridge box. His sword was buckled on.

"It can't last much longer, Sallie Rose. We'll hold and defend our positions for as long as we possibly can, but the end is coming. We can't survive this forever; they're too strong. It's only a matter of time, I'm afraid. Don't forget to pray for us. We'll need that."

She stood on tiptoe to kiss him. "Godspeed your way."

"Amen." Jeremy gathered her close for a final farewell hug and a lingering kiss. "Well then."

"I'll see you when I see you." Salina mustered her best smile for him. "You know where to find me."

"Aye," he saluted before settling himself in his saddle. "Tell Bentley I'll meet him around in front."

Salina hunkered down on the porch with one arm around E.J. and the other around Glory. The three of them waved good-bye until the handful of horsemen disappeared from sight. *It can't last much longer...* Jeremy's words rang in her ears. The war had been going on for so long, it was almost difficult to remember what peace actually tasted like. Salina prayed it would come soon, for in the meantime their lives hung in the balance until the outcome was finally resolved—one way or another.

☆☆☆☆☆☆☆

Christmas, 1864

Once more, Salina found herself at the Union supply base located at City Point. She was thankful for the miraculous opportunity to see her mamma and her little brother, but she was constantly alert, always on guard.

In turn, Annelise was thrilled to finally meet her grandchildren. Duncan's reward was in seeing the shared joy in the reunion between his wife and his stepdaughter. He decided it had been worth the number of strings he'd had to pull and the favors he'd had to call in to secure the necessary papers from the provost.

Listening intently as Mamma read a recent letter from Ethan, Salina gleaned few details concerning her brother's life far away at the remote outpost in Dakota Territory. It was a dry epistle, one containing only facts, devoid of any intimate thought or feeling. Ethan was routinely working with the post's regimental surgeon, but beyond that, he was merely existing from one day to the next.

Departing the small cabin that Duncan's rank garnered as both home and office, they walked over to the boarding house where Aurora Dallinger lived. Since most of the boarders had gone back to their Northern homes for the Christmas holiday, space was available to accommodate Duncan, Annelise, and Yabel; Salina and her two; plus Lottie and Lance Colby with their boy, Caleb. Mr. and Mrs. Drake Dallinger, returned from their sojourn in London, were also present. Toasts of good cheer were accomplished with eggnog and warm mulled wine.

Salina was taken aback by Lottie's amicable welcome. She was relatively sure the kiss Lottie placed on her cheek was well-meant, but she couldn't help but feel a degree of Judas-like betrayal in it.

Lottie laughed outright, delighted to have shocked Salina altogether. They had never gotten along well in their years of growing up, primarily because Lottie had cultivated an intense and oftimes spiteful contention between them. "I've changed, cousin. Honest I have."

"She has," Colby vouched for his wife with a nod.

The old animosity was starkly absent from Lottie's demeanor, and Salina indeed sensed that something about her cousin was profoundly...*different*. Perhaps, Salina allowed, Lottie had finally grown up and come to her senses.

Colby relinquished his son to his wife's care. He stood before Salina with his shoulders squared. "Life has its odd twists and turns."

"I should say so," Salina agreed. "I reckon I ought to thank you for not shooting my husband when you had the chance."

"Your husband—*my cousin*," Colby rolled his pale blue eyes, a reflection of his unimaginable disbelief. "If this conflict ever ends and we've both survived, there are a few things I'd like to discuss with your husband. Do you know a man called Ridge Southerland?"

Though Colby proved to be related by both marriage and blood, Salina sharply reminded herself that he still served the Union first and foremost—confidences were out of the question. "I have some knowlege of the man."

"He's another whom I should like to converse with at some length," Colby confessed. "In truth, I just might take up the invitation which was extended to me to come visit the South Union ranch in Kansas someday."

On Jeremy's behalf, Salina felt a prickling stab of jealousy. Of course Lance Colby would be made welcome at South Union by the Southerlands, since he was Maida's *legitimate* son. Jeremy did not enjoy similar status in the eyes of the family to which he belonged. Salina forced herself to smile at Colby. "My cousin apparently has had a drastic change in her attitude and outlook on life, but really, Colby—can you see her on a *ranch*?"

Colby's eyes narrowed as they came to rest on the figure of his wife. "Lottie's shown me that she's full of surprises in the past year. I won't rule out any possibility where she is concerned."

In Salina's mind, the picture of Lance and Lottie together was a testament to the adage "All's well that ends well". Salina was genuinely happy for them.

The Christmas tree in the corner of the room was bedecked with dozens of small tallow candles, and larger ones flickered in the sconces along the walls. The soft light illuminated the gold-leaf pattern of the flocked wallpaper, lending a cozy, shimmering ambience to the room. Salina yearned to feel even a fleeting sense of contentment in being here with friends and family. Her two children were absorbed in playing amiably with her little brother Yabel and her cousin's son—the four youngsters supplied a boundless measure of laughter, giggles, and unaffected squeals that made the grown-ups remember to smile during this time of what should have been a festive occasion. Salina's troubled thoughts, however, took her away from the warmth and glow of her present surroundings to her husband and where he might be on this bitter cold and gray day. Her mind then wandered to the frontier fortress where Ethan was stationed with the 1st U.S. Volunteers.

Salina's reverie was disturbed when Mamma brought in a tray loaded with crystal cups of wassail. The singing started, and the traditional carols proved a partial balm to her soul as she lent her voice to the songs extolling the birth of the Christ child.

When everyone was seated around the dining table, eager to partake of the meal Aurora and Elinor had contrived, Duncan preceded his prayer of thanksgiving with a reading from the second chapter of Luke. Two particular verses especially ministered to Salina's heart:

> *And the angel said unto them, Fear not: for, behold,*
> *I bring you good tidings of great joy, which shall be to*
> *all people. For unto you is born this day in the city of*
> *David a Saviour, which is Christ the Lord.*

A peace settled in Salina's soul, for as much joy as news of the end of the war might bring, Salina was reminded that the greater joy was that their Heavenly Father had given His only Son as their Savior. She bowed her head, earnestly praying that He would draw close to her and protect those she loved, and reverently thanking Him for making a way for eternal life. Salina heard, almost as clearly as if Taylor Sue had been standing by her side, the heartening phrases: *Be strong and courageous* and *All things work together for good to them that love God, to them who are the called according to his purpose.* The Lord was faithful, He had not forsaken her, and Salina intuitively knew that in the days to come she would cling to His strength more than she had ever done before.

It was that God-given strength that allowed Salina to sit by after supper and quietly listen to the others discuss their varied views on the Southern defeats at Winchester, Fisher's Hill, Tom's Brook, and Cedar Creek—the results contributing to the subsequent reelection of President Lincoln to a second term in office. Their elation over the Union victories at Franklin and Nashville in Tennessee was apparent. Lately rumors reported that Mosby had been killed somewhere in Northern Virginia, but Salina didn't believe them. Word had come yesterday, on Christmas Eve, of the wire to Lincoln that General Sherman had sent shortly after his arrival on the Georgia coast: "...I beg to present you, as a Christmas gift, the city of Savannah..." Mutely Salina wondered how long before Grant would make a similar attempt to bequeath the city of Richmond to the Union's Commander-in-Chief. Jeremy's words echoed anew with louder volume, *It can't last much longer...*

☆☆☆☆☆☆☆

New Year's Eve, 1864
Linden Row on Franklin Street
Richmond, Virginia

Staring openmouthed, Salina's incredulity was obvious as she read the document Ridge placed in her hands:

RICHMOND, December 21, 1864.

Hon. JAMES A. SEDDON,
Secretary of War:

SIR: I have the honor to submit for your information the following statement:

In the present emergency, when the resources of the country are so far exhausted, it becomes a question of paramount importance as to where recruits can be had for our armies, and every effort should be made to fill up our decimated ranks. With this view I would suggest the following plan as affording one field of recruiting not yet resorted to. The only section where men of Southern birth can be raised in large numbers, who sympathize with us and who would join us in this struggle, is Southern California and New Mexico. A considerable number might be raised on the Rio Grande. The only plan for getting those men from Southern California is to send an expedition for the recapture of Arizona. This would open the route into Southern California and enable those who are disposed to join us to do so, and I am confident that one or two brigades of New Mexicans could be raised. As to the number of men that could probably be raised in Southern California (including the mines), I am governed by the opinion of prominent men from that country, who are well acquainted with the sentiment of the people, such as Judge Terry, Colonel Showalter, and many others, who assert that from 15,000 to 20,000 men could be raised... In order to accomplish this it would be necessary to send an expedition of 2,500 men and retake Arizona and, if possible, New Mexico. The troops used for this purpose could be returned to Texas so soon as the forces raised could be organized for holding the Territories. This plan for recruiting when I was in command of Arizona was perfectly feasible, and I know of no reason why it might not be accomplished now.

Salina looked up at Ridge, intending to speak, but he cut her off. "Read on."

Salina's eyes settled on another section of pertinent information contained in the missive:

As to the resources of New Mexico and Arizona and their ability to sustain the forces sent or raised there I

*have no question. An abundance of wheat, corn, and
stock is raised in the country to subsist any force the
Government would send there, except, perhaps, the beef,
which can be driven from Texas with great ease.*

*...I cannot do more, in the brief space of a letter, than
call your attention to this important matter and leave for
the Government to take such action as it deems best.*

I have the honor to be, very respectfully,
JNO. R. BAYLOR.

"It's really going to happen?!" she breathed. "You're really
going to be part of another attempt to retake territory in the West in
the name of the Confederacy?"

"Well, it hasn't been approved yet," Ridge replied. "At present
a number of considerations are still being investigated. All objections will have to be overcome and the proper endorsements
obtained. Then there's the supplies, the silver mines..."

"President Davis and the Secretary of War will have to make
some decision about it soon, though," Brisco piped up.
"Something's got to be done. As Baylor said, it's a question of
paramount importance."

"Do you know where Jeremy is?" Ridge quietly asked Salina.

"I know he and his men were with Mosby by last report. But,
Ridge, Jeremy won't go with you to California—even if you did
manage to find him," Salina said with certainty. "Jeremy will stay
and defend Virginia to the last."

"Out of duty and honor to country or loyalty to Mosby's
cause?" Ridge tapped his index finger against his pursed lips.

"Maybe both," Salina nodded. "When are you leaving again?"

"As soon as we get the go-ahead," Brisco answered in
Ridge's stead. "Damaris is still out there, you know. She's with
Esther Nichols in San Francisco. Those two have been a tremen-
dous help in our efforts."

"But this mentions Southern California, not San Francisco."
Salina held up the copied document.

"The plans are a bit more extensive than Baylor and Seddon
are currently aware of," Ridge confided, reclaiming the paper she
held. "I'm willing to let them believe what they want to believe—
but there is much more to it than they've been allowed to know.

There are still operations in the planning stages for the Powder Mill and other key points that would work to our advantage."

As she had done on previous instances, Salina shook her head and politely declined further involvement or interest in learning more. "Please don't say anything more. I do appreciate the fact that you still place your trust in me, but I don't want to be a part, and you know my reasons why." Her glance lifted from Ridge's face to the ceiling, reinforcing the fact that the two sleeping little ones upstairs meant more to her than anything else.

Ridge tactfully retreated. He knew there was nothing he could do to change her mind, but she couldn't blame him for trying. "I stopped off at South Union on my way back here from California," he said, changing the subject entirely. "My mother requested that I give you this." He handed Salina an envelope bearing her name. "I've taken the liberty of telling her about you and answering questions about Jeremy."

"Did you see Evan as well?" Salina softly inquired. Jeremy's father remained an awkward topic.

"Aye," Ridge nodded. "He's running the ranch since Pa's accident."

Salina's surprise was plain. "Has something happened to your father?"

"You mean Drake didn't tell you about it when you saw him at Christmas?" Ridge stroked the outline of his goatee. "Maybe word hasn't reached Drake yet—for I'm sure he'd have left for South Union by now."

"He did mention that he would be leaving shortly after the New Year," Salina offered. "What happened?"

"Pa got thrown from a horse," Ridge told Salina. "Broke his arm and his hip and banged up one knee. Ephraim was home on leave to visit but has since had to go back to his regiment. Evan's been forced out of his despondency and has shouldered most of the work on the place himself. It's good for him; keeps him occupied."

Salina arched a brow in query.

"Ruth-Ellen has privately denounced Evan," Ridge explained. "She turned my brother out of their rooms in the east wing of the house and is trying to poison the boys—Little Evan and Jonathan— against him. It's bitter to watch, let me tell you. She'll hardly speak to him, let alone see him. Yet on Sundays she'll go to town and sit in the same pew and pretend that all is right with the world. It turns my stomach."

"Appearances must be very important to her," Salina guessed, tearing the envelope open.

Before she could read the letter, however, Ridge placed a hand on her arm, drawing her attention back to him. "I know you wrote to my ma when I was sick—as Brisco instructed you to do," he tossed a glance at his partner. "Her relief was great when you verified that I had not died, like the papers said I did."

"Then the letter served its purpose," Salina nodded.

"It's her wish that this letter in turn will serve its own purpose," Ridge nodded. "I'll bid you good day."

"Ridge, wait," Salina halted his departure. "How long will you be in town?"

"Few days at best. I've got a lot of work to do and not much time to do it in."

"You and Brisco are welcome to stay here," Salina hospitably offered. "There's plenty of room."

"I'll think on it. In the meantime, you have some reading to do." He tipped his hat. "If Brisco and I aren't back here tonight, it's not meant as a slight against your generous hospitality. But if we don't return, you just be ready in the morning because we'll be here in time to escort you to church."

Salina looked askance at Ridge.

Ridge grinned. "I'm not the hardened sinner you must think me, Salina. I might have been once, but God is faithful—He answers prayers. Just ask my mother or Damaris someday. They'll tell you."

☆☆☆☆☆☆☆

Mrs. Jeremy Barnes
Richmond, Virginia

My dear Salina—

Many thanks for your recent letter. Its contents were received with much relief. You were kind to explain the situation concerning Eldridge and send us word that he had not died. He is here with us now, and his visit has been a most welcome one. I owe you a debt of gratitude for your compassion toward our family.

It would give me a great deal of pleasure to meet you one day. I have heard much of you, both from Drake and from Eldridge. To hear them tell it, you must be quite a remarkable young lady, made more so by the fact that you are the helpmate of my grandson. I trust you will not judge us harshly, in light of Evan's unwillingness to name Jeremy as his legitimate heir. There are present difficulties which extend beyond the circumstances of Jeremy's birth, but alas I will not take up your time with a lament of our own troubles. They will work themselves out in the end, in God's time if not in ours.

If in the future you should find yourself in need, I beg you would consider coming to South Union. I will leave it to your good judgment, but know the invitation is there and will never be withdrawn. Keep it in mind should the occasion arise when you deem it prudent to accept.

I don't know how often you see Jeremy, what with him involved in the fighting, but when you next find yourselves together, please convey to him my best regards. He is very much like his father when Evan was that age. The acorn did not fall far from the tree, let me tell you. I know you must love him a good deal, and I praise God that He saw fit to bless Jeremy with a woman of your character and ability to love so deeply. He deserves that after what he has been made to endure in his twenty-odd years.

Wishing you all the best and peace for the coming year,
I remain devotedly your friend and servant,
Marrietta Southerland

South Union Ranch
Kansas
December 4, 1864

Setting the letter aside, Salina drew her knees to her chest and wrapped her arms around them. She rested her cheek on one knee, her head turned toward the frosty glass panes. From her vantage point in the window seat, she observed the panorama below. Snow had drifted steadily downward during the night, and presently at least two inches of layered flakes whitened the roof of the porch, the naked trees limbs, the wrought-iron gate, and the streets and gutters. It was a beautiful sight, almost tranquil, but the serenity of the scene did not interlace itself in Salina's mind, where her thoughts were all a-jumble.

Salina heard the chiming of the clock and belatedly realized she had yet to dress for Sunday service. Brisco and Ridge would be arriving soon, and she wasn't near ready, let alone Glory and E.J.

In her cold room, Salina donned a white shirt and velvet waist over a woven skirt of green, black, and red plaid. She tamed her curls within the confines of a mesh snood and pulled on a second pair of woolen stockings before lacing up her boots.

Glory and E.J. were bundled and ready to go when Brisco and Ridge arrived, each of them taking a child and thus freeing Salina to keep her hands warm in her coat pockets.

At St. Paul's, Dr. Minnegerode performed the New Year's Day service. President and Mrs. Davis were there, General Lee's daughters, and a handful of others Salina recognized. It was apparent that the stress of the future of the Confederacy was wearing on the First Lady, and even more so on her husband. Salina knew that Varina Davis had lost a little boy in a calamitous fall from a balcony at the executive mansion in late April last year and had given birth to another girl, "The Daughter of the Confederacy," in June. In addition to matters of home, the issues of State pervaded Mrs. Davis's life. Mrs. Davis remained steadfast amid talk and demands to arm the slaves in order to have manpower enough to fight off the Yankees and stoically ignored rumors abounding from the "croakers" who wanted President Davis removed from office—some strongly suggesting that General Lee should be installed as a dictator.

To Salina's way of thinking, 1864 had been a year of both triumphs and tragedies, but her intuition told her that the light of the Confederacy was dwindling.

The New Year—1865—started on a dismal note: The feast that was to have been supplied to Lee's troops around Petersburg had not materialized. Shortages of food combined with the increased price of gas had hit the citizens of Richmond hard; there wasn't enough food to share with the hungry soldiers.

There were but a few balls and parties throughout the months of January and February, several of them likened to the last dance that preceded Napolean's defeat at Waterloo. It made Salina shiver to think on it.

A rare letter arrived from Clarice, whose anecdotes of life in Culpeper with her mother and Aunt Ruby were all good and well, but the best news was that the rumors stating that Mosby had died were just that, rumors.

Mosby had been visiting Lakeland, the home of one of his rangers near Rector's Crossroads, when Yankees from a New York regiment descended on the place. One of the shots fired through the dining room window struck Mosby in the stomach. Mosby was left for dead but was later smuggled away by oxcart to the house of a neighbor two miles distant. Members of the Lake family, along with several captured rangers, were questioned by the Federal authorities, but they played very convincing roles in their part of the charade and denied knowing the identity of the man who'd been "killed" that icy cold night. Mosby's escape was a success. He was summarily delivered to his father's house near Lynchburg and was currently on the mend. Salina judged the news a happy contradiction to the Richmond papers that had erroneously reported Mosby's death!

At the end of January, Brisco and Ridge, who had been staying intermittently at the house in Linden Row, departed for good, headed west with their endorsements and orders to continue their endeavors toward the retaking of Arizona and the capture of California. Ridge had continued to share with Salina the plans, and Salina had bestowed, albeit reluctantly, some little input here and there when he asked her for her opinions. She could not bring herself to tell him that in her heart she felt that this Western campaign would never be launched.

Chapter Twenty

$\mathcal{F}$lora Stuart sent a letter to Salina telling her that she, Jimmie, and Virginia had survived the winter and that the Stuart family were collectively recovering from the injurious December attack of Stoneman's raid on the saltworks at Saltville and the nearby towns of Abingdon, Marion, and Wytheville. Flora, with her sister-in-law Mary Heddon, kept school for the Stuart cousins and for the children of the neighboring Preston family. Her missive explained she was faring as well as she possibly could in the cabin she and the children shared with Mary Heddon and her brood, and she hoped Salina was doing well also.

Salina put her hand to her still flat belly. She was well, in spite of the onset of the morning sickness that had again begun to afflict her. This time, she easily determined the symptoms of her ailment, and she was not so terrified of the experience. In fact, the notion of another little one on the way reinforced her will to survive and gave her hope amid increasingly hopeless circumstances. Salina had penned a letter to tell Jeremy, but she had no idea of where to send it, and so she kept the news to herself.

Less than a month later, Salina learned that Mrs. Davis and her children had been packed up and escorted from the Rebel capital, headed for points south. Before the week was out, Mrs. Hoffman and her little girl also departed Richmond. The handwriting, Salina's neighbor maintained, was clearly on the wall.

What Salina did not know was that her own mamma had boarded a steamer, at Duncan's insistence, and in the company of Yabel, Aurora, Elinor, Lottie, and Caleb—in addition to a dozen other officers' wives—sailed back to the safe environs of Washington City.

E.J.'s first birthday was call for celebration, followed a few weeks later by Glory's. Salina had just enough sugar to make a small cake for each of them on their respective days. As time passed, their words were coming more rapidly, and except on the days of Salina's hosptial visits, their babbling articulations were often the only conversation she had. Salina was grateful that Captain Sally allowed her to bring the children along, since the recovering men seemed to enjoy the presence of the little ones. No one could resist the children's smiling faces.

After several consecutive days of rain, Salina belatedly noticed that on the second day of April spring had arrived in Richmond. Having forgotten to do so the day before, she changed the calendar from the expired month of March to show the April page. The day promised to be pleasantly warm, and Salina decided that after church she would take Glory and E.J. into the garden to enjoy the sun, the budding trees, and the fragrant breezes. As she pushed the pram toward St. Paul's, she listened to the joyful chorus of chirping the birds provided. Perhaps she would let the little ones help her dig up the flower beds to ready them for planting. It was a diversionary tactic at best—anything to pass time.

During the church service, Salina was distracted by a courier who delivered a message to President Jefferson Davis in his pew. The pallor of the president's somber face turned ashen upon reading the note that had been handed to him. Davis collected his hat and hastily exited.

Clusters of folks lingered on the sidewalk and in the street in front of St. Paul's. The news from Petersburg was not good: Grant's troops had broken Lee's lines. When the bell tower took up chiming its all too familiar tocsin, Salina felt the impending doom in the chill that stole down her spine. Since 1861, Richmond had stood proud, thwarting all the campaigns the Union had hurled against her. This time, however, the mournful warning bespoke the impending fall. Word spread concerning the Confederate government's decision to move off to the west and south—out of the immediate path of the invaders—thereby abandoning Richmond. With piercing dread, Salina understood that the Yankees were making their inevitable approach.

Savannah had been conquered; the last ports at Wilmington and Fort Fisher had been bottled up. Sherman was moving north from Georgia up through the Carolinas—Charleston had been abandoned and Columbia sacked. The Confederacy was crumbling. The dull murmur of the distant thunder of battle that had started the day before continued. The low rumble underscored the bombardment General Grant unleashed on the Rebel lines in the trenches around Petersburg. Finally, after ten long months of seige, the stranglehold had reached the breaking point.

Unable to sleep that night, Salina sat wide awake in the window seat overlooking Franklin Street. *The name of the Lord is a strong tower: the righteous runneth into it, and is safe*, she quoted from Proverbs. It appeared that every street, alley, and avenue leading from town was choked with vehicles, horses, mules, carts, and the crush of panicked people. Wagons and carriages laden with trunks, furniture, and every earthly belonging of rich and poor alike multiplied the congestion of the roads a hundredfold. A mass exodus was in progress; the Mayo Bridge spanning the James River was clogged to the point of standstill, even as the frenzied populace struggled to surge across to flee the tottering capital. Salina wept bitterly—it was a dark day, one that she was glad that Daddy and men like Stonewall Jackson and Jeb Stuart had not lived to see for themselves.

Salina tried to envision the kind face of General Lee's wife. For the past fortnight, Mrs. Lee was about the only person Salina knew to be possessed of a demeanor of true tranquility, encouragement, strength, and hope. But surely Mrs. Lee's heart must be breaking, too, for in spite of her own heroic facade, her sons and her husband were at the front, and she must be feeling their pain as well as her own.

As order filed out of Richmond, lawlessness came marching in. Salina bolted the doors of the brick townhouse and kept her guns within easy reach. Looters joined forces with a seedy assortment of deserters, camp followers, and newly liberated prisoners. These miscreants broke into deserted homes, ransacked empty shops, smashed windows, and stole whatever they could carry off. The government whiskey stores had been poured out by military order as the last of the soldiers withdrew from the capital, but the slovenly wretches greedily scooped the liquor from the gutters with grimy hands, buckets, cups, or whatever they could find. Reeling drunk from the undiluted spirits, they pillaged and plundered at will, knowing full well there was nothing, no one, to stop them. All men who were able had been sent to join Lee's battered forces at Amelia Court House. The citizens of Richmond were utterly defenseless against the ribald crowd acting no better than pirates or brigands.

A violent concussion rattled all the windows in the townhouse. Glory and E.J. both felt the blast of the explosion and wailed in fright. While comforting her children, Salina witnessed billowing columns of smoke rising to the heavens. The air turned pungent with the acrid smell of burning tobacco. Either the retreating soldiers had set fire to the riverside storehouses or the looters had carelessly initiated the blaze. A swift breeze fanned the uncontrolled flames eastward, and within the hour, a second massive explosion rocked the foundations of the city. The fiery conflagration was, in a morbid way, almost spectacular. Showers of brilliant sparks shot up, chased by a sharp banging and rapid popping that sounded like hundreds of firecrackers. Ammunition stored belowdecks in the navy ships anchored at the dockyard near Rocketts Landing went off, adding volume to the cacophonous disturbance.

Salina's heart pounded. She had no place to go, nowhere to run with her little ones. She had told Jeremy she would wait for him here in Richmond; this is where he would come to look for her. Her lips moved rapidly in prayer as the fires encroached, moving closer to Capitol Square less than ten blocks away, their destructive flames spewing heat, ash, and devastation.

Rocking a youngster in either arm, Salina had almost managed to calm her children into tentative slumber when the racket of what sounded like a hundred cannon rent the air with furious shrieks. The fire, she surmised, had at last reached the powder magazine, and for but a moment, the ear-splitting sounds of the ghastly detonation almost drowned out the roar and crackle of the fire. E.J.'s and Glory's cries resumed; tears trickled down Salina's cheeks.

By morning, Richmond's business district was wholly consumed, along with Tredegar Ironworks and the last remaining shops on the riverfront. The sun, when it rose, was an ethereal, glowing ball suspended in the murky, smoke-filled atmosphere. Salina remembered that Revelation told of a day when the sun would appear blood red, and that day would foreshadow the end of the world. Salina's world was ending, shattered into broken pieces about her. God alone knew what would become of them.

☆☆☆☆☆☆☆

Two days later, Salina learned that a shift in the wind had brought flames to the roof of the church just across Franklin Street from "The Mess." Mrs. Lee, Mildred, Agnes, and Mary had adamantly stayed put. They, like Salina, had nowhere else to go. The general's wife, even if she hadn't been an invalid, would no doubt have chosen to stick it out rather than run; she and her daughters elected to meet disaster and the Yankees head on without flinching, without budging. Salina took the example of Mrs. Lee's dignity to heart.

Somehow the appearance of Duncan Grant on the front stoop of the brick townhouse provided no great surprise. "In truth," Salina admitted candidly, "I'd rather been expecting you. They've already taken down our flag and replaced it with the Stars and Stripes of your country. We are conquered."

"It will be your country again, too, Salina," Duncan predicted. "The Army of Northern Virginia cannot hold out forever."

Even as they stood staring at each other, the animosity drained out of Salina. In reality, Duncan was not the personification of the North, and like the Rebel army, Salina was running out of strength to keep the fight alive. Her attention was drawn from Duncan's care-worn face to a throng coming down the street. The Union's President, Abraham Lincoln himself, was making a tour through the vanquished city. His expression was not one of haughty subjugation but was one of purpose. Four long years had passed with futile attempts to wrest this place from the hands of the unbending Southerners. Now Lincoln walked along the cobbled streets of the broken capital city, observing, comtemplative, while hundreds of Negroes swarmed and paraded behind him, blessing his name.

Lincoln's glance of acknowledgment met Duncan's gaze. A tip of his stovepipe hat made Salina believe that he had not forgotten her from the interview that had ultimately resulted in a dismissal of charges of treason and her presidential pardon. She reticently dipped her head, lowering her eyes until the Union leader passed.

"Elizabeth Van Lew was seen gathering papers that had been scattered across the lawns at Capitol Square," Duncan remarked.

"Oh, I'm quite sure she was," Salina answered sharply. "In fact, I'm certain her traitorous ways will manifest themselves openly now. She has no call to go around dressed as or acting like 'Crazy Bet' anymore. No, sir. She'll be entertaining General Grant himself, escorting him through the ruins or presenting him with the key to the city! You watch and see."

Duncan ignored the biting sarcasm in Salina's tone. She hurt, and he understood that. Her father had given his life for a lost cause; on occasion she had willingly risked her own neck to fight against the Federals; her husband was still out there with Mosby's battalion, and Jeremy Barnes was not the type who would take defeat lightly. Duncan ordered a guard posted at the house, assurance to himself of her safety. Then he gave her ration cards so that she could obtain food for herself, E.J., and Glory. "Don't be stubborn, Salina. It is within my power to help you. Let me do that."

The ration cards were crumpled in the fist that disappeared into the pocket of Salina's apron. Her chin wavered and her eyes filled with tears. "You must view me as a rude, defiant ingrate." She swallowed her pride. "I don't mean to be."

"I know," Duncan nodded compassionately. "I know."

The governor of Richmond had surrendered the city. The executive mansion at Twelfth and Clay Streets was overtaken and became the headquarters of the occupying army. Lincoln was a visitor there; he sat in the same chair Jefferson Davis had used. Salina absently wondered then what might happen to the Davises should they be caught. And what of other top Confederate leaders—government officials and military personnel alike? Would they be tried and hung as traitors against the United States?

Abraham Lincoln gave no written edict concerning such matters, but he was reported to have told General Weitzel, "If I were in your place, I'd let 'em up easy—I'd let 'em up easy."

☆☆☆☆☆☆☆

April 11, 1865
Fort Rice, Dakota Territory

Ethan Hastings couldn't believe his ears. He'd heard his comrades buzzing over the news: The war was over! General Lee had surrendered at Appomattox Court House! When Ethan saw the reports with his own eyes, the rumor gained truth and substance: Two days prior the Army of Northern Virginia had laid down its arms and was in the process of being paroled. The Rebels were being sent home after four bloody years—almost to the day—of murderous conflict. There was still time to get the spring planting done...

The wash of mawkishness brought on by the disparaging news was short-lived. Ethan didn't know when he'd decided, but he knew he wasn't going home. For so long he'd dreaded facing his sister and his brother-in-law when this was all over with. He doubted whether either of them would understand what had made him choose as he had. If he didn't go home, he would be relieved of making excuses or explanations; if he did, he would face one last clash that was an eventuality as certain as the day of his mustering out would be. He would not stay in Dakota Territory forever, he determined, nor would he return to Virginia. Taylor Sue was buried there.

Ethan did not allow himself to indulge in dreams for his future. For the present, he was bound by the Oath and assignment with the 1st U.S. Volunteers. Until that obligation was fulfilled, all thoughts of what he might do—including traveling west to California—were shelved.

Ethan read the accounts of the fighting and of the route of retreat Lee had taken once Petersburg was lost. The South's tenacious resistance had produced a trail of blood from Five Forks, Namozine Church, Amelia Springs, High Bridge, Saylor's Creek, and Farmville to the place where Lee and Grant had finally met face-to-face.

On the ninth day of April, in the parlour of the McLean House at Appomattox Court House, the opposing generals had come to an agreement on terms. Lee had done the best he could for his soldiers. General Orders No. 9 was addressed to the remnant of his command:

> *After four years of arduous service marked by unsurpassed courage and fortitude, the Army of Northern Virginia has been compelled to yield to over-whelming number and resources.*
>
> *I need not tell the brave survivors of so many hard fought battles, who have remained steadfast to the last, that I have consented to this result from no distrust of them.*
>
> *But feeling that valor and devotion could accom-plish nothing that could compensate for the loss that*

would have attended the continuance of the contest, I determined to avoid the useless sacrifice of those whose past services have endeared them to their countrymen.

By the terms of the agreement, officers and men can return to their homes and remain until exchanged. You will take with you the satisfaction that proceeds from the consciousness of duty faithfully performed, and I earnestly pray that a Merciful God will extend to you His blessing and protection.

With an unceasing admiration of your constancy and devotion to your country, and a grateful remembrance of your kind and generous consideration for myself, I bid you an affectionate farewell.

R.E. Lee
Gen'l

Rebel troops under General Joseph E. Johnston were still in North Carolina, but Ethan had the feeling that they would not be long in following Lee's course of action. The Confederacy was all but dead.

"God help us," he muttered under his breath. It was the first time he'd prayed in a long time.

☆☆☆☆☆☆☆

April 14, 1865
Good Friday

"General Grant has sent back his regrets, and he and his wife will not be accompanying Mrs. Lincoln and me to Ford's Theatre tonight," Lincoln told Duncan. "I've received a handful of other regrets as well. For all the joyous celebration and lauded congratulations of last night while this city was rejoicing in long-awaited triumph, people are staying away in droves today. I was almost ready to call off going myself, but since the Grants are unable to attend, Mrs. Lincoln feels it would be in poor taste to disappoint a public who has already been notified that we will be there this evening. I've extended an invitation to Major Rathbone and his fiancée to accompany us, and if they don't accept, I may come back to you, Duncan. Do you suppose your wife would be interested in going to a play?"

"With all due respect, sir, my wife and I already have tickets for this evening's performance," Duncan replied. "If Major Rathbone does not accept, though, Annelise and I would be pleased to join you and your wife. I'm confident, however, that the major will not turn down your invitation, sir."

Lincoln shrugged his shoulders. "We'll see. At any rate, I shall watch for you tonight, since I know you will be there."

"Very well, sir," Duncan saluted. "My wife and I will look forward to seeing you later on."

The play was already thirty minutes in progress when the Lincolns arrived at Ford's Theatre on Tenth Street. A popular actress and comedienne named Laura Keene had the starring role in a production called *Our American Cousin*, which halted mid-peformance as the orchestra struck up the tune of *Hail to the Chief.* The entire audience, from orchestra level to the dress circle, the parquet, and the family circle, was on its feet to welcome the President. Lincoln responded kindly with a smile and a bow.

As the distinguished party settled into their seats in the bunting-draped box, Annelise whispered to Duncan, "He still looks sad, doesn't he?" For the past five days she had been trying to accept the South's surrender. She privately mourned the action General Lee had been forced to take to bring about the resolution of the conflict, and she prayed for her daughter, who by the last of Duncan's reports was still in Richmond, awaiting Jeremy's return. The precise whereabouts of Mosby and his band had not been determined, but certainly Salina's husband was still with the partisan battalion.

Duncan pondered Annelise's observation. Not only did Lincoln look sad, but he had aged dramatically during his presidential term, his countenance irrevocably marred by the scars of the war. Lincoln felt bereft for each life lost in the struggle, and his relief that no more lives were required to reestablish the Union was unequivocal.

The play resumed. Act II was completed without further ado, and the third act commenced.

In the second scene, calamity struck. Uproarious laughter impelled by a line spoken by one of the characters masked a mortal gunshot. John Wilkes Booth, a renowned actor with ardent Southern sympathies, fired a derringer at close range into the back of Lincoln's head. Then Booth stabbed Major Rathbone before leaping from the State box to the stage below. *"Sic Semper Tyranus!"* he shouted above the din. Booth got up from where he fell, his spur having caught in the red, white, and blue striped bunting, and hastily limped out of the theatre, disappearing into the night.

The meaning of the Latin phrase, which was Virginia's state motto, was "Thus Always to Tyrants." Duncan's storm-gray eyes flew to the luxuriously appointed box, immediately identifying the slumped figure of the nation's leader.

"The President has been shot!" someone yelled out.

Mary Todd Lincoln's hysterical shrieks signaled the onset of pandemonium. Cries for revenge mingled with pleas for medical assistance, and both grew in volume.

In short order the theatre was cleared of patrons. Duncan clutched Annelise's hand tightly as they waited with hundreds of others to find out what had happened and what would happen next.

Lincoln, borne on an improvised stretcher, was carried from Ford's to the Petersen House, just across the street from the theatre. Union soldiers pressed the crowd back, making the way clear for the stretcher-bearers to get through.

Duncan's heart sank. *If he dies, the South will be punished harshly.* As far as Duncan could tell, Lincoln was all that stood between peaceful measures and the politicians who held that the Southern states ought to suffer cruelly for their waywardness. Hundreds of thousands of Union men had given their lives, and the defunct Confederacy would not only be forced to take the full blame for the war but also be made to pay dearly.

Duncan had the presence of mind to escort Annelise home before he went back to the Petersen House. He was curtly interviewed by Secretary of War Edwin Stanton, who had already launched the preliminary steps of investigation to hunt down the assassin.

The front of the Petersen House was filled with bureaucratic activity while the back bedroom contained the medical staff attending the waning President. Duncan dutifully paid his last respects amid a string of Lincoln's friends and other dignitaries. It was useless to keep a vigil there, though, Duncan realized. He had not been called upon in an official capacity and was only underfoot. He would be summoned if his services were needed. Returning to the War Department, Duncan stayed at his desk until the dour announcement came the next morning.

"Lincoln is dead," he grimly informed Lance Colby when the junior officer appeared. In his mind's eye he could see the lengthy frame of the President laid out diagonally across the bed, the pillow stained with blood oozing from the mortal wound. "Seven twenty-two a.m., the man breathed his last. God rest his soul."

☆☆☆☆☆☆☆

April 20, 1865
Millwood, Virginia

The appointed site for the rendezvous was the Clarke Hotel. This was the second time in as many days that Mosby had agreed to a truce and a meeting with a Federal representative. The reports of the surrender at Appomattox had been told to him only by the enemy—nothing from his own army had confirmed those reports—and the partisan leader was not altogether sure whether the Yankees were telling the absolute truth. Mosby knew they would like nothing better than to kill him and to eradicate his command, and therefore he wasn't taking any chances.

General Grant had initially given his approval that the terms of Lee's surrender would apply also to Mosby's men. Mosby delayed in acceptance. He wanted to wait only until he could get clarifying orders from Johnston's army. He would rather disband his men than surrender them; he would give them the freedom of choice: If they opted for their paroles, he wouldn't stop them from taking them.

Jeremy, Bentley, and Boone were among those on the fringes near the front gate, waiting anxiously to hear the outcome of the meeting. While Mosby met with the Union representative, another of the rangers rode up in haste, claiming a trap had been sprung. A Yankee column had been sighted moving up the road toward Millwood, and that was all it took for Mosby to break off the talks. Thinking it to be a trick, Mosby marched out.

"Sir," the partisan commander coolly addressed the Federal officer, "if we are are no longer under the protection of our truce, we are, of course, at the mercy of your men. We shall protect ourselves." Outside the hotel, Mosby gave the order for his men to mount up and follow him. The men rode away, revolvers at the ready, unsure yet as to what course of action to take next.

The Yankees believed that Mosby might have had a hand in the assassination of Abraham Lincoln. Mosby had had none whatsoever, but one of his former riders, a man named Lewis Paine, had played an active part in the murder conspiracy with John Wilkes Booth. Paine had been arrested and was in custody, along with the other assassination suspects: George Atzerodt, David Herold, Edman Spangler, Michael O'Laughlin, Samuel Arnold, Mary Surratt, and

Dr. Samuel Mudd. Upon learning of the tenuous connection between Paine and Mosby, General Grant had rescinded the offer to include the 43rd Battalion of Virginia cavalry in the terms he'd agreed to with Lee. "If Mosby does not avail himself...end it and hunt him and his men down. Guerillas will not be entitled to quarter."

Kidd Carney, C.J., and Tristan Scarborough met up with Bentley, Boone, and Jeremy. They listened to Jeremy's account of the meeting at Millwood. Some of the rangers were urging the battalion be kept intact. If they didn't go to fight with Johnston farther south, there was Mexico to be considered. "Essentially, we are fugitives," Jeremy said. "What do you all want to do?"

"Wait and see," Bentley sagely advised. "If word does reach Mosby from Johnston's headquarters, and if he decides to go that route, then I say we follow him to the end."

"To the end," the others echoed.

"Let's finish this," C.J. nodded, holding up his canteen in toast. "It's not over until it's over."

The next day at Salem, however, Mosby met with approximately two hundred of his men—all that remained of a force that had once boasted a strength of eight hundred. The company commanders solemnly formed ranks. Mosby wordlessly inspected them, then waited silently as William Mosby, brother and adjutant to the commander, read aloud:

> *Soldiers:*
> *I have summoned you together for the last time. The vision we cherished of a free and independent country has vanished, and that country is now the spoil of a conqueror.*
> *I disband your organization in preference to surrendering to our enemies. I am no longer your commander. After an association of more than two eventful years, I part from you with a just pride in the fame of your achievements and grateful recollections of your kindness to myself. And now, at this moment of bidding you a final adieu, accept the assurance of my unchanging confidence and regard. Farewell!*
>
> John S. Mosby
Colonel

"It's over now," Boone lamented.

"Unless we follow him to Johnston," Kidd Carney pointed out.

"Or Mexico, *amigos*," Tristan reminded them.

But before any great length of ponderance could be conducted, news arrived of Johnston's surrender at Bentonville, North Carolina. The end had indeed come.

On the heels of their last supper together, the men who had faithfully ridden with Jeremy reluctantly parted ways. Boone Hunter lit out for Culpeper, Bentley for his home in Danville, C.J. said he would return to San Antonio most likely, and Kidd Carney was off to Orange Court House. Only Tristan Scarborough accompanied Jeremy southward to Richmond; he'd be heading on to Charlotte from there—after he had seen Aurora Dallinger at City Point one last time.

☆☆☆☆☆☆☆

Jeremy drew a ragged breath as he tethered his raw-boned horse at the front gate of the brick townhouse in Linden Row. He was disappointed that Salina did not rush to the front steps to greet him. For more than a score of miles he'd been rehearsing what to say to her when she threw herself into his arms—how he would explain what had happened to their country and a cause that had not survived. They had few options open to them, and he needed to find out what she wanted to do.

The face of a woman he didn't recognize answered the beveled-glass door.

"Good day, ma'am," Jeremy drawled, politely removing his hat.

"Humph!" The woman cast an intolerant look of disdain at Jeremy's worn butternut uniform. "State your business."

"I'm looking for Mrs. Jeremy Barnes," he replied, his ears stinging with her clipped New England accent.

"Barnes? I know no one named Barnes," the woman snapped tersely. "Be gone with you—don't let me catch you loitering, or I'll send for the provost guard."

"Excuse me, ma'am—if you please," Jeremy put a hand against the door to keep it from being slammed in his face. "A young Virginia lady with two small children lived in this house the last time I was here. Would you know where they've gone?"

"Even if I did, I don't know that I would tell the likes of you!" The beveled panes rattled with the force of the slam.

Jeremy turned away from the door, confused and puzzled. The city of Richmond was a wreck, he'd seen for himself the devastation of flame and fire. But the burning had apparently halted before reaching the lower part of Franklin Street, leaving the residences there unharmed. Yet where was his wife?

Jeremy led the Morgan behind him, walking down Franklin toward Capitol Square with the intent of inquiring after Salina at "The Mess." He knew his wife had spent hours there knitting with the Lees—perhaps she'd left word for him with them. But at Third Street, he turned right and continued on to Main. At Robertson Hospital, where he knew Salina had worked, he requested an interview with Captain Sally Tompkins.

"She was sure you'd come," the hospital administrator nodded, disclosing her anticipation of Jeremy's eventual arrival. "She left this for you." Captain Sally handed over a short note, one obviously written in haste:

> *My Darling—*
>
> *I know I said I would meet you here in Richmond, but the Yankees have descended in force and en masse. The people who rented the townhouse to the Careys sold the place, lock, stock, and barrel out from under me with no warning, to an enterprising couple from Connecticut. I was evicted post haste, for they arrived the very morning after we'd heard of the surrender at Appomattox. Dr. Brewer helped me acquire a small handcart which I loaded with our meager belongings. I have ample space for the children to be tucked in, and they seem to look upon this next adventure almost as a lark. I bade farewell to Dr. Brewer and to Maria, to the Lees, and to Captain Sally. They have been my only solace these past few days. At the time of this writing, we none of us have heard anything concerning Mosby or the rangers.*
>
> *Without a roof over my head in Richmond, I had to make prompt decisions. I am going to Ivywood. Uncle Caleb and Aunt Priscilla will not turn me away; they will no doubt extend an offer of shelter at least until you come for me, for us. Come to us there. I intend to use the last of the money Drake sent for passage by rail—I may well have to bribe my way north. Come as soon as you can.*
>
> *Your own,*
> *Salina Rose Hastings Barnes*

Post Script—Hugs await you from Glory and E.J. Come quickly.

"Captain Sally, I do thank you," Jeremy folded the note and tucked it into is pocket. "I'm headed back to Northern Virginia."

"I figured you would be. Do give my compliments and kind regards to your wife, sir. I—along with the men she so faithfully cared for—am forever indebted to her for the service of her willing hands. She proved the value of her worth time and again as an able nurse." Sally Tompkins's praise was accompanied by an encouraging smile. "God go with you, Captain."

Jeremy rolled his eyes. "Little good the rank does me now."

"About as much as mine does me," Captain Sally nodded in understanding. "Take care of yourself."

"You do the same, ma'am." Jeremy gave her a salute.

Before departing Richmond, Jeremy detoured to Hollywood Cemetery. He placed a small bouquet of spring flowers on the grave of his sister-in-law and murmured a farewell. At Stuart's marker, Jeremy removed his hat. The fingers of his right hand touched the black mourning band circling his left sleeve. "We did the best we could, but it wasn't enough, General. We had the heart, the devotion, the duty, and the honor along with a good measure of valor, but just not the victory. The odds simply weren't in our favor, and I reckon God's will must lie on a different path from the one we chose. I will go on seeking His purpose. Praise and honor and glory belong to Him."

Jeremy could hear the surging roar of the James River rapids. "I take no greater pride than having served with you, General, and I trust we'll meet again someday." He replaced his hat and performed a final salute.

Chapter Twenty-one

Ivywood
Near Fairfax Court House, Virginia

*W*ith sorrowful eyes, Salina pored over the pages of the ledgers and journals that had belonged to Daddy, and to Grandpa Henry before him. The books contained a documented history of Shadowcreek—a meticulous accounting of the improvements on the land, upkeep of the buildings, yield of the annual crops, inventory of all the animals, as well as a log of the slaves bought, sold, and freed.

As of this morning, the deed was gone, no longer in possession of any of the Hastings, but owned by someone else. That singular piece of paper—signed and witnessed in the Fairfax County Courthouse—was all that proved beyond reasonable doubt that Henry Hastings had legally obtained the land from the Barnes family in lieu of money owed as a result of unpaid gambling debts incurred by John Barnes's father.

John Barnes had been driven to kill for the document that was the title to the coveted estate. Salina mourned to think of all they had gone through to fight for, protect, and retain those lands, only to lose them in the end at auction for unpaid back taxes. The harsh, reverberating slam of the auctioneer's gavel and the resonant echo of "Sold!" rang in Salina's ears.

There had been nothing Salina could do to prevent the sale of her beloved Shadowcreek. The last of the leftover money Jeremy had given her from the Greenback Raid had dwindled until it simply wasn't enough. Salina was almost glad that Drake had not been on hand, or she might've cast all her pride aside and begged him outright to purchase the estate on her behalf—which he probably would have done for her without question. But Drake hadn't been here to forestall the sale, and besides, the sum would have been far greater than either she or Jeremy could ever afford to repay.

Uncle Caleb would have liked to have acquired the tract of acreage that bordered his own, but his fortunes were not what they were prior to the war either. He prudently let himself be content in that he hadn't lost any of his own property, for Ivywood remained intact, thanks to a number of astute investments.

Salina pushed aside her painful reflections. The past was something that could never be recaptured, a time they would never be able to restore. It was hers to wait until Jeremy came to fetch her and the children, and then together they would make plans for what to do and where to go.

In Salina's pocket was a letter from Marietta Southerland that contained a renewed invitation for Jeremy to bring his family to South Union in Kansas at his earliest convenience—Evan Southerland wanted to see him.

The baby in Salina's womb moved, and Salina put her hand atop her enlarged belly. The sensation emphatically reinforced the fact that she was nurturing another life within her—one her husband had yet to learn of. Staring absently out the window, Salina yearned impatiently, "Oh, Jeremy, please come to us soon."

A delighted squeal lifted on the afternoon breeze. Salina instantly recognized it as Glory's infectious laughter. Then she heard her daughter gleefully shout, "Daddy!"

Salina's heart lurched. She knelt on the window seat cushion and pushed the draperies aside. Glory was absolutely right—it *was* her daddy's horse trotting up the oak-shaded lane leading to Ivywood's manor house. Salina hastened down to the veranda, wanting to be there to welcome him.

"Daddy! Daddy!" Glory lifted her arms, eager to be picked up and hugged, as Jeremy dismounted.

"Glory Stuart," Jeremy grinned wearily, his tired countenance filled with love for his little girl. It didn't matter that he'd ridden thirty-five miles straight, stopping only when necessary to feed and water the Morgan, that his hips were sore and his knees unsteady, or that the ill-fitting boots he wore had rubbed blisters on his feet. All that paled, for he adored hearing the sound of *Daddy* coming from Glory's lips—treasured it just as much as he did the feel of her little arms wrapped around his neck. He squeezed her tight and kissed her cheek. "Where's your brother?"

"Eee-Jay, Unca-Lance, C'leb—see hosses." Glory pointed a finger in the general direction of the stables.

Bonnie Lee and Annie Laurie Baxter each nodded, affirming that Lance Colby had taken the boy cousins to see the Armstrong horses.

"Girls," Jeremy nodded to Mary Edith's twins, his untrained eyes unable to tell Glory's cousins apart.

"'Lo," the twins greeted their Uncle Jeremy shyly. Neither remembered him.

"Glory, where's your mamma?"

The sandy-blond little girl pointed to an upstairs window.

Jeremy saw only an empty sill with curtains fluttering against the open sash. The face and form he longed to see were missing. But then he felt Salina's presence, and when he turned about, she was indeed there, her pretty face wreathed in smiles. Salina mouthed Jeremy's name, but no sound came forth. Joyful relief mingled with gladness, thanksgiving, and love welled up her eyes.

Jeremy's expression was one of shock when he saw the condition his wife was in, though after a moment of reflection, his lopsided grin appeared, narrowly preceded by a brash chuckle. Salina had no need to make any sort of announcement, not when the fruitful evidence of their union was so plainly discernible. Effortlessly Jeremy shifted Glory to his hip and embraced Salina with his free arm. He planted a kiss on top of her head and whispered in her ear, "Due in September?"

"Aye, September." She stood on tiptoe, kissing his bearded jaw. "I'd have written to tell you..."

"But I've been on the move since the last time we saw each other in Richmond, and chances were slim that a letter would've reached me," Jeremy completed her sentence for her. "That's over and we're together—which is all that matters to me right now." He let his hand fall from her shoulder to the swell of her abdomen. "This is the best welcome-home present you could have given me, Sallie."

"I'm glad." Salina placed her hand on top of his. She looked up at him, so very thankful that he'd come back at last, and at Glory, who contentedly laid her head against her daddy's shoulder. "Come inside," she suggested. "You look like you could use a nap, and then maybe a bath and something to eat."

"I've got to see to my horse," Jeremy started to say.

"I'll see to your horse," Salina argued.

"No," Lance Colby's voice startled them both. "Why don't let you let me see to *my* horse, eh, cousin?" He raised an eyebrow in consternation as he inspected the Morgan with a critical eye. *"What have you done to my horse?!"*

"I'm afraid I've worn him out," Jeremy lamented, concerned for the faithful steed. "He's in need of shoes and a better diet of feed than what I've been able to get for him as of late."

Lance untied the lead strap from the veranda railing. "Don't worry about him, Jeremy. I'll see to him."

But the Morgan refused to budge.

"Are you stealing back your horse?" Jeremy wanted to know, fondly rubbing the velvety nose of the mount who'd diligently carried him through some difficult days.

Lance Colby took the rejoinder for the olive branch it was intended to be. "We'll discuss rightful ownership later. Salina, take your husband inside. Make him rest. I want him alert and paying attention after supper. I've got a few issues to settle with him, once and for all."

Jeremy refused to be meekly led away. "Oh, really?"

"I've no intention of fighting you," Lance spoke with determination, "but I do expect to get some straight answers out of you. Later." He clucked to the Morgan and led the horse to the stables.

"Where are the boys?" Salina called after Lance.

"Down for naps—as your husband should be," he quipped. "Get along with you—both of you."

☆☆☆☆☆☆☆

Initially, Salina was denied access to the library, where Lance and Jeremy closeted themselves for more than an hour. She could hear tone through the heavy paneled doors, but not specific words. Uncle Caleb was allowed in, but he exited the bookshelf-lined room within ten minutes.

"No, Salina, they're not ready to invite you in yet," Caleb Armstrong warned. "That is no place for a young lady at this particular point. Go on to bed. Jeremy said he'll join you in a while."

"They're behaving?" Salina was concerened.

Caleb laughed. "As well as gentlemen can be expected to, given their circumstances. Suffice it to say that they are getting reacquainted."

Salina was still awake when Jeremy came to the guest bedchamber. She was at the vanity, brushing out her hair, her pale face illuminated by the soft light of a hurricane lamp on the dressing table.

"Lance told me about the auction, Sallie. I'm so very sorry. I know how much that place meant to you."

"But you mean more," Salina stated evenly.

Jeremy sat down on the tapestry seat of the cedar chest at the foot of the bed. "It means a lot to me to hear you say so."

Salina caressed his cheek, savoring the feel of his whiskers against her palm. Her fingertips brushed the faint scar near his eye. "The Widow Hollis was the last person I expected to see at Shadowcreek this morning. But it shouldn't have surprised me so—she would naturally feel it was her obligation to try to restore the land to her family's possession. I'm of the opinion she is as mad as John Barnes, but with just a hint of lucidity thrown in. She made me uncomfortable, but I knew she couldn't hurt me. Not anymore."

"Aye," Jeremy nodded. "She can't hurt any of us. Lance said he followed her to Fairfax Station, made sure she got on the train and was really gone. She won't be bothering us, Sallie. She might be John Barnes's half sister, but she lacks the depth of his insanity."

"She once insisted that my daddy was a murderer; she accuses you of being the same," Salina confided. "She's not someone I would completely turn my back on, for she may still have a dagger up her sleeve."

Jeremy shook his head. "Your family doesn't own the land anymore. You have nothing more that she wants."

"I doubt that even if Duncan had been here he could've postponed the auction," Salina whispered. "It would've been a moot point. The amount of the taxes was more than double the amount I've got tucked away."

"You know who it was who got the final bid?"

"Some lawyer from Boston, bidding on behalf of an undisclosed client." Salina shrugged. "Yankees at Shadowcreek. It's enough to turn my stomach." She looked intently at her husband. "What are we going to do?"

"I don't know yet," Jeremy confessed.

"What were you and Lance discussing at such length?"

"Our blood," came Jeremy's cryptic answer. "We are cousins, married to cousins. We met as enemies and survived to be kin."

"Speaking of kin..." Salina produced the letter from Jeremy's grandmother, which Jeremy read.

His jaw was so tightly clamped shut that the nerve along his cheek jumped in agitation. "What does he think I am, at his beck and call?" Jeremy ground out, angered by the insinuation that he should come running to Kansas because Evan Southerland willed it.

Salina didn't have to be told who Jeremy's *he* meant. "We've got nothing, Jeremy, except fifty-seven dollars and twelve cents. You didn't officially surrender, you haven't signed a parole or taken the Oath. You'll never be able to get work of any kind around here unless you do—the Yankees will see to that—and I know you well enough to know that you won't comply, simply as a matter of principle. Drake is there at South Union, Jeremy, and he has made you an offer of working for him. You won't ever know what Evan wants unless you face him. We haven't got anything to lose by going, and unless we go, we don't know what we stand to gain."

"What makes you think we could gain anything by going all the way to Kansas?"

"Just suppose, for the sake of argument, that your father has reconsidered. What if Evan is ready to own up to the fact that you are his firstborn? You might gain your rightful name."

"The letter says nothing of the sort," Jeremy snapped. "Where is this coming from?"

"I don't know. It's just a feeling I have." Salina rubbed her arms to ward away the sudden chill that overtook her.

Jeremy remained silent for a long, drawn-out moment. Salina's feelings and intuition had so often been right in the past, why should now be any different? But Jeremy refused to let himself get his hopes up. "Are you sure you're up to traveling all that way—like this?" He laid a protective hand on her abdomen.

"I traveled from Pennsylvania through Maryland and back to Richmond like this last time," she reminded him.

"Have you been sick?"

"Not nearly so bad as I was with Glory," Salina answered. "Jeremy, if you consent to accepting that invitation, I am more than ready to go with you." She smiled saucily. "I reckon you could say that I do still love a good challenge."

"I'll think on it." Jeremy wasn't ready to make a commitment of that magnitude.

☆☆☆☆☆☆

Through the rest of the month of May, Salina and Jeremy stayed on at Ivywood with Glory and E.J. Lance Colby was at the estate from time to time, though his attentions were divided between there and Washington, D.C. He was remotely involved with the trial of the Lincoln conspirators. John Wilkes Booth had been tracked down and killed in a tobacco barn in Virginia. The fate of the other members having connection with the assassination plot was yet to be determined. Jefferson Davis, the former Confederate President, had been captured and imprisoned at Fortress Monroe. In the wake of Johnston's surrender at Bentonville, North Carolina, Florida had surrendered, as had the Confederate forces of the Trans-Mississippi Department in the Far West.

Randle Baxter was home from the sea, and he and Jeremy had gone with Caleb Armstrong to buy horses—surplus stock the U.S. quartermaster was selling off at the Geisboro stables. The mounts were older and had seen much wear and tear in battles, yet they would be serviceable enough for farmwork.

As the weeks slipped by, Salina observed her husband. It wasn't so much bitterness that ate at him, kept him aloof. It was disappointment, disillusion, and maybe something else that she couldn't quite put her finger on. She waited until the children had been tucked into their trundle bed one warm June night, and then she proposed that they take a walk together. Lottie had promised to keep an ear out for their little ones, though Salina was quite sure that they would sleep contentedly with no cause for alarm.

Their moonlit walk inevitably led them to the border of the Ivywood property, to where Uncle Caleb's land adjoined Shadowcreek.

"We could've been happy here, grown old together," Jeremy said. "If..."

Salina shook her dark head. "If wishes were horses, beggars could ride."

Jeremy squeezed Salina's hand. "I got a wire from Drake. Lije Southerland is recovering from a stroke. He wants to see me."

"I can have us packed tonight," Salina offered. "We could be headed west before dawn."

Jeremy shook his head. How many times had Salina been prepared to be on the move, ever ready for the next adventure? "You are something else, darlin'," he grinned. "And I'm blessed to have you."

"We deserve each other, remember?" Salina affectionately laid her head against his shoulder.

"I'd never dreamed you'd be so willing to leave Virginia," Jeremy countered.

"Virginia's not the same anymore." Salina's reply was tinged with regret. "She's occupied by a conqueror, scarred and barren. I will always be a Virginian and love my native state, but there is nothing left for us here, Jeremy. Shadowcreek is lost. Why shouldn't we make the most of the opportunity that Drake and the Southerlands are offering? What is keeping us here besides our stubborn pride?"

"It almost makes me feel like I'm running away. Skedaddling. Where is the honor in that?"

"It is your duty to honor Lije Southerland's request. The man is your grandfather, you know that."

"He's asked for Lance as well, and Lance is going to go. I told him he was welcome to travel with us."

Salina could not restrain her smile. She was pleased that Jeremy had made a firm decision. Anything would be better than this inactivity they had been mired in since he'd come back after Mosby's disbanding of the 43rd Battalion.

"I've even thought about going to California, Sallie. I still have some connections there..."

"We'll stop off in Kansas first, though. What if we give it a year, Jeremy?" Salina pondered. "If things haven't turned out according to your liking by then, we'll move on, farther west."

"A year," Jeremy murmured. By then their child would be born, and it would be easier for Salina to travel. He had that to consider. At least they could get to Kansas by rail, so she wouldn't be quite so uncomfortable as she might be if she had to go the entire distance by wagon alone. Jeremy didn't cotton to the idea of getting all the way to South Union only to be rejected again, but he held his tongue on that score. Salina was right. It was high time for him to face Evan Southerland, once and for all. Come what may. "All right. I'll wire Drake back and tell him to expect us in St. Joseph."

By the bright light of the three-quarter moon they surveyed the unkempt Shadowcreek lands, walked hand in hand up the slope of the hill where the main house had stood and then down to the stream. Salina didn't cry. She wore her strength like a mantle, and Jeremy stood quietly by her side while she privately bid farewell to the land she loved.

"I will miss this place." Her hoarse voice was hardly audible above the rush of the water and the whispering of the leaves in the trees overhead.

"As will I," Jeremy confessed. His arm about her tightened in a reassuring hug. "Come on. Let's go tell Lance that we're ready to go."

Chapter Twenty-two

South Union Ranch
Kansas
Mid-June 1865

$\mathcal{D}$rake and Lance reined up in front of the main gate of the Southerland property. Behind them in the wagon, Jeremy halted as well. A wash of chills rippled down the length of his back and across his squared shoulders.

Out of the corner of her eye, Salina saw the cold shiver run through her husband as his apprehension flitted across his face. She knew he had misgivings, and his reluctance was plain. "Be strong and courageous," she whispered. "You know as well as I that the Lord must have a reason for leading us here."

Jeremy nodded. He'd been entertaining notions of turning tail and heading back to St. Joseph. He reckoned that his arrival here was going to cause pure havoc in the Southerland family, and in truth he didn't want that. He was plumb tired of fighting—period. Yet he believed that this last battle was one he must fight if he ever hoped to have any peace in his life. As each mile had passed between St. Joseph and the ranch, he'd resigned himself to that, but it hadn't curbed the trepidation churning within him. This was going to be awkward at best.

Salina slipped her hand into the crook of his arm. Jeremy took comfort from the quiet, calm strength she exuded. He smiled, winked his thanks. No matter what happened, he could rely on her to faithfully stand by him.

"As far as the eye can see—and then some." Drake's sweeping gesture encompassed acre upon acre of gently undulating ranchland. "All of it belongs to the Southerlands."

"How far to the main house?" Lance Colby inquired, rubbing his grumbling stomach. "Think the cook'll let us eat when we get there?"

"Marietta Southerland won't let you go to bed hungry," Drake said from experience. "We're losing daylight." He looked pointedly at Jeremy. "Unless we pick up the pace a bit, we won't make it there before dark." He nudged his steed forward.

About half a mile from the gate, Jeremy spied a rough log cabin house nestled in a hollow.

"That's Lampwick," Drake answered his friend's unspoken query. "Lije Southerland has sectioned off his holdings into six separate parcels—one for each of his sons. Each parcel has a house or cabin built on it. Lampwick is one of the six section houses; the others are Eastbourne, Red Gate, Westerland, Sagebrook, and Cottonwood Alley. There used to be an area called Stage Run Springs, but the stage doesn't run through here anymore. That portion has been abandoned, just as Red Gate has been."

Two miles from Lampwick stood an empty three-story Victorian house with paint peeling from the exterior side boards and a wide, falling-down porch. Roof shingles were loose, several shutters hung askew, and the dingy white picket fence bordering the overgrown yard possessed the singular feature for which the place was named: a red gate sagging on rusted hinges. Two broken windows on the upper floor gave the house a melancholy expression.

"How come this place was abandoned?" Salina's curiosity got the better of her.

"It belonged to Evan," Drake replied. "Ruth-Ellen and her sons moved to the main house when he went off to fight in the war. No one's lived here since."

In his mind's eye, Jeremy envisioned Salina here, their new baby riding her hip, cooking smells emanating from the kitchen, laundry on the clothesline flapping in the breeze, and himself coming in from a hard day's work with the cattle and horses to play with the little ones. *She'd insist I take a bath before I set myself down to supper...* A wistful smile lit his eyes. Maybe if he saved enough money working for Drake here he could buy her a place they would call their own.

The distance of a mile stretched between Red Gate and the main house of South Union. Jeremy blinked in the gathering darkness. The main house was an exact replica of Red Gate—only it must have been three times the size, at least, and in perfect upkeep. No peeling paint, no rusty or sagging hinges here.

Lance whistled appreciatively. "Impressive. One wouldn't think to find such refinement way out here in the middle of nowhere."

"Your grandmother might be a rancher's wife, but she knows how to maintain a proper household," Drake grinned. "You'll find no lack of protocol or etiquette here."

The woman herself was descending the porch steps even before the horses were tied to the hitching post. "Glory, glory! Saints be praised!" She approached the covered wagon and riders with a broad smile and open arms. "You've come at last!"

Salina and Jeremy looked at each other, stifling their incredulous laughter. *Glory, glory!* was the phrase Jeremy habitually exclaimed—so much so that their daughter's name had been inspired by it. His grandmother apparently was possessed of the same habit.

Glory, having heard her name called, tugged on Jeremy's sleeve. "Daddy."

"Yes, darlin'."

"Wanna see."

Jeremy pulled Glory from the back of the wagon onto his lap. "There. See?"

Glory nodded, satisfied. She always wanted to know what was going on around her, afraid that she might miss out on something. She pointed a finger at Marietta Southerland. "Hi!"

"Hello!" Marietta returned the greeting. "Jeremy, it is good to see you again. And you must be Salina."

"Hello, Mrs. Southerland." Salina couldn't help but reciprocate the woman's infectious, beaming smile.

"I'm so glad you've come. And this must be Lance."

"Ma'am." Lance Colby politely tipped his hat.

"*Ma'am?*" Marietta's warm laughter encompassed all of them. "I'm your grandmother!"

"Yes, ma'am, I know," Lance acknowledged. "It's just going to take some time to get used to all this."

"Amen," Jeremy echoed his cousin's sentiments.

"Why don't you all go inside," Drake suggested. "I'll get the boys to help me with the horses."

"I'll go with you." Jeremy jumped down from the buckboard and gingerly lifted Salina to the ground. Next he put Glory down, but instead of running off, she stayed close by her mamma's skirts. Jeremy said to his wife, "E.J.'s still asleep, but I'll bring him up once I've unhitched the team."

"Why don't you give him to me?" Marietta suggested. "I'll carry him up to the rooms I've prepared for you and yours."

"Very well," Jeremy acquiesced. As he passed Salina, she whispered, "Please hurry."

"Where's your courage, Sallie?" Jeremy taunted lightly. "They won't hurt you, you know."

"I know. I just prefer to have you by me, that's all," Salina insisted.

Glory, feeling the same way, slipped her hand into her mamma's for reassurance.

"She's a beautiful child," Marietta complimented. "Sort of reminds me of your mama, Lance."

"I'm hoping you'll tell me about her," Lance remarked. "I didn't have a chance to know her at all."

The interior of the L-shaped house was equally as impressive as its exterior. Rich appointments, luxurious decor, but no pretention. The house reflected its mistress's exquisite tastes and no-nonsense attitudes.

Emmett and Edmund, Marietta's youngest sons, showed up in the parlour first. They kept Lance company while Marietta took Salina upstairs to a suite of rooms on the second floor.

"I hope the trip wasn't too tiresome for you," Marietta said, laying the sleeping E.J. down in the center of the wide sleigh bed that dominated the room. "Do you mind my asking how far along you are?"

"This baby is due in September," Salina replied, reciprocating Jeremy's grandmother's cordiality.

"We haven't had babies in this house since Little Evan and Jonathan were born. I adore little ones," Marietta exclaimed. "They are so precious."

"Little Evan and Jonathan—they are Jeremy's half brothers?" Salina recalled their names from the Southerland dossier.

"Aye," Marietta nodded. "Unfortunately Little Evan has taken his mother's side in this and has already determined that he will have nothing to do with Jeremy. Jonathan, on the other hand, is most curious to meet his older brother. Jeremy and Jon favor each other, cut from the same cloth. I've no doubt they'll get along well together."

"Has Jeremy's father acknowledged he is Jeremy's sire?" The direct question slipped out before Salina could prevent it.

"Not officially." Marietta appreciated the young lady's forthright manner. She was one who firmly believed it better to have things out in the open and not discussed in disdainful whispers. "But I know my son, Salina, and he wouldn't have wanted Jeremy to be here unless he planned to do something about him. Now, I have confided in you, but I beg you to say nothing to Jeremy just yet. I'm not asking that you harbor secrets from him, but I think it would be best to let this thing get worked out between them in their own time and fashion."

"Agreed." Salina breathed easier, relieved to learn that her intuition had not been in error. "How is your husband? Drake told us that he'd suffered a stroke."

"Lije is doing somewhat better. Thank you for asking. He has regained the use of his right side, but the doctor gives little hope that he will ever be able to use his left arm again. The left side of his face is permanently paralyzed—I used to think he had a lopsided grin before, but now it's really a one-sided expression."

Salina smiled. "I've always believed Jeremy's grin could be described as lopsided."

"Salina, be prepared—when you meet Evan you will see for yourself what Jeremy will look like a score of years from now. There's little difference between them aside from the discrepancy in their ages and the placement of their scars. I knew Jeremy was Evan's son from the moment I saw him. Those eyes they share are a dead giveaway."

"It must have been a mighty powerful shock for you to learn that Evan wasn't dead," Salina commented.

"Indeed it was! A welcome one, mind you. And so was learning of two more grandsons—and to learn that I have great-grandchildren besides." Marietta cast a loving smile at Glory, who quickly disappeared behind Salina's skirts again. "They aren't twins, are they?"

"No. Jeremy and I have adopted E.J. He's my brother's son, actually. He and Glory are very dear to us. This next one will be, too."

"South Union is almost self-sufficient, but we still make an occasional trip to town when the occasion warrants. If you need anything between now and your confinement, you'd best let me know. We are isolated out here—so I insist that you come back to this house rather than stay out at Red Gate when your time comes," Marietta instructed.

"Red Gate?"

Marietta covered her mouth. "There I go, putting the cart before the horse again."

"Drake showed us that place on the way here. Is it to be Jeremy's?"

A single nod affirmed Salina's perceptive conjecture. "Since Evan is alive and Lije's health is failing, Evan will rightfully take over matters at the main house. I believe he is going to deed Red Gate and its acreage to Jeremy. The place needs work, that's a given, but we'll all pitch in, rest assured. I'll not allow you to over-work yourself and chance bringing that baby on early."

"I've already done that once," Salina confided. "Glory was born in cavalry headquarters a month before I thought she would be."

"We'll have to take extra special care of you, then," Marietta declared firmly. "Salina, I am so very glad you and Jeremy decided to come home to South Union. Don't ever forget that."

☆☆☆☆☆☆☆

At breakfast the next morning, Salina, Jeremy, the children, and Lance were introduced to the rest of the Southerlands—all but Ruth-Ellen, who refused to join them. Lije, sitting at his place at the head of the table, looked over his family proudly, his sapphire eyes still as lively as ever. Though he struggled a bit in feeding himself, Marietta, seated to his right, was on hand if he conceded to need-ing assistance.

Ephraim and Elton sat opposite of each other; Emmett and Edmund sat acoss from Jeremy and Lance. Elton had spent two years in prison at Salisbury, North Carolina, and he was still too thin for Marietta's liking. Marietta passed the bacon and eggs around to him a third time. "Ma, I can't eat that much," her second son protested. "But thanks just the same."

Practically everywhere Salina looked, she saw the vivid, sapphire hue of the Southerland eyes. Uncles and nephews were trying not to gape openly at one another, but a full-scale inspection, sizing one another up, was in progress. Jonathan had eyes of that same deep blue, Salina noted, but Little Evan did not. That one had eyes as dark as coal and filled with loathing whenever they chanced to rest on Jeremy.

Jeremy either pretended not to notice the hateful looks his brother tossed in his direction or simply made it a point to ignore them. He understood that he was more than a threat to Little Evan.

If Evan actually acknowledged Jeremy, he would usurp Little Evan's standing as firstborn son and the privileges of that position.

Evan Southerland arrived late for the meal. Elton pushed the bacon and eggs toward his brother, and Evan nodded curtly. The table, which was usually loud with exuberant chatter, became deathly silent. Even Glory and E.J. were quiet while Salina fed them, the little ones feeling the oppressive air of qualm and mistrust as keenly as the adults did.

Drake entered the dining room a few minutes later, amazed to hear nothing more than the scrape of silverware against the china and the rattle of glassware. "Sun's been up for almost an hour, Barnes, get going. There's work to be done, so quit your lollygagging. I hired you to do a job."

Jeremy set his napkin beside his cleared plate. He thanked Marietta for the tasty breakfast, kissed Salina's brow and both of his childen. "I'll be back for supper," he told Salina.

As he walked passed Evan's place, the two men exchanged a wary glance. Jeremy followed Drake out the door.

"It's like a tomb in there," Drake commented dryly, pulling on his gloves.

"What's there to say?" Jeremy queried. "It's awkward, Drake. I freely admit it. Certainly you didn't expect it to be any different, did you?"

"What did *you* expect?" Drake wondered.

Jeremy shrugged his broad shoulders. "I tried not to expect anything, not to bring with me any preconceived ideas, and so far, that's proved to be a sound policy. Besides, I've got you, Mr. Foreman, to remind me that I'm not a son of this house. I'm just another hired hand."

"For now," Drake agreed. "Give it time, Jeremy. Don't give up on the Southerlands just yet. They really are good folks, you'll see."

"So, what kind of routine have you got set up around here? What chores do you have lined up for me?"

"There are literally fences that need to be mended," Drake told him. "We'll start out at Red Gate."

☆☆☆☆☆☆☆

August 1865

Elinor Dallinger dismounted in front of Red Gate, stunned at the transformation of the place. For the past six weeks Drake and Jeremy had poured every free hour they had into making the dilapidated place into a liveable home. The results to date were satisfactorily pleasing. "Good afternoon, Jeremy!" she called, waving to the man perched on the roof.

Jeremy paused to remove three nails from between his teeth. "Afternoon, Ellie. Salina's inside. Make yourself at home."

"Thank you!" Elinor called gaily. She went up the new porch steps and opened the repaired screened door. "Salina?"

"I'm in the kitchen," Salina answered.

Elinor plopped her basket down on the checkered tablecloth. "I've had a letter from Aurora—she and Tristan Scarborough are to be married on New Year's Eve. Can you believe it?"

"I thought Tristan had gone back to Charlotte." Salina's eyes were wide.

"Evidently they've been keeping up a steady stream of correspondence since their last meeting," Elinor said glibly. "I know she took prodigious care of him at the hospital at City Point, saved his life. But I had no idea that Tristan had been able to spark her heart. She mourned Mason's death for a long, long time."

"Well, I am very happy for them," Salina smiled. "Excuse me, I just need to get these biscuits out of the oven." She continued with her baking, urging Elinor to take a seat at the table. "Was there any other mail from town?"

"A letter for Jeremy from Kidd Carney, and one from Bentley. I posted the letter you'd written to Clarice."

"Thank you for doing that for me. I do appreciate it."

"What else are neighbors for," Elinor brushed off Salina's thanks. The two women chattered amiably over cups of lemonade, discussing Aurora's upcoming wedding. Elinor departed shortly thereafter to drive to the main house to deliver the rest of the mail.

The kitchen was filled with the enticing aroma of baking bread when Jeremy came in through the back door. Salina was sitting at the kitchen table sorting through stacks of papers, taking advantage of Glory and E.J. being down for their afternoon naps.

Biting into the bacon sandwich Salina had fixed for his dinner, Jeremy glanced over the documents. "What's all this?" he asked before he'd swallowed.

"Old traveling passes, my pardon from Lincoln, maps, copies of the affidavit from your mother, newspapers, your poems, Curlie's sketchbook, letters from Mamma and Flora Stuart... Daddy's things."

Jeremy set down the sandwich, his fingers targeting one of the copies of Justine's affidavit. "Tell me again what happened to the original."

"Captain Sally Tompkins found it in Ridge's jacket pocket when he was recuperating at Robertson Hospital after his ordeal in Libby. She gave it to Brisco, who in turn entrusted it to me. I made those copies before I sent the true document to your grandmother for safekeeping."

"So Gram has the original."

"Aye, she should," Salina nodded, her mind working at a rapid pace. "Do you think she's showed it to your father?"

Jeremy shook his sandy head. "I don't know. But I intend to find out."

"Are you going to confront your father?" Salina ventured to ask.

"Maybe. In time. Not today."

Salina shivered.

"What?" Jeremy looked askance at her.

"I don't know," Salina shrugged. "It's just that ever since we got here, things have been stirred up, unsettled. On the surface, things proceed as usual, but underneath, the tension is so thick." She hugged her elbows. "Don't you get the feeling that we're just waiting for the other shoe to drop?"

Jeremy's wife had pinpointed exactly how he felt. Something had been brewing from the day Lance had left to return East.

"Do you like it here?" Salina suddenly questioned.

"I like it well enough," Jeremy allowed. "It's still too early to decide for sure. But I do know that I'd much rather be here at Red Gate, removed from the cauldron boiling up at the main house—let me tell you! I had coffee up there earlier today. First time I've had a chance to talk to Elton at all. We danced around any mention of the war, the same as he and Ephraim are wont to do."

"That limits the subject matter for conversation severely. What did you find to say to each other?"

"We discussed the prospects of increasing the size of the herd next year. Apparently Evan wants to make a trip down to Texas to purchase longhorn steers." Jeremy saw the look of trepidation on his wife's face. "Don't fret, I'm not leaving you here for any length of time." He kissed the back of her hand. "Not yet, anyway."

Salina inclined her head and playfully scowled. "You leave me alone here every day for hours on end while you and Drake work with horses and do all the things required to keep this place running."

Jeremy conceded. "But I come home to you every night."

"I know this ranch is a big place, but I'm surprised that you haven't yet run into Evan somewhere during the last month. He's deliberately staying away, isn't he? Avoiding us at all costs."

"It doesn't matter what Evan does. I don't care," Jeremy declared. He tapped his finger on a copy of the affidavit. "This proves who I am whether he does anything about it or not. Can you live with that?"

"Can you?"

"Yeah," Jeremy nodded. "It's fine. The mystery is solved: I know who my father is, what my name should've been. That'll have to be enough." He glanced about the near-empty room. "Gram says you ought to take a look at the unused furniture stored up in the attic and take your pick of what you want when you go to dinner at the main house on Sunday. She'll send Emmett and Edmund out to help you put the stuff where you want it."

"Where will you be?" Salina wanted to know.

"I have to accompany Drake to a neighboring ranch—just for the day. Somebody's selling a stallion that he's had an eye on." Jeremy took a checkered napkin and wiped the breadcrumbs from his mustache and the corners of his mouth. "Do you reckon we'll ever feel like this is home, Sallie?"

"My home is where you are," Salina answered. In truth, she was settling in at Red Gate comfortably. She already had an affection for the place, but she was resolutely trying not to become too enamored of living here in the event that Jeremy decided that they would move on to California at the end of the year. She prayed that some sign would be revealed to Jeremy. Something that would be a clear, irrefutable indicator that this was where they were meant to be.

Hours later, after Jeremy was asleep in her arms, she prayed more specifically, "God, please, let him share his father's name if we're to stay. That's the sign I'm looking for; if You'll grant that, then I'll know that this is where You've transplanted us and that that is the reason for our being here. Fill us both with Your strength and show us how to accomplish Your purpose. I ask this in Jesus' name. Amen."

In the middle of the night, Jonathan arrived at Red Gate. "Come—as quick as you can! Grampa's taken a turn for the worse, and I can't find my pa anywhere. Gram's with Grampa now, Drake and Ellie are up at the house; the rest of the family's there, too. You ought to be there, Jeremy—just in case."

"Ride back and tell Drake that we're on our way," Jeremy yawned. "Jon..."

His half brother paused, waiting.

"If Drake thinks our being there will make things worse, tell him to leave a lantern on the porch and we'll stay away."

Jonathan Southerland shook his head. "Drake's the one who sent me to fetch you. Grampa was calling for you by name, Jeremy. He's expecting you."

While Jeremy hitched up the wagon, Salina hastily bundled up the children, all the while thinking how odd it was that Jeremy was considered a part of the Southerland clan, though nothing had been done to remedy the fact that his name was not theirs. Again she prayed, seeking the Lord for His sign.

"What happened?" Salina asked Drake and Elinor when Jeremy went into Lije's room at his grandfather's request.

"I'm not sure, but I'd guess it's more of Ruth-Ellen's same nonsense," Drake muttered angrily. "She certainly hasn't grasped the concept of forgiving and forgetting in the least!"

Elinor was able to elaborate a bit. "Marietta said that Ruth-Ellen had upset Lije again. This time she accused him of changing his will. She claims that if Lije doesn't banish Jeremy from the ranch and make Evan do his duty by acting like the father of her sons, she'll take Little Evan and Jonathan away from here."

Salina shook her head.

"The doc said Lije's heart was failing him. Chances are he won't make it through the night," Drake said softly. "I wish Ridge was here."

"But he's still in California," Salina whispered. "Oh, Drake, was the strife worth our coming here?"

"Jeremy belongs here," Drake insisted. "Don't you doubt that."

"I do, though," Salina confessed. "This family was first divided by the war; it is now divided because of Jeremy's very life. Jeremy may hide his feelings about it from you, Drake, but I know it hurts him."

"Patience, Little One. Patience," Drake encouraged.

Belatedly, Salina remembered that of all people, Drake would be able to understand firsthand what it meant to have a family divided over one's very existence. Hadn't virtually the same situation happened when he fulfilled Aurora's request to go to Boston? When his father had publicly acknowledged Drake as his heir, it had set the entire Dallinger household on its ear. Grandmamma's grudging acceptance had come over time.

Drake seemingly read her mind. "It will all work out in the end. Trust me."

☆☆☆☆☆☆☆

The Southerland patriarch's death was a blow to all of them, especially Drake, who felt this loss in a far greater sense than he had that of his own father. Lije Southerland was the one man who'd been able to teach Drake the meaning of integrity and devoutness, not necessarily by preaching but by action and deed. His steady influence would be sorely missed. Drake was wise enough to know now that Lije's well-meaning interference had not only saved his life but ultimately saved his soul as well.

"He was good to me," Drake whispered to Elinor at Lije's funeral. "Better than I deserved—I never could quite figure why he singled me out and bestowed favor."

"For a purpose," Elinor nodded comfortingly. "All things work together for good, Drake."

Salina's head snapped up at hearing Elinor's admonition to her husband. It reminded her of Taylor Sue. "Be strong and courageous," Salina whispered aloud, to no one but herself.

"What did you say, darlin'?" Jeremy leaned his head toward hers.

"Be strong and courageous," Salina repeated. She hadn't known Lije Southerland for very long, but she realized that she, too, would miss the man. "With your permission, I think I'll invite your grandmother to stay with us for a bit, give her a reprieve of sorts."

"She'd like that," Jeremy nodded. "Besides, then you won't be alone while I go to town with Drake and Elton. There are some legalities that have to be taken care of with the attorney."

"Evan inherits."

"But Drake runs the place," Jeremy reminded her. "Evan's all but abdicated his role as the incumbent head of this family. He doesn't want to be in charge, and he's just as happy to leave things to Drake's management. Knowing Lije, he probably made some sort of provision for Drake."

"He's a good foreman, and he's more content here than he ever would be in Boston," Salina observed. "This place prospers because of him."

"Elton and Ephraim are aware of that," Jeremy nodded. "I doubt that they'll change the order of things."

While the reverend read the funeral text over the casket, Jeremy stole a glance at the man who was his father. Evan Southerland had followed on the fringes of the procession that trailed from the main house to the place Marietta had selected for Lije's gravesite. Evan's pained face told plainly that his heart was grieved.

☆☆☆☆☆☆☆

"Evan Southerland, I demand to know where you're off to! Don't you leave me here without saying a word!" Ruth-Ellen realized her poor choice of words when her husband turned around to face her, anger blazing in his shrewd sapphire eyes. Evan snatched up his slate and ground the chalk down heavily. The thick white lines he hastily drew spelled out *RED GATE.*

Both the slate and the chalk landed with a clatter on the dining room table. Evan stalked past his estranged wife without a backwards glance. He was hurting her by doing this, but he'd be darned if he continued to let Salina's husband hurt for another day. Jeremy had suffered all his life for mistakes Evan had never owned up to. Evan was aware that his efforts might be a case of too little, too late, but he would shirk his duty no longer. Since the day of Lije's funeral, he'd come to believe that he'd failed his father by not being man enough to shoulder his responsibilities. Evan was determined to change that. His head was clearer now than it had been for months, and he knew what he must do to make amends.

For weeks Evan had covertly watched his oldest son as he worked, sunup to sundown. Jeremy performed his chores around the ranch on a daily basis, then headed out to continue with the reconstruction of the house he and Salina were living in with their children—his grandchildren. It was as plain to see that Jeremy had a knack with horses as it was to see that his wife loved him with everything she had. Little Evan shunned his older brother completely, but Jonathan followed Jeremy around, helping where he could, learning what he didn't already know. Jeremy was patient with his younger brother, probably realizing that the little son he had would be shadowing him in but a matter of time. Evan used to have that kind of camaraderie with his own father, and since Lije's passing, he found he yearned to know this man Jeremy Barnes better. Each day that passed was time wasted. He doubted they would ever be close, but at the very least perhaps they could grow to be friends.

Ephraim caught a glimpse of his oldest brother lighting out of the stable, spurring a black Morgan in a northerly direction. He didn't have to guess where Evan was headed.

"Ruth-Ellen." Ephraim hesitantly touched his sister-in-law's slumped shoulders. "Evan was supposed to meet me here. He knows I've got to head out to catch a train to Kansas City. Is he coming back?"

Ruth-Ellen raised her head and looked at Ephraim with red-rimmed, watery eyes. "I'm supposed to tell you to take Little Evan with you to the auction in his place. He's going to town with Elton, Drake, and Jeremy instead." She wrung her hands. "I did everything I could to stop him, but he's going to claim his son in spite of my protestations. He's going to make Jeremy Barnes his legitimate heir!"

"It's his right as Jeremy's father to do that," Ephraim conceded. "You know Evan. It was only a matter of time before he succumbed to honor. He would see this as doing the honorable thing."

"I don't know Evan at all anymore!" Ruth-Ellen raged. "But then, I doubt if I ever did. He never let me get close to him. He always held himself apart. I thought I knew him, but I was wrong."

"The war changed him," Ephraim acknowledged. "It left its mark on all of us. And I'm sure Pa's death has taken its toll..." his voice trailed off, his eyes scanning the empty horizon in the direction Evan had ridden.

"He's going to give Jeremy his name," Ruth-Ellen grumbled. "Evan feels it's the least he can do..."

"And so it is," Ephraim agreed. His sister-in-law would never understand, and he made no attempt to make her see it from Evan's point of view.

☆☆☆☆☆☆☆

"Glory, get up in your chair and I'll let you lick the spoon." Salina patted the sandy-blond head of the little girl clinging to her knees. Having finished preparing the icing to glaze the fresh-baked cinnamon rolls, she shifted the weight of E.J. from one hip to the other. E.J.'s chubby little legs straddled her thickened waist, one leg lightly resting against the swell of her belly.

Relinquishing the icing-coated spoon into Glory's anxious hands, Salina saw a rider's approach through the kitchen widow. She called into the study, "Jeremy? Darlin', somebody's coming up the hill. What time was Elton supposed to be here? He's early, isn't he?"

Jeremy Barnes recognized the man who tethered his horse at the fence and opened the red gate at the edge of the hedge-lined walk. It was not his Uncle Elton.

"It's your father!" Salina breathed in astonishment, eyes round as saucers. "Oh, Jeremy, what's *he* doing here do you suppose?"

Jeremy shoved his hands deep into the pockets of his jean-cloth trousers, his fingers clenched tightly into fists. "He's probably here to tell us that now that Lije is dead, we're no longer welcome around here."

"Marietta would never let him run us off." Salina laid a hand on Jeremy's arm, looking up into his narrowed eyes. "Whatever he has to say, please, just hear him out."

Jeremy cast a sidelong glance at his wife. "He won't be *saying* anything."

"Slip of the tongue—just like when I used to expect you to *see* things when you were blind," Salina retorted. "Greet him, and make him feel welcome. I'll put a pot of coffee on to brew." She handed E.J. into Jeremy's arms. "Watch him for a minute, would you? I need both hands." She stood on tiptoe to kiss Jeremy's whiskered cheek. "Don't be frightened; I'll stand by you, you know that."

"I do know that." Jeremy brushed a trace of flour from her cheek and kissed her.

Salina saw her reflection in the halltree mirror. "Maybe a clean apron would be appropriate, too."

"You don't have to impress him, Sallie. You look beautiful to me."

"Thank you for saying so," she laughed, walking to the pantry to exchange her dirty apron for a clean one anyhow, tucking the errant strands of curls escaped from her chignon back behind her ears.

When she took the serving tray into the study, she was sure that neither her husband nor his father had done anything but stare at each other. She wanted to shake her own head to clear it, but she knew that would be to no avail. She was not seeing double—they were definitely related.

"This is my wife, Salina." Jeremy made the stilted introductions. "Salina, may I present Evan Southerland."

Evan bowed over her hand and kissed it. He pantomimed to convey his request for paper and pencil.

Jeremy retrieved the writing implements while Salina set out the mugs and and coffee pot. "Shall I pour?"

"We'll take care of it, darlin', thank you."

She looked up at Jeremy for confirmation: Did he want her to stay with him, or should she leave? His second nod indicated that he would be all right, she could go. He wasn't afraid of this man.

Evan took the sheets of paper and the pencil. He began writing: YOU'VE DONE WONDERS WITH THIS PLACE SINCE YOU MOVED IN.

"I finally finished patching the hole in the roof day before last. I suppose we'll have to wait and see if it holds when the rains come," Jeremy replied.

Evan nodded.

"You must have reason for seeking me out. What can I do for you?"

ALLOW ME TO ACCOMPANY YOU TO TOWN. I'VE A PIECE OF BUSINESS TO STRAIGHTEN OUT, AND I MAY NEED AN INTERPRETER.

"I'm sure Ephraim or Elton can serve in that capacity for you."

Evan shook his head. *THEY ARE MY BROTHERS, BUT THEY ARE NOT MY SONS.*

"Well, then I suppose you'd be needing Little Evan or Jon to help you."

ONLY YOU CAN HELP ME.

"But I'm not your son," Jeremy said lowly. "At least you don't consider me as such."

CIRCUMSTANCES HAVE CHANGED. I STAND COR-RECTED.

"Oh?" Jeremy arched an eyebrow in query. "Was there some-thing specific that served to alter your belief?"

EVEN WITHOUT WRITTEN VERIFICATION, EVIDENCE STILL BEARS OUT THE RELATIONSHIP BETWEEN US.

"In Maryland you insisted there must be *written* documentation before you would believe the charges Justine laid at your door. Did you manage to come up with the proof you sought?"

Evan produced the original copy of the affidavit signed by Justine Newman Prentiss Barnes Wentworth. *SHE WASN'T ALWAYS AS COLD AND HEARTLESS AS SHE HAS COME TO BE.*

"You can believe that if you want to," Jeremy shrugged. "I know better."

I REGRET THAT SHE DIDN'T TELL ME. I HONESTLY WOULD HAVE DONE THINGS DIFFERENTLY HAD SHE INFORMED ME THAT I HAD A SON ALL THOSE YEARS AGO.

"So, you accept that you are my father?"

I DO. AND AS SUCH, I SHOULD LIKE VERY MUCH TO START BY HAVING YOU SHARE MY NAME. YOU ARE A SOUTHERLAND, AND I KNOW YOU ARE AS PROUD AS THE REST OF US. IT IS MY HOPE THAT YOU WILL LEARN TO FORGIVE ME FOR MY OWN RELUCTANCE AND HARD-HEARTEDNESS. MY FOLLY AND ARROGANCE PRE-VENTED ME FROM DOING WHAT WAS RIGHT.

"You want me to take the name of Southerland?" Jeremy quelled the sudden elation rising in him. He'd been burned by this flame before, and he wasn't overanxious to touch it again. "You're going to give me your name?"

Evan nodded, quickly scribbling, *IF YOU WILL HONOR ME BY ACCEPTING IT AND MAKING IT YOUR OWN. I LEAVE THE CHOICE IN YOUR HANDS.*

Jeremy blinked back the sting of tears. "I appreciate what you're trying to do..."

PLEASE, Evan wrote, *I'VE DENIED YOU LONG ENOUGH. THAT WAS MY MISTAKE. TWENTY YEARS I CANNOT MAKE UP FOR IN A SINGLE DAY, BUT I BEG YOU WILL GIVE ME A CHANCE TO BUILD A RELATIONSHIP BETWEEN US. YOUR MOTHER ROBBED US OF THAT. WON'T YOU MEET ME IN AN EFFORT TO REMEDY OUR SITUATION?*

With his arms folded across his chest, Jeremy took his time in digesting Evan's scrawled words. "What did you have in mind?"

Evan handed an envelope to Jeremy. It contained a written account of Jeremy's history endorsed with his witnessed acknowledgment. He added the signed affidavit. The documents verified that Jeremy was Evan's undisputed offspring and would put to rest once and for all any question of paternity. *FOR STARTERS, I PLAN TO SUBMIT THESE TO THE JUDGE. ONCE YOUR NAME IS LEGALLY CHANGED, THEN WE'LL MOVE ON FROM THERE, ONE STEP AT A TIME.*

"Why?" Jeremy was struggling to understand. "What finally changed your mind?"

BEFORE HE DIED, YOUR GRANDFATHER SAID SOMETHING TO ME ABOUT KNOWING THE TRUTH AND ITS POWER TO SET ONE FREE. THIS TRUTH WILL SET US BOTH FREE. IT CAN AID IN THE HEALING OF THE GUILT I'VE BEEN HARBORING, AND I WOULD HOPE IT WILL HELP DIMINISH THE RESENTMENT YOU FEEL. I DON'T WANT YOU TO HATE ME.

"I don't hate or resent you," Jeremy argued. "Yes, I was disappointed when you didn't want to believe who I was when we first met. But not anymore. It was ludicrous for me to expect instant acceptance from you—just as it's overwhelming to receive it now."

BUT I WANT YOU TO KNOW THAT YOU HAVE IT NONETHELESS. I CANNOT REASONABLY EXPECT YOUR INSTANT ACCEPTANCE EITHER. IT IS SOMETHING WE WILL HAVE TO WORK ON OVER TIME—TOGETHER. I HANDLED THIS SITUATION POORLY ALL THE WAY AROUND. ALL I'M ASKING IS THAT YOU BE PATIENT WITH ME.

"And you must be patient with me as well," Jeremy reciprocated. "Between us, I'm sure we'll find a way to work this all out."

I AM CONFIDENT WE WILL.

Jeremy folded Evan's testament and put it back into the envelope with his mother's statement. After a few minutes of intensely contemplative silence between the two men, Jeremy extended a proffered hand toward his father.

Evan shook Jeremy's hand to seal the pact between them, but then he started to weep. He put his arms around Jeremy and hugged him fiercely. Working his damaged throat, Evan determined to speak with his own words a harsh, strangled sound: "You...are...indeed...my...son."

☆☆☆☆☆☆☆

Glory stood at the front door, blocking Jeremy's path. She didn't want him to go away.

Jeremy hunkered down to his daughter's level and put his arms around her. "Glory. Daddy's got to go away for a little time. I'll be back in four days." He held up the appropriate number of fingers. "Four."

"Four," she repeated somberly, her attention focused on the collar of his suit jacket rather than his eyes. Her little fingers traced the edge of the seam.

"Glory Stuart, look at me," Jeremy instructed.

The girl obeyed.

"I love you, darlin'."

Glory nodded.

"I need you to look after your mamma for me, keep Gram company, and make sure E.J. stays out of trouble. Will you do that for me?"

Glory's sandy-blond head bobbed again.

"Good. I'm counting on you to be a trooper." Jeremy hugged her close.

"But why you go, Daddy? Why no take Glory too? Want to ride with you."

"Not this time, darlin'. Another time. Stay with Mamma and be my good girl. I'll bring you back something special, okay?"

"Okay," Glory relented. "Bye-bye, Daddy. I love you." She kissed him.

Jeremy stood up. He took the saddlebag Salina had packed for him. "And what will you bring back for me?" she impishly queried.

"A new name," he winked at her.

Salina had her sign.

As promised, Jeremy returned to Red Gate four days later. He had in his possession a modified birth certificate for himself, a revised marriage certificate, and proper documentation officially changing the children's names from *Barnes* to *Southerland*. The witness signatures were validation, and duplicates were on file with the county clerk's office. The deed to Red Gate was made out to *Jeremy Evan Southerland*.

Jeremy pulled Salina onto his lap. He watched her study each piece of paper, and then she turned to meet his dancing sapphire eyes. "Well, *Mrs. Southerland*, what do you make of all this?"

Salina laughed blithely. "It is a direct answer to my prayers. The Lord is faithful, Jeremy."

"Glory, glory—so He is."

Two days later, the proverbial fatted calf was killed and a celebration at the main house began in earnest. Salina praised God for the way He had seen fit to heal the wounds, to help this family mend after all each of its members had been through. A sudden pain ripped across her lower back, indication that her time had come.

When the birthing was done and she held her newborn daughter in her arms, Salina looked up at her husband. "Another girl."

"Aye," Jeremy nodded, leaning down to kiss her brow. He brought out Salina's Bible, and in the front he proudly made the inscription: *Grace Hastings Southerland, born September 26, 1865.* "There."

Salina smiled. Tiredly, she asked, "Where are E.J. and Glory?"

"Out in the hall with Gram and my father. Are you up to company?"

Salina adjusted the quilts around her and smoothed her tousled curls. "I suppose I am. You can let them in."

Jeremy kissed her tenderly. He opened the door and beckoned to his children, "Come meet your new sister."

Glory and E.J. were in awe of the sweet little baby that wriggled in the crook of Jeremy's arm.

Evan Southerland was invited in and allowed to hold his new granddaughter. The wonder that shone in his eyes was mirrored in Jeremy's. Salina's eyelids drooped, her long lashes came to rest on her flushed cheeks. She was at peace and content.

Epilogue

May 29, 1907
Richmond, Virginia

*T*he liveried coachman halted the carriage in front of a row of brick townhouses near the intersection of Franklin and First Streets. Glory Stuart Southerland Alexander glanced at the three-story structures with their white-columned stoops and black wrought-iron fences. "Is this where you lived during the war, Mamma?"

"Aye," Salina Southerland replied with a reminiscent nod. "On and off, until the end."

Glory's eyes transferred from the brick edifice to the nostalgic expression on her mamma's face. Glory could detect old memories, both triumphant and tragic, reflected in the still keen, sparkling emerald eyes.

"I brought you home to this house; E.J. was born here, and Grace was conceived here," Salina recalled. She looked toward Capitol Square, then at all the buildings that had sprung up over time. "The evacuation fire almost destroyed this town..."

The streets seemed as full of congestion now as they were forty-three years ago, Salina thought—the difference being that streetcars and horseless carriages had taken the place of uniformed troops, horses, and wagons. During their morning tour of the former Confederate capital, Salina had pointed out several sites to Glory, some still standing and some not: Chimborazo, Robertson Hospital, Richmond Theatre, Libby Prison, the executive mansion, Tredegar Iron Works, Hollywood Cemetery, the Spottswood Hotel, and where the Brewers used to live. "More than forty years." Salina shook her silver-gray head in wonder. "Hard to believe there were days when I didn't know if we were going to make it or not. The months when there was no word from your daddy, the nights when we prayed that the Yankees wouldn't overrun the city." She brought her meandering thoughts back into the present. "That certainly was another lifetime ago."

"Indeed," Glory nodded sagely. Her firsthand experience with armed conflict came on the day she saw E.J. off to fight in the Spanish-American War back in 1898. E.J. Southerland was a graduate of the Virginia Military Institute, and his training and expertise had been in demand. He had followed the call of duty to fight for his country.

On the way back to the Jefferson Hotel, the driver of the carriage took a detour so Salina and Glory could view the statues on Monument Avenue of President Davis and General Robert E. Lee. The ceremonies for the unveiling of the new statue erected in memorial to General Stuart would commence on the morrow.

The Jefferson was a remarkable hotel, lately reopened after the reconstruction required to repair fire damage as well as increase the number of guest rooms. Marble pillars, potted palms, antique furniture, and an eclectic combination of architectural styles produced a rich ambience. The mezzanine, grand staircase, and stained-glass skylights offered a visual feast for the eyes, the famed Valentine statue of Thomas Jefferson was most impressive, and the live alligators inhabiting the sunken rills alongside the statue were certainly a point of interest.

A portion of the Palm Court served as headquarters for Confederate veterans checking in to register for the events pertaining to the reunion. The unveiling of Stuart's statue was a part of the opening ceremonies of a week-long celebration.

"There's Daddy," Glory pointed, easily picking out her father's tall frame among the crowd. Even at the age of sixty-four, his sandy-blond hair now gone entirely gray, Jeremy Southerland still stood proud and distinguished, his broad shoulders squared.

"Captain Barnes!" A man called out to Jeremy, but Jeremy seemed not to hear, and he did not halt his approach toward Salina and Glory.

"Daddy," Glory turned her father around to face the man who was calling after him. "That man is trying to get your attention."

"Captain Barnes," the man repeated, grinned, and snapped a salute. "It's been two score years, but I hope you haven't forgotten me."

"Kidd Carney." Jeremy, too, flashed a grin as the former comrades-in-arms vigorously shook hands. "Pardon me for seeming to ignore you. I've not used the name of Barnes since practically the last time we saw each other. It's Southerland now—just plain Jeremy Southerland—no rank or title attached."

"It's still awfully good to see you, sir," Kidd Carney nodded. "And you, too, Miss Salina."

"Carney." Salina smiled warmly and made the introductions to Glory.

"Ah, you're the little lass who was named for General Stuart," Kidd Carney inferred. "Then it's only fitting that you should be here." He introduced the Southerlands to his wife, the former Miss Hollis of Orange Court House, and their grown children.

Uncle Boone and Aunt Clarice had come down from Culpeper, and Uncle Tristan and Aunt Rorie had traveled from Massachusetts to be present for the festivities. Drake and Elinor would arrive on a later train.

Glory sighed, taking in the sights and all the details, wishing once more that her own children, Salina and Jeremy's grandchildren, could have attended—but they were grown, with lives of their own, and had not much interest in what seemed to them to be "ancient history."

Throughout supper that night, Glory listened as the veteran Rebels retold stories of the War Between the States that she'd heard hundreds of times at her daddy's knee. The intensity in Jeremy's eyes burned bright, the old scar from his Gettysburg wounding a long-faded reminder of that monumental conflict.

The next day's activities started early. Salina, Glory, the aunts, and Carney's wife met in the lobby of the Jefferson and departed together. Mrs. Carney had an aquaintance in Richmond who had kindly extended an invitation for all of them to come watch the proceedings from the balcony of her home near the intersection of Lombardy and Franklin Streets.

Drake did not march in the parade with Jeremy, Kidd Carney, Boone Hunter, and Tristan Scarborough. The elderly quartet were among the five hundred original horse soldiers still living. Drake became the self-appointed chaperone to the ladies and accompanied them while taking in the sights.

Homes along the parade route were decorated with bunting and fluttering flags; verandas, balconies, and rooftops accommodated spectators. Water stations at strategic intervals supplied refreshment to the aged, banner-waving cavalrymen. The bands played, the press of the multitudes increased, and a resurrected patriotism filled the air. A choir of six hundred children sang Confederate songs and formed a human depiction of the battle flag of the Army of Northern Virginia.

The morning paper printed a notice that declared that J.E.B. Stuart, grandson of the general, was to have performed the unveiling. The ten-year-old had suffered appendicitis, however, and had been hospitalized. It was believed that none of the Stuart family would be in attendance, due to the severity of the boy's condition.

But Flora Stuart had not stayed away after all, and with her she brought her granddaughter, Virginia Stuart Waller, age eight, to take part in the ceremonial exercises on May thirtieth. Dressed in her habitual black, Flora was proud and pleased to finally see erected the monument that had its inception a scant two days after her husband's death in May of 1864. It had taken all these years—planning committees, fund-raisers, donation collection, and design selection—for the City of Richmond to fulfill its resolution to honor Stuart in exchange for her agreement to allow his burial at Hollywood. Throughout the proceedings, Stuart's widow sat poised on the platform among the dignitaries with her granddaughter at her side.

The dedication address was given by Theodore Garnett, who had been one of Stuart's aides. Salina remembered him. She also remembered Major Venable and had recognized Miss Mary Lee, one of General Lee's daughters, seated on the platform. Later Salina learned that Mrs. General William Mahone and Mrs. General Stonewall Jackson were also in attendance—Mary Anna Jackson had remained in her carriage, however, since she had not been feeling well.

"Comrades of the Veteran Cavalry Association of the Army of Northern Virginia, United Confederate Veterans, Fellow Citizens of Richmond, Ladies and Gentlemen," Garnett began.

"In response to a call as inspiring as the bugles of Stuart on the field of battle, I am here to attempt the impossible task which has been assigned me by my old comrades.

"Forty-three years, to this same flowery month of May, have passed away since 'The cannon of his country pealed Stuart's funeral knell,' and that same period has elapsed since the city of Richmond registered its high resolve to place a monument here to his undying name.

"To the honor of this city, and in proof of her gratitude for his sacrifice of life in her behalf, the city of Richmond, coming to the aid of the Veteran Cavalry Association of the Army of Northern Virginia, sees to-day the realization of hopes so long cherished by his faithful followers..."

Garnett's poignant summary of the general's glorious service as chief of the Confederate Cavalry stirred and revived Jeremy's recollections of hearing the thunder of roaring cannon, tasting the remains of spent gunpowder, feeling the heart-stopping rush and shock of headlong charges. Those four bloody years had sorely tested men's honor, requiring of them immeasurable dedication, courage, strength, and fortitude. The diminishing remnant of those cavaliers had lived long enough to see their commander's memory given due recognition.

"Where's your mamma?" Jeremy asked Glory when he rejoined her after the unveiling.

"She made her way through the crowd to see Flora Stuart," Glory replied. "We're to meet her there."

Jeremy put an arm about his daughter's shoulders. He and Glory paused together at the foot of the bronze equestrian statue, a magnificently sculpted impression of the animated, legendary cavalry leader half-turned in his saddle atop the back of a spirited mount. Glory had always been proud that her parents had elected to incorporate the bold name of Stuart into her own.

She read the inscription aloud:

> *His grateful countrymen will mourn his loss and cherish his memory. To his comrades in arms he has left the proud recollection of his deeds and the inspiring influence of his example.*

"There was some good that came of it all, General. Some little good indeed," Jeremy murmured.

Later that same evening, Jeremy strolled down Main Street with Glory on one arm and Salina on the other. Bright electric lights illuminated the thoroughfare from Fifth Street to Fifteenth Street. Their unhurried promenade allowed the Southerlands a chance to enjoy the incandescent spectacle.

"Do you ever miss the thrill of those days, Daddy? The glory?"

Jeremy squeezed his oldest daughter's gloved hand and winked at her. "Are you suggesting that forty some odd years of ranching on the Kansas plains hasn't had any adventure to it?"

Salina smiled at her husband's jesting. Ranching was its own brand of adventure.

"I'm serious, Daddy," Glory insisted. "I was too young to remember the war, but I know all the stories—as if they'd happened yesterday. Between you and Mamma, you certainly had your share of adventure."

That faraway look that infused the depths of Jeremy's sapphire eyes made Glory believe that the echoes of artillery fire, the pounding of galloping horses' hooves, and the metallic clank of silver sabres were still vivid in his mind. His reminiscences oft included the likes of Lee, Mosby, Stuart, Jackson, his little band of men, Uncle Ethan, and the grandfather, Garrett Hastings, whom Glory had never known.

Jeremy's sigh was contemplative. "God was faithful then, just as He is now. He supplied your mamma and me with the heart and determination we needed to survive those years of trial by fire. He also gave us you, to remind us of the good and precious times along the way in spite of the darkness of the hour. I reckon by war's end, you could say we'd sampled our portion of both strength and glory. And it was enough."

"Aye." Salina was in full agreement with her beloved old Horse Soldier. "It was enough."

Author's Note:

It is my goal to be as accurate as possible when it comes to the historical part of my stories. I have been fortunate to work with various historians, battlefield tour guides, authors, historical society members, descendants, reenactors, curators, and fellow Civil War buffs to collect reliable information. My own Civil War library has more than eight hundred books in it, but there are some volumes that I find myself turning to time and again for reference. If the readers are interested in digging deeper into the historical aspects, here are some suggestions for further investigation:

Books

* *43rd Battalion Cavalry—Mosby's Command* by Hugh C. Keen and Horace Mewborn
* *Ashes of Glory: Richmond at War* by Ernest B. Furgurson
* *The Civil War: A Narrative (Red River to Appomattox)* by Shelby Foote
* *Diary of a Southern Refugee During the War* by Judith W. McGuire
* *Escape from Libby Prison* by James Gindlesperger
* *Everyday Life in the 1800s* by Marc McCutcheon
* *Farewell My General* by Shirley Seifert
* *First Lady of the South: The Life of Mrs. Jefferson Davis* by Ishbel Ross
* *The Galvanized Yankees* by Dee Brown
* *General Lee's City: An Illustrated Guide to the Historic Sites of Confederate Richmond* by Richard M. Lee
* *Glory at a Gallop: Tales of the Confederate Cavalry* by William R. Brooksher & David K. Snider
* *Hampton and His Cavalry in '64* by Edward L. Wells
* *I Rode with Jeb Stuart: The Life and Campaigns of Major General J.E.B. Stuart* by Major Henry B. McClellan
* *I Rode with Stonewall* by Henry Kyd Douglas
* *The Lee Girls* by Mary P. Coulling
* *Mosby's Confederacy: A Guide to the Roads and Sites of Colonel John Singleton Mosby* by Thomas J. Evans and James M. Moyer
* *Mosby's Memoirs* by Colonel John S. Mosby

Motherhood in the Old South: Pregnancy, Childbirth, and Infant Rearing by Sally G. McMillen

Mr. Lincoln's City: An Illustrated Guide to the Civil War Sites of Washington by Richard M. Lee

Point Lookout Prison Camp for Confederates by Edwin W. Beitzell

Ranger Mosby by Virgil C. Carrington

Riding with Stuart: Reminiscences of an Aide-de-Camp by Theodore S. Garnett, edited by Robert J. Trout

Songs of the Civil War, edited by Irwin Silber

They Followed the Plume by Robert J. Trout

Articles

*"Confederate War Horses" by Todd Kern, in Crossroads to History (Part I, Oct. 1997; Part II, Nov. 1997)

*"The Great Rebel Beefsteak Raid" by Francis A. O'Brien, in America's Civil War (July 1996)

*"Sabotage at City Point" by Ella S. Rayburn, in Civil War Times Illustrated (April 1993)

*"In the Beginning: A History of the Paradise Park Site" by Thomas L. Reedy and Alice M. Reedy, in the Santa Cruz Historical Society Journal (1974)

Manuscripts/Letters

*Lee Collection at the Virginia Historical Society

*Journal of Mrs. Hugh (Mary) Lee at the Handley Library Archives

*Hunter Holmes McGuire Collection at the Handley Library Archives

*Stuart Collection at the Virginia Historical Society

CDs/Tapes

*The Civil War CD-ROM/The War of the Rebellion: A Compilation of the Official Records of the Union and Confederate Armies (Guild Press of Indiana)

Come Before Winter by James Taylor

Homespun Songs of the Christmas Season by Bobby Horton

Homespun Songs of Faith by Bobby Horton

Homespun Songs of the C.S.A. (Volumes 1-5) by Bobby Horton

Lincoln (Original Soundtrack Recording) by Alan Menken

Little Rose Is Gone by James Taylor